The Official
OLYMPIC GAMES
COMPANION

Published in co-operation with the International Olympic Committee

The complete guide to the
OLYMPIC WINTER GAMES
1998 Edition

Compiled and Edited by
Caroline Searle and **Bryn Vaile**
Matchtight Media

BRASSEY'S SPORTS
London ~ Washington

The articles published in the Official Olympic Games Companion do not necessarily reflect the opinion of the International Olympic Committee

First English Edition 1998

Brassey's Sports is an imprint of Brassey's (UK) Ltd.

UK editorial offices: Brassey's, 33 John Street, London WC1N 2AT, UK
Email: brasseys@dial.pipex.com
Web: http://www.brasseys.com

UK and non-American orders orders:
Marston Book Services, PO Box 267, Abingdon OX14 4SD, UK

North American orders:
Brassey's Inc., PO Box 960, Herndon, VA 22070, USA

Library of Congress Cataloging in Publication Data
Available

British Library Cataloguing in Publication Data
A catalogue record for this book is available from the British Library

ISBN 1 85753 244 9 Flexicover

Designed and originated by BPC Information Ltd, Abingdon, Oxfordshire, UK

Printed in Great Britain by BPC Wheatons Ltd., Exeter, UK

PREFACE

The XVIII Olympic Winter Games in Nagano, Japan, will forever hold a special place in Olympic history as the last Olympic Winter Games of the twentieth century. The people of Nagano and the whole of Japan have been striving to make this an excellent Olympic celebration, and we have every confidence that their services will be outstanding.

The occasion of these Games has given rise to many publications, including this fine companion volume which charts the history of the Olympic Movement since the first Olympic Winter Games in Chamonix, France, in 1924. On its pages, great moments and figures from the past 'Games of snow and ice' come to life.

Readers will also share in the excitement of the XVIII Olympic Winter Games in 1998, where spectators and a global television audience will enjoy sixteen days of high-performance competition in Nagano. Some new sports, including snowboarding and women's ice hockey, will add to the programme.

In addition to thrilling sport, the prefecture of Nagano and the country of Japan offer us great natural beauty, which has been preserved consistently in preparing for the competitions. Each sport venue has been selected so that it will be in harmony with its environment and indigenous wildlife.

I would like to congratulate the publishers and the editors of this book for their efforts in producing this special volume.

Juan Antonio Samaranch
President of the International Olympic Committee

CONTENTS

Preface by Juan Antonio Samaranch, President of the IOC   (iii)
Contents   (iv)
Acknowledgements   (vi)
Editors' Introduction   (vii)

PART ONE: Historical Background   1
    From Chamonix to Nagano   2
    Magical Olympic Moments   27
    World Forces and the Olympic Winter Games   36
    Women and the Olympic Winter Games   39
    Writing in Ski Gloves   44
    Participation of Nations by Sport   46
    National Medals Totals in Each Olympic Winter Games   47
    Table of Past Games and Locations   49
    All-time Medals Table 1924-1994   50

PART TWO: Nagano 1998   51
    About Nagano   52
    Nagano Schedule   56
    Walkabout—Olympic Winter Village Life   57
    Discontinued Events   59
    1998 Sports and Events List   60
    International Time Zones   61
    Abbreviations for Weights and Measures   63
    Medals Records   63
    Country Abbreviations   64

PART THREE: The Winter Sportsfile   65
    Biathlon   66
    Bobsleigh   80
    Curling   97

Ice Hockey   108
Luge   134
SKATING
Figure Skating   145
Speed Skating—Long Track   169
Short Track Speed Skating   187
SKIING
Alpine Skiing   197
Cross-country Skiing   224
Freestyle Skiing   242
Nordic Combined   251
Ski Jumping   259
Snow Boarding   269

PART FOUR: The Olympic Family and Movement   275
The IOC: A Vast and Complex Global Organization   276
Cities Bidding to Host the Olympic Winter Games   282
Olympic Solidarity   283
The Olympic Fight Against Drugs in Sport   285
The Next Olympic Century   289
The Pursuit of Excellence   290
Olympic Committees and Sports Federations   292
Olympic Museum, Lausanne   294

APPENDIX
Authors and Editors   295

ACKNOWLEDGEMENTS

The directors of Brassey's, particularly sports publishing director Alan Steel, together with the editors, Bryn Vaile and Caroline Searle, wish to acknowledge the invaluable help of the International Olympic Committee in compiling and editing "The Official Olympic Games Companion: Nagano 1998 Edition".

In particular, thanks are due to: the IOC "Reader" Wolf Lyberg for his patience, generosity of spirit and rapid response time; Nikolai Gueorgueiv for much of his original IOC material; Ruth Beck-Perrenoud, of the IOC Museum and Research Centre, for her energy in researching and welcoming the editors to Lausanne: the IOC photographic archive department.

We would also like to acknowledge the British Olympic Association and following:

Sports Federations:
A debt of gratitude is owed to the international federations of all of the Olympic Winter sports for their provision of original material and their checking of many sections.

The editors have also been grateful for additional help from: The British Olympic Association (for the use of its library and resources); the British Ski Federation (Mike Jardine and his staff) for their unfailing help; international federation press officers Ingeborg Kollbach, Hakan Sundstrom and Harro Esmarch for their expert knowledge; and Benjamin Wright, the ISU's historian, for his analytical eye.

The Authors:
Who are listed with biographical notes on pages 295, 296.

Editorial team:
Our thanks go to Pauline Turpitt of Matchtight Media for inputting all the past medallists from original sources as well as the hours spent checking and cross-referencing them and preparing other data sections.

Photographs:
We must acknowledge the assistance given by the Allsport team in the UK including James Nicholls and Paul Sales.

Reference sources:
The Official Reports - compiled by the relevant Organizing Committee—of every Olympic Winter Games since 1924.

The Official British Olympic Association Reports and Team Handbooks for every Olympic Winter Games since 1924.

The United States Olympic Books, 1976, 1980

"Analyse du Programme des Jeux Olympiques d'Hiver 1924–1998, Nikolay Gueorguiev - Lausanne, Musee Olympique, 1995, ISBN 92-9149-004-0

"Olympic Review: XXVI-15, June-July 1997", special feature on women in sport.

"The Book of Facts on the Olympic Winter Games 1908–1994", a study made for the IOC by Wolf Lyberg (update June 1994/100).

"Les Medailles des Jeux Olympiques d'Hiver; IIIeme Tome", Nikolay Gueorguiev, Lausanne 1990.

"Olympics Facts and Feats", Stan Greenberg, Guinness Publishing, 1996.

"Guide to Nagano", the Organising Committee for the XVIII Olympic Winter Games (NAOC).

"Skating in the Olympic Games", International Skating Union, Davos Platz, Switzerland, June 1994.

"The Olympic Story 1980: The Pursuit of Excellence" - AP and Grolier, Grolier Enterprises Inc 1980.

"J.O. d'Hiver 1976. La Suisse".

"El Olimpismo despues de Lake Placid", Andres Merce Varela

"The Olympic Games 1984" by Lord Killanin and John Rodda - Willow Books

"The Complete Book of the Winter Olympics: 1994 Edition", David Wallechinsky, Aurum Press

"A complete Pictorial Record, Olympics 1976, Montreal, Innsbruck", by Graham Fulton Smith, James M Sampson and Willy B Wange

"The Olympic Games at the Threshold of the 21st Century", George Candilis

"Olympic Winter Games, Albertville, 1992, Guide to the Athletes", published by the Commission of the European Communities, Brussels, 1992

Photographs:
Allsport UK Ltd, Keyston/Hulton Getty, Vandystadt.

EDITORS' INTRODUCTION

Caroline Searle   **Bryn Vaile**

The "Official Olympic Games Companion: 1998 Nagano Edition" has been compiled in association with the International Olympic Committee. Its aim has been to bring some of the magic of the Olympic Winter Games to the reader by covering the personalities, sports and events which have made up the history of those Games since 1924. In addition, we have taken a look at the forthcoming Nagano Olympic Winter Games, the work of the IOC and the Olympic Movement on a four-year cycle and the issues facing the modern Games.

The Companion is in four parts. Part 1 takes the reader through the great moments of Olympic Winter Games history in both a sporting and political sense. An insight is given into the role played by women and the media as well as the world forces which have sometimes shaped the Games and the Movement. All-time medals tables and other interesting statistics are incorporated in this section.

Part 2 centres on the final Games of the twentieth century which will be held in Nagano, Japan, in 1998. There is a complete list of sports and events, a description of the venues as well as a day by day schedule (as at August 1997).

The Winter Sportsfile is the major part of the companion and appears in Part 3. It includes: a sport-by-sport guide to potential 1998 stars; a brief history of each sport's origins and development; a guide to rules, equipment and 1998 venues; the format and schedule (as at August 1997) under which each sport will take place in Nagano and some past Olympic anecdotes. A series of international contributors and the International Sports Federation have helped in producing this section.

(vii)

Within each sport, tables are presented for all-time medals by nation (sorted in order of most golds first and then by most silvers and/or bronzes where gold tallies are equal) and a major tabulation of every Olympic Winter Games medal winner since 1924.

Part 4 comprises information about the Olympic Family and Movement. It sets out to answer questions about the role of the IOC and its work. Who organizes the Games? What is planned for Sydney 2000 and where are the next Olympic Winter Games? What happens to the funds generated and what moves are being made to curb drug-use in sport?

The Companion contains more than 100 contemporary and historical photographs, many in colour, which convey an impression of some of the leading personalities and defining moments of the Olympic Winter Games.

We have very much enjoyed compiling this Companion, reliving some of the magical moments of the Olympic Winter Games. We hope some of that enjoyment is conveyed to the reader. As editors, we would welcome any suggestions for improvement or additional useful features for incorporation in future volumes.

Caroline Searle, Bryn Vaile

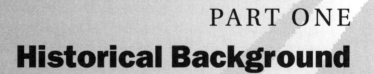

PART ONE
Historical Background

FROM CHAMONIX TO NAGANO

The History of the Olympic Winter Games

Athletes from around the world celebrated the re-birth of the modern Olympic Games in Athens in 1896. Five more editions of this ever-growing international sports festival would take place, spanning 28 years, before a parallel Olympic Winter Games took place in Chamonix, France, in 1924.

In the early part of this century the Scandinavians dominated winter sports. Every four years from 1901 to 1917, as well as after the tragic intervention of the First World War, they organized a winter sports festival called the "Nordic Games". A week-long and tremendously atmospheric festival of winter sports was also held every year at the Holmenkollen in Oslo with competitions in nordic skiing and ski jumping.

Hardly surprising, then, that the Scandinavians were none too happy at the thought of a new competition usurping their role. Equally, for this reason, Baron Pierre de Coubertin, the Olympic founding father, was concerned that an Olympic Winter Games might disturb the unity of the Olympic Movement.

Yet, as the popularity of winter sports spread outside of Scandinavia, there were calls for a Winter Games. Ice skating was added to the programme of the summer Games in 1908 in London. And, as early as 1911, a delegate at the International Olympic Committee (IOC) congress in Budapest was bold enough to ask the Swedish member whether his country, already set to host the 1912 Olympic Games, had also developed a winter sports Games.

The Swede rebuffed the question by referring to the already-planned "Nordic Games" due in 1913. Immediately, a long debate took place as to whether this event should become the Olympic Winter Games. The idea was eventually shelved but in Paris in 1914 another IOC congress added the sports of figure skating, ice hockey and skiing to the list of optional sports to be considered by any future organizer of the summer Olympic Games. As a result in Antwerp, in 1920, figure skating re-appeared and ice hockey took place in the form of its inaugural world championships.

By this time Baron Pierre de Coubertin, still conscious of Scandinavian resistance, had shifted his opinion. Not only had the winter sports, he believed, developed in popularity but they were truly amateur and needed great athleticism. He felt that they were being diminished by exclusion from the Olympic Games. On the other hand, he realized that, for practical reasons, they could not be organized at the same time and place as the summer Games.

"Are we going to force Holland to buy a mountain chain just for the occasion", he wrote in his memoirs of the 1921 IOC Congress in Lausanne, Switzerland. "We can make artificial ice but not snow nor mountain peaks". The solution appeared to be a separate event which was somehow linked to its "older brother", the summer Games.

So the Baron suggested a separate commission to study the Olympic Winter Games. It was decided that Chamonix, in 1924, would organize an "International Week of Winter Sports" which would receive IOC patronage.

In Prague in 1925 the IOC produced a charter for the Winter Games. These were to take place in the same year as the Games of the Olympiad. The country selected to host the Games of the Olympiad would have first right to stage the Olympic Winter Games in that year as long as they had suitable facilities.

Even the Scandinavians, wary of the new power exerted by Switzerland and Canada, rallied to the cause and the Olympic Winter Games were born. Retrospectively, in 1926, the Chamonix "week" was awarded the title of the inaugural Olympic Winter Games.

From that point onwards, the Winter Games took place in the same year as the Olympic Games until 1992. However, in 1986 the IOC took the decision to put the two Games on an alternating cycle every two years in order to spread the immense burden of preparation which was otherwise falling in a single year on the shoulders of its own administrators and those of many of its National Olympic Committees.

So, in 1994, the 12th Olympic Winter Games took place in Lillehammer, Norway, two years after the Games of the XXVth Olympiad in Barcelona in 1992. The next Olympic Winter Games will be in Nagano, Japan, in 1998, two years after the Games of the XXIVth Olympiad in Atlanta, USA.

1924–1936

The organizers of the first Olympic Winter Games in Chamonix went to their beds troubled men on the night of January 24th. For days the temperatures in the French resort had risen alarmingly and rain had fallen. However, they awoke on the all-important January 25th, opening ceremony day, to a sharp frost. After that the weather behaved itself impeccably.

Austria, Belgium, Canada, Estonia, USA, Finland, France, Great Britain, Hungary, Italy, Lithuania, Luxembourg, Norway, Poland, Sweden, Switzerland, Czechoslovakia and Yugoslavia were the pioneering nations who lined up for the Chamonix opening ceremony.

The resort's ice rink, incorporating a 400m speed skating track, two ice hockey rinks and a figure skating area, was in a beautiful setting with mountains all around. It was against this setting that Charles Jewtraw of the USA won the first gold of the Games in the 500m speed skating. However, a Norwegian and a Finn were the two heroes of the Games. The former, Thorleif Haug, won three golds and a bronze in the Nordic events and the latter, Clas Thunberg, won three golds a silver and a bronze in speed skating.

Gillis Grafstrom of Sweden—already Olympic champion from 1920 in Antwerp—won the men's figure skating whilst in the women's figure skating Herma Plank-Szabo of Austria took a lead over Beatrix Loughgran of the USA in the opening compulsory figures and went on to win gold. Superior team-work gave the Canadians an easy victory over the USA in the final pool of the ice hockey by 6-2.

The bobsleigh track, winding down between closely-spaced firs, was extremely spectacular. It had 18 curves during a run of 1433m (1567yds) and was designed to be a severe test for the drivers. This resulted in several accidents in training and during the competition. On the first run the top bobs from Italy and Switzerland both overturned. Switzerland's second bob created a lead after the first run and held on to it to give them victory.

In the ski-jumping Anders Haugen of the USA jumped the furthest but when the style points were taken into consideration, Jacob Thams of Norway was awarded the gold with Haugen dropping to fourth place. A military ski race of 30km was won by Switzerland.

Baron Pierre de Coubertin attended the Games' closing ceremony on February 5th, 1924 to present the prizes and to declare the Games closed.

258 athletes from 16 nations competed in 1924. By 1928 the growth in winter sports meant that 464 competitors from 25 nations

Ice hockey in 1924

Ivar Ballangrud: dominated speed skating in 1936

1936 speed skating competitions

assembled in St Moritz, Switzerland, for the second Olympic Winter Games. These, however, were one of the first of many Olympic Winter Games to be troubled by the vagaries of the weather. Some events had to be cancelled due to a sudden thaw to ensure the Games finished on time. Even the opening ceremony took place in the teeth of a severe blizzard.

Figure skating was a key sport in these Games. Gillis Grafstrom of Sweden won his third successive Olympic title. Even he, however, was overshadowed by the dramatic performance of 15 year-old Sonja Henie of Norway who won the women's title. On arrival in St Moritz, three weeks before the Games, it was obvious that the Norwegian youngster had talent but that it needed some refinement, particularly for the compulsory figures. During those three weeks she took lessons from the British coach Alex Adams.

Afterwards Adams said of Henie: "The child has an extra sense, she can never be out of balance. I could teach her anything, because you can turn her any way you like in the middle of any movement without disturbing her perfect poise". Henie, inspired by the top Russian ballerinas of the day, was certainly an extraordinary talent.

She was ahead after the compulsory figures in 1928 and went on to give an electric display in the free programme. As one observer commented: "The exquisite finish with which this little skater performs her spins and jumps, puts her in a class as a free skater quite by herself". Although Fritzi Burger of Austria also gave a "delicious exhibition", Henie won the gold, the first of three in consecutive Games. She had become an overnight star who went on to a glittering Hollywood career.

Disappointment surrounded the 1928 bobsleigh event because of the thaw. The 14 nations soon learnt that the competition would consist of two runs over two days rather than four runs in four days. There was a dispute over starting orders for each day and the track was exceedingly slow, diminishing the excitement of the event. An American millionaire's son, William Fiske won the five-man event gold ahead of his compatriot Jennison Heaton.

The weather also played havoc with the ice hockey tournament which was won by the Canadians, represented by a Toronto University team. They were given a bye into the final pool whilst the other eleven nations contested preliminary matches in order to limit the number of games played. In that final pool Canada beat Sweden (11-0), Switzerland (13-0) and Great Britain (14-0).

Per Erik Hedlund of Sweden won the 50km cross-country race. Choice of wax had proved crucial in this event which was raced in extraordinarily mild temperatures reaching 25C (77F). It was a gruelling competition in the heat and Hedlund's time was almost 70 minutes slower than Haug's winning time four years before.

After seven competitors had competed in the heats of the 10,000m this event had to be abandoned because the temperature had risen so quickly. Irving Jaffee of the USA was winning at the time.

Lord Northesk of Great Britain won bronze in the skeleton event at these Games after his compatriot, Colonel Moore-Brabazon, had broken two ribs in a training accident.

Switzerland were momentarily in the lead of the military patrol race when their skier broke a pole. Norway overtook them to take gold and so did Finland who won silver. Sigmund Ruud of Norway had jumped 72.5m a year before the Games but could only manage 60 and 64m in St Moritz to take silver behind Alf Andersen also of Norway in the ski-jumping. Ruud's brother, Birger, was later to win gold in 1932 and 1936.

Lake Placid, New York State, hosted the 1932 Olympic Winter Games. If the poor weather again meant problems—with snow being moved into venues by the truckload—it was the sport of speed-skating which really caused a storm at these Games.

The Europeans were used to a format whereby skaters raced against each other in pairs with the fastest time winning. Controversially and against huge protests, in Lake Placid, the Americans decided to adopt a format which was popular in the USA and Canada incorporating a mass start. America and Canada took ten of the 12 available medals much to the annoyance of the top Europeans. Irving Jaffee, beaten by the weather in 1928, took both the 5000 and 10,000m titles.

Two-man bobsleigh was introduced at this Games and was won by Americans Hubert and Curtis Stevens. They reached speeds of up to 60mph (96kmph). William Fiske won the four-man event for the USA. One of his crew, Eddie Eagan, had previously won Olympic boxing gold in Antwerp in 1920.

America and Canada fought a thrilling ice hockey final. After normal time and three periods of extra time the score stood at 2-2. The draw gave Canada the title. Had America previously beaten Germany, however, the gold would have been theirs on goal-average.

Schafer of Austria deprived Sweden's Gillis Grafstrom of a potential fourth consecutive gold in the men's figure skating competition. Henie won her second gold for Norway in the women's event in which two "British children"—Cecilia Colledge and Megan Taylor both aged 11—took part.

The 50 racers who took part in the 50km ski race only actually skied 48.239km after the organizers altered the course due to problems with the earlier warm weather. Norway took a clean sweep of the ski-jumping medals in an event where the slushy out-run soaked many competitors after their jumps. Birger Ruud took his second gold.

Whilst the 1932 Games had 252 competitors from 17 nations, those held in Garmisch-Partenkirchen in 1936 reflected both the accessibility of the venue and the growth of winter sports through 668 competitors and 28 participating nations. This was also the first Games to include Alpine skiing and the weather, for once, gave no problems.

Birger Ruud, already twice the Olympic ski-jumping champion, won the downhill section of the only Alpine event, the first in this sector of skiing at the games, the Alpine Combined, but was pushed into fourth place after the slalom by Franz Pfnur of Germany.

Ivar Ballangrud won three golds and a silver in the speed skating whilst his compatriot, Henie, again won the figure skating but this time only after being pushed hard by Colledge of Britain. Henie turned professional immediately after the Games.

Perhaps the shock of the 1936 Games, however, was the eclipse of Canada in the ice hockey tournament after a successful run of three Olympic Winter Games. Even more surprisingly, they were beaten by Great Britain who fielded a team mainly of British-born Canadians.

Japan was to stage the 1940 Olympic Winter Games but had to waive its claim in 1938 due to the Sino-Japanese war. For a while it seemed like the 1940 version would return to Garmisch before world war made that impossible.

1948–1960

28 nations, including 669 competitors, took part in the first post-war Olympic Winter Games in the Swiss resort of St Moritz. War had not killed the Olympic spirit even if the weather threatened to do so again in 1948 with warm winds causing the postponement of some ice hockey matches and the 10,000m speed skating.

Ice hockey was also threatened from another direction. Two teams turned up from the USA—one backed by the Amateur Hockey Association, a member of the International Ice Hockey League, the other by the American Olympic Committee. One marched in the opening ceremony but the other played all the matches. The ensuing tri-partite row, between the ice hockey authorities, the St Moritz organizers and the International Olympic Committee, looked certain at one stage to lead to the cancellation of the tournament. In the end, it went ahead and Canada won on goal-average from Czechoslovakia. America were placed fourth but their results were later declared null and void.

Sweden dominated the cross-country skiing events, breaking the previous Finnish and Norwegian monopoly of the Finns and Norwegians. They took gold and silver in the classic 50km race and all three medals in the 18km race as well as winning the relay. A Finnish skier crashed into a tree and broke his thigh during the 50km race which took place on an icy course. Nils Karlsson of Sweden was dubbed the "Nurmi of skiing" at these Games not only for his St Moritz medals but also for his many previous world championship wins.

Another of the Norwegian Ruud brothers, this time Asbjorn, competed in the 1948 ski-jumping competitions. Sigmund Ruud had won silver in 1928 whilst Birger Ruud, already Olympic champion in 1932 and 1936, was runner-up in St Moritz. Norway took all three medals in the event again with Petter Hugsted as the winner.

Gretchen Frazer of the flying pigtails won America's first skiing gold at any Olympic Winter Games with the slalom title. Another American, Richard Button, proved that acrobatics were becoming as important as artistry in winning the men's figure skating title at the age of 18.

The only Olympic speed skating event to be staged in normal conditions in St Moritz was the 1500m in which the first three racers bettered the Olympic record. Once again, because of the Cresta Run, there was a skeleton event. These Games also featured demonsration events in Military Patrol and pentathlon.

A special atmosphere pervaded the Olympic Winter Games in 1952 when the event was staged for the first time by Norway, considered the spiritual home of skiing. Almost flawless organization was provided for the 694 competitors from 30 nations. Tens of thousands of spectators turned out to every event including the previously unheralded cross-country and long track speed skating events. An Olympic record paying crowd of 103,432 watched the ski-jumping finals at Holmenkollen swelled by probably 20,000 more non-paying spectators.

For the first time at these Games the Olympic flame was kindled not in Greece but in Morgedal, birthplace of the pioneer of modern skiing, Sondre Norheim. Norway had already won a gold in the giant slalom through Stein Eriksen, "The White Wizard", before the Games' opening ceremony had taken place.

Bobsleigh competitions were also underway before the official opening. Both the two- and four-man events were won by Germany but with crews so heavy that the International Federation later revised their rules.

A 32 year-old Italian moutaineer, Zeno Colo, won the men's downhill with some tactical cunning on soft snow. Eriksen was beaten into second place by an Austrian in the special slalom—an event invented by the British Alpine skiing pioneer Sir Arnold Lunn. A "fragile, likeable girl" called Andrea "Andy" Mead Lawrence won a golden double in the slalom and giant slalom.

Sweden, the dominant nation four years before, fell from grace in the cross-country skiing, earning only two bronze medals. Norway and Finland thus re-established their supremacy. Hallgeir Brenden, a top athletics mile-runner, won the 18km for Norway whilst Finland's Eero Kolehmainen won the 50km. Finland won the relay whilst Norway won the Nordic Combined and took gold and silver in the ski-jumping.

Hjalamar Andersen delighted the home crowd with three golds in the speed skating. Richard Button retained his figure skating crown for America, producing the first "triple" jump of all time in competition in an event which also featured a 12 year-old French prodigy, Alain Giletti, who was seventh. Jeanette Altwegg of Great Britain won the women's title.

Sweden at one stage led the mighty Canadian ice hockey team by 2-0 but lost 3-2. Canada took the title as at every Games since 1920 except 1936. The USA were second but were criticized from many quarters for "over-robust" play.

Italy, due to host the 1960 Olympic Games in Rome, were anxious to make a good impression on international sport in hosting the 1956 Olympic Winter Games in Cortina d'Ampezzo. So anxious that they spent £2.5 million in preparing the venue for its 820 competitors from 32 nations.

Money, however, cannot buy snow. Instead teams of workers had to move snow from the upper to the lower slopes of Cortina to make many of the ski events possible due to lack of falls earlier in the season. A massive ice stadium was constructed and witnessed 76 competitors surpassing the existing Olympic records during the Games.

Several other Olympic landmarks were recorded in 1956. These were the first Winter Games in which the Soviet Union competed, they were the first to be televised and the first in which an Alpine skier won three individual gold medals.

Anton "Toni" Sailer, a tinsmith from Kitzbuehel, not only took all three men's titles but won them by truly fantastic margins—6.2

Richard Button: twice a figure skating gold medallist in 1952 and 1956

American Skier Andrea 'Andy' Mead Lawrence

Nash and Dixon: Bobsleigh winners in 1964

Jean-Claude Killy: triple Alpine gold medallist in 1968

seconds in the giant slalom, 4.0 seconds in the slalom and 3.5 seconds in the downhill on an icy wind-swept course. He was given a hero's welcome on his return to Austria in nearly every city and later went into the films and theatre. Madeleine Berthod of Switzerland won the women's downhill.

At these Games Norway failed to win a gold medal in speed skating for the first time since the controversial 1932 Games. The newly-arrived Soviets took many of the titles backed by some prodigious sports science support. They were impressive, too, in the ice hockey where they won the title— the first of many subsequent victories. The Soviet Union also won the cross-country relay and her women won gold and silver in the women's 10km.

Sixten Jernberg of Sweden won a gold, two silvers and a bronze in the cross-country races to mark the beginning of a remarkable career. Italy enjoyed gold and silver in the two-man bob and silver in the four-man event on their home track. The Finns, using the new "arms-back" style won gold and silver in the ski-jumping.

Some said that the IOC had bowed to "American salesmanship" in awarding the 1960 Games to Squaw Valley in the USA. This resort in the Sierra Nevada was built from nothing into a fitting Olympic host venue from that day onwards by American millionaires.

Its opening ceremony was orchestrated by Walt Disney—who seemed to conjure up sunshine from a blizzard just in time for the event to begin—and a team of unlikely college boys became overnight national heroes in wresting the ice-hockey title from the mighty Soviets. Earlier the tournament had been marred by Swedish complaints against the Canadians after they were defeated 5-2 in a particularly rough game.

There were also many pre-Games complaints (which faded as competition began) including those about the high altitude at which the cross-country races would have to take place and about the refusal of the organizers to build a bobsleigh track. Despite this the Games proved a great success. Women's speed skating events were added to the programme, with Lidya Skoblikova winning two golds, as was the sport of biathlon.

The cross-country relay had a thrilling finish with Finland coming from over 20 seconds behind on the last leg to win against arch-rivals Norway by half a ski-length. But perhaps the biggest shock of these Games was the victory of Germany's Georg Thoma in the Nordic combined event. This diminutive postman was the first non-Scandinavian ever to take this Olympic title.

American Penny Pitou had been favourite to take the women's

slalom title but fell on the second run when seemingly certain of victory. The race was won by Canada's Anne Heggtveit. Jean Vuarnet won the men's downhill using metal rather than wooden skis. At these Games around 10% of the top skiers were using metal skis and it was a subject of great debate.

Carol Heiss, who read the competitors' oath at the opening ceremony won the women's figure skating gold medal for the USA and her compatriot, David Jenkins, won the men's title. Soon after the Games, Heiss married Hayes Allen Jenkins, Olympic champion in 1956 and brother of David.

1964–1980

A record number of 1091 competitors from 36 nations took part in the Olympic Winter Games of 1964 in Innsbruck, Austria, in front of over a million spectators. Again the weather was unhelpful. No snow was visible on the streets of Innsbruck throughout the 12 days of competition with the city experiencing its mildest winter for 58 years. No events, however, were cancelled although some had to be re-scheduled to avoid the sun later in the day.

Tragedy struck before the Games with the deaths in training of Australian skier Ross Milne and British luger Kay Skrzypecki. Otherwise these were spectacular Games with a budget of £12 million spent by the Austrian organizers including the first computerized results systems.

IOC President Avery Brundage again criticized the commercialization of the Winter Games, taking particular umbrage with the Alpine skiers whose ski brands got huge publicity when they were displayed in the finish area of every race.

The irony of the situation, however, was that the two Britons — Robin Nash and Tony Dixon — who won their nation's first and only gold to date in the sport were allegedly very rich men. As British journalist John Rodda explained in an "Olympic Essay": "The bobsleighers, at least from the western world, are the amateurs Brundage stood up for. They are such good amateurs because they are all very rich and can afford to gavant around the bob-runs of Europe. So it wasn't a glass of soft drink when Nash and Dixon won gold. It was a ride down from Igls into Innsbruck in a vintage Rolls Royce and champagne all the way". Nash and Dixon were helped to victory by Italian veteran Eugenio Monti who provided them with a bolt for their bob when their own had sheered.

Elsewhere, women made their mark on these Games. Austria took a clean sweep of the downhill medals led by Christl Haas. And the

French Goitschel sisters, Christine and Marielle, aged 19 and 18 respectively, from Val D'Isere did battle for Alpine golds. Christine beat her sister in the slalom but Marielle won gold in the giant slalom and her sister shared second place with American Jean Saubert. Egon Zimmerman won the men's downhill for Austria on a challenging course at Axamer Lizum where care was needed to avoid the woods on the fringes.

Alain Calmat of France fell heavily twice to leave German Manfred Schnelldorfer with the men's figure skating title. In the women's event, Dutchwoman Sjoukje Dijkstra won the gold, her nation's first Olympic gold in any event since Fanny Blankers-Koen's athletics golds in 1948.

Germany won all the men's luge medals in a sport which was making its Olympic debut and proved a fascination to the spectators who were more used to the forward-prone position of skeleton tobogannists rather than the lugers who sat up and steered by weight transference only. The Soviet Union won the ice hockey tournament without losing a single match. Sixten Jernberg of Sweden won his third and fourth Olympic golds in the 50km cross-country skiing race and the relay. Perhaps the outstanding Games performance, however, came from speed skater Skoblikova. The Soviet athlete won four golds. Norway and Finland shared the jumping medals including the new, "small" 70m hill.

If 1956 had belonged to Toni Sailer, Grenoble in 1968 was the domain of "King Killy", Jean-Claude Killy. The French skier was outstanding amongst the 1158 competitors from 37 nations. He won all three Alpine skiing golds with inimitable style—the kind of French style which also marked the opening ceremony during which artificial roses were dropped on the stadium by helicopters, guns fired Olympic flags which floated down into the arena on mini parachutes and coloured smoke was weaved into the five Olympic rings by aeroplanes.

Killy's wins, however, were not without controversy. The first, the downhill, was won by just eight hundredths of a second from his compatriot Guy Perillat. A second, in the giant slalom, proved comfortable. It was the slalom which was spoilt by a dispute. Austria's Karl Schranz was allowed a second run after he alleged his first run, during which he missed a gate, was marred, he said by an official crossing the course in the fog. He was faster than Killy on the second run and was momentarily awarded the gold. However, this was later taken away after a French protest, upheld by the jury, claimed that the official had been too far away to cause him any distraction in the first run. Schranz and the whole of Austria protested, to no avail.

Canadian Nancy Greene recovered from an ankle injury to win the women's giant slalom and take silver in the slalom. Marielle Goitschel of France won her second Olympic gold, this time in the slalom and Olga Pall took the downhill title for Austria. An Italian, Franco Nones, broke up the Scandinavian hegemony in the cross-country skiing by winning the 30km gold.

The bobsleigh events were again the subject of controversy. Whilst France had spent millions on creating a perfect indoor ice arena in Grenoble, the bob track at Alpe d'Huez left a lot to be desired. It had been built on exposed slopes with no shade from the sun and safe bobbing had to take place very early in the morning—often just before dawn. There were, however, sentimental victories in both the two- and four-man events for 40 year-old Italian Eugenio Monti who had previously won nine world titles but never an Olympic gold.

Austria, Germany and Poland shared the spoils in the luge events which had to be reduced from four to two runs because of the unusually mild weather. Three East German women were disqualified from the competition for heating their runners prior to racing. Expert opinion indicated that the outdoor speed-skating venue was likely to produce slow times. This was disproved when 52 skaters bettered the previous Olympic records. Anton Maier of Norway set the only world record of the Games in the 5000m whilst Holland replaced the Soviet Union as the leading nation in the women's events.

The graceful Peggy Fleming, of the USA, won the women's figure skating title and Austria's Wolfgang Schwarz won the men's event. Equally gracefully, Soviet pairs skaters Oleg Protopopov and Ludmila Belousova retained their pairs title at the ages of 35 and 32 respectively. They drew gasps from the crowd for their skilful split lutz lift and trademark one-handed death spiral, incorporated into a smooth, balletic performance.

One of the most thrilling moments of the whole Games, however, came in the ice hockey clash between Czechoslovakia and the previously almost invincible Soviet Union. The Czechs pushed the Soviets onto the defensive early in the match and were 3-1 up by the end of the first period, scoring three goals in four minutes. The Soviets hit back with a goal early in the second period but then found themselves soon two down again. In a tense and often desperate third period with end-to-end action there was no score until, with four minutes to go, and leading 4-2 at that stage, Czechoslovakia scored once more. The Soviets replied with two rapid-fire goals but too late to save them from a final 5-4 defeat.

Away from the slopes and the rinks there were two political rows. The first came when the IOC tried to ban advertising on all skis and equipment. Eventually a compromise was reached when skiers were asked to remove their equipment before being photographed or filmed. The second surrounded the introduction of a special elimination slalom to reduce starting numbers in the slalom event. Killy led a revolt of many top skiers. In the end, the situation was saved when the elimination race was cancelled due to bad weather.

Emperor Hirohito of Japan declared the 1972 Sapporo Olympic Winter Games open. These were again a Games which had a huge budget (£17 million), somewhat to the embarrassment of the IOC, and were extremely well organized. 1006 competitors represented 35 nations and Dutch speed skater Ard Schenk, in winning three golds, was arguably the star of the show.

Before the Games could begin, however, Austrian Alpine skier Karl Schranz was again at the centre of controversy. He was banned by the IOC from taking part in the Games for allowing his image to be used in advertising. This brought the row between the IOC and the "professional skiers" to a head. Several nations threatened a boycott as Schranz returned home to crowds welcoming him in the streets.

Austria withdrew its team only to re-instate them after Schranz pleaded that they should not miss their Olympic opportunity because of him. Schranz was one of an alleged black-list of 40 names held by the IOC but he had been singled out according to IOC President Avery Brundage because: "He was the most blatant and the most verbose we could find". Schranz had given a media interview on the eve of the Games in which he had said that if Brundage's ideas of amateurism were followed then the Olympic Games would only be for rich men.

Back on the slopes Italy's Gustav Thoeni won the first giant slalom to be decided on an aggregate of two runs. Bernhard Russi of Switzerland took the men's downhill after being dubbed by Schranz the "best man left in the field". Spaniard Francisco Fernandez-Ochoa sprung a surprise by winning the slalom, the first from his country to win any Olympic Winter Games medal. Sapporo's changeable weather had provided a headache for the ski-technicians over choice of wax. Perhaps the Swiss fared best in this respect with six medals, including three golds of which two were won by Marie Therese Nadig in the giant slalom and downhill.

Poland won its first Nordic skiing medal with gold in the 90m ski-jump for Wojciech Fortuna. There are few more gratifying moments than home victories in the Olympic Games. The Japanese spectators, however, were in for a rarer treat than that when they took a clean sweep of the medals from the 70m hill.

Galina Koulakova, a Soviet physical education teacher won

individual golds in the 5km and 10km cross-country races as well as the team relay. Norwegian Magnar Solberg successfully defended his biathlon title. West Germany took gold and silver in the two-man bobsleigh event.

Alongside the achievements of Schenk, American Anne Hemming shone in the speed skating competitions setting two new Olympic records in one event. She was baulked in her first 500m sprint and was allowed a second run in which she clocked an even faster time to take gold.

Exemplary compulsory figures exponent Ondrej Nepela took Czechoslovakia's first figure skating gold in the men's event. Good figures also helped Austria's Beatrix "Trixi" Schuba win the women's gold. Moscow's Alexei Ulanov and Irina Rodnina won the pairs event in a close finish from their compatriots and rivals Andrei Souraikin and Ludmila Smirnova. Ulanov and Smirnova were later to marry each other.

When Denver, Colorado, USA, pulled out of staging the 1976 Olympic Winter Games, Innsbruck was delighted to step into the breach. The voters of Denver had, in 1973, refused further funds for staging the Games after a state referendum and the IOC chose Innsbruck over Lake Placid, Tampere in Finland and the Mont Blanc region of France.

The Austrian city had the facilities, the know-how and the willingness to stage the Games. With just three years to prepare the Austrians staged one of the most successful Games ever. The IOC had a new President, Lord Killanin, and there was perhaps a more relaxed atttitude to professionalism under his new tenure. He was more sensitive to the needs of modern sport to generate income to fund its events and individual competitors. The choice of Austria also went some way to building bridges between the IOC and one of the top winter sports nations following Schranz's disqualification from Sapporo.

These were billed as the "simple Games" and expenditure was limited to a minimum in upgrading the facilities used in 1964. However, security was one key area of additional expense following the tragedy of the 1972 summer Olympic Games when Israeli athletes had died after being taken hostage by Arab terrorists.

On the opening day of competition Franz Klammer, renowned for his rodeo-style skiing, won the men's downhill for the host nation. He was down on defending champion Bernhard Russi at the mid-point but skied the bottom half of the course with legendary courage and natural ability to win. Austria also won the final gold of the Games with Karl Schnabl's 90m ski-jump victory.

Rosi Mittermaier won two golds and a silver for Germany in the Alpine events. She failed to take a clean sweep by just 12 hundredths of a second when Canada's Kathy Kreiner won the giant slalom. East Germany won all the bobsleigh and luge titles as well as the Nordic Combined title through Ulrich Wehling, the second of three successive golds that he was destined to win in this event.

The Soviet Union dominated much of the cross-country skiing as expected. More unexpectedly, American Bill Koch won a silver in the 30km race. No media representative from his nation's huge press corps was there to witness the achievement.

Ice dancing was introduced for the first time to the programme. John Curry won the men's figure skating competition with Toller Cranston of Canada in third place. Both had previously criticized ice skating judging in the press for downgrading balletic style. Curry, who went on to be successful and admired in professional ice shows, later died, allegedly of Aids, and Cranston went on to become a successful artist.

The ice hockey tournament was without Sweden and Canada. Czechoslovakia were hit by influenza and a drugs incident, leaving the Soviets to claim their sixth consecutive title. A triple tie for third place between Germany, Finland and the USA was decided on goal average in favour of Germany.

In 1980, 1072 competitors from 37 countries descended on Lake Placid, New York State, for the second time in Olympic Winter Games history—a venue which this time round had invested millions in snow-making equipment. It was a worthwhile investment as the area suffered its worst snow-drought since 1887.

The Olympic Village which welcomed the athletes of the world was described in the official report of the Games as: "a rolling 36-acre site eight miles from Lake Placid providing a campus-style setting for 2,000 athletes and officials". Its later inmates might have taken umbrage at the idyllic description as it was to become a state penitentiary after the Games.

Two American victories set the Games alight for the home spectators and a network TV audience. A fledgling USA ice hockey team, as in 1960 composed from the collegiate ranks, took on and defeated the six-times Olympic champions from the Soviet Union. And Eric Heiden, a speed skater, achieved immortality by winning all five speed skating golds. In doing so, he set one world record and five Olympic records. His sister, Beth, won a bronze in the women's 3000m.

As Anne-Marie Moser-Proell, Austria's skiing world champion, stood at the top of Whiteface Mountain waiting for the downhill to start she knew this was her last chance of Olympic gold. This was the skier who had won everything else that mattered including six overall world cup titles.

Her coach Alois Bumberger rubbed the skier's knees to keep them warm and warmed the inside of her boots with a hairdryer. There was a howling wind and, despite the fact that it was 11am, the temperature had not risen above -14C. To ski the course at Whiteface, especially in those conditions, required courage and aggression at the top to maintain speed on the bottom sections.

Moser-Proell stormed out of the gate and attacked the first section, keeping tighter to the gates than any skier before. Her time of 1:37.52 was nothing short of remarkable given the severity of the course and the conditions. Moser-Proell had won gold at last. No other skier on that tricky day could better her. The Austrian's lone gold was charismatic whilst the two won by Leichtenstein's Hanni Wenzel in the slaloms as well as a silver in the downhill were nothing short of folklore. Hanni's brother Andreas also took a silver in the giant slalom, making them the first brother and sister team to win medals at the same Games and putting little Leichtenstein in sixth place on the final medal table.

In men's Alpine skiing the name of the Games was Sweden's Ingemar Stenmark who won both the slalom titles. The Swede had created an almost invincible aura by winning nearly every race in the preceding two years. He had a bad first run in the giant slalom but stormed back in the second run to win, using his trademark second run charge.

After the first run of the slalom, Stenmark was also behind. This time Phil Mahre of the USA gave the home crowd hope of gold by leading after the first race. However, it was not to be and Stenmark again came charging home.

In the 70m ski jumping competition several competitors had already completed their first jumps when the judges declared that conditions were too dangerous, moved the starting point lower and began the competition again. Anatoli Aljabiev of the Soviet Union hit all the targets in the 20km biathlon event to win despite not being the fastest skier around the course. A new 10km "sprint" competition was added to biathlon at the Games and was won by East Germany's Frank Ullrich.

Meinhard Nehmer, Ullrich's compatriot, won the four-man bob gold and two-man bronze in Lake Placid. These medals were in addition to the two golds he won in 1976. Another East German,

Bernhard Glass, won the men's luge singles and East Germany again took gold in the men's doubles through Norbert Hahn and Hans Rinn. The same pairing had also won the Olympic doubles title in 1976.

Great Britain won the men's figure skating title for the second successive Games. Robin Cousins had lived and trained in Denver, Colorado, for two years prior to the Games. He worked with Carlo Fassi, the legendary trainer who had also coached Olympic champions Peggy Fleming, Dorothy Hamill and John Curry. After the compulsory figures, Cousins was lying in fourth place. He skated such a dynamic short programme that he catapulted into second place and rounded the competition off with a superb free programme.

Soviet pairs skaters Irina Rodnina and Alexander Zaitsev won, for Rodnina, a third successive gold in Lake Placid. Rodnina accepted the gold medal on the rostrum with tears in her eyes. She had taken time off the year before to have a baby boy and did not know whether to return to the sport. The gold medal gave her the answer.

Anett Potzsch won the women's figure skating title despite "losing" the free programme contest with America's Linda Fratianne. Another East German female skater also won gold in those Games, Karin Enke, aged 18, in the 500m speed skating. It was the beginning of an illustrious career for Enke, who later became Enke-Kania, with three golds, four silvers and a bronze between 1980 and '88.

Nikolai Zimyatov's gold medal for the Soviet Union in cross-country skiing's 30km race was the first of the Lake Placid Games and put the Soviet Union at the head of the all-time medal table for the first time. At the same Games he also won relay and 50km gold.

1984–1994

Sarajevo, Yugoslavia, hosted the 14th Olympic Winter Games for 1274 competitors from 49 nations. Everything worked out well in the end. But there were many delays to the Alpine skiing competitions as 130mph winds whistled around the Bjelasnica and Jahorina venues. The Austrian men's team even went home to train. American Bill Johnson told them not to bother to come back because he was going to win. Unfancied beforehand, he did just that when the race took place a week behind schedule.

America had never won a men's Alpine skiing gold medal before. Austria, meanwhile, had a disastrous Games by their high standards. There had been rifts in the camp on the eve of the Games, just as in 1980 when Leonhard Stock was selected at the last minute, causing an internal row. However, whereas Stock won gold in Lake Placid there was no such outcome in Sarajevo.

Johnson's compatriot Debbie Armstrong won the women's giant slalom with another American, Christin Cooper in second place. And America completed their golden hat-trick when Phil Mahre won the men's slalom. His twin brother Steve, younger by four minutes, won the silver in the same event. In the men's giant slalom Jurij Franko won a silver medal for the host nation, their first medal in Olympic skiing history. Michela Figini, at 17, became the youngest ever Alpine skiing gold medallist when she won the women's downhill for Switzerland.

A 28 year-old Finnish physiotherapist became the cross-country star of the Games. Marja-Liisa Haemalainen won three golds on the tracks of the Igman-Veliko Polje plateau. Some spectators at the Malo Polje ski-jump venue for the 90m event could have been forgiven for believing that Finn Matti Nykanen was going to land amongst them as he won gold with two huge jumps. Nykanen had earlier been beaten to gold in the 70m event by Germany's Jens Weissflog. Nykanen went on to win from both hills in 1988 whilst, remarkably, Weissflog struck gold again on the 120m hill ten years later in Lillehammer, Norway.

Biathletes Erik Kvalfoss of Norway and Peter Angerer of West Germany both won a gold, silver and bronze apiece across the three events. Some of Great Britain's team at the Games had recently seen active service in the Falklands conflict as they were all soldiers. In downtown Sarajevo the speedskaters battled blizzards on the outdoor track with East German women, including Karin Enke, winning all the medals bar three bronze.

Indoors at the same venue the Soviet Union re-established their ice hockey supremacy. Vladislav Tretiak, their goal-keeper, ended his Olympic career after winning gold in Sapporo, Innsbruck and Sarajevo. Only his Lake Placid silver ruined an otherwise perfect set.

Britain, however, again made its impact on a Winter Games by winning a figure skating gold—this time in the ice dance event through ex-Policeman and insurance officer Christopher Dean and Jayne Torvill. They skated to near perfection with a balletic and imaginative style to win twelve sixes from the judges. Tiny Scott Hamilton won the men's figure skating title for the USA whilst Katarina Witt of East Germany was the women's winner.

Sarajevo was the first Eastern European city to host the Games. It had previously been famous as the place where Archduke Ferdinand was assassinated in 1914 bringing about the First World War. Prior to the Games two top skiers, Ingemar Stenmark and Hanni Wenzel, were banned as professionals and there were angry disputes over whether some ice hockey players who had played in America's National Hockey League should be allowed to compete.

Nakiska on the slopes of Mount Allan lived up to its North American Indian name when it became the "meeting place" of ski rivalries during the 15th Olympic Winter Games in Calgary, Canada. 1423 competitors from 57 nations took part. Three rivalries stood out from the crowd.

In Alpine skiing the quietly religious Pirmin Zurbriggen was favourite to take the downhill gold and possibly more besides to become the most successful male skier at the Games. Dubbed the "choirboy", he was eventually beaten to the accolade by the contrastingly boisterous Italian "playboy" Alberto Tomba who won both slalom titles. Tomba went on to win gold again four years later in Albertville as well as silver in Lillehammer. He may also compete in Nagano in 1998.

At the Saddledome ice-rink two further rivalries were to unfold. Katarina Witt, 1984 champion, and credited with bringing major sex appeal to the ice, was pitted against the athletic black skater Debbie Thomas of America. It was all on the free programme. Witt, on the ice first, skated a cautious but technically good programme to the strains of Carmen. Thomas, skating last, had also chosen Carmen but could not rise to the pressure producing a stumbling progamme and ended up with bronze behind Canada's Liz Manley.

In the parallel men's event two "Brians", Orser and Boitano of Canada and the USA respectively, were gold contenders. Both men sported mock military costumes but there the similarity ended in the free progamme which Boitano entered marginally in the lead. Whereas Boitano skated an inspired free progamme and flung back his head at the end to savour the moment, Orser faltered on an early triple and pared down his final triple axel to a double to fade into silver. In the pairs event Ekaterina Gordeeva and Sergei Grinkov of the Soviet Union skated to near perfection to take gold.

Drama unfolded in the Olympic Oval when speed skating's reigning world champion, Dan Jansen of the USA, learned just hours before his race at the 500m distance that his 27 year-old sister had died of leukemia. He stumbled in this race and in the 1000m, clearly affected by the tragedy. 29 skaters set world records during the Games, proving that the indoor arena was the fastest in the world. Holland's Yvonne van Gennip was the discovery of the Games. She recovered from surgery on her right foot just two months before Calgary to win three golds.

At the Canmore biathlon venue East German Frank-Peter Roetsch became the first man to win both individual titles in one Games. East Germany also took all three luge gold medals on offer at the Games.

The "meeting place" -Nakiska- of two weather fronts had brought high winds and soaring temperatures at times to Calgary during the sixteen days of competition. This was sorely felt at Canada Olympic Park for both the bobsleigh and luge events.

Sand and grit was constantly blown into the track causing several delays. The legendary Wolfgang Hoppe of East Germany, winner in 1984, was beaten into silver medal in both bobsleigh events by the Soviet Union and Switzerland respectively. The Soviet Union won the ice hockey title again, only ruining their previously unbeaten record with a 2-1 defeat to Finland once they knew the gold was theirs.

There were two "comic heroes" of these Winter Games. In the ski-jumping a British plasterer named Eddie "The Eagle" Edwards warmed North American audiences, but chilled the purists, with his "have-a-go" attitude despite finishing last twice. And Jamaica, as unlikely a nation as possible, entered a bobsleigh team in the four-man event. They crashed spectacularly on the last day but emerged unscathed.

Albertville, venue for the 1992 Olympic Winter Games, almost stretched the Olympic rings to breaking point. Its 1801 competitors from 64 nations were forced to do more travelling than ever before to numerous venues scattered about several mountain regions. It was, according to many observers, a Games "without a heart". Although it was the result of years of lobbying by former Games triple skiing gold medallist Jean-Claude Killy, by then a successful businessman.

Alberto Tomba, Italy's flamboyant 1988 gold medallist returned to win a gold and silver, helicoptered in from his training base in Italy. Austrian Petra Kronberger won the combined and the slalom titles. Patrick Ortlieb, of Austria, and Canada's Kerrin Lee Gartner won the two downhills. Both victories were unexpected. Neither had even won a world cup downhill before. New Zealander, Annelise Coberger, also sprung a surprise by winning slalom silver, her country's first Olympic skiing medal of any kind.

Mighty Switzerland could only manage one Alpine bronze whilst Norway took two golds. Marc Girardelli, of Luxembourg won his first Olympic medals with two silvers in the giant slalom and Super-G.

Russia's cross-country skier, Raissa Smetanina, won her 10th medal in five Games 12 days before her 40th birthday. When asked her secret she replied: "I was born on February 29th. In reality, I am only ten years old". Norway's Vegard Ulvang won three golds and a silver in the cross-country.

South Korea made an impact on the new sport of short track speed skating. They were winners of the men's 1000m through Kim Ki Hoon as well as the men's relay. Cathy Turner of the USA won the inaugural women's event, a 500m, whilst Canada won the women's relay.

Britain had hopes of winning the two-man bobsleigh event at La Plagne when Mark Tout, much later banned from the sport on drugs charges, and Lenny Paul were in the lead after the first two runs. Their hopes were foiled on the final day as they slipped to sixth place after four runs. Gustav Weder of Switzerland won the two man event and Austria took the four-man title.

Pre-Games figure skating favourites Christopher Bowman of the USA and Canada's Kurt Browning both fell, leaving Viktor Petrenko to take the gold. America's Kristi Yamaguchi won the women's figure skating title from the athletic Midori Ito. Sizzling brother and sister duo of Isabelle and Paul Duchesnay, coached by 1984 champion Christopher Dean who was married to Isabelle, were the crowd favourites in the ice dance but failed to impress the judges beyond awarding them the silver behind Marina Klimova and Sergi Ponamorenko of the "equipe unifiee".

Athletes from the former Soviet Union competed at these Games under this heading whilst those from the former East Germany took part once more under the banner of a combined Germany. The sport of freestyle skiing made its Olympic debut with a moguls contest.

American Tommy Moe had been a top-flight junior racer but one who had never really fulfilled his potential. Until, that is, the Olympic Winter Games of 1994 in Lillehammer. There Moe shocked 1727 competitors from 67 nations—as well as the majority of his own press —by winning the men's downhill by four hundredths of a second from home favourite Kjetil Andre Aamodt. He went on to win silver in the men's super-G on his birthday.

Germany's Marcus Wasmeier won that event and the giant slalom. His compatriot, Katja Seizinger won the women's downhill. In the women's super-G Russia's Svetlana Gladischeva won silver, her country's best ever Olympic Alpine finish. But the women's events took place under the shadow of the death of Austria's Ulrike Maier in training just two weeks before.

You could always tell when it was a big cross-country skiing day in Lillehammer. Pre-dawn a huge line of slow-moving coaches packed with spectators wound their way up the hill to the Birkebeineren stadium and the pavements were full of families skiing their way in the same direction. Some fans even camped overnight in temperatures dropping to below -20C to get a glimpse of their heroes.

The atmosphere was something special and those 100,000 and more Norwegians had something to cheer about when their country took the first three of five available golds. Bjorn Daehlie won the 10km and 15km after a surprise opening defeat to his younger compatriot, Thomas Alsgaard, in the 30km, and tied for the most number of golds won by any Olympic cross-country skier.

"This is the best", he said afterwards. "I won three golds and a silver in Albertville but there were only 10-15,000 people on the course. To win here? Before all these people? My country? I was hoping to do this but afraid that I would not".

Manuela di Centa, nicknamed the "sparrow" back home, won two golds, two silvers and a bronze in the women's cross-country in which she shared the spoils with Russia's Lyubov Egorova. Marja-Liisa Kirvesniemi (formerly Haemalainen) of Finland also got amongst the medals at her record sixth Games.

Norway were also dominant in another of their traditional sports, the long track speed skating, where Johann Olav Koss won three golds and set three world records and then donated his "Olympia-toppen bonus" to Olympic Aid. American Bonnie Blair won the 500m women's title for the third successive time. Another popular victor was her compatriot, Dan Jansen, who after an emotional time in Calgary six years earlier, was facing his last chance of gold and duly won the 1000m title.

A 13 year-old South Korean named Kim Yoon Mi was part of her country's winning short track speed skating relay team and became Olympic Winter Games history's youngest ever gold medallist. Kim Ki Hoon retained his 1000m title at the Games. Cathy Turner of the USA won the women's 500m for the second time despite a dispute with the Chinese silver medallist.

The figure skating competitions were packed with glamorous ex-champions who had returned, under new rules, from the professional ranks. Russians Gordeeva and Grinkov were amongst them and regained their 1988 pairs title. Britain's Torvill and Dean again proved crowd pleasers but won only bronze in a competition where the gold went to Oksana Grichtchuk and Evgeni Platov. 1988 men's winner Brian Boitano fnished sixth and double former Olympic women's champion Katarina Witt was seventh in the women's event, won by Oksana Baiul of the Ukraine.

Figure skating was dogged throughout the Games, however, by drama surrounding two Americans, Nancy Kerrigan and Tonya Harding. Kerrigan, who finished in silver medal position, had been attacked at a pre-Games event in the USA by a man wielding a crowbar and suffered a knee injury. It was alleged, and later proven, that the man was connected with the Harding camp. Harding finished a tearful eighth and was later charged with related offences back home.

Freestyle aerials made their Olympic debut in Lillehammer. Veteran Swiss Gustav Weder won the men's two-man bobsleigh. Germany's Harald Czudaj sprung a surprise in the four-man event by winning the title in the second-ranked German bob. Italy won the women's singles and men's doubles on the luge track. Sweden won the ice hockey final in one of the most thrilling matches of the Games by 3-2 against Canada. It took more than three and a quarter hours of normal play, overtime and two stages of a penalty shoot-out to settle it.

These were wonderfully organized Games, played out in peerless weather conditions and in state-of-the-art facilities. Lillehammer was also the first Olympic Winter Games to be held in a different year to the Games of the Olympiad. The stage is now set for Nagano, Japan, 1998. What next for the event that has grown so much since its humble beginnings at the Chamonix International Winter Sports Week of 1924?

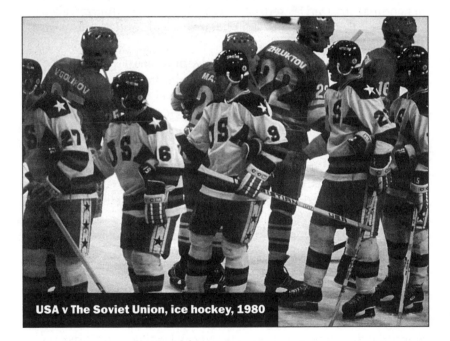

USA v The Soviet Union, ice hockey, 1980

MAGICAL OLYMPIC MOMENTS

by Joseph Metzger and Caroline Searle

The Olympic Winter Games without Alpine skiing? Unthinkable? No. In fact the discipline was not included prior to 1936 in Garmisch-Partenkirchen, the Bavarian health and sports resort. There Franz Pfnuer and Christl Cranz fulfilled home dreams against the backdrop of the ski-finish area which looked more like a classical arena.

However, these Games, sadly, were a prelude and dress-rehearsal for the greater Nazi propaganda exercise of the summer Games of that year. During the second world war many great skiers and up-and-coming stars were killed. But the Olympic spirit and the Games survived.

When the Olympic flame was re-kindled in 1948 in St Moritz. The hero of those Games was a Frenchman named Oreiller. The Savoyarde won the downhill and the combined — the latter considered a greater accolade in those days. He was the first "golden" boy from Val D'Isere. His skiing was in a different class and his hometown kept his name alive on the world cup circuits for ever by naming a downhill course after him.

Outside of Alpine skiing, which in modern terms is the "blue riband" of the Games, there had already been a host of magical Olympic moments. It is a shame that, without the kind of global TV audiences enjoyed by the Games of today, they sometimes remain dimmed in the memory.

Perhaps the initial hero of the Olympic Winter Games was Norway's Thorleif Haug who, in Chamonix in 1924, won two cross-country races as well as gold in the Nordic Combined and a bronze in the ski jump. Finland's Clas Thunberg won two speed skating golds and a silver as well as a gold for his combined performance at the inaugural Games.

One of the early stars of the Olympic Winter Games, however, was undoubtedly, Sonja Henie of Norway. Inspired by the top Russian ballerinas of the day, Henie won figure skating gold in 1928, aged just 15. Henie's style and rigorous training not only brought her a total of three golds in consecutive Games but also sparked a revolution in skating. She went on to create a glamorous career in Hollywood. Gillis Grafstrom of Sweden won his third consecutive Olympic gold in figure skating in 1928, having won the title when figure skating was part of the summer Games of 1920.

Norwegians took all the ski-jump medals in Lake Placid in 1932. The defining leap was Birger Ruud's second attempt which brought him gold—a feat he was to repeat in 1936 as well as taking a silver in 1948 aged 36. Another Norwegian, alongside Henie, was outstanding in the 1936 Games. Speed skater Ivar Ballangrud won three golds and a silver in those Games.

In Oslo in 1952, Austria's Trude Jochum-Belser repeated her gold medal Alpine skiing success of Garmisch in 1936. Understandably, she was overshadowed by local hero, Stein Eriksen. A previously fanatical cross-country nation suddenly had an Alpine hero to cheer. He won the giant slalom and was runner-up in the slalom. His charm and elegance also won him a subsequent Hollywood career.

In the 1952 women's Alpine skiing events a fascinating battle opened up between Austria's glamorous Dagmar Rom and Andy Mead-Lawrence, America's 1950 world champion, housewife and mother of two. The American was to succeed, winning the special slalom despite a fall.

Germans Andreas Ostler and Lorenz Nieberl proved they were Olympic heavyweights in more sense than one when winning two medals apiece in bobsleigh in these Games. Richard Button, reigning Olympic figure skating champion, successfully defended his title.

Nothing could have prepared Alpine fans, however, for 1956 and Cortina D'Ampezzo, Italy. Here, Anton "Toni" Sailer made a clean sweep of the Alpine golds—the first skier ever to do so. He was nicknamed "The Black Blitz from Kitz". The tinsmith from Kitbuehel delivered highlight after highlight. Everything this tall, handsome man touched turned, quite literally, to gold.

When he won the giant slalom by the incredible margin of six seconds over his compatriot Anderl Molterer, everybody rubbed their eyes in disbelief and questioned the veracity of the time-keeping. Sailer quelled the doubts by edging out Japan's Chiharu Igaya in a thrilling slalom battle on a difficult and demanding course.

Only the downhill, Sailer's best event, remained. He was a born downhiller and the famous Tofana course stood between him and glory. Then, misfortune struck. With a minute to go to the start, Sailer discovered that a lace in his binding had worked loose. Coolness under severe pressure is the mark of a great champion and, at that moment in time, Sailer proved he was amongst the all-time greats. Calmly, he waited for his coach, Hans Senger, to resolve the problem and went on to win—again by a large margin. Sailer was equally successful in his "second" career in films and the theatre.

Meanwhile, America achieved its own clean sweep in these Games by taking all three medals in the men's figure skating. A touch of showbusiness, mixed with native American history, awaited the Olympic family in Squaw Valley in 1960. Given the opportunity to stage the Games this resort rose from nothing to cope with the world's greatest sporting festival in a matter of months. Built by millionaires near Lake Tahoe, California, bordering on Nevada and its famous gambling cities.

If the facilities were a success, the weather remained a lottery. Different kinds of snow fell daily. Sometimes wet, sometimes dry. In the end, the French with new ski materials adapted the best. Jean Vuarnet won the men's downhill rather than the pre-race favourite, Adrien Duvillard. Willy Bogner, heir to a German fashion dynasty, seemed to have the slalom gold within his grasp in 1960 but let it slip at the bottom of the second run. Turning to a career as a film-maker, Bogner was later killed in an avalanche alongside two great skiers from those Squaw Valley Games, Buddy Werner and Barbl Henneberger.

America's heart at the 1960 Games, however, belonged to ice hockey and the incredible achievement of its own team in winning gold against the odds and against the mighty Soviets in a desperately close 3-2 finish.

When the Olympic Winter Games turned to Innsbruck in 1964 a global TV audience turned on for the first time, too. A cook from Lech, Austria, Egon Zimmerman, spoiled the soup for everyone else—including flu-weakened local hero Karl Schranz—by winning the giant slalom on the Patscherkofel. His mother was delighted with the happy outcome. She had begged him not to race following the death of Australian skier Ross Milne in training just weeks before the Games.

But there was more to come for ski-crazy Austria. Pepi Stiegler won the men's slalom gold and Christl Haas, Edith Zimmerman (no relation to Egon) and Traudi Hecher swept the women's donwhill medals. The first clean sweep in Olympic history in the discipline.

Grenoble, 1968, and France's Jean-Claude Killy had three in a row on his mind. Austrian Gerhard Nenning might have take issue with those intentions. He had won all the pre-Olympic downhills but could not handle the burden of expectations. Killy, on the other hand, had the kind of magic quality that all truly great racers possess—to be at their best when it counts. Downhill gold by a whisper from compatriot Perillat was followed by victory in the giant slalom. A third gold emerged from the foggy slalom course following a dispute over the disqualification of Karl Schranz of Austria—an incident which is well-documented elsewhere in this book.

For Schranz who recorded the event's fastest time after being permitted a second run it was like falling from heaven to hell. One moment he was accepting gold on the rostrum, the next he was out of the medals. For Killy it was the inverse process. He was promoted to the status of a demi-god in his own country.

The margin of glory in bobsleigh's two-man event in Grenoble was the smallest imaginable. The West German and Italian sleds finished with identical times after four runs. Gold was finally awarded to Italy as they had achieved the fastest single run. Such can sometimes be the margin between victory and defeat in Olympic sport.

Some great Olympic moments can also go relatively unnoticed at the time. Such was the fate of Italian Franco Nones who became the first non-Scandinavian ever to win an Olympic cross-country medal when he took the 30km event gold in Grenoble. Contrast that with the 12,000 fans who packed the cross-country finish area to cheer home Sixten Jernberg at the climax of his astonishing Olympic career in 1976 in Innsbruck.

A golden triple was always unlikely in Sapporo, 1972. Not even a foolhardy bookmaker, however, would have taken bets on Francisco Fernandez-Ochoa from Navacerrada, a small village in the Sierra de Guaderrama, 60km from Madrid, winning an Alpine skiing gold medal. A solid but unexceptional international skier but fuelled by an ambition to make history, Ochoa produced two storming slalom runs to become the first Spaniard to win an Olympic Winter Games gold.

There was, however, a clean sweep of the medals in one event—the 70m ski jump. Fittingly, it was the host nation's Yukio Kasaya, Akitsugu Konno and Seiji Aochi who achieved gold, silver and bronze respectively in front of an ecstatic and packed crowd.

Sapporo was also the setting for Norway's Magnar Solberg to win his second gold in biathlon. Four years earlier he had produced a faultless shooting peformance to beat hot title-favourite Alexander Tikhonov of the Soviet Union. In 1972 he missed twice on the range but had the speed in the tracks to win.

If Ochoa won the 1972 slalom out of the blue, nothing could have been a greater contrast in Innsbruck in the 1976 downhill. The whole of Austria was focused on a sunny Sunday in February on just one man. Franz Klammer. It was high noon and the streets were deserted. The local hero was almost "condemned to win" by his own winning streak prior to the Games.

He looked unbeatable. Yet pre-race conjecture centred not on Klammer's abilities but on a new type of skis with a hole in the tip. Would the red-hot favourite dare to try them on the big day? In the end, he did not. But he did produce one of the most thrilling Olympic downhill runs in history. Trailing defending champion Bernhard Russi of France at the intermediate timing point he came from behind with some truly dynamic and aggressive skiing to finish almost a second ahead. It was Klammer at his best and on request. Few will ever forget the performance.

Klammer's victory lessened the impact that another stunning Innsbruck feat might otherwise have had. In the women's events Rosi Mittermaier missed out on a clean sweep of the three gold medals on offer by a mere 12 hundredths of a second when she was beaten in the giant slalom.

One of female Alpine skiing's greatest names finally became an Olympic champion four years later at the last possible time of asking when Anne-Marie Moser Proell won the downhill at the 1980 Lake Placid Games on Whiteface mountain. In that one victory the several times world champion laid the Olympic ghosts which had threatened her for so long.

Proell's final triumph coincided with a first victory for Sweden's Ingemar Stenmark. The shy skier from Taernaby let his skiing talk for him with a touch of pure poetry. Everything he did on the slopes looked so easy. He seemed to be able to change gear at will. If he had not declared himself professional after the 1980 Games he may have repeated his golden double of slalom and giant slalom in 1984.

In all other senses, however, the 1980 Games were marked forever by a dramatic ice hockey victory for the previously unfancied team of collegiate players from the USA against the might of the Soviet Union as well as by a long track speed skater called Eric Heiden. Heiden, who went on to become a professional cyclist, won all five gold medals on offer at the Games. He credited his victory to a detailed pre-Games training programme as well as a desire to make people sit up and take notice of his otherwise sparsely-publicized sport.

The Soviet Union had won five out of six possible Olympic golds since arriving on the Olympic ice hockey scene in 1956. America's team was the youngest on average that it had ever fielded at the Games. Perhaps the ultimate tribute in a remarkable tournament should be paid to the goal-tender, Jim Craig. He made 36 saves in the USA's 4-3 defeat of the Soviet Union. America also rallied from a 2-1 deficit against Finland in the final.

The talk of the 1984 Sarajevo Games, however, was another American—an Alpine skier called Bill Johnson. In true "Wild West" fashion he fired back at all his critics by winning the downhill as he had so brashly predicted. Sarajevo belonged to the Americans with Debbie Armstrong winning the giant slalom and the Mahre twins taking gold and silver in the men's slalom.

At the ice rink in 1984 the world belonged briefly, however, to Britain. Ice dancers Jayne Torvill and Christopher Dean scored six perfect sixes for artistic impression and a further three for technical merit for their free dance interpretation of Ravel's "Bolero". The difference in style of choreography to all preceding ice dance competitions made this performance a defining Olympic moment. As the fated lovers from the story fell to the ice with the music dying in the background the crowd rose as one in unanimous acclaim. Torvill and Dean later attempted an Olympic comeback in Lillehammer in 1994. Again they were the crowd favourites but, this time, were awarded the bronze medal.

A Swede called Thomas Gustafson was also in form in 1984. He won the 10,000m speed skating event even though he had left the arena with a female companion convinced that his time might put him in the top six but would probably not win him a medal. Gustafson returned to the Olympic arena in 1988 where he won two more golds.

Calgary, where Pirmin Zurbriggen of Switzerland won the 1988 downhill, was the first Games to experience "Tomba-mania"—the circus of attention which followed Italy's charismatic slalom specialist who was better than anyone else when it came to the final run of his events. Nobody else could explode into action like he did, earning him the nickname "Tomba La Bomba". He won two golds and his touring band of fans partied all night each time. If the quiet, religious Zurbriggen was dubbed a "choirboy" then Tomba was most definitely a playboy. He was followed by a swarm of girls and the media wherever he went. He came back to the Games in 1992 to win the giant slalom and add a silver. Tomba was also a silver medallist in Lillehammer and will probably be skiing in Nagano.

The 1988 Games also fixed the moment when global sympathy rested with America's long track speed skater Dan Jansen. Pre-Games favourite in the shorter distances, he learned that his sister had died of

Alberto Tomba

Torvill and Dean

leukemia just hours before he was due to skate. Jansen, clearly unable to concentrate, fell in both races. Medals also eluded him in 1992.

So Lillehammer was his last chance of glory. He failed at 500m and everything rested on the 1000m. Jansen brought the complete crowd in Lillehammer's Viking Ship venue to its feet when he was on world record pace at 600m and went on to win. His lap of honour carrying his small daughter will be one of the abiding images of those Games. Another speed skater, Norway's Johann Olav Koss—dubbed "Koss the Boss"—was in stunning form in taking three golds on his home territory. His gesture of donating £32,000 (US$53,400) to Olympic Aid for Sarajevo also caught the public imagination.

Back to 1988, however, and the feats of the often irascible Finn Matti Nykanen who took two titles by flying further than anyone else from the "little and large" ski jump hills. He was supreme in his technique, threatening almost to land amidst the very crowd who gasped in amazement at his skill. That same crowd, however, gasped in fear with Britain's Michael "Eddie the Eagle" Edwards as he launched himself off the hills to finish last in each competition. A virtual novice, he became the folk-hero of the Games epitomising the love held by North Americans for "have-a-go" heroes.

On the cross-country tracks at Canmore, East Germany's Frank-Peter Roetsch became the first athlete in his sport to take both individual golds in one Games.

Calgary, too, was the scene for two of figure-skating's greatest Olympic battles. In the men's event two Brians—Boitano of the USA and Orser of Canada—entered the final night's free programme with a chance of gold. Boitano was the 1986 world champion, a title he surrendered to Orser a year later. Orser should have been bolstered by home support and had the advantage of skating second of the two. However, Boitano skated to near-perfection in one of the greatest Olympic Winter Games performances. Orser, skating last, nearly missed an early jump and never recovered.

A parallel script had been written for the 1988 women's event between an athletic black American, Debbie Thomas, and East Germany's seductive ice queen and 1984 Olympic champion Katarina Witt. Witt, slow and slinky, emerged from the short programme in first place with Thomas, upbeat and funky, close behind. Both chose the music from Carmen for their free programme. There the similarity ended. Witt opted for caution and artistry. She skated first and had to wait for Thomas who was skating last. But Thomas' earlier exuberance seemed to disappear that night as she completed a stumbling performance to give Witt the title. Witt also made headlines in Calgary in an alleged romantic allegiance with Tomba, the skier.

In 1992 in Albertville, the mountains might have danced to a Tomba beat once more. But Petra Kronberger of Austria was also in stunning form with two golds—one in the Alpine Combined and the other in the slalom. If Kronberger's win might have been expected, few would have chosen Patrick Ortleib of Austria to win the the men's downhill and Kerrin Lee-Gartner of Canada to win the women's version. Neither had previously won a downhill world cup title.

In similar fashion in Lillehammer, two years later, American Tommy Moe became yet another underdog in the rich tapestry of Olympic history to win gold on the day that mattered when he took the downhill title.

This was a Games, too, when Norway stamped itself on the medal table like no other host nation before. Perhaps the magic of this Games, however, was more than just sporting performances. Here was a Games which was relatively compact, where the sun shone daily and where the crowds were enthusiastic, knowledgeable and friendly. Vladimir Smirnov of Kazakhstan can confirm this. In front of over 100,000 people he won the 50km race at the cross-country venue. To do so, he beat some of the home favourites. Yet the crowd screamed and willed him to victory, chanting his name. They knew it might be the last chance that this popular and world-class athlete had of winning Olympic gold.

Perhaps, however, they got it wrong. Smirnov looks set to compete once more in Nagano where he may add to his Olympic tally. Tomba might shine once more. And a tense battle may be fought between figure skaters Tara Lipinski and Michelle Kwan, both of the USA. Japan has its host of good ski-jumpers and Nordic Combined exponents to bolster its hopes and Wolfgang Hoppe of Germany will be hoping to sign off in gold after a long and distinguished Olympic bobsleigh career.

Bjoern Daehlie, of Norway, may achieve greatness of even more significant proportions if he adds more than two golds to the four cross-country Olympic titles which he has already won.

Who can tell? On whom will the magic of the Olympic Games fall in 1998? Whose destiny is it to write Olympic history once more?

WORLD FORCES AND THE OLYMPIC WINTER GAMES*

"Sport transcends all political and racial situations". "When we let politics, racial questions or social disputes into our actions, we're in for trouble". Both quotes are attributed to Avery Brundage, IOC President from 1952 to '72.

The sentiments are noble. Yet history proves that the Olympic Games have always been subject to political influences. Indeed Brundage's successor, Lord Killanin, once said: "I have never denied or ignored the intrusion of politics into the Olympic Movement".

At the very beginning, the founding father of the modern Games, Baron Pierre de Coubertin, is alleged to have threatened to stage the 1896 Games of the Olympiad in Hungary as a measure to coerce the Greeks into making a commitment to host the inaugural Games.

More major political influences have impinged on many celebrations of the Olympic Games this century. Much has been recorded about the propaganda use Adolf Hitler made of the 1936 Olympic Games in Berlin. Several months earlier, however, there were similar scenes at the Olympic Winter Games in Garmisch-Partenkirchen.

Perhaps the IOC should have foreseen the troubles ahead. In 1931 they had awarded the Games to Germany by postal vote. A year later a German newspaper suggested that the Games should be for white athletes only. Adolf Hitler came to power in 1933. In June of that year the IOC President, Count de Baillet-Latour, a Belgian, was given the guarantee that Germany would respect the Olympic Charter, otherwise, it was stated, Germany would have to forego the Games.

Nazi ideology was as diametrically opposed to the Olympic ideal as was possible and, as the Germans' persecution of the Jews reached appalling proportions, the problems intensified as the Games grew closer. The Jewish question was at the heart of the matter.

Baron Pierre de Coubertin did not attend the opening ceremony

*Includes extracts from an article on this topic written by Iain Macleod

(he died a year later) which was led by Adolf Hitler with his ministers Dr Goebbels and General Goering. The intimations of racism, despite a German-jew being part of the host nation's ice hockey team, became apparent as the venue preparations were completed.

Signs on the toilets at first read: "Dog and Jews not allowed". Baillet Latour insisted on their removal before the Games began. Some athletes were later criticized, including Sonja Henie the figure skating star, for giving Hitler salutes on the rostrum. Some key German victories during the Games helped to fuel the Nazi propaganda machine.

The 1940 Olympic Winter Games was then awarded, at the IOC's 1936 Session in Berlin, to the Japanese venue of Sapporo—as that nation were also to host the summer Games of the same year in Tokyo. This blithely ignored Japan's invasion of Manchuria in 1931. When, in July 1937, Japan invaded China leading to the second Sino-Japanese war, the IOC's blushes were saved by the Japanese who withdrew as hosts, citing the huge expense involved. Australia and Britain had already agreed to boycott the Tokyo Games by that stage.

The IOC then designated St Moritz as the 1940 host for the Olympic Winter Games and, in June 1939, awarded the 1944 Olympic Winter Games to Cortina d'Ampezzo in Italy. However, in September 1939, Germany invaded Poland and for the next six years the Games became an irrelevance. When the IOC had its first post-War Executive Committee meeting in London, in August, 1945, there was much debate as to whether the Games should go on. However, the new President, a Swede, J.Sigfrid Edstrom, believed that they should and St Moritz was awarded the Games once more.

Edstrom and his successor, Avery Brundage, did much to reunite the Olympic Movement. Brundage even expressed the opinion in 1944 that German and Japanese athletes should be allowed to compete at the next Games. It was not a popular sentiment at the time but was consistent with his view that politics should not intervene in sport. Eventually, the 1948 Games went ahead but without Germany and Japan.

Cold war politics, the division of Germany and Korea, as well as disputes between China and Taiwan, all took a toll on the Olympic Movement, although they had a minor impact on the Winter Games when compared to the Games of the Olympiad.

Soviet athletes competed at the Olympic Winter Games in Cortina in 1956 for the first time.

In 1964, at the IOC Session in Innsbruck, the IOC voted to revoke South Africa's invitation to the Tokyo Games as they had not complied with requests to oppose publicly all racial discrimination. South Africa were not to return to the Olympic Winter Games family until the Games of Lillehammer in 1994.

In 1976 security had to be stepped up in Innsbruck—a Games which had originally been awarded to Denver, Colorado, USA, and then rebuffed by the voters of the city—after the Munich Olympic Games (1972) when 12 members of the Israeli Olympic delegation lost their lives after being taken hostage by terrorists from the Black September organization.

In the 1970s the Winter Games were affected by the oil crisis and the environmental protection movement. Both in Sapporo and in Lake Placid, the Games were the target of protests by ecological movements. This continued at later Games over the use of ammonia to cool the bob and luge tracks. In more recent years the IOC and host venues for the Games have adopted a proactive stance towards protection of the environment.

The Lake Placid Games of 1980 took place amidst frenzied discussions over potential boycotts of the summer Games of that year in Moscow. Soviet troops had invaded Afghanistan just weeks before the Winter Games. Later, this proved to be the start of an era of tit-for-tat boycotts of the summer Games of 1980 and 1984.

At its 1977 Session in Prague, the IOC had amended its charter and took measures to suspend or otherwise discipline any National Olympic Committee which entered its athletes in the Olympic Games and then withdrew them for political reasons. At the time, the gesture was haunted by immediate failure.

However, with President Samaranch at the helm—excepting the 1984 boycott of the Los Angeles Games—the Olympic Movement has entered a more stable era. Potential disaster was averted when staging the 1988 Olympic Games in South Korea, technically still at war with its northern neighbour. Albertville, Barcelona, Lillehammer and Atlanta have all enjoyed almost-full complements of attending nations.

Nagano is also set to benefit from that stability to stage the biggest Olympic Winter Games yet.

WOMEN AND THE OLYMPIC WINTER GAMES

"The prodigious and spectacular development of sport in this century has accorded an increasingly important place to women athletes", said Nawal El Moutawakel-Bennis, 1984 Olympic 400m hurdles champion and member of the IOC's Working Group on 'Women in Sport' in a recent publication.

"But the woman athlete must be placed in her setting and environment for us to better understand the different constraints which may impede her rise to success and her self-development. Sport is certainly not an activity that all women can take for granted".

With her two statements El Moutawakel-Bennis summed up the modern-day dilemma for women hoping to reach the top in sport. Certainly, from the International Olympic Committee's current viewpoint, it is imperative that the number of female competitors at the Games of the Olympiad and the Olympic Winter Games should increase. So should the number of women involved in the administration and coaching of sport.

Suggested quotas per federation and per National Olympic Committee have also been set by the IOC. President Samaranch recently exorted the Olympic Family "to make every effort to fill 10% of the posts in their legislative and executive bodies with women by the year 2000 and 20% by the year 2005".

The IOC, often criticized in the past for its own tardy incorporation of women has been busy in recent years co-opting new female members and will soon reach the 10% quota within its own organization.

In Atlanta, for the centennial Games, one third of the total athletes were women, representing 169 countries. A century before, in Athens, the first Games were totally devoid of female competitors. Indeed, writing in the Olympic Review of 1912, the founder of the modern Olympic Movement, Baron Pierre de Coubertin, described the Games as: "the solemn and periodic exaltation of male athleticism, with internationalism as a base, loyalty as a means, art for its setting, and female applause as reward". In other words, for de Coubertin, women had no place on the sports field.

It was hardly surprising, therefore, that the number of female athletes at early summer Olympic Games was small. Not only were they fighting against the perceptions of the Olympic founder but also against the prevailing culture of the period.

A small number of women took part in golf and tennis in 1900 whilst archery was added in 1904. The big breakthrough, in terms of summer sports, came in 1912 when the International Swimming Federation began to promote women's involvement actively.

Women also competed in figure skating in 1908 and 1920 when the sport was part of the summer Games rather than the Olympic Winter Games. For this fact, 51% of the population can be grateful because this ensured women appeared in the first Olympic Winter Games in Chamonix in 1924. Their route to wider winter participation was to prove slightly more tortuous, often blocked by ideology.

In 1936 women were permitted to take part in Alpine skiing—the first time that this discipline appeared on the Olympic programme for either men or women. Yet the first women's races in cross-country skiing did not appear, staggeringly, until 1952 and in long track speed skating until 1960.

From that point a rapid improvement took place. When the sport of luge made its Olympic debut in 1964, women were part of the programme with a singles event.

In 1976 the addition of ice dance to the programme gave the opportunity to more females to participate. Short track speed skating, introduced to the Olympic Games in general in 1992, has female events.

Biathlon admitted its first female competitors in 1992 whilst ice hockey will do so in 1998—although some reports claim that women competed in ice hockey in 1920. Curling and snowboarding are new Olympic sports in 1998 and both will have female representation.

This means that the total number of events at the Olympic Winter Games for women has risen from two in 1924 to 29 in 1998. And the total number of female athletes from 13 to 522.

Whilst the participation of women at the Olympic Winter Games since 1924 may have been small in terms of numbers, their impact has been enormous. Sonja Henie of Norway, who won three Olympic figure skating golds in 1928, '32 and '36, was the first true superstar of the Winter Games.

She brought a new athleticism, grace and style to the sport. Not

Rosi Mittermaier is congratulated on her 1976 Alpine golden double

Figure skating pair, 1908

Bonnie Blair, three times 500m speed skating gold medallist

only was it enough to win her three gold medals—the first in 1928 when she was aged 15—but it also launched her on a career in Hollywood. Henie thus became one of the first Olympic Winter Games athletes, and certainly the first female of the genre, to make over $1 million in commercial activities after the Games.

Over the years Henie has been followed by a pantheon of female figure skating stars, culminating in Oksana Baiul's fairytale performance in Lillehammer last year after which her tragi-comic smile turned to tears when she realized that she had won.

In between, the Games have savoured the sporting performances, and artistry, of Americans Dorothy Hamill and Peggy Fleming. Another American, Tenley Albright, won the title in 1956 despite having surgery on an ankle and Carol Heiss Jenkins was the 1960 winner—a promise she had made to her dying mother after winning silver in 1956. More recently, the former East German Katarina Witt won two consecutive golds in 1984 and '88. She brought a seductive element to her performances which helped popularize the sport once more worldwide.

In speed skating American Bonnie Blair is one of the most successful Winter Olympians of all time. She was the first skater to win the 500m title at three successive Games between 1988 and '94. Blair also took 1000m gold in 1992 and '94. Blair was a short track speed skater before turning to the long track version of the sport. Lidya Skoblikova of the Soviet Union won four golds at the 1964 Games as well as two in 1960 in this sport.

Cross-country skiing has also had its share of prolific female medallists. Raissa Smetanina of Russia won four golds, five silvers and one bronze in a career which spanned from 1976 to '92.

Rosi Mittermaier, Anne-Marie Moser-Proell, Pernilla Wiberg, Petra Kronberger and Andy Mead Lawrence are amongst the names who have set women's Alpine skiing alight over the years.

In 1998, however, one of the most fascinating battles for gold of the whole Games may come between two American teenagers, Michelle Kwan and Tara Lipinski. Women's ice hockey should make a few headlines, too, in the continually growing impact of female athletes on the Olympic story.

WOMEN'S EVENTS AT THE GAMES

Year	No. of events on programme	No. of events for women*	%
1924	16	2	12.5
1928	14	2	14.28
1932	14	2	14.28
1936	17	3	17.64
1948	22	5	22.72
1952	22	6	27.27
1956	24	7	29.16
1960	27	11	40.74
1964	34	13	38.23
1968	35	13	37.14
1972	35	13	37.14
1976	37	14	37.83
1980	38	14	36.84
1984	39	15	38.46
1988	46	18	39.13
1992	57	25	43.86
1994	61	27	44.26
1998	64	29	45.31

* including mixed events from 1924 to 1998

WRITING IN SKI GLOVES

by Morley Myers

Crossing your fingers for luck while wearing ski gloves is no easy feat. In really cold weather, they could become fused, making it impossible to use chopsticks which will be de rigueur when eating like the locals at next year's Olympic Winter Games in Nagano, Japan.

But finger-crossing is often the only recourse left to the media when confronted with the spectre of covering the Winter Games. Unlike their summer relation these are Games which are at the mercy of the weather which can play havoc with the schedule, upsetting the best laid plans of organizers and press alike.

Not enough snow and the ski events, centrepiece of the Games, have to be postponed. Too much snow... ditto... with the additional likelihood of transportation grinding to a halt and people being stranded like lost polar ice explorers. Recovering temporarily misplaced personnel, shuffling assignments and re-working storylines becomes second nature to the media.

Yet it remains very much a scaled-down operation with the media "army" having to deal with only 68 events in seven sports over 16 days in Nagano, compared to 271 events in 26 sports in 17 days at the Atlanta Olympic Games in Atlanta in 1996. Seventy nations will be competing in Nagano, but only 55 have applied for media accreditations which will total around 2700.

Writing for winter sports fans, however, is very specialized, aiming for a niche market. Apportioning coverage of each sport from the viewpoint of the national media is largely dependent on medal potential, but internationally, it is alpine skiing, figure skating and ice hockey which fuel the Games.

The debate still continues as to whether figure skating is a sport or a slice of "showbiz", but there is no escaping the impact it had on the

1994 Lillehammer Winter Games where the postscript to the Nancy Kerrigan—Tonya Harding drama of the wounded knee court-case attracted unprecedented publicity. Even so, it is the constant source of backstage heated rivalry which has always made figure skating good "copy" and a media "must" at the Games.

Traditionally, though, it is also the alpine skiers who are the Winter superstars and the battle for supremacy on the slopes makes this sport the top priority for sports editors. The World Cup season provides the perfect build-up to the Olympic Alpine events where the main focus is on the men's downhill, the "Gold Riband" of the Games.

The only certainty in an often unpredictable event this time round is that the winning time will be the fastest ever recorded because the race is being staged on an extra short course of less then 3000m.

The International Ski Federation (FIS) wanted the starting point raised from 1680m, but NAOC rejected the request on environmental grounds.

Equally, the location of the Alpine courses in Shiga Kogen (55kms) and Hakuba (44kms) will test the resources of the media transportation service as well as the endurance of reporters, especially if events are cancelled because of bad weather.

Ice hockey has always had a big following at the Games, but those in Nagano will be something special with the world's best players taking part in the tournament for the first time. Such greats as Wayne Gretzky will be on parade as the NHL (National Hockey League) professionals show their paces in a competition fit for any world championship. It is a genuine leap forward—much more so than the hyped-up Summer Olympic appearance of the US basketball "Dream Team"—and is likely to lead to tremendous pressure on media seating. The presence of the NHL players will also bring a completely new element to Olympic hockey reporting with stories of big money transfers, contract negotiations and NHL team news providing fresh fields.

The debut of women's ice hockey is likely to be treated tongue-in-cheek by much of the media along with curling, while there will be routine coverage—based on national bias—for the many other events, including nordic skiing, ski jumping, freestyle skiing, snowboarding (on its Olympic debut), speedskating, biathlon, bob and luge.

Television and radio share many of the problems of the written media at the Olympic Winter Games, but the consequences of bad weather can be more devastating, particularly relating to programming. There were 3200 hours of coverage of the 1996 Olympic

(Summer) Games, 10 times more than for Nagano. Yet if coverage of one of the scheduled sports at Atlanta had gone wrong, there were 25 others to replace it. The winter scenario is very much different with just a handful of choices. The programming is much thinner, so the vagaries of the weather have enormous consequences.

Figure skating and alpine skiing shoulder most of the weight for TV coverage of the Winter Games. Stock feature material has to be at the ready and if the bad weather really takes hold, then more TV viewers will know about the intricacies of curling than they ever thought possible.

PARTICIPATION OF NATIONS BY SPORT

Year	Biathlon	Bobsleigh	Figure skating	Ice hockey	Luge	Skeleton	Alpine skiing	Free-style	Nordic skiing	Speed skating	Short track
1908	*	*	5	*	*	*	*	*	*	*	*
1920	*	*	8	7	*	*	*	*	*	*	*
1924	*	5	11	8	*	*	*	*	12	10	*
1928	*	14	11	13	*	6	*	*	15	14	*
1932	*	8	12	4	*	*	*	*	12	6	*
1936	*	1	17	15	*	*	26	*	23	16	*
1948	*	9	12	9	*	6	26	*	15	15	*
1952	*	10	15	9	*	*	28	*	19	14	*
1956	*	14	15	10	*	*	31	*	21	18	*
1960	9	*	15	9	*	*	23	*	22	17	*
1964	15	11	16	16	12	*	32	*	25	23	*
1968	16	11	17	14	14	*	33	*	25	19	*
1972	14	11	18	11	13	*	28	*	20	18	*
1976	18	13	18	12	16	*	33	*	24	19	*
1980	18	11	20	12	14	*	30	*	25	20	*
1984	25	16	21	12	17	*	42	*	33	24	*
1988	23	23	26	12	22	*	43	*	35	21	*
1992	28	25	28	12	22	*	50	19	41	23	17
1994	32	30	28	12	25	*	45	21	53	21	19

NATIONAL MEDALS TOTALS IN EACH OLYMPIC WINTER GAMES

	Gold	Silver	Bronze		Gold	Silver	Bronze		Gold	Silver	Bronze
1924 Chamonix				GBR	1	1	1	CAN	-	1	2
NOR	4	7	7	USA	1	-	3	JPN	-	1	-
FIN	4	4	2	CAN	-	1	-	GDR	-	-	1
AUT	2	1	-	FRA	-	-	1	POL	-	-	1
SUI	2	-	1	HUN	-	-	1	HUN	-	-	1
USA	1	2	-								
GBR	1	1	2	**1948 St Moritz**				**1960 Squaw Valley**			
SWE	1	1	-	SWE	4	3	3	URS	7	5	9
CAN	1	-	-	NOR	4	2	3	USA	3	4	3
FRA	-	-	3	SUI	3	4	2	NOR	3	3	-
BEL	-	-	1	USA	3	3	3	SWE	3	2	2
				FRA	2	1	2	FIN	2	3	3
1928 St Moritz				CAN	2	-	3	FRG	2	3	1
NOR	6	4	5	AUT	1	3	4	CAN	2	1	1
USA	2	2	2	FIN	1	3	2	GDR	2	-	-
SWE	2	2	1	BEL	1	1	-	SUI	2	-	-
FIN	2	1	1	ITA	1	-	-	AUT	1	2	3
CAN	1	-	-	CZE	-	1	-	FRA	1	-	2
FRA	1	-	-	HUN	-	1	-	NED	-	1	1
AUT	-	3	1	GBR	-	-	2	POL	-	1	1
SUI	-	-	1					CZE	-	1	-
GBR	-	-	1	**1952 Oslo**				ITA	-	-	1
CZE	-	-	1	NOR	7	3	6				
BEL	-	-	1	USA	4	6	1	**1964 Innsbruck**			
GER	-	-	1	FIN	3	4	2	URS	11	8	6
				FRG	3	2	2	AUT	4	5	3
1932 Lake Placid				AUT	2	4	2	NOR	3	6	6
USA	6	4	2	ITA	1	-	1	FIN	3	4	3
NOR	3	4	3	CAN	1	-	1	FRA	3	4	-
SWE	1	2	-	GBR	1	-	-	SWE	3	3	1
CAN	1	1	5	NED	-	3	-	GDR	2	2	1
FIN	1	1	1	SWE	-	-	4	USA	1	2	3
AUT	1	1	-	SUI	-	-	2	NED	1	1	-
FRA	1	-	-	FRA	-	-	1	FRG	1	-	2
SUI	-	1	-	HUN	-	-	1	CAN	1	-	2
GER	-	-	2	**1956 Cortina**				GBR	1	-	-
HUN	-	-	1	URS	6	4	6	ITA	-	1	3
				AUT	4	3	4	PRK	-	1	-
1936 Garmisch				FIN	3	3	1	CZE	-	-	1
NOR	7	5	3	SUI	3	2	1				
GER	3	3	-	SWE	2	4	4	**1968 Grenoble**			
SWE	2	2	3	USA	2	3	2	NOR	6	6	2
FIN	1	2	3	NOR	2	1	1	URS	5	5	3
SUI	1	2	-	ITA	1	2	-	FRA	4	3	2
AUT	1	1	2	FRG	1	-	-	ITA	4	1	1

	Gold	Silver	Bronze
AUT	3	4	4
NED	3	3	3
SWE	3	2	3
FRG	2	2	3
USA	1	5	1
FIN	1	2	2
GDR	1	2	2
CZE	1	2	1
CAN	1	1	1
SUI	-	2	4
ROM	-	-	1

1972 Sapporo

	Gold	Silver	Bronze
URS	8	5	3
GDR	4	3	7
SUI	4	3	3
NED	4	3	2
USA	3	2	3
FRG	3	1	1
NOR	2	5	5
ITA	2	2	1
AUT	1	2	2
SWE	1	1	2
JPN	1	1	1
CZE	1	-	2
POL	1	-	-
ESP	1	-	-
FIN	-	4	1
FRA	-	1	2
CAN	-	1	-

1976 Innsbruck

	Gold	Silver	Bronze
URS	13	6	8
GDR	7	5	7
USA	3	3	4
NOR	3	3	1
FRG	2	5	3
FIN	2	4	1
AUT	2	2	2
SUI	1	3	1
NED	1	2	3
FRA	1	2	1
CAN	1	1	1
GBR	1	-	-
CZE	-	1	-
SWE	-	-	2
LIE	-	-	2
FRA	-	-	1

1980 Lake Placid

	Gold	Silver	Bronze
URS	10	6	6
GDR	9	7	7
USA	6	4	2
AUT	3	2	2
SWE	3	-	1
LIE	2	2	-
FIN	1	5	3
NOR	1	3	6

	Gold	Silver	Bronze
NED	1	2	1
SUI	1	1	3
GBR	1	-	-
FRG	-	2	3
ITA	-	2	-
CAN	-	1	1
HUN	-	1	-
FRA	-	-	1
CZE	-	-	1
JPN	-	-	1
BUL	-	-	1

1984 Sarajevo

	Gold	Silver	Bronze
GDR	9	9	6
URS	6	10	9
USA	4	4	-
FIN	4	3	6
SWE	4	2	2
NOR	3	2	4
SUI	2	2	1
FRG	2	1	1
CAN	2	1	1
ITA	2	-	-
GBR	1	-	-
CZE	-	2	4
FRA	-	1	2
JPN	-	1	-
YUG	-	1	-
LIE	-	-	2
AUT	-	-	1

1988 Calgary

	Gold	Silver	Bronze
URS	11	9	9
GDR	9	10	6
SUI	5	5	5
SWE	4	2	2
FIN	4	1	2
AUT	3	5	2
NED	3	2	2
FRG	2	4	2
USA	2	1	3
ITA	2	1	2
FRA	1	-	1
NOR	-	3	2
CAN	-	2	3
YUG	-	2	1
CZE	-	1	2
LIE	-	-	1
JPN	-	-	1

1992 Albertville

	Gold	Silver	Bronze
GER	10	10	6
EUN	9	6	8
NOR	9	6	5
AUT	6	7	8
USA	5	4	2
ITA	4	6	4
FRA	3	5	1

	Gold	Silver	Bronze
FIN	3	1	3
CAN	2	3	2
KOR (South)	2	1	1
JPN	1	2	4
NED	1	1	2
SWE	1	-	3
SUI	1	-	2
CHI	-	3	-
LUX	-	2	-
NZL	-	1	-
CZE	-	-	3
ESP	-	-	1
KOR (North)	-	-	1

1994 Lillehammer

	Gold	Silver	Bronze
URS	11	8	4
NOR	10	11	5
GER	9	7	8
ITA	7	5	8
USA	6	5	2
KOR	4	1	1
CAN	3	6	4
SUI	3	4	2
AUT	2	3	4
SWE	2	1	-
JPN	1	2	2
KAZ	1	2	-
UKR	1	-	1
UZB	1	-	-
BLR	-	2	-
FIN	-	1	5
FRA	-	1	4
NED	-	1	3
CHI	-	1	2
SLO	-	-	3
GBR	-	-	2
AUS	-	-	1

TABLE OF PAST GAMES AND LOCATIONS

Year	Venue	Nations	Athletes m	w	Sports	No. of sports
1924	Chamonix	16	258	13	Bobsleigh, curling, ice hockey, military patrol, skating (w/mx)*, skiing	6
1928	St Moritz	25	464	26	Bobsleigh, ice hockey, skating (w/mx) (w/mx), skeleton, skiing	5
1932	Lake Placid	17	232	21	Bobsleigh, ice hockey, skating (w/mx) (w/mx), skiing	4
1936	Garmisch	28	668	80	Bobsleigh, ice hockey, skating (w/mx), skiing (w)	4
1948	St Moritz	28	669	77	Bobsleigh, ice hockey, skating (w/mx), skeleton, skiing (w)	5
1952	Oslo	30	694	109	Bobsleigh, ice hockey, skating (w/mx), skiing (w)	4
1956	Cortina	32	820	132	Bobsleigh, ice hockey, skating (w/mx), skiing (w)	4
1960	Squaw Valley	30	665	143	Biathlon, ice hockey, skating (w/mx), skiing (w)	4
1964	Innsbruck	36	1091	200	Biathlon, bobsleigh, ice hockey, luge (w), skating (w/mx), skiing (w)	6
1968	Grenoble	37	1158	211	Biathlon, bobsleigh, ice hockey, luge (w), skating (w/mx), skiing (w)	6
1972	Sapporo	35	1006	206	Biathlon, bobsleigh, ice hockey, luge (w), skating (w/mx), skiing (w)	6
1976	Innsbruck	37	1123	231	Biathlon, bobsleigh, ice hockey, luge (w), skating (w/mx), skiing (w)	6
1980	Lake Placid	37	1072	235	Biathlon, bobsleigh, ice hockey, luge (w), skating (w/mx), skiing (w)	6
1984	Sarajevo	49	1274	274	Biathlon, bobsleigh, ice hockey, luge (w), skating (w/mx), skiing (w)	6
1988	Calgary	57	1423	313	Biathlon, bobsleigh, ice hockey, luge (w), skating (w/mx), skiing (w)	6
1992	Albertville	64	1801	489	Biathlon (w), bobsleigh, curling (w), ice hockey, luge (w), skating (w/mx), skiing (w)	6
1994	Lillehammer	67	1739	522	Biathlon (w), bobsleigh, ice hockey, luge (w), skating (w/mx), skiing (w)	6
1998	Nagano				Biathlon (w), bobsleigh, curling, ice hockey, luge (w), skating (w/mx), skiing (w)	7

Men participate in all sports.
w and mx indicate that there are events for women and mixed pairs in the sport.

ALL-TIME MEDALS TABLE 1924–1994

Country	Gold	Silver	Bronze	Total
Soviet Union 1	79	57	59	195
Norway	73	77	64	214
United States	53	56	39	147
Sweden	39	26	34	99
East Germany 2	39	36	35	110
Finland	36	45	42	123
Austria	36	48	44	128
Switzerland	27	29	29	85
West Germany 2	26	27	23	75
Italy	25	21	21	67
Canada	19	20	24	64
Germany	19	17	14	50
France	16	16	21	53
Netherlands	14	19	17	50
Russia 3	11	8	4	23
Unified Team 4	9	6	8	23
Great Britain	7	4	12	23
Korea	6	2	2	10
Japan	3	8	8	19
Czechoslovakia	2	8	16	26
Liechtenstein	2	2	5	9
Poland	1	1	2	4
Belgium	1	1	2	4
Spain	1	-	1	2
Kazakhstan 3	1	2	-	3
Ukraine 3	1	-	1	2
Uzbekista 3	1	-	-	1
Yugoslavia	-	3	1	4
Hungary	-	2	4	6
China	-	4	3	7
Belarus 3	-	2	-	2
Luxembourg	-	2	-	2
North Korea	-	1	1	2
New Zealand	-	1	-	1
Slovenia 3	-	-	3	3
Australia	-	-	1	1
Bulgaria	-	-	1	1
Romania	-	-	1	1
TOTAL	547	551	542	1639

1 Up to and including 1988
2 Up to and including 1988. Thereafter see under Germany
3 From 1994 onwards
4 For 1992 only

PART TWO
Nagano 1998

ABOUT NAGANO

Nagano City has a population of 360,000. It is surrounded by mountains, including the Northern Japanese Alps. Prior to winning the right to stage the 1998 Olympic Winter Games, Nagano was known as the site of the historic buddhist Zenjoki Temple which attracted a multitude of visitors for centuries. In the southern part of the city there is also the site of an ancient battle where two local warlords, Takeda Shingen and Uesugi Kenshin, fought each other in the sixteenth century at Kawanakajima.

The Chikuma, Sai and Susbana rivers flow through the city which is surrounded by a region famous for growing apples and peaches. 3000 athletes and officials will be housed in the Olympic Village in the Imai district of Kawanakajima, during the Games. This new town development will be used as housing once the Games are over. There will also be a satellite Village in Karuizawa for the sport of curling.

A cluster of venues within Nagano will host competitions in ice hockey, all the skating disciplines as well as the opening and closing ceremonies. Ice hockey will take place in the "Big Hat" to the southeast of the city centre as well as the "Aqua Wing, located in Nagano Sports Park. "Big Hat", so-named for the shape of its exterior, will host all the main matches including the medal encounters as well as the majority of the men's group games.

Figure skating and short track will find a home in the city's "White Ring" stadium again to the south-east of the centre. "White Ring" also gets its name from its exterior appearance which is supposed to represent a water droplet. The stadium is in Nagano's Mashima district.

Long track skating, meanwhile, will be housed within the "M-wave" stadium straddling the city's Asahi and Mamejima districts to the east of the centre. The M-wave is an impressive structure mimmicking the contours of the surrounding mountains. It contains a 400m track and, just as its 1994 Lillehammer Games fore-runner, the emphasis inside is on natural materials.

Bobsleigh and luge's dramatic "Spiral" track with its unique dual uphill sections is located in Iizuna Kogen. This is an area which

Nagano skyline

The Winter Games Host in 1998: Nagano

Shiga Kogen—one of the key venues

spreads out along the base of Mt Iizuna, northwest of Nagano City. Iizuna Kogen is characterised by lakes, forests and marshes as well as being home to a spectacular array of birdlife. The area will also play host to the dramatic Olympic discipline of freestyle skiing.

Nagano's final city-based venue is the dramatic "ceremonies" stadium in Minami Nagano Sports Park in Tofukuji. The stadium will be the focus for 50,000 spectators as well as a global TV audience of millions when the Games open on the morning of 7 February, 1998. The two hour ceremony will have a dramatic artistic programme alongside the "official and symbolic Olympic elements" of lighting the Olympic flame, raising the Olympic flag, taking the athletes' oath and singing the Olympic hymn.

Alpine skiing's speed events—the downhill and super-G—for men and women will be staged in the Happo'one skiing area of Hakuba. The men's downhill—on a specially shortened course to protect the natural environment at the top of the slopes—will start on the Usagiaira course, finishing on a portion of the Kokusai course. The women's equivalent event will begin on the Kurobishi course and end on the Sakka course. Both super-G races will take place on the same courses but with lower starting points.

Hakuba Village, home to 9300 people, will also be the location of the ski-jumping events during the Games. Two spectacular hills have been built against the backdrop of the mountains in this popular tourist area which includes the "Hakuba Grand Snowy Gorge". Hakuba is also on the route of Japan's famous "Chikuni Highway" or salt road. The route was used in ancient times to transport salt from the Japan Sea and there is an annual salt festival in Hakuba.

The ski jump hills will be used as part of the Nordic Combined event. Cross-country skiing will also find its home in the Kamishiro area of Hakuba where dramatic and testing trails have been prepared.

Shiga Kogen, Yamanouchi Town, well known as a winter ski resort and a summer recreation area, will play host to the technical disciplines of Alpine skiing as well as the new Olympic discipline of snowboarding. The slopes of Mount Higashidate will be home to the giant slalom races for Alpine skiing whilst the slalom races for Alpine skiing and snowboarding's giant slalom will take place on the slopes of Mount Yakebitai. Kabayashi Snowboard Park will be the venue for snowboard's innovative half-pipe event.

The Shiga Kogen highlands are the pride of Yamanouchi. They form, with the town, part of a national park and are considered an area of outstanding natural beauty. Some of the peaks in the region reach over 2000m (6562ft) in height and were formed by volcanic activity.

Two other satellite venues have been brought into use for the Games. The first of these, the biathlon will take place in Nozawa Onsen. Originally, this sport was to have been hosted in Hakuba but this would have meant disturbing rare Goshawk nests so the venue was changed. Nozawa Onsen is famous for its hot springs and was a ski resort as far back as 1924. A million skiers a year now tackle its slopes. Although the village itself only has a population of 5000 people, it has already sent 11 competitors to the Olympic Winter Games since 1956.

Karuizawa Town's pleasantly cool summer climate has made it a summer resort for those wishing to escape the heat. Many Japanese have summer houses there following in the footsteps of British missionary Alexander Croft Shaw who first saw the area's potential. The surrounding woodlands are a haven for wildlife.

At the 1998 Olympic Winter Games, Karuizawa Town will play host to curling—another Olympic newcomer alongside snowboarding and women's ice hockey. Karuizawa, however, already has its place in Olympic history. This was the venue for the equestrian events during the 1964 Olympic Games in Tokyo. Therefore, it will be the first venue in the world to host winter and summer Games events.

Four owlets are Nagano's mascots for the 1998 Olympic Winter Games. There are four to represent the four year Olympic cycle and their youth has been chosen to depict the "fun" of the Games. Owls have been selected, too, as they are cherished for their "wisdom" by peoples around the world. The four owls are called Sukki, Nokki, Lekki and Tsukki.

An Olympic torch relay will bring a flame ignited in December 1997 at the Temple of Hera, at Olympia in Greece to Nagano. In January 1998 the flame will begin a journey through 47 Japanese prefectures en route. Once in Nagano prefecture it will travel through 120 municipalities carried by torch bearers with running escorts. Some sections of the journey will be taken on skis and by sleigh before the flame enters the opening ceremony stadium on February 7, 1998.

February 7, 1998 will be the culmination of a dream which began in July 1986 at the first meeting of the Nagano Winter Games Bidding Committee. The desire to bid was approved by the Japanese Cabinet in 1989 and Nagano won the right to stage the Games during a vote taken at the 97th IOC Session in Birmingham, England, in June 1991.

NAGANO SCHEDULE

FEBRUARY 1998

SPORT	VENUE	7	8	9	10	11	12	13	14	15	16	17	18	19	20	21	22	No. of days
OPENING CEREMONY	Minami Nagano Sports Park	7																1
VICTORY CEREMONY	Central Square		8	9	10	11	12	13	14	15	16	17	18	19	20	21	22	15
Alpine Skiing																		
Downhill	Happo'one Course1/Course 2 - Hakuba		8						14									2
Combined downhill	Happo'one Course1/Course 2 - Hakuba			9						15								2
Slalom	Mt Yakebitai - Yamanouchi													19		21		2
Giant slalom	Mt Higashidate - Yamanouchi												18		20			2
Super-G	Happo'one Course1/Course 2 - Hakuba				10			13										2
Combined slalom	Happo'one Course1 - Hakuba					11						17						2
Cross-country Skiing	Snow Harp - Hakuba		8	9	10		12		14		16		18		20		22	9
Ski Jumping	Hakuba ski jumping stadium					11				15		17						3
Nordic Combined	Hakuba							13	14					19	20			4
Freestyle Skiing																		
Moguls	Iizuna Kogen ski area		8			11												2
Aerials	Iizuna Kogen ski area										16		18					2
Snowboarding																		
Giant slalom	Mt Yakebitai - Yamanouchi		8	9														2
Half pipe	Kanbayashi snowboard park - Yamanouchi						12											1
Speed Skating	M-Wave - Nagano City		8	9	10	11	12	13	14	15	16	17		19	20			12
Figure Skating	White Ring		8		10		12	13	14	15	16		18		20	21		10
Short Track Speed Skating	White Ring											17		19		21		3
Ice Hockey	Big Hat/Aqua Wing	7	8	9	10	11	12	13	14	15	16	17	18		20	21	22	15
Bobsleigh	Spiral								14	15					20	21		4
Luge	Spiral		8	9	10	11		13										5
Biathlon	Nozawa Onsen			9		11				15		17		19		21		6
Curling	Kazekoshi Park arena - Karuizawa			9	10	11	12	13	14	15								7
CLOSING CEREMONY	Manami Nagano Sports Park																	1

WALKABOUT

by Wilf O'Reilly*

It is like a children's dream village. Only for "adults." It is where the rich and famous mix with the poor and not so well known. It is the place where almost all social, cultural and economic barriers are brought down. From free food to eye vision tests and condom supplies. It all happens here. If you have not guessed by now, I am talking about the "Olympic Village."

My first encounter with the Olympic Village was in 1972. I saw it on the TV and, at the age of eight, I just thought everyone turned up. In that year though, the terrible tragedy of the terrorist attack and hostage-taking brought it to the forefront for the world's media and for me. It also showed what a powerful stage the Olympic Games is.

Clearly, as I later learned, you do not just turn up. Immense planning is necessary to meet the needs of such a number of athletes. Even down to the village's environmental friendliness.

As a three times Olympian, the village has a special ambiance about it. After a long, tiring trip to the host city I wait to get my accreditation. But from the moment I walk through the first security check, it makes me feel important. With this "thing" that hangs around my neck (my accreditation tag on a chain) I can go almost anywhere.

I head off to find my room. I am fortunate enough to have a single room. Not that this is a problem for me to share a room, but I think it helps me to focus better on the job. Then the next port of call is the restaurant.

This is where the first part of the fun starts. Where do I find the restaurant? The adventure begins. I bump into Katerina Witt on my way to the restaurant, then Alberta Tomba and Nancy Kerrigan (including her security guards). By now I am completely lost. So I decide to forget the pains and grumbling in my stomach and check out this amazing place.

The only problem is, unlike the Summer Games, it is twenty degrees below. But my eagerness to explore further is addictive. My first impression of the village is its size. Akin to trying to cross the road in the middle of Tokyo. People all walking in different directions busying themselves with their own concerns. It looks similar to a circus performance with all their brightly coloured uniforms.

As I walk towards a mass of people gathered around a man and a woman, I cannot make out who they are. I take no notice and carry on walking. I later find out that they were Don Johnson and Melanie Griffith. This place is amazing!

Walking over newly formed snow I slip and fall heavily. With sore wrists and a bruised hip I suddenly realize that I am hungry after all. Limping off in the direction of the restaurant I can see it is snowing in the mountains in the distance. It will not be long before the snow has changed the appearance of the village.

It is then that I feel this energy that is far too incredible to put into words. Total relaxation. I am trance-like yet fully aware of what is going on around me. Then, in that split second, I know I am going to win. Trying to rationalize, I ask myself how I can possibly know this? I have not done a single training session in the competition arena and I know I am going to win. Still shaking from this frightening experience I head back to the restaurant.

Sitting down to my first meal in the Olympic Village is a treat. As a lover of hot, spicy food (particularly Indian) I am pleasantly surprised at the selection on offer. Because there is so much on offer people tend to take a bit of everything. Athletes are bigger than average eaters and pile a range of different dishes on the same plate. My first mistake! It is all free and open twenty four hours a day. I would advise anyone to only select one main style. Although, after about the fourth or fifth day, you get pretty bored with the same food with its cyclical menu changes.

Belly full and raring to go (I don't know where at 21.30) I walk with a group of other skaters back to our rooms. I lie on my bed listening to how quiet the whole village seems. All these athletes in the Olympic Village and yet so quiet you can hear the snow fall outside. I cannot sleep so I decide to get dressed again and continue my walkabout of the village.

Whilst getting dressed I notice a greeting card addressed to occupier of the room. It is from one of the local school children. He is asking me to send him a card stating who I am and my sport. Walking out into the cold night air I cannot help thinking how nice it would be to answer this request by telling him that I am going to win. I guess this would be too confident.

I walk past the restaurant towards the main entrance. Security guards are standing around the gate making the odd jump in the air to keep their feet warm. I notice two teams of hockey players coming through the security check. From the expressions on their faces it is clear to see that one team has lost and the other has won. What a difference success can make.

For me this energy draining experience resulted in two gold medals in 1988. I will never forget my first "walkabout" in the Olympic Village nor the good and bad memories I was fortunate to experience whilst I was there over my three Games.

It is said that when you go on a walkabout you go to find yourself. I certainly did. And that schoolboy? He got his card from me and even to this day I still get the occasional Christmas card from him.

* *Wilf O'Reilly won two golds when short-track speed skating was a demonstration sport in 1988.*

DISCONTINUED EVENTS

Sport	Year of participation
Military patrol	1924-1948
Speed skating — all round championship	1924
Luge - skeleton	1928, 1948
Figure skating — special figures (m)	1908 (part of summer Games)
Speed skating — 4 races combined (m)	1924
Biathlon — 3 x 7.5km relay (w)	1992
Biathlon — 4 x 7.5km relay (w)	1994
Speed skiing	1992
Ski ballet	1992
Nordic:	
15km classical (m)	1924–1988
10km classical (w)	1952–1988
20km freestyle (w)	1984–1988

1998 SPORTS AND EVENTS LIST

BIATHLON

Men – 3 events

20km
10km
4x7.5km relay

Women – 3 events

15km
7.5km
4x7.5km relay

BOBSLEIGH

Men

Two man
Four man

CURLING

Men's Tournament

Women's Tournament

ICE HOCKEY

Men

14-team tournament

Women

6-team tournament

LUGE

Men

Single
Double

Women

Single

SKATING

Men – 9 events

Speed skating
500m
1000m
1500m
5000m
10,000m

Short-track speed skating
500m
1000m
5000m relay

Figure skating
Men's individual

Women – 9 events

Speed skating
500m
1000m
1500m
3000m
5000m

Short track speed skating
500m
1000m
3000m relay

Figure skating
Women's individual

Mixed - 2 events
Pairs
Ice-dancing

SKIING

Men – 17 events

Cross country skiing
10km classical
15km pursuit/free
30km free
50km classical
4x10km relay: classical-free

Jumping
90m individual
120m individual
120m team

Nordic Combined
Individual Combined (90m
jumping + 15km)
Team Combined (90m jumping
+ 3x10km relay)

Alpine skiing
Downhill
Slalom
Giant slalom
Super giant slalom
Alpine Combined

Freestyle skiing
Moguls
Aerials

Snowboard
Giant slalom
Half-pipe

Women – 12 events

Cross country skiing
5km classical
10km pursuit/free
15km free
30km classical
4x5km relay: classical-free

Alpine skiing
Downhill
Slalom
Giant slalom
Super giant slalom
Alpine Combined

Freestyle skiing
Moguls
Aerials

Snowboard
Giant slalom
Half pipe

INTERNATIONAL TIME ZONES

Hours ahead (+) or behind (-)
Greenwich Mean Time—no account is taken of Summer Time

Afghanistan	+4	East	-3	Czech Republic	+1
Albania	+1	Acre	-5	Denmark	+1
Algeria	+1	Brunei	+8	Djibouti	+3
Angola	+1	Bulgaria	+2	Dominica	-5
Antigua	-4	Burkina Faso	GMT	Dominican Republic	-4
Argentina	-3	Burundi	+2	Ecuador	-5
Armenia	+3	Cameroon	+1	Egypt	+2
Aruba	-4	Canada:		Equatorial Guinea	+1
Australia:		*Newfoundland*	-3	Estonia	+3
Canberra, NSW	+10	*Atlantic*	-4	Ethiopia	+3
Victoria, Queensland	+10	*Eastern*	-5	Fiji	+12
Tasmania	+10	*Central*	-6	Finland	+2
Northern Territory	+10	*Mountain*	-7	France	+1
South Australia	+9	*Pacific*	-8	Gabon	+1
Western Australia	+8	*Yukon*	-8	Gambia	GMT
Austria	+1	Cape Verde Islands	-1	Georgia	+4
Azerbaijan	+4	Cayman Islands	-5	Germany	+1
Bahamas	-5	Central African Republic	+1	Ghana	GMT
Bahrain	+3	Chad	+1	Gibraltar	+1
Bangladesh	+6	Chile	-4	Great Britain	GMT
Barbados	-4	China, People's Republic	+8	Greece	+2
Belarus	+3	Colombia	-5	Grenada	-4
Belgium	+1	Comoro Islands	+3	Guam	+10
Belize	-6	Congo	+1	Guatemala	-6
Benin	+1	Cook Islands	-10	Guinea	GMT
Bermuda	-4	Costa Rica	-6	Guyana	-3
Bhutan	+6	Cote d'Ivoire	GMT	Haiti	-5
Bolivia	-4	Croatia	+1	Honduras	-6
Bosnia Herzegovina	+1	Cuba	-5	Hong Kong	+8
Botswana	+2	Cyprus:		Hungary	+1
Brazil		*North*	+3	Iceland	GMT
West	-4	*South*	+2	India	+5

Indonesia:		Nepal	+5	Sweden	+1
West Zone	+7	Netherlands	+1	Switzerland	+1
Central Zone	+8	Netherlands Antillies	-4	Syria	+2
East Zone	+9	New Zealand	+12	Taiwan	+8
Iran, Islamic Republic	+3	Nicaragua	-6	Tajikistan	+5
Iraq	+3	Niger	+1	Tanzania	+3
Ireland	GMT	Nigeria	+1	Thailand	+7
Israel	+2	Norway	+1	Togo	GMT
Italy	+1	Oman	+4	Tonga	+13
Jamaica	-5	Pakistan	+5	Trinidad & Tobago	-4
Japan	+9	Palestine	+2	Tunisia	+1
Jordan	+2	Panama	-5	Turkey	+3
Kazakhstan		Papua New Guinea	+10	Turkmenistan	+5
Ama-Ata	+6	Paraguay	-4	Turks & Caicos Islands	-5
Ouralsk	+5	Peru	-5	Uganda	+3
Kenya	+7	Philippines	+8	Ukraine	+3
Korea	+9	Poland	+1	United Arab Emirates	+4
Korea DPR	+9	Portugal	GMT	USA:	
Kuwait	+3	Puerto Rico	-4	Eastern	-5
Kyrgyzstan	+6	Qatar	+3	Central	-6
Lao	+7	Romania	+2	Mountain	-7
Latvia	+3	Russia:		Pacific	-8
Lebanon	+2	Moscow	+2	Alaska	-9/10
Lesotho	+2	St. Petersburg	+3	Hawaii	-10
Liberia	GMT	Omsk	+6	Uruguay	-3
Libya	+1	Vladivostock	+10	Uzbekistan	+5
Liechtenstein	+1	Rwanda	+2	Venezuela	-4
Lithuania	+2	Saint Lucia	-4	Vietnam	+7
Luxembourg	+1	Saint Vincent	-4	Virgin Islands	-4
Macedonia	+1	Salvador (El)	-6	Yemen	+3
Mdagascar	+3	Samoa	-11	Yugoslavia	+1
Malawi	+2	San Marino	+1	Zaire:	
Malaysia	+8	Saudi Arabia	+3	Kinshasa	+1
Maldives	+5	Senegal	GMT	Shaba	+2
Mali	+1	Seychelles	+4	Zambia	+2
Malta	+1	Sierra Leone	GMT	Zimbabwe	+2
Marshall Islands	+12	Singapore	+8		
Mauritania	GMT	Slovakia	+1		
Mauritius	+4	Slovenia	+1		
Mexico	-6	Solomon Islands	+11		
Moldova	+3	Somalia	+3		
Monaco	+1	South Africa	+2		
Mongolia	+8	Spain	+1		
Morocco	GMT	Sri Lanka	+5		
Mozambique	+2	Sudan	+2		
Myanmar	+6	Surinam	-3		
Namibia	+2	Swaziland	+2		

ABBREVIATIONS FOR WEIGHTS & MEASURES

g	*gram(s)*	in.	*inch(es)*
kg	*kilogram(s)*	kmph	*kilometres per hour*
oz	*ounce(s)*	mph	*miles per hour*
lb	*pound(s)*	OR	*Olympic Record*
st	*stone(s) (= 14lbs)*	WR	*World Record*
mm	*millimetre(s)*	2:11:46.23	*hours: minutes: seconds.*
cm	*centimetre(s)*		*divisions of seconds*
m	*metre(s)*	(m)	*men*
km	*kilometre(s)*	(w)	*women*
yd	*yard(s)*	4x7.5km etc	*a relay of four legs each*
ft	*feet*		*covering 7.5km etc*

MEDAL RECORDS

1 Most golds won by a single competitor = 6
Record is held jointly by Lidya Skoblikova in speed skating:
1960   1500m & 3000m
1964   500m, 1000m, 1500m & 3000m

and Liubov Egorova in Nordic skiing:
1992   10,000m, 15,000m & 4x5000m relay
1994   5000m, 10,000m & 4x5000m relay

2 Most golds won by a single competitor at one Games = 5
Record is held by Eric Heiden in speed skating:
1980   500m, 1000m, 1500m, 5000 & 10,000m

3 Most medals won by a single female competitor = 10
Record is held by Raissa Smetanina in nordic skiing:

Gold:	10,000m & 4x5000m relay	1976
	5000m	1980
	4x5000m	1992
Silver:	5000m	1976
	10,000m & 20,000m	1984
	10,000m	1988
Bronze:	20,000m	1988

4 Most medals won by a single male competitor = 9
Record is held by Sixten Jernberg in nordic skiing:

Gold:	5000m	1956
	30,000m	1960
	50,000m & 4x10km relay	1964
Silver:	15,000m & 30,000m	1956
	15,000m	1960
Bronze:	4x10km relay	1956
	15,000m	1964

63

LIST OF COUNTRY ABBREVIATIONS

AHO	Antilles Netherlands		ISR	Israel
ALG	Algeria		ISV	Virgin Islands
AND	Andorra		ITA	Italy
ARG	Argentina		JAM	Jamaica
ARM	Armenia		JPN	Japan
AUS	Australia		KAZ	Kazakhastan
AUT	Austria		KGZ	Kyrgystan
BEL	Belgium		KOR	Korea
BER	Bermuda		LAT	Latvia
BIH	Bosnia & Hercegovena		LIB	Lebanon
BLR	Belarus		LIE	Lichstenstein
BOL	Bolivia		LTU	Lithuania
BRA	Brazil		LUX	Luxembourg
BUL	Bulgaria		MAR	Morocco
CAN	Canada		MDA	Rep. of Muldava
CHI	Chile		MEX	Mexico
CHN	China		MGL	Mongolia
CRC	Costa Rica		MON	Monaco
CRO	Croatia		NED	Netherlands
CYP	Cyprus		NOR	Norway
CZE	Czechoslovakia [*2]		NZL	New Zealans
DEN	Denmark		PHI	Philippines
EGY	Egypt		POL	Poland
ESP	Spain		POR	Portugal
EST	Estonia		PRK	Dem. People's Rep. of Korea
EUN	Unified Team		PUR	Puerto Rico
FIJ	Fiji		ROM	Romania
FIN	Finland		RSA	South Africa
FRA	France		RUS	Russian Federation
FRG	Germany (West) [*1]		SEN	Senegal
GBR	Great Britain		SLO	Slovenia
GDR	Germany (East) [*1]		SMR	San Marino
GEO	Georgia		SUI	Switzerland
GER	Germany [*1]		SVK	Slovakia
GRE	Greece		SWE	Sweden
GUA	Guam		SWZ	Swaziland
GUA	Guatemala		TPE	Taipei
HON	Honduras		TUR	Turkey
HUN	Hungary		UKR	Ukraine
IND	India		URS	Soviet Union
IRL	Ireland		UZB	Uzbekistan
IRN	Iran		YUG	Yugoslavia
ISL	Iceland			

USA

[*1] Germany from 1896 to 1964 inclusive, German Democratic Republic and Federal Republic of Germany from 1968 to 1988 inclusive. Germany from 1992.
[*2] Czechoslovakia up to and including 1992. Henceforth two separate nations - Slovakia (SVK) and Czechoslovakia (CZE).

Inside M-wave

NAGANO
1 9 9 8

Nagano

XVIII Olympic Winter Games, Nagano
SNOWLETS™

Snowlets

Kimonos

Face paint for the fans

BOBSLEIGH

The 1994 Olympic women's relay

An explosive start from Italy, led by Gunther Huber

Japan on their home track

LUGE

Luge singles

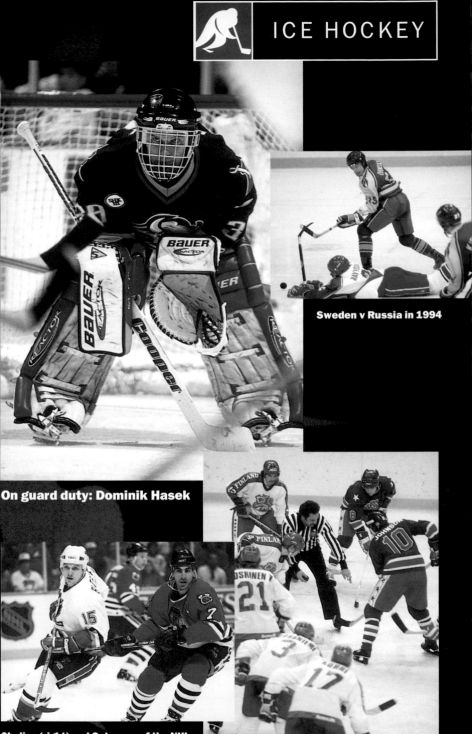

ICE HOCKEY

Sweden v Russia in 1994

On guard duty: Dominik Hasek

Chelios (right) and Gutsayev of the NHL

USA beat Finland in the final 1980 match

FIGURE SKATING

Boitano—triumphed in the 1988 battle of the 'Brians'

Dorothy Hamill—exuberant former American Olympic champion

Sultry Katarina Witt—star quality in 1984 and 1988

Todd Eldredge—artistry on the ice

Torvill and Dean—nine perfect
sixes in Sarajevo, 1984

Michelle Kwan—1996 world champion

Gordeeva and Grinkov—golden couple
before tragedy struck

Dan Jansen

Tony de Jong—the young Dutch star

ALPINE SKIING

Kristian Ghedina
in flight

Sweden's slalom maestro, Stenmark

Ortlieb takes a tumble

Norway's Kjetil Andre Aamodt negotiates a gate

Picabo Street of America

CROSS COUNTRY

Dæhlie, the world's darling

Women's relay start

Men's 15km race

Jens Weissflog—two golds ten years apart for Germany

Espen Bredesen of Norway seemingly flies into the crowd

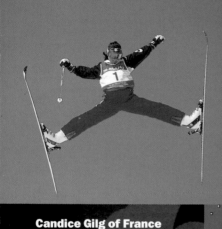

Candice Gilg of France

FREESTYLE SKIING

Kirstie Marshall shows aerials skills

SNOWBOARDING

NORDIC COMBINED

Ogiwara and Kono—local colour

Image in the snow

PART THREE
The Winter Sportsfile

BIATHLON

Stars all over the Biathlon Sky

by Thore-Erik Thoresen

Selecting medal favourites for the biathlon events in Nagano is an impossible task. In a sport where the number of participants is increasing at the same speed as the margins are decreasing, the easiest and safest way of making predictions might appear to be to paper a wall with the starting lists in each event, fire a shot gun at close range and hope to hit a winner.

Since Lillehammer, the number of nations chasing medals in international championships has been constantly rising. In the 1994 Olympic Games, six nations shared the 18 medals with only Russia, Germany and Canada hitting gold.

At the 1995 world championships, in Anterselva, Italy, eight nations won medals. Four of them—France (3); Germany (2); Poland and Norway—were the golden nations.

In the Slovakian venue of Osrblie in the winter of 1997, eleven nations took medals. Six of these struck gold: Germany (3); Russia (2); Sweden (2); Italy; Norway and Belarus.

A forecast based on the Osrblie results would put 30 year-old Swede and double gold winner, Magdalena Forsberg-Wallin at the top of the favourites list for women. Old results are sometimes of no value when you lie down to fire your shots at the targets 50m away or stand on shaky legs, heart beat rocketing and trigger-finger unsteady whilst aiming at the same distance to hit 115mm targets with a smallbore rifle which will have cost from £1200 (2004 US$) upwards.

As well as Forsberg-Wallin, it would be impossible to avoid names such as Olga Romasko and Petra Behle as medal favourites. Russian Romasko, a 29 year-old professional soldier from Krasnoiars, hit gold in the last two world championships. German 29 year-old, Petra Behle, has matured through the years since she, as Petra Schaaf, won her first of a total of nine gold medals in the Chamonix world championships in 1988. Biathlon, of course, did not make its Olympic debut for women until 1992.

Amongst the men, the picture is even more blurred. Russian Sergei Tarasov, who was seriously ill and hospitalized during the Albertville Games, came back to collect his gold medal in Lillehammer. Tarasov has been on the podium in the last two world championships. Meanwhile Germans Sven Fischer, Ricco Gross and Frank Luck are a well-blended mixture with championship experience who seldom leave a major event without visiting the podium. They start as relay favourites chased by Russia, Italy, Norway, France and Belarus.

The German women have also won the last two world championships relays. As a result, the Russians are more than eager to defend their Lillehammer gold.

The difficulties of prediction, however, were recently highlighted by the President of the International Biathlon Union (IBU), Anders Besseberg, of Norway: "It's almost an impossible task before Nagano. There are more than 20 racers who could win in each individual event".

Since biathlon entered the Olympic family, at the Squaw Valley Games of 1960, where Sweden's Klas Lestander was the historical first gold medal winner, the sport has seen wholesale changes. There was a time when the participants disappeared into the wood to fire their shots at different distances and did not come back into view before they crossed the finishing line more than an hour and a half later, with competitors, public and the media waiting hours for the results.

Now the sport steps forward today in a modern TV-adapted format using all available electronic support to give the viewers as well as the spectators a running update. There was a time when the results could be changed whilst the winner was showering and preparing for the medal ceremony. A single shot may have been interpreted "out" instead of "in" on the paper target. Nowadays, the competitors fire at electronic targets showing hits or misses while computers give you the exact time and position.

There are no changes to the current competition format in Nagano. However, by the time of the 2002 Salt Lake City Games, the new-style individual pursuit competitions may have come to the fore.

Background

The term biathlon comes from the Greek meaning "two tests". In this sport, competitors race across country on skis stopping at various stages to shoot at targets with a rifle. Penalties are given for any target missed and the fastest time wins.

This sport originates from the times when man hunted on skis for food in the winter months. There are early cave paintings dating from 3,000 BC showing hunters with bows and arrows travelling on primitive skis made from wood. The juxtaposition of tough physical exercise with the need to stop suddenly, steady oneself and aim, make it a fascinating spectacle.

Biathlon made its Olympic debut in 1960 at Squaw Valley in the USA with a 20km event and has remained on the programme ever since. A four-man 7.5km relay was added in 1968, followed by an additional individual event, the 10km race, in 1980. These were all for men. Women's biathlon made its Olympic debut in 1992 with both a 7.5km and a 15km individual race and a relay race. Since 1994 the women's biathlon 7.5km relay has had four legs, rather than three as in 1992. The first women's world championship was in 1984.

Early Olympic races involved a number of shooting stations with targets at varying distances. This has now been standardized for each race. In 1978 the weapon used was changed to a .22 calibre rifle.

An earlier form of biathlon, called Military Patrol, appeared on the Olympic Games programme in 1924 and was a demonstration event in 1928, '36 and '48. These drew heavily on nations who had regular ski-borne soldiers. A team of men, guided by an officer, raced across country for 30km and fired at targets at the end of the race. For each target missed a 30 second penalty was added. This sport was dropped after the 1948 Games due to the anti-military atmosphere of that era.

Modern technology has transformed this sport bringing home the drama of the shooting to the TV audience. Use of the skating style of skiing has increased the pace of the races and the relay race, which often culminates in a close dash for the line, has an exciting mass start.

The 1960 Games, biathlon's debut year, were marked by an opening ceremony organized by Walt Disney and by top American artistes, such as singer Danny Kaye, entertaining the athletes after dinner in the Olympic Village.

In 1994, in Lillehammer, the Russian 20km winner, Sergei Tarasov was only three seconds ahead of his rival, Germany's Frank Luck. A shooting miss in the 10km event denied Tarasov a golden double. Also in 1994 Belarus' Svetlana Paramygina lost her chance of gold when she fell just metres from the finishing line. She held on to silver, however, just a tenth of a second ahead of Valentyna Tserbe of the Ukraine.

Alexander Tikhonov of the former Soviet Union won a record four relay gold medals at four successive Games between 1968 and 1980. In

1988, in Canada, East Germany's Frank-Peter Roetsch was the first man to win both individual titles at the Games. Women's biathlon is yet young. However, Anfissa Reztsova of Russia and Canada's Myriam Bédard have already won two golds and a bronze apiece.

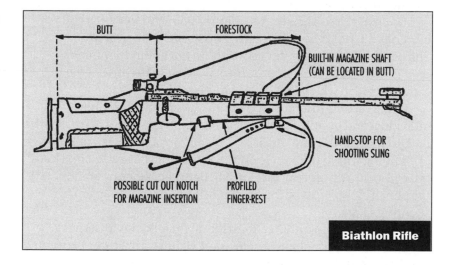

Biathlon Rifle

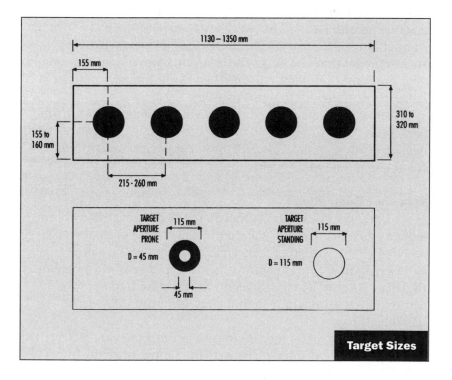

Target Sizes

Equipment

Biathlon competitors use skis which are designed for cross-country skiing. These are narrower and shorter than their Alpine skiing counterparts. They have upturned tips and taper towards the rear. It is important that skiers choose the right type of wax for the snow conditions.

There are also special cross-country skiing boots which clip into bindings on the ski by the toe only. This leaves the heel free to move. The boots come up over the ankle but are not as rigid as alpine ski boots. Most skiers wear some form of head-gear because of the extreme cold in which they often compete.

When race courses are set there are maximum allowable individual and overall climbs. For instance, in the men's 20km race the longest individual climb must not exceed 75m and the overall amount of climbing within the course must be between 600 and 750m. There must also be a distance of at least 3km between shooting stations and the penalty loop must be in a level area immediately adjacent to the shooting range.

Each skier carries a .22 calibre rifle on their back with a special harness. This does not have a telescopic sight and it weighs between 3.5 (7.7) and 4.5kg (9.9lbs). Biathletes fire at targets from a shooting "ramp", made of solidly-packed snow, on which synthetic shooting mats are placed. There must be at least 27 shooting lanes for Olympic competition and each is 2.5 (8ft 2in.)–3.0m (9ft 10in.) wide. Wind flags are installed at the side of every third lane to help competitors judge their shooting. Competitors are allowed 45 minutes on a practice range before their race to zero their rifles.

Electronic targets are used at the Olympic Winter Games. If the black target area—a circle—is hit, it is covered by a white disc. Target diameters are: 45mm (1.77in.) for the prone position and 115mm (4.5in.) for the standing position.

Rules and Regulations

At the 1998 Olympic Winter Games there will be six biathlon events: individual races for men at 20km and 10km and for women at 7.5km and 15km. Both will have a 7.5km relay. Participants ski along specially prepared cross-country trails carrying a rifle, firing at targets which are set up at varying stages of each race. Each competitor carries twenty rounds (ten for the sprint) of ammunition in the individual races.

In the 20km race for men there are four firing stations each with five targets set at a distance of 50m (164ft). Competitors fire from the prone position at the first and third station and from the standing position at the second and fourth. A time penalty of one minute is added for each target missed. The best biathletes hit all five targets within 15 seconds of beginning to shoot. The fastest time wins because of the staggered start. Top athletes will complete the course in around 53-55 minutes without missing a target.

In the men's sprint, or 10km, race competitors have to ski a penalty loop of 150m (492ft) for each of the targets missed. This gives them the option of taking more risks with their shooting, relying on their speed of skiing to make up the time lost. In this race there are two firing stations each of five shots—the first, 3km into the race, is from the prone position and the second, standing. Top athletes complete this event in around 24 minutes.

Shooting stations of five targets apiece are spaced between the 3km and 12km points in the women's 15km race. The first and third are tackled in the prone position and the other two in the standing position. A minute is added for any targets missed. Top times in this race are likely to be around 55 minutes. The women's sprint is a 7.5km race with two firing stations—the first prone, the second standing—penalty loops of 150m are skied for missed targets. The fastest finishers will complete the course in around 23 minutes.

Relay teams consist of four competitors each of whom skis 7.5km and fires once prone and once standing. A striking difference in relay races is the mass start with skiers on the first leg jockeying for position before arriving at the first firing range. Each competitor also has eight rounds of ammunition to hit the five targets. A penalty loop is only incurred if all eight rounds have been fired and a target has still been missed. In the changeover zone the next skier is sent on his or her way with a pat on the back. The winner is the first team to cross the line and top teams cover the course in around an hour and 20 minutes.

Starting order for each race is decided by randomly drawing the names of the competitors from four draw groups. Seedings for these groups are based on prior results.

In relay events, previous Nations Cup results are used to determine from which row each team will depart during the mass start—a little like Formula One cars on a grid. During a race team officials can run alongside competitors for up to 50m (164ft), except near the firing zone, to give drinks or impart race information. A jury is appointed for the Olympic Winter Games to resolve any dispute over the rules.

On competition days, ten forerunners must ski the entire course before a race begins to set the tracks and clear any obstacles. All features of the course must be clearly signposted—for example where there is a steep descent or tight bend. There must also be a sign telling competitors when they are 100m (328ft) from the finish.

Biathlon has strict rules concerning amateur status. Its athletes are not allowed to be professional participants or trainers / coaches in any other sport. They must not display their rifles or skis in the finish area for advertising purposes and they cannot accept sponsorship unless through their federation or Olympic committee. Their image must not be used in advertising.

Nagano Format

A quota system has become necessary to limit the total number of athletes at the 1998 Olympic Winter Games to 210. The sport's international governing body—the International Biathlon Union— has awarded start places per nation according to world ranking in the 1996/'97 season with only the top eight nations in the world being given four places, the next seven nations being awarded three places and so on. This system applies to men's and women's races.

Each athlete, however, must have qualified by competing in at least one individual or sprint race at a world championships, world cup or continental championships. They must have also finished within 25% of the average time of the first three placed athletes in that race. Younger athletes may also have qualified by finishing in the top half of the four world junior championships prior to the Olympic Winter Games. The top 20 men's and women's nations will be able to enter a team in the respective relay events.

Venue

The 1998 Olympic biathlon venue is located just south of the Nozawa Onsen ski resort in Toyosato district. Originally, the event was due to take place in Hakuba but it would have meant disturbing some goshawk nesting grounds.

Two 4km trails, designated A and B, are laid out in an area 1km (0.38miles) square. The trails are 7m wide and meander within the vicinity of the grandstand and shooting range.

A Sporting Legend

Magnar Solberg (Norway)

At the age of 61, Magnar Solberg can look back and view a rich life. In the winter of 1997 he was one of the first to be chosen as an "ambassador" for the world championships in nordic events, held in his hometown, Trondheim. Almost 30 years earlier, Solberg, born on February 2, 1937, was named as the last and final selection for the Norwegian team at the Grenoble Games. His strengths were his steady nerve and solid aim.

At the Games he produced a clear 20 shot run and grabbed the gold from hot favourite, Alexander Tikhonov of the Soviet Union.

To quit after this would have been easy. Solberg chose to continue. Inconsistent and often disappointing results followed. In 1972, again chosen for the Norwegian Olympic biathlon team, and again not counted among the hottest favourites, Solberg travelled to Sapporo. In Grenoble he had hit all the 20 targets; in Sapporo he had two misses but, this time, had the speed in the tracks—enough speed to win gold 12.1 seconds ahead of East German, Heinz-Jörg Knauthe.

Magnar could not have suspected that these two gold medals would be Norway's only success, in the classic 20km Olympic distance, until the 1994 Games of Lillehammer.

"For me it was a great advantage to be a policeman, changing watches and day-time training", Solberg says, explaining his success not in terms of his steady nerve but as a result of his detailed training sessions. "There were jobs to be done all the way and I prepared for all of them. How to slow down before reaching the shooting range, how to act there and how to adapt my speed in the trails to the shape I was in. You never think much in a serious competition, you do the things you have been through time and time again in preparation". After leaving the international scene, Magnar Solberg tried to return some years later. "It was a scary experience, the body was not functioning as it had in the old days", smiles the busy champion of Grenoble and Sapporo. He retired from the force a couple of years ago, going into business as an insurance valuer. Where life can still be good, especially when the snow lies temptingly outside the windows.

A Sporting Legend

Myriam Bédard (Canada)

Few would have dared to forecast better than a bronze for Myriam Bédard in Les Saisies, France, in 1992. Few, perhaps, except her compatriots. Bédard entered the Albertville Games, aged 22, having produced some promising results since entering the international biathlon arena. However, there is often many a slip between potential and success. Her eventual bronze in Albertville was a success. But her two golds two years later were breathtaking. In those two years female biathlon had changed from merely incorporating competitors from the ranks of fading cross-country hopes to those who were clean and clear biathlon specialists.

In Lillehammer, Bédard first won the 15km gold thanks to her clean shooting. Then came the 7.5km sprint. The 24 year-old student was forced to ski two penalty rounds for her misses before entering one of the sport's most dramatic finishes. That put her down by 1.1 seconds to Svetlana Paramygina of Belarus. Most people have time to do little in such time. Bédard took an Olympic gold medal, helped by Paramygina slipping just before the line.

A Sporting Legend

Anfissa Reztsova (EUN) *

Aged 27, and mother of a three year-old daughter being looked after at home by grandparents in Vladimir outside Moscow, Anfissa Reztsova at last climbed to the top of the Olympic podium in 1992. For years Reztsova had tried for success in cross-country skiing. Her best performances had been a 5km silver in Oberstdorf at the 1987 world championships and an Olympic 20km silver, the following year in Calgary.

Then, as her nation converted from the Soviet-Union to "EUN" (Équipe Unifiée), and Reztsova had problems in securing her place in the national cross-country team, female biathlon "was invented".

"I tried a gun shortly after Calgary", smiled Reztsova the day before her success was completed. She liked shooting after her first try, but combining her new "hobby" with her old "job" took time and gave her great problems initially. There were difficulties, particularly in the standing position even if she fared better with her prone shooting.

In the end, Reztsova's speed on skis proved crucial. Three penalty rounds could not stop her from winning the 1997 7.5km gold almost 16 seconds ahead of another converted cross-country specialist, Antje Misersky, of the former German Democratic Republic. The latter went on to win Olympic history's first female 15km gold.

(At the 1992 Olympic Games competitors from the former Soviet Union competed as the "équipe unifiée)

A Contemporary Heroine
Nathalie Santer (ITA)

One of Nagano's darkest horses must be the Italian, Nathalie Santer. Santer entered the Olympic arena, along with the first Olympic female biathlon competitors in 1992. She finished in a promising eighth place. By the approach to the Lillehammer Games, two years later, the hotel-owner's daughter from Toblach at the gates of Cortina, was amongst the favourites. Two world cup victories in Badgastein had put her there. Yet, instead of a sparkling performance in Lillehammer, Santer finished 25th in the 15km and seventh in the sprint competition. Hers, it appeared, was still an undeveloped talent.

If her preparations have gone without injuries or other complications, Santer can continue her road to the top in Nagano. At the end of the 1996/'97 season at the world championships for military personnel, this Italian forest guard won the 15km race. Not even four shooting misses could prevent her from hitting gold. And amongst her opponents were familiar faces, ones which she will meet again in Nagano.

Once an unpredictable starter, Santer looked more mentally-balanced, consistent and wiser last season. And, of course, another year older.

A Contemporary Hero
Ole Einar Bjoerndalen (Norway)

Former Olympic biathlon champion Eirik Kvalfoss always had an alternative to the phrase "speed skills". "It isn't the speed", he said, "but the sudden stop that kills". For Ole Einar Bjoerndalen (born on January 27, 1974), life has been full of speeding and stopping.

Multi-talented, he could have gone on to reach several goals as a cross-country specialist, winning many Norwegian age-group championships as a junior. Being born in the small village of Simostranda—where hobbies are limited to either the juke box-and coke-evenings—or biathlon, Ole Einar chose wisely as did his older brother, Dag.

Ole Einar's results going into the Lillehammer Games suggested him capable of much more than a 36th and 28th placing in the 20km and sprint respectively. The Norwegian biathlon failure at their own Games was a catastrophe. Spurred on, young Bjoerndalen established himself permanently among the world's best biathlon exponents in 1995 and 1996. He was one of the fastest skiers and by the end of the 1996/'97 season, Bjoerndalen had won the sprint part of the world cup and finished second to German Sven Fischer in the overall world cup standings.

The secrets behind his skills and talent are partly due to his father. Bjoerndalen has tremendous balance. As a child he was taught how to walk on his hands and, by the age of 14, he was a skilled tightrope walker. In Nagano he must learn to operate without a safety net.

A Contemporary Heroine

Ursula ("Uschi") Disl (Germany)

She returned from last season's world championships in Osrblie with only a relay gold medal. That's what makes Ursula "Uschi" Disl so dangerous going into Nagano. She has one of biathlon history's finest collections of medals. Only one is missing. An Olympic gold.

With hobbies spanning from book-reading to biking and from kayaking to billiards, the 27 year-old police border guard, born in tiny Dietramzell—a village with little more than a hundred houses, just outside Munich—Disl was a member of the German team that won Olympic silver in Albertville (1992) and Lillehammer (1994), where she also won an individual 15km bronze.

In Orsblie Disl and her team prepared for their world relay gold at a champagne reception the night before for compatriot, Ricco Gross's, victory. Their relay performance was also truly sparkling, winning by a minute and a half from Norway in second. Disl went on to finish the season as world cup sprint champion and second to Swede Forsberg-Wallin in the 15km.

MEDALLISTS *(by nation)*

Country	Gold		Silver		Bronze		Overall
	m	w	m	w	m	w	total
URS/EUN	10	1	6	1	5	2	25
GER	3	1	4	3	1	1	13
GDR	3	-	4	-	4	-	11
NOR	3	-	2	-	2	-	7
RUS	2	1	1	-	1	-	5
FRG	1	-	2	-	2	-	5
SWE	1	-	-	-	4	-	5
FIN	-	-	4	-	1	-	5
FRA	-	1	-	1	1	1	4
CAN	-	2	-	-	-	1	3
ITA	-	-	-	-	2	-	2
BLR	-	-	-	1	-	-	1
UKR	-	-	-	-	-	1	1

**Sweden's Magdalena Forsberg-Wallin
double world gold medallist**

NAGANO SCHEDULE

Biathlon

Venue: Nozawa Onsen

Date	Description	Start	Finish
9 Feb	15km (w)	13:00	15:00
11 Feb	20km (m)	13:00	15:00
15 Feb	7.5km (w)	13:00	14:30
17 Feb	10km (m)	13:00	14:30
19 Feb	4x7.5km relay (w)	13:00	15:00
21 Feb	4x7.5km relay (m)	13:00	15:00

Biathlon [Men]

Year	Gold	Country	Time	Silver	Country	Time	Bronze	Country	Time
10km									
1980	Frank Ullrich	GDR	32:10.69	Vladimir Alikin	URS	32:53.10	Anatoli Aljabiev	URS	33:09.16
1984	Eirik Kvalfoss	NOR	30:53.8	Peter Angerer	FRG	31:02.4	Matthias Jacob	GDR	31:10.5
1988	Frank-Peter Roetsch	GDR	25:08.1	Valeri Medvedtsev	URS	25:23.7	Sergei Tchepikov	URS	25:29.4
1992	Mark Kirchner	GER	26:02.3	Ricco Gross	GER	26:18	Harri Eloranta	FIN	26:26.6
1994	Sergei Tchepikov	URS	28:07	Ricco Gross	GER	28:13	Sergei Tarasov	URS	28:27.4
20km									
1960	Klas Lestander	SWE	1:33.21.6	Antti Tyrvainen	FIN	1:33.57.7	Alexander Privalov	URS	1:34.54.2
1964	Vladimir Melanin	URS	1:20:26.8	Alexander Privalov	URS	1:23:42.5		Olav Jordet	NOR
	1:24:38.8								
1968	Magnar Solberg	NOR	1:13:45.9	Alexander Tikhonov	URS	1:14:40.4		Vladimir Goundart	
URS	1:18:27.4								
1972	Magnar Solberg	NOR	1:15:55.5	Heinz-Jörg Knauthe	GER	1:16.07.6	Lars-Göran Arwids	SWE	1:16.27.03
1976	Nikolai Kruglov	URS	1:14:12.2	Heikki Ikola	FIN	1:15:54.1		Alexander Elizaro	
URS	1:16:05.57								
1980	Anatoli Aljabiev	URS	1:08:16.3	Frank Ullrich	GDR	1:08:27.7	Eberhard Rosch	GDR	1:11:11.73
1984	Peter Angerer	FRG	1:11.52.7	Frank-Peter Roetsch	GDR	1:13.21	Eirik Kvalfoss	NOR	1:14.02.4
1988	Frank-Peter Roetsch	GDR	56:33.3	Valeri Medvedtsev	URS	56:54.6	Johann Passler	ITA	57:10.1
1992	Evgeni Redkine	EUN	57:34.4	Mark Kirchner	GER	57:40.8	Mikael Lofgren	SWE	57:59.4
1994	Sergei Tarasov	URS	57:25.3	Frank Luck	GER	57:28.7	Sven Fischer	GER	57:41.9
Relay (4x7.5km)									
1968	Alexander Tikhonov	URS	2:13:02.4	Ola Waerhavg	NOR	2:14:50.2	Goeran Arwidson	SWE	2:17:26.3
	Nikolai Pousanov			Olav Jordet			Tore Eriksson		
	Viktor Mamatov			Magnar Solberg			Olle Petrusson		
	Vladimir Goundartsev			Jon Istad			Holmfrid Olsson		
1972	Alexander Tikhonov	URS	1:51:44.9	Esko Saira	FIN	1:54:37.2	Heinz-Jörg Knauthe	GER	1:54:57.67
	Rinnat Safine			Juhani Suutrinen			Joakim Meischner		
	Ivan Biakov				Heikki Ikola				Dieter Speer
	Viktor Mamatov			Mauri Roeppaenen			Horst Koschka		
1976	Alexander Elizar	URS	1:57:55.6	Henrik Floejt	FIN	2:01:45.5	Karl-Heinz Menz	GDR	2:04:08:61
	Ivan Biakov			Esko Saira			Frank Ullrich		
	Nikolai Kruglov			Juhani Suutarinen			Manfred Beer		
	Alexander Tikhonov			Heikki Ikkola			Manfred Geyer		
1980	Vladimir Alikin	URS	1:34:03.2	Mathias Jung	GDR	1:34:56.9	Franz Bernreiter	FRG	1:37:30.26
	Alexander Tikhonov			Klaus Siebert			Hansi Estner		
	Vladimir Barnaschov			Frank Ullrich			Peter Angerer		
	Anatoli Aljabiev			Eberhard Rosch			Gerd Winkler		
1984	Dimitri Vassilie	URS	1:38:51.7	Odd Lirhus	NOR	1:39:03.9	Ernst Reiter	FRG	1:39:05.1
	Yuri Kachkarov			Eirik Kvalfoss			Walter Pichler		
	Alguimantas Shalna			Rolf Storsveen			Peter Angerer		
	Sergei Bouliguin			Kjell Soebak			Fritz Fischer		
1988	Dmitri Vassiliev	URS	1:22:30	Ernst Rieter	FRG	1:23:37.4	Werner Kiem	ITA	1:23:51.5
	Sergei Tchepikov			Stefan Hoeck			Gottlieb Taschler		
	Alexander Popov			Peter Angerer			Johann Passler		
	Valeri Medvedtsev			Frierich Fischer			Andreas Zingerle		
1992	Ricco Gross	GER	1:24:43.5	Valeri Medvedtsev	EUN	1:25:06.3	Ulf Johansson	SWE	1:25:38.2
	Jens Steinigen			Alexander Popov			Leif Andersson		
	Mark Kirchner			Valeri Kirienko			Tord Wiksten		
	Fritz Fischer			ergei Tchepikov			Mikael Lofgren		
1994	Ricco Gross	GER	1:30:22.1	Valeri Kirienkko	URS	1:31:23.6	Thierry Dusserre	FRA	1:32:31.3
	Frank Luck			Vladimir Dratchev			Patrie Bailly-Salins		
	Mark Kirchner			Sergei Tarasov			Lionel Laurent		
	Sven Fischer			Sergei Tchepikov			Herve Flandin		

Biathlon [Women]

7.5km

Year	Gold	Country	Time	Silver	Country	Time	Bronze	Country	Time
1992	Anfissa Reztszova	EUN	24:29.2	Antje Misersky	GER	24:45.1	Elena Belova	EUN	24:50.8
1994	Myriam Bédard	CAN	26:08.8	Svetlana Paramygina	BLR	26:09.9	Valentyna Tserbe	UKR	26:10

15km

Year	Gold	Country	Time	Silver	Country	Time	Bronze	Country	Time
1992	Antje Misersky	GER	51:47.2	Svetlana Pecherska	EUN	51:58.5	Myriam Bédard	CAN	52:15
1994	Myriam Bédard	CAN	52:06.6	Anne Briand	FRA	52:53.3	Ursula Disl	GER	53:15.3

3x7.5km

Year	Gold	Country	Time	Silver	Country	Time	Bronze	Country	Time
1992	Corinne Niogret	FRA	1:15:55.6	Uschi Disl	GER	1:16:18.4	Elena Belova	EUN	1:16:54.6
	Veronique Claudel			Antje Misersky			Anfissa Reztszova		
	Anne Briand			Petra Schaaf			Elena Melnikova		
1994 (4x7.5km)									
	Nadejda Talanova	URS	1:47:19.5	Ursula Disl	GER	1:51:16.5	Corinne Niogret	FRA	1:52:28.3
	Natalia Snytina			Angie Harvey			Veronique Claudel		
	Louiza Noskova			Sion Greiner-Petter-Memm			Delphyne Heymann		
	Anfissa Reztsova			Petra Schaaf			Anne Briand		

Russia's Sergei Tarasov: hospitalized 1992, gold 1994

BOBSLEIGH

Stars to watch
What goes down also comes up

by Ingeborg Kollbach

When the world's leading bobsleighers first tried out the new artificial bobsleigh and luge track, "The Spiral", on Mount Iizuna in Nagano City in February 1997, they were baffled. It is different from all other tracks. It not only goes down, but at two points, also comes up! The first uphill straight leads from corner seven to eight, the second from corner 11 to 12.

The 1997 world cup final, the first international "bob" competition on the new track, proved a success. It was also a real Olympic test for the organizers and track operators. During training and competition, the weather conditions were seriously changeable. Sunshine turned to snow then to warm weather and rain. The track workers did a tremendous job and instead of having just the two final races of the 1996–'97 world cup season, the Nagano organizers also agreed to stage a substitute four-man race which had been cancelled in Calgary.

Canada's Pierre Lueders, the 1995 and 1996 world silver medallist in the two-man, not only won the final two-man event in Nagano, but also the world cup classification. The 26 year-old driver from Edmonton was the fastest in both heats clocking 54.10 and 54.33 with brakeman Dave MacEachern. Switzerland's Reto Goetschi, who came to Nagano as newly crowned world champion three weeks earlier on his home track in St Moritz, took second place finishing both heats in fourth position. Goetschi went on to win the four-man event from American Brian Shimer, who had been victorious in the substitute four-man race the previous day.

The results of the competitions on the Spiral track on Mount Iizuna were puzzling. Even though the final classifications were not a surprise, the performances in the individual heats were. Hardly any driver (apart from Lueders and Goetschi) had two consistent runs. Germany's veteran driver Wolfgang Hoppe, who won the first of his record 33 international medals back in 1983, said shaking his head, "You don't know where you lose the time. You don't make an obvious mistake, you think you are driving well but then you find out you are eleventh!" Pierre Lueders, for instance, finished eighth in the four-man, finishing tenth and third in the respective heats.

The Olympic and the world championship competitions have a different format to the world cup. They have four runs over two days rather than two runs in one day. There is a real psychological difference. At the 1992 Olympic Winter Games, Great Britain's Mark Tout was leading after the first day in the two-man ahead of Italy's Günther Huber and Austria's eventual four-man champion, Ingo Appelt. None of the three finished in a medal position after four runs. The medals went to Switzerland's Gustav Weder (gold) and the two Germans, Rudolf (Rudi) Lochner (silver) and Christoph Langen (bronze).

Two years later in Lillehammer it was an altogether different situation in the two-man as well as in the four-man. All the medals were achieved by athletes who had been leading at the end of the first day. Nagano will see a new Olympic champion, at least in the two-man event. Gustav Weder, the 1992 and 1994 gold medallist, has retired from the sport. Germany's Harald Czudaj, the reigning Olympic four-man champion of Lillehammer, must first of all overcome the tough internal competition to qualify for the Games. The Germans have many potential medallists in the four-man. In addition to Czudaj, veteran driver Wolfgang Hoppe wants to end his unique career in Nagano with yet another medal to add to his Olympic collection after two golds in 1984, three silvers (two in 1988, one in 1992) and one bronze (1994).

Christoph Langen is another strong contender. He was injured in the pre-Olympic season but dominated the 1995-'96 season winning all four European and world titles plus the two-man and combined world cup and finishing second in the four-man. Dirk Wiese, the 1997 world silver medallist, who was defeated in the Calgary substitute race in Nagano only by American Brian Shimer, is also in the wings as are up-and-coming athletes like Matthias Benesch, Rene Spies and Andre Lange. With only two sleds per country per event any German driver who qualifies must be considered a potential medal candidate.

International competition in bobsleigh has become much closer in the past few years. It is no longer just the Swiss, the Germans and the Austrians who win races. The Italians are back in medal contention with Günther Huber (1994 Olympic bronze medallist, 1997 world silver medallist two-man) after a 25-year drought in the world championships. The Canadians have a good chance, with Pierre Lueders, to add a further medal to their only victory so far (1964, Victor Emery in the four-man). France achieved its third world bronze medal through Eric Alard in the two-man in 1995 (after two bronzes in the four-man in 1934 and 1947). And the Americans are back on the medal road with Brian Shimer gaining two third places in the 1997 world championships.

Reto Goetschi achieved two-man silver in his first Olympic competition in Lillehammer in 1994. The 32 year-old Swiss is considered Weder's successor in the country where bobsleigh was born more than 100 years ago. Switzerland is also the most successful nation in bobsleigh. In the Olympic Winter Games Swiss sleds have taken home 25 of a possible 90 medals—nine gold, eight silver and eight bronze. Marcel Rohner, one year older than Goetschi, is another Swiss medal hope, particularly in the four-man as the 1996-'97 world cup winner.

Background

In the last two decades of the nineteenth century a new phenomenon appeared in the Alps—the bobsleigh—courtesy of a group of British sportsmen who were looking for something which went faster than the normal toboggans of the day. The first "bobs" were built in 1886 and were raced down icy, winding roads. Bob clubs were formed, the bob itself was developed and the need for purpose-built tracks and standardized rules became evident.

At its Rome meeting of April, 1923, the International Olympic Committee stimulated the formation of an international federation to coordinate the sport because the organizers of the inaugural Chamonix Olympic Games wanted to run a bobsleigh event but were faced with a plethora of different rules. The FIBT (Federation Internationale de Bobsleigh et Tobogganing) was formed in November 1923 in Paris.

The first Olympic competition was a four- or five-man event in Chamonix. In 1928 this was changed to a five-man machine only to revert to a four-man event in 1932 when the two-man bob was added to the programme. In 1928 William Fiske, the son of an American millionaire, won the title, aged just 16. Both competitions have

Wolfgang Hoppe (GER), veteran medallist who would like Nagano gold

Bobsleigh 1936-style with the Swiss gold medal winners

Brian Schirmer (USA) has put America back on the medal trail

Swiss on the spiral: Heir-apparent Goetschi tries out the track

appeared at every Olympic Games since 1932, except in 1960 when the Squaw Valley organizers refused to build a track.

The top nations have always tried to steal a technological march over their opponents in this sport where the difference between gold and silver can be measured in mere hundredths of a second. In 1933 countries were forbidden to heat the runners of their sleds before competing. And in 1947 competitors were forbidden from wearing shoes with "nails" in the soles to give them better grip at the push-start.

There have also been a number of different combined maximum weight limits for men and machines over history, most particularly after the 1952 Games where both gold medals were won by German crews. Their combined four-man weight was over 1040lbs (472.5kg) and their two-man crew weighed 521lbs (236.6kg), stirring complaints from other nations.

In 1984 the Soviet Union team arrived at the Games with a revolutionary new design in sleds borrowed from Formula One. Nicknamed variously the "bullet" and the "hammerhead shark", the new bob was cigar-shaped with fins. One commentator described it as having: "the fins on the outside and the Russians on the inside".

At a meeting in St Moritz, in February 1932, women were given the right in principle to drive a two-man bob and form part of a four-man crew. This decision was rescinded in 1933 by the FIBT and there are no women's events in the 1998 Olympic Winter Games.

From 1924 through to 1992 the Olympic Games also doubled as the sport's world championships. Medal-winning teams were, therefore, issued with two sets of medals.

"Skeleton", a type of toboggan race, was a sport governed by the FIBT and was an Olympic event in 1928 and 1948 at St Moritz. The American Jennison Heaton won the gold medal in the skeleton alongside a bobsleigh silver in 1928. His brother, John, was an Olympic silver medallist twice, in 1928 and 1948.

Edward ("Eddie") Eagan won a gold medal as part of American William Fiske's 1932 four-man crew in Lake Placid. Twelve years earlier, Eagan had won Olympic boxing's first light-heavyweight gold when the division was introduced in Antwerp. He is the only athlete to have won Olympic gold medals at both the winter and summer Olympic Games. In 1932 America also won the inaugural two-man event through brothers Hubert and Curtis Stevens.

In 1968 the top West German and Italian two-man sleds finished with identical aggregate times after four runs. The gold, however, went to Italy as they had achieved the fastest single run with the fourth run being decisive. Italians also won the two-man 1956 gold medal in

Cortina in a newly-designed sled which had an enclosed front pod.

Jamaica entered a four-man bobsleigh team at the 1988 Olympic Winter Games in Canada, crashing badly on one of the runs. However, the novelty of a team from such an unlikely bobsleigh country was attractive to the film-makers who turned their story into the movie, "Cool Runnings".

The start is all-important in bobsleigh. Competitors sprint and push the bob—using handles which later retract inside the machine—before leaping in for the descent. This practice has given the sport a few lighter moments when athletes have either missed the sled as they leap in, or have found themselves sitting the wrong way round. On its descent, a bob can reach speeds of 130kmph (80 mph) and the crew is submitted to huge G-forces as it rounds the curves in the track.

Meinhard Nehmer is the only bobsleigh driver to have won three Olympic golds, winning the two- and four-man in 1976 and the four-man in 1980. Bernhard Germeshausen is the only bob athlete to have won medals in the same Games as driver and brakeman. He was two-man silver medallist as a driver in 1980 and gold-medallist as a crewman in the four-man. Wolfgang Hoppe is the most successful driver of all time with 33 Olympic, world and European medals as he entered the 1997/'98 season.

Equipment

A bobsleigh is a sled with four steel runners—one pair at the front and another pair at the rear which are a maximum of 270cm (8ft 10in.) long for the two-man and 335cm (10ft 11in.) long for the four-man bob. A bob may have a cowled front end but must be open at the rear (see diagrams). The cowling may not be made of Plexiglas, transparent material or any material which will splinter on impact. The bobsleigh has a supporting frame and axles which are made of steel.

Push bars protrude at the start of a race from the hull. Those for the second and third men in the four-man event must be retractable. Whilst those for the driver may be retractable and that for the brakeman, in both cases, must be immovable. Each bob is equipped with a harrow-type brake which can be applied after the finish. Braking during the race means automatic disqualification.

The driver steers the bob by means of steering handles and cords attached to a steering mechanism for the front axle. The driver is the only one who has a clear view of the track and must select the fastest line through the curves. His crew sit crouched behind him, taking care not to touch him. They tilt their heads to help round the curves more effectively.

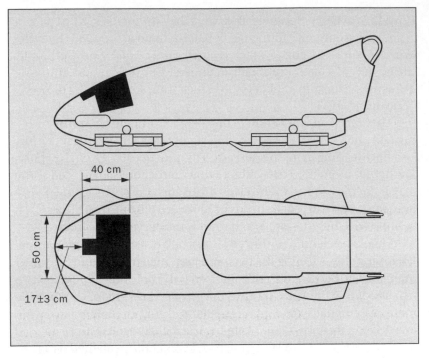

The total weight of the bob and its crew must not exceed 390kg (860lb) (two-man) and 630kg (1389lb) (four-man). A crew may add weights to bring their bob up to this limit if desired. Bobsleigh athletes wear aerodynamic clothing and compulsory crash helmets. Their boots have brush-like spikes on the front portion of the sole.

A bobsleigh track consists of a series of straights and bends. It may have an uphill stretch with bends in the last 100m. Once across the finish line there is a straight stretch in which crews can apply their brakes.

The push-off stretch runs from a 150cm (4ft 11in.) -long wooden block at the rear to the first photo-electric cell. This is followed by a 50m (164ft) -long stretch before the next photo-electric cell during which the crew must get into the sled which by now is travelling at around 35–40kmph (22–25mph).

Each bend in the track must allow for a variety of trajectories of travel and can impart up to 5G in centrifugal force on the bobsledders. There are guard rails on the bends which are designed to guide the bob back into the track. Lighting is provided on the track for evening training sessions and there are solar protection devices on the areas where the sun might otherwise shine during the daytime. Catwalks are placed above the track in certain areas for use by the jury and by coaches.

Rules and Regulations

The aim of bobsleigh is to complete a run down the track in the fastest possible time by having the best push start and by finding the best line through the bends. As recently as the 1997 world championships the Swiss team, who had made a clean sweep of the medals in the four-man event, were disqualified because their axles did not conform to regulations. They appealed against the decision but the appeal was turned down.

Technical regulations governing the design, weight, construction and dimensions of a bob are very strict. In part, these regulations were designed by the FIBT to cap the costly search for the ultimate racing machine which was favouring the richer nations. Under these regulations a bob's runner temperature is taken prior to each run to make sure that they have not been heated up and the overall bob and crew weight is taken. There is a technical delegate and a jury to ensure regulations are enacted.

There are four runs over two days in each of the two- and four-man events during Olympic competition—rather than the two runs in one day of a normal world cup competition. The winner is the sled which records the fastest aggregate time over the four runs. Eight training runs are offered before each event.. Starting order in the competition proper is done in groups, both by draw and by results (see Nagano Format later).

The two-man bob consists of a driver and brakeman. The four-man bob has a driver, a brakeman who sits at the rear and two other crew members who sit between them—called the second and third man. The crew and driver in both events are allowed a 15m (49ft 2in.) run-in to the start-line so as to push the bob and gain initial momentum before leaping in. This explosive starting procedure, which must be completed within 60 seconds of the start signal, is extremely important to the finish time and athletes train hard to be in peak physical condition. Many bob crews are recruited from the ranks of track and field athletics— particularly decathletes and sprinters—for this purpose.

All members of the crew must complete a run down the track for it to be valid. If any member of the crew puts a foot on the ice outside the start section, the bob is disqualified. Equally, it is disqualified if a crew member falls out at any time. Braking is not allowed in any section of the course except the straight after the finish line.

Nagano Format

Two bobs per nation per event (and one extra bob in official training runs) are permitted to enter the 1998 Olympic Winter Games in

Nagano as long as the drivers have taken part in and completed all the runs in at least five international competitions on three different tracks in the two seasons between the last and the upcoming Olympic Winter Games season. They must also have scored a certain number of world, European or America Cup points in the current or previous season.

In exceptional circumstances crews may have gained entry for the Games if they come from nations where there is a regular national championships with ten or more crews participating or if they are the best driver from a continent where the continent would otherwise not be represented. The host nation may also enter a bob.

Starting order is decided, within groups, for the first run. The top ten world-ranked drivers are put into the first group to gain the best ice conditions. For the second run the top 15 drivers start in reverse order of times achieved on the first run—i.e. the 15th-ranked crew goes first and so on. The second group is in descending order from 16th to last. The start order for run three is the top ten in reverse order and the final run is in reverse order of aggregate time for the first three runs with the 15th-placed bob going first once more.

Venue

The 1998 Olympic Winter Games bobsleigh competitions take place on a track dubbed "The Spiral" in the foothills of Mount Iizuna in the Asakawa district in the northern part of Nagano. This is the first artificially-refrigerated track in Asia. It is 1700m (5577ft) long, with 15 curves and a drop of 113m (370ft). It is unique because it has two uphill stretches.

Located on the north-east facing slopes of the mountain, the track has been built with environmental issues in mind. The potential for ammonia leakage has been minimized by use of a revolutionary new cooling system which uses ammonia only in the machine houses to cool a freezing agent which is then pumped through pipes embedded in the track. Ice temperature is controlled through over 50 sensors linked to a computer.

A Contemporary Hero
Wolfgang Hoppe (GDR)

Wolfgang Hoppe of Germany was born on November 14, 1957. He is the most successful bobsleigh driver of all time. Since 1983, when he won his first world bronze medal in the two-man with Dietmar Schauerhammer for the former German Democratic Republic (GDR) at Lake Placid, Hoppe has collected no fewer than 33 Olympic, world and European medals. The most recent was gold in the four-man at the 1997 world championships. Hoppe, a father of two, has gained medals at every world championships since 1983—a unique feat.

At the 1984 Olympic Winter Games in Sarajevo he had his greatest success, winning both Olympic titles. Four years later, in Calgary, he achieved both silver medals. On the track in La Plagne, in 1992, he was defeated by just two hundredths of a second by Austria's Ingo Appelt in the four-man. In Lillehammer, in 1994, he took the four-man bronze medal. At the last two Olympic Winter Games, Hoppe only competed in the four-man. The veteran driver will definitely retire after the Nagano Games when he will be 41.

A Contemporary Hero
Christoph Langen (GER)

Christoph Langen of Germany was born on March 27, 1962. He suffered a ruptured Achilles' tendon at the world cup event in La Plagne at the end of November 1996 and underwent surgery a week later. The injury prevented him from taking part in the 1996-'97 world cup series. Yet the former brakeman turned driver had dominated the 1995-'96 season. He was 1996 world champion in both the two- and four-man, world cup winner in two-man and combined and beaten into second place in the four-man only by compatriot Wolfgang Hoppe.

The 6ft 2in. (1.88m) athlete collected his first Olympic experience in Calgary 1988 as brakeman on Anton Fischer's two-man and four-man sled, finishing seventh and eleventh respectively. In 1991 he became world four-man champion in Altenberg as brakeman on Hoppe's first all-German sled. A year later, at the 1992 Olympic Games, Langen drove his two-man to the bronze medal, then failed to qualify for the 1994 Lillehammer

Games. The former boyfriend of Susi Erdmann, 1994 Olympic silver medallist in luge, is keen to prove in Nagano that he is still a driver to be feared.

A Contemporary Hero
Günther Huber (ITA)

Günther Huber of Italy was born on October 28, 1965. He won Italy's first world championships medal for 25 years when he finished in the silver medal position in the two-man at St Moritz in 1997. A week earlier Huber had become European champion in the two-man event with brakeman Antonio Tartaglia. In 1994 he gained his first international medals with silver in the two-man and gold in the four-man at the Europeans and then Olympic bronze in the two-man in Lillehammer. He has been coached by three-times Olympic gold medallist, Meinhard Nehmer, since the 1994-'95 season.

Considered one of the best and most sensitive drivers, Huber won the 1996-'97 world cup title in the combined classification (two- and four-man), was beaten into second place in the two-man by Canada's Pierre Lueders because the Canadian had more wins (they were tied on points) and finished third in the four-man. Günther Huber's brothers, Norbert, Wilfried and Arnold are Olympic, world and European medallists in luge. Günther has explained why he took to bobsleigh rather than luge: "The competition amongst us was too tough. We could never have competed together because of limited starting places". In the meantime, Arnold Huber has also switched to bobsleigh.

A Contemporary Hero
Pierre Lueders (CAN)

Pierre Lueders of Canada was born on September 26, 1970. He is the youngest among the world's top bobsleigh drivers. He was born in Edmonton of German parents who emigrated to Canada in 1967. Pierre Lueders began his career in the world cup with a sensation in the first race of the 1992-'93 season in Calgary. He defeated Switzerland's reigning Olympic and world champion Gustav Weder into second position in the two-man and took fourth place in the overall two-man rankings.

The young Canadian, who speaks fluent German, went on to win the bronze medal in the 1993 world junior championships. At the Lillehammer Games he was already considered one of the favourites in two-man but finished in seventh place. In 1995 at Winterberg, and on his home track in Calgary in 1996, Lueders won world silver medals. At the 1996-'97 world cup final in Nagano he not only won the last two-man race but also the overall title from Günther Huber. Both drivers had accumulated 224 points, but Lueders had four wins in seven events that season, Huber only one.

A Sporting Legend

Meinhard Nehmer (GDR)

Meinhard Nehmer of East Germany was born on January 13, 1941, in Boblin. He is the only bobsleigh driver ever to have won three Olympic gold medals. He achieved both titles at the 1976 Olympic Winter Games in Innsbruck and repeated his four-man victory in Lake Placid in 1980, also taking bronze in the two-man. The German Democratic Republic (GDR) had only joined the international bobsleigh family in 1973 and Nehmer's double gold just three years later signalled the first of altogether 85 (27 gold, 38 silver and 20 bronze) international bobsleigh medals (Olympic, world and European) won by East Germany until unification with the Federal Republic of Germany (FRG) in 1990.

The former javelin thrower (267ft 4in. /81.5m) was already 35 years old when he gained the first of his altogether 15 international medals in just four years. He became the third driver to gain both gold medals at the same Games in 1976 after Andreas Ostler (GER) in 1952 and Italy's Eugenio Monti in 1968. In 1984 Wolfgang Hoppe (GDR) became the fourth and, until now, final driver to achieve such a feat.

Nehmer retired from active sports after Lake Placid, aged 39, but remained involved in bobsleigh as an adviser in sled-construction and as a test driver. After the unification the rather quiet man, who lives on Germany's largest island, Rügen, in the Baltic Sea, and enjoys fishing, became ice coach to the American team in 1991. Two years later he led Brian Shimer to bronze in the four-man, America's first world championship medal for 24 years since Les Fenner's 1969 bronze in four-man. After the 1993-'94 season Nehmer left the American team and, since then, has been Italy's ice coach.

A Sporting Legend
William Guy Fiske (USA)

William Guy Fiske, born in the USA in 1911, was just 16 years old when he achieved his first Olympic title at the second Olympic Winter Games in St Moritz, in 1928, driving his five-man sled with Nion Tocker, Charles Mason, Clifford Gray and Richard Parke to victory. Fiske, the son of an American millionaire, repeated that feat four years later in Lake Placid. He is the youngest bobsleigh driver ever to win an Olympic gold medal. And Fiske was also the first of just three drivers in Olympic history to have won gold medals in consecutive Games. The others are Meinhard Nehmer (GDR) in 1976 and '80 and, most recently, Switzerland's Gustav Weder in 1992 and '94.

Fighter-pilot William Guy Fiske died in the "Battle of Britain" in 1940, one of the first Americans to die in the Second World War. He volunteered and joined the British Royal Air Force, was hit but managed to land safely suffering burns to the hands and ankles. He was taken to hospital in Chichester, where he died of delayed shock on August 17, 1940.

A Sporting Legend
Edward "Eddie" Eagan (USA)

Edward "Eddie" Eagan, born in the USA in 1898, was the second man on William Guy Fiske's winning four-man bob at the 1932 Olympic Winter Games in Lake Placid. Twelve years before—in Antwerp in 1920—Eagan was the Olympic champion in the light-heavyweight boxing division. Until today he is the only athlete to have won Olympic gold medals in the Summer and Winter Games. Antwerp, 1920, was the first time that there had been a light-heavyweight division at the Games. Eagan went on to become a successful businessman and even played guitar in a band. He died in 1967.

A Sporting Legend
Eugenio Monti (ITA)

Eugenio Monti of Italy was born on January 23, 1928. He is—and will probably remain forever—the most successful bobsleigh driver in the history of the world championships. The little Italian won no fewer than eleven world titles (plus three silvers and two bronze) in the span of twelve years (1956–'68).

Monti was awarded the "Fair Play Trophy Pierre de Coubertin" at the 1964 Olympic Winter Games in Innsbruck, when he gave a bolt to competitor Anthony Nash of Great Britain, who had damaged his sled. Nash eventually became Olympic champion in two-man together with Robin Dixon, while Eugenio Monti and his brakeman Sergio Siorpaes took bronze in two- and four-man.

Monti gained two Olympic silver medals in Cortina, 1956, and was probably denied more Olympic medals when—for the only time—bobsleigh was not held at the 1960 Games in Squaw Valley. He returned in 1964 to win two bronze medals and topped his career with his two Olympic victories in Grenoble in 1968. Monti and brakeman Luciano De Paolis were actually tied in first place with West Germans Horst Floth and Pepi Bader after four heats in the two-man in 4:41.54 on the natural track at Alpe d'Huez, but were awarded the gold medal because they had the faster time in a single heat of 1:10.05 compared with 1:10.15 and their fourth run was decisive. Before he became a bobsleigher, Monti was Italian national champion in slalom and giant slalom in 1950.

A Sporting Legend
Gustav Weder (SUI)

Gustav Weder was born on August 2, 1961. Weder announced his retirement from bobsleigh six weeks after retaining his Olympic two-man title in Lillehammer in 1994. The most successful driver of recent years, Weder started his medal collection at the 1989 European championships in Winterberg, Germany, with gold in the two-man and finished it with the Olympic silver medal in the four-man in Lillehammer. In between "Gusti" gathered altogether 24 medals (14 golds, five silver and five bronze), including his first Olympic two-man gold in Albertville in 1992, but retired without fulfilling his ambitious dream of winning an Olympic four-man title. When he retired, the Swiss driver said: "I think I'm too old to go on to Nagano 1998 to make my dream come true". Gustav Weder is now a much sought-after constructor of sleds thus passing on the knowledge he gathered during his very successful career.

A Sporting Legend
Bernhard Germeshausen (GDR)

Bernhard Germeshausen, of East Germany, was born on August 21, 1951. He is the only bobsleigher to have won medals in the same Olympic Games as a driver and crewman. Germeshausen drove his two-man to silver and was in third position on Meinhard Nehmer's winning four-man in Lake Placid, 1980. The former decathlete (7,534 points) had previously collected another two Olympic gold medals as Nehmer's brakeman in two- and four-man in 1976. After Lake Placid he went on to become double world champion as a driver in Cortina d'Ampezzo in 1981 before retiring. In addition to his three Olympic golds and one silver, Germeshausen collected six world titles, two world silvers and one world bronze.

MEDALLISTS *(by nation)*

Country	Gold	Silver	Bronze	Total
SUI	9	8	8	25
GDR	5	5	3	13
USA	5	4	5	14
ITA	3	4	3	10
FRG	3	3	2	8
GER	1	2	4	7
AUT	1	2	·	3
GBR	1	1	1	3
URS	1	·	2	3
CAN	1	·	·	1
BEL	·	1	1	2
ROM	·	·	1	1

NAGANO SCHEDULE

Bobsleigh [Men]

Venue:	Spiral		
Date	Description	Start	Finish
14 Feb	Two-man	15:00	18:30
15 Feb	Two-man	15:00	18:30
20 Feb	Four-man	15:00	18:15
21 Feb	Four-man	15:00	18:15

Bobsleigh [Men]

Year	Gold	Country	Time	Silver	Country	Time	Bronze	Country	Time
Skeleton									
1928	Jennison Heaton	USA	181.8	John Heaton	USA	182.8	David Earl of Northesk	GBR	185.1
1948	Nino Bibbia	ITA	5:23.2	John Heaton	USA	5:24.6	John Crammond	GBR	5:25.1

2-man bobsleigh

Year	Gold	Country	Time	Silver	Country	Time	Bronze	Country	Time
1932	Hubert Stevens Curtis Stevens	USA I	8:14.74	Reto Capadrutt Oscar Geier	SUI II	8:16.28	John Heaton Robert Minton	USA I	8:29.15
1936	Ivan Brown Alan Washbond	USA I	5:29.29	Fritz Feierabend Joseph Beerli	SUI II	5:30.64	Gilbert Colgate Richard Lawrence	USA II	5:33.96
1948	Felix Endrich Fritz Waller	SUI II	5:29.2	Fritz Feierabend Paul Eberhard	SUI I	5:30.4	Frederick Fortune Schuyler Carron	USA II	5:35.3
1952	Andreas Ostler Lorenz Nieberl	GER I	5:24.54	Stanley Benham Patrick Martin	USA I	5:26.89	Fritz Feierabend Stephan Waser	SUI I	5:27.71
1956	Lamberto Della Costi Giacomo Conti	ITA I	5:30.14	Eugenio Monti Renzo Alvera	ITA II	5:31.45	Heinrich (Max) Angst Harry Warburton	SUI I	5:37.46
1964	Anthony Nash Robin Dixon	GBR I	4:21.9	Sergio Zardini Romano Bonagura	ITA II	4:22.02	Eugenio Monti Sergio Siorpaes	ITA	4:22.63
1968	Eugenio Monti Luciano De Paolis	ITA I	4:41.54	Horst Floth Pepi Bader	GER	4:41.54	Ion Panturu Nicolae Neagoe	ROM	4:44.46
1972	Wolfgang Zimmerer Peter Utzschneider	FRG	4:57.07	Horst Floth Pepi Bader	GER I	4:58.84	Jean Wicki Edy Hubacher	SUI I	4:59.33
1976	Meinhard Nehmer Bernhard Germeshausen	GDR	3:44.42	Wolgang Zimmerer Manfred Schumann	GER I	3:44.99	Erich Schärer Josef Benz	SUI I	3:45.70
1980	Erich Scharer Josef Benz	SUI II	4:09.36	Hans Gerhardt Bernhard Germeshausen	GDR II	4:10.93	Meinhard Nehmer Bogdan Musiol	GDR I	4:11.08
1984	Wolfgang Hoppe Dietmar Schaurhammer	GDR II	3:25.56	Bernhard Lehmann Bogdan Musiol	GDR I	3:26.04	Sintis Ekmanis Vladimir Aleksandrov	URS II	3:26.16
1988	Ianis Kipours Vladimir Kozlov	URS I	3:53.48	Wolfgang Hoppe Bogdan Musiol	GDR I	3:54.19	Bernhard Lehmann Mario Hoyer	GDR II	3:54.64
1992	Gustav Weder Donat Acklin	SUI I	4:03.26	Rudolf Lochner Markus Zimmerman	GER I Günther Eger	4:03.55	Christoph Langen	GER II	4:03.67
1994	Gustav Weder Donat Acklin	SUI I	3:30.81	Reto Goetschi Guido Acklin	SUI II	3:30.86	Günther Huber Stefano Ticci	ITA I	3:31.01

4-man bobsleigh

Year	Gold	Country	Time	Silver	Country	Time	Bronze	Country	Time
1924	Eduard Scherrer Alfred Neveu Alfred Schläppi Heinrich Schläppi	SUI	5:45.54	Ralph Broome Thomas Arnold Alexander Richardson Rodney Soher	GBR	5:48.63	Charles Mulder René Mortiaux Paul van den Broek Victor Verschueren	BEL	6:02.29
1928 (5 man)	William Fiske Nion Tocker Charles Mason Clifford Gray Richard Parke	USA II	3:20.5	Jennison Heaton David Granger Lyman Hine Thomas Doe Jay O'Brien	USA	3:21	Hanns Kilian Valentin Krempl Hans Hess Sebastian Huber Hans Nägle	GER II	3:21.9
1932	William Fiske Edward Eagan Clifford Gray Jay O'Brien	USA I	7:53.68	Henry Homburger Percy Bryant Paul Stevens Edmund Horton	USA II	7:55.70	Hanns Kilian Max Ludwig Hans Mehlhorn Sebastian Huber	GER I	8:00.4

Bobsleigh

Year	Gold	Country	Time	Silver	Country	Time	Bronze	Country	Time
1936	Pierre Musy Arnold Gartmann Charles Bouvier Joseph Beerli	SUI II	5:19.85	Reto Capadrutt Hans Aichele Fritz Feierabend Hans Bütikofer	SUI I	5:22.73	Frederick McEvoy Jr James Cardno Guy Dugdale Charles Green	GBR I	5:23.41
1948	Francis Tyler Patrick Martin Edward Rimkus William D'Amico	USA II	5:20.1	Max Houben Freddy Mansveld Louis-Georges Niels Jacques Mouvet	BEL	5:21.3	James Bickford Thomas Hicks Donald Dupree Bill Dupree	USA I	5:21.5
1952	Andreas Ostler Friedrich Kuhn Lorenz Nieberl Franz Kemser	GER	5:07.84	Stanley Benham Patrick Martin Howard Crossett James Atkinson	USA I	5:10.48	Fritz Feierabend Albert Madörin André Filippini Stephan Waser	SUI I	5:11.70
1956	Franz Kapus Gottfried Diener Robert Alt Heinrich Angst	SUI	5:10.44	Eugenio Monti Ulrico Girardi Renzo Alvera Renato Mocellini	ITA II	5:12.10	Arthur Tyler William Dodge Charles Butler James Lamy	USA I	5:12.39
1964	Victor Emery Peter Kirby Douglas Anakin John Emery	CAN	4:14.46	Erwin Thaler Adolf Koxeder Josef Nairz Reinhold Durnthaler	AUT	4:15.48	Eugenio Monti Sergio Siorpaes Benito Rigoni Gildo Siorpaes	ITA II	4:15.60
1968	Eugenio Monti Luciano De Paolis Roberto Zandonella Mario Armano	ITA I	2:17.39	Erwin Thaler Reinhold Durnthaler Herbert Gruber Josef Eder	AUT I	2:17.48	Jean Wicki Hans Candrian Willi Hofmann Walter Graf	SUI I	2:18.04
1972	Jean Wicki Edy Hubacher Hans Leutenegger Werner Camichel	SUI	4:43.07	N Zordo Gianni Bonichon Adriano Frassinelli C Fabbro	ITA I	4:43.83	W Zimmerer P Utzschneider S Gaisreiter W Steinbauer	GER I	4:43.92
1976	Meinhard Nehmer Jochen Babok Bernhard Germeshausen Bernhard Lehmann	GDR I	3:40.43	Erich Schärer Ulrich Bächli Rudolf Marti Josef Benz	SUI II	3:40.89	Wolfgang Zimmerer Peter Utzschneider Bodo Bittner Manfred Schumann	GER I	3:41.37
1980	Meinhard Nehmer Bosdan Musiol Bernhard Germeshausen Hans Gerhardt	GDR I	3:59.92	Erich Schaerer Ulrich Baechli Rudolf Marti Josef Benz	SUI I	4:00.87	Horst Schoenau Roland Wetzig Detlef Richter Andreas Kirchner	GDR II	4:00.97
1984	Wolfgang Hoppe Roland Wetzig Dietmar Schauerhammer Andreas Kirchner	GDR I	3:20.22	Bernhard Lehmann Bogdan Musiol Ingo Voge Eberhard Weise	GDR II	3:20.78	Silvio Giobellina Heinz Stettler Urs Salzmann Rico Freiermuth	SUI I	3:21.39
1988	Ekkehard Fasser Kurt Meier Marcel Faessler Werner Stocker	SUI	3:47.51	Wolfgang Hoppe Dietmar Schauerhammer Bogdan Musiol Ingo Voge	GDR I	3:47.58	Ianis Kipours Gountis Ossis Iouri Tone Vladimir Kozlov	URS II	3:48.26
1992	Ingo Appelt Harald Winkler Gerhard Haidacher Thomas Schroll	AUT	3:53.9	Wolgang Hoppe Bogdan Musiol Axel Kuhn Rene Hannemann	ALL I	3:53.92	Gustav Weder Donat Acklin Lorenz Schindelholz Curdin Morell	SUI I	3:54.24
1994	Harald Czudaj Karsten Brannasch Olaf Hampel Alexander Szelig	GER	3:27.38	Gustav Weder Donat Acklin Kurt Meier Domenico Semeraro	SUI I	3:27.84	Wolfgang Hoppe Ulf Hielscher Rene Hannemann Carsten Embach	GER I	3:28.01

CURLING

Stars to Watch
Canada favourites at Karuizawa

by Håkan Sundström

There will be a new official sport at the Olympic Winter Games in 1998: curling. This is the sport where huge and heavy stones slide across the ice whilst players sweep their path with brushes to allow them to travel more easily. The inaugural Olympic curling tournament will take place in the town of Karuizawa, 70km (43.5 miles) south of Nagano.

Many nations have left the nomination of their teams to the last minute. However, curling is a sport where the Canadians often dominate even if their 1998-style teams may be a little lighter on experience than usual. Canada's women are still likely to include three former world champions: Sandra Schmirler (1993, '94 and '97); Connie Laliberte (1984) and Marilyn Bodogh (1986 and '96). Their men could include four former world champions: Ed Werenich (1983 and '90), Russ Howard (1987 and '93); Kerry Burtnyk (1995) and Jeff Stoughton (1996).

The Scandinavian nations are also world forces in this sport. Sweden's men became world champions in April of 1997 by beating Germany in the final of the event held in Berne, Switzerland. The same team will be on duty in Nagano: Peter Lindholm, Tomas Nordin, Magnus Swartling and Peter Narup. Their women, world champions in 1992 and '95, will include: Elisabet Gustafson, Katarina Nyberg, Louise Marmont and Elisabeth Persson.

Denmark and Norway will send teams skipped by world champions. Helena Blach-Lavrsen, the Danish female skip, was world champion as long ago as 1982. Her Norwegian counterpart, Dordi Nordby, was world champion in 1990 and '91 and Norway's men will be led by Eigil Ramsfjell who has three world titles from 1979, '84 and '88.

The host nation might also steal a medal in the women's event. Japan only became interested in curling in the 1990s but its players have developed impressively in that time. Last winter, Japanese teams reached the semi-finals at both the world women's and junior championships. Their men are an unknown quantity having never qualified for a world championships. They have won a place in the Olympic tournament as host nation.

Background

Curling is a traditional Scottish sport going back to the sixteenth century. The sport was codified as early as 1838 by the Royal Caledonian Curling Club. It involves sliding large, granite stones down a rink marked out on a sheet of ice. Points are scored by the team getting their stones closer to the centre of the target area or "house" than the opposition.

Early stones did not have handles like their modern counterparts. They were natural stones which were deemed suitable because of their shape, size and smoothness. They were often taken from river beds where the water had smoothed and rounded them. Later, finger grips were carved in the stone. The first metal handles date from the eighteenth century.

Curling appeared, some say unofficially, on the programme of the inaugural Olympic Winter Games in Chamonix in 1924 when Great Britain won the gold medal. It was also an Olympic demonstration event in 1932, '36, '64, '88 and '92. Women took part in the demonstration tournaments of 1988 and '92. The decision to add curling to the Olympic programme took place in Barcelona in 1992.

It was not until April 1, 1966, that the International Curling Federation was formed by seven countries—ostensibly as an international committee of the Royal Curling Club before being declared an independent entity in 1982. In 1968, the first world championships took place for men. The inaugural women's world championship was in 1979. In 1991 the name of the Federation was changed to the World Curling Federation (WCF). Prior to the advent of the world championships the Scotch Cup was the premier international event.

Canada, the USA, Scotland, Sweden, Switzerland and Norway are the world's strong nations. Canada won the first five world championships for men from 1968 to 1972. Currently, the WCF has 31 affiliated nations.

Equipment

Sixteen stones—in two sets of eight differentiated by the colour of their handles—are the essential ingredients of curling. These are made of Welsh or Scottish granite. No stone must be of greater weight than 19.96kg (44 lbs) or of greater circumference than 91.44cm (36in.) or of less height than 11.43cm (4.5in.). A handle is attached to every stone to lift, deliver and release it. Both sides of the circular stone have concave areas which are referred to as "cups". The outer portion of the cup has a small sliding surface, called the rim, on which the stone actually slides.

Each player starts delivery of the stone from a fixed foothold called a hack. This is made of rubber fixed to a wooden strut. Players also wear special shoes—one of which has a slippery sole which allows the player to slide into the delivery of the stone, whilst the other has a rubber sole for traction. Once the player has delivered the stone, a rubber cover is put over the sole of the "slider" shoe.

In the modern sport, two types of broom are used to clear the stones' path. These are a new-style synthetic pad and a "push broom". The "broom" is made of thick hog or horse-hair bristles. The object of sweeping is also to create a thin film of moisture between the stone and the ice to act as a lubricant. This makes the stone travel faster and makes it less likely to deviate from a straight line or "curl".

The rink itself (see diagram) is 44.5m (146ft) long and 4.381m (14ft 2in.) wide. There is a "house" at either end which consists of concentric rings. The inner, white circle, is called the centre and has a radius of 6 in. (0.1524m). This is surrounded by a series of three other rings coloured blue, white and red from the inside out. The outer red ring has a radius of 6ft (1.8288m). A centre line runs from one end of the rink to the other through both houses and a tee line runs perpendicular to this through the centre of each house. Immediately behind each house there is a backline. The hog line is marked 10m (33ft) from the hack across the rink at each end. A stone must pass the second hog line to be in play.

Each team must wear identical uniforms with a player's name and country in large letters across the back of the shirt or sweater. The team throwing the light-coloured stones must wear light-coloured clothes and vice-versa for the dark-coloured stones.

Rules and Regulations

Curling is a sport played by two teams of four players. Each player has two stones to play or "deliver" during an "end". Players deliver their stones alternating with the opposition until all sixteen stones have been delivered.

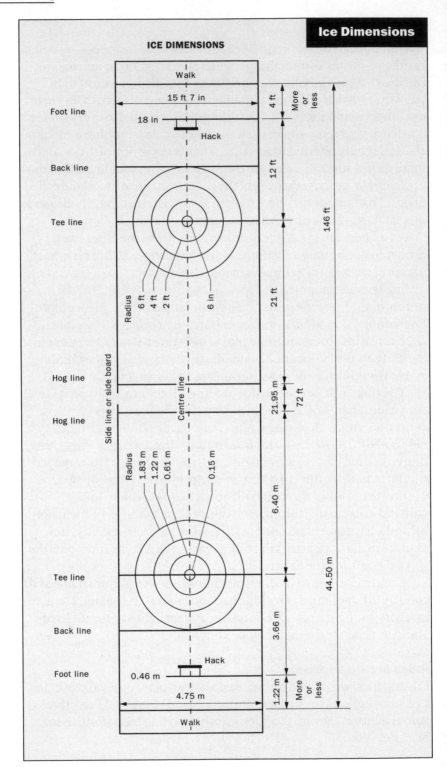

They use the hack to push off from and their arm to "throw" the stone along the ice in a fluent sliding motion. To be in play, a stone must be delivered before the first hogline, travel fully across the second hogline and come to rest at least on the outer edge of the backline. Any which hit the sidelines or fall short of these criteria are removed immediately.

The basic aim is to complete each end with more stones closer to the centre of the house than the opponent because a point is scored for each stone which is closer than those of the opposition at the finish of each end. A game is ten ends and each team is allowed 75 minutes of playing time in total with one minute between ends. If a team runs out of playing time, they forfeit the game.

The loser of the initial coin-toss between the teams goes first, giving the winner the advantage of the last stone in the end. The team that wins the first end, throws first in the second end. If no team scores during an end, the winner of the previous end begins the next. After ten ends, if two teams are tied another complete end is played as a tie-breaker.

Each team consists of the "Lead", the "Second", the "Third" and the "Skip". The Lead starts every end whilst the Skip has the last throw in each end because he or she is the most experienced player and the last throw may be crucial to the outcome. The Skip also decides the team's strategy and calls all the shots, often marking where a player should aim with his or her broom.

Just as in lawn bowls, curlers can attempt to knock their opponents' stones away from the target. Curlers are also permitted to impart a "turn" on their stone by using the handle.

Nagano Format

Eight men's and eight women's teams will participate in the 1998 Olympic curling tournament. Japan, as hosts, have gained automatic qualification to one of the eight places in each event. The other nations have qualified by means of the points scored in relation to their results at the last three world championships (1995-'97). The respective line-ups are: men—Canada, Scotland (playing as Great Britain), Sweden, Germany, USA, Norway and Switzerland; Women—Canada, Norway, Sweden, USA, Germany, Denmark and Scotland (playing as Great Britain).

Initial competition in each event will be based on one round-robin group with each team playing all the other teams. The top four teams will then move into knock-out semi-finals and a final. Losing semi-finalists will play-off for the bronze medal. If two teams are tied at the end of the group matches, the result between those two teams will be used to decide between them.

Venue

Curling takes place at the Kazakoshi Park Arena in Karuizawa, near Lake Shiozawa. For the Olympic Games, the ice will be divided into four rinks. In summer the Arena converts to a swimming pool. Karuizawa is famous in Japan for producing ice hockey players and speed skaters.

Norwegian men's team

A Contemporary Hero
Peter Lindholm (SWE)

Born in Ostersund, Sweden, on June 2, 1970, Peter Lindholm began curling in 1980 with his home town team-mates Magnus Swartling and Peter Narup. The trio played together as juniors and were very successful. Peter skipped the Swedish team at three consecutive world junior championships between 1988 and 1990 winning a medal at each including gold without losing a game in 1989.

On leaving the junior ranks Peter and his team were regarded as amongst the most talented Swedish players of all time. They won the national championships in 1993 and '95 to qualify for the world championships but could not qualify, once there, for the semi-finals and beyond. Their track record in other international events, however, was good with wins at the Bund Trophy in Berne and the Crown of Curling, in Kamloops, Canada.

The big breakthrough came in 1997 when Peter skipped his Swedish team to world championships gold, beating Germany in the final. Peter is also celebrated for his fair play on the ice. At the 1990 world junior championships and the 1995 world men's championships he won the "Sportsmanship Award".

A Contemporary Hero
Eigil Ramsfjell (NOR)

This Norwegian architect, born in Oslo in March 1955, was world champion in 1979, '84 and '88. He started curling in 1970 in a team skipped by Kristian Soerum. The team became Norwegian champions for the first time in 1976, competing in the world championships of that year and the next without reaching the play-offs.

In 1978 Ramsfjell was a world silver medallist, beating the favourites, Canada, in the semi-finals but losing to the USA in the final. A year later, in front of 11,000 spectators Norway, again skipped by Soerum, won the world title by beating Switzerland in the final. It was Norway's first ever world title.

Ramsfjell played for two more years with Soerum. In 1980 they reached the world final but lost to Canada and in 1981 they lost to the USA in the semi-final. In 1982 Ramsfjell decided to set up his own team, becoming Norwegian champion and taking world bronze. Having gained experience as a skip he went on, in 1984, to win the world title in Duluth, USA, beating Switzerland once more in the final.

Two barren years followed where Ramsfjell failed to qualify for the world championships. In 1987 he won world bronze but 1988 was his best year. In Calgary, in February, he won Olympic demonstration gold. Two months later he took world gold in Switzerland by beating Canada in the final. In December of that year he reached the European championships final but lost to host nation, Scotland.

Ramsfjell also qualified for the world championships of 1989, '90, '91, '95 and '96 winning bronze in both '89 and '91. No other player in the history of curling has played at so many world championships—15 in total so far with 103 wins from 161 games. In 1993 Ramsfjell finally became European champion after losing four finals during the 1980s. No other player is more experienced or more successful than him.

A Contemporary Heroine
Elisabet Gustafson (SWE)

Nee Johansson, Elisabet Gustafson was born in Umea, Sweden, in May 1964. She began curling in 1980 and has enjoyed great success as a junior and senior over the past two decades with Katarina Nyberg, Elisabeth Persson and, later, Louise Marmont.

In 1992, Gustafson and her friends played their first world championships in Garmisch Partenkirchen and when the week was over were crowned as champions. In December of that same year they won the European title in Perth—one they successfully defended a year later although only taking bronze at the world championships both in 1993 and '94.

Canada hosted the 1995 world championships and nearly 7000 spectators packed into the arena in Brandon, Manitoba. Gustafson's team won a thrilling final against Canada who were skipped by local girl, Connie Laliberte.

European bronze in 1995 and silver in 1996 have been Gustafson's most recent medals. Gustafson is married to Tomas Gustafson, triple Olympic gold medallist in speed skating. She is a qualified doctor who has prepared for the current season by running marathons and playing golf.

A Contemporary Heroine

Sandra Schmirler (CAN)

Sandra Schmirler, a leisure centre supervisor from Regina who was born in Biggar, Saskatchewan in June 1963, was world champion in 1993, '94 and '97. The most recent of the wins came in Berne, Switzerland, in April 1997, when Schmirler was already three months pregnant with her first child. Schmirler was expected to return to competition and skip her team to victory in the Canadian Olympic trials for Nagano.

Ironically, for two years prior to the 1997 win, Schmirler had been forced off the international scene because her regular team-mates were having children.

Nee Peterson, Schmirler began curling in 1975. In 1990 she recruited a team at Regina Caledonian Curling Club with Janice Betker, Joan McCusker and Marcia Gudereit.

By 1993 they had won their first Candian national championships title to book their passage to Geneva for the world championships where they beat Germany in the final. To defend their title a year later, the Canadians beat Scotland in the final, having only lost one game during the event to Denmark in the groups.

Returning to the international scene in 1997 by means of a third Canadian national title, Schmirler's team were outstanding during the world championships with only one loss—to Germany at the round robin stage. In the final they beat Norway who were skipped by twice world champion, Dordi Nordby.

MEDALLISTS *(by nation)*

Country	Gold		Silver		Bronze		Overall
	m	w	m	w	m	w	total
NOR	1	-	1	1	-	1	4
SUI	1	-	1	-	-	-	2
GER	-	1	-	-	-	-	1
USA	-	-	1	-	1	-	2
SWE	-	-	1	1	-	-	2
CAN	1	1	-	-	1	1	4

NAGANO SCHEDULE

Curling

Venue: **Kazakoshi Park Arena**

Date	Round	Start	Finish
9 Feb	rounds 1 & 2 (w)	9:00	12:00
		19:00	22:00
10 Feb	round 1 (m)	14:00	17:00
	rounds 2 & 3 (m)	9:00	12:00
		19:00	22:00
11 Feb	round 3 (w)	14:00	17:00
	rounds 4 & 5 (w)	9:00	12:00
		19:00	22:00
12 Feb	round 4 (m)	14:00	17:00
	rounds 5 & 6 (m)	9:00	12:00
		19:00	22:00
13 Feb	round 6 (w)	14:00	17:00
	round 7 (w)	9:00	12:00
	round 7 (m)	19:00	22:00
14 Feb	tie-break (m & w)	14:00	17:00
	tie-break (m & w)	9:00	12:00
	s/final	18:00	20:00
	s/final	14:00	17:00
15 Feb	play-off (bronze) (m & w)	9:00	12:00
	FINAL (w)	13:00	16:00
	FINAL (m)	17:00	20:00

Curling

DEMONSTRATION EVENT

Year	Gold	Country	Points	Silver	Country	Bronze	Country
1924		GBR			FRA		SWE
1932	Errick Willis Robert Pow James Bowman William Burns	CAN (Manitoba)	4-0	W W Thompson John Walker Peter Lyall E F George Albert Maclaren John Leonard T Howard Stewart William Brown	CAN (Ontario) CAN (Quebec)		
1936	Wilhelm Sibermayr Anton Ritzi Otto Ritzi Wilhelm Pichler Rudolf Rainer	AUT I		Georg Redel Ferdinand Erb Johann Eibach Josef Lenz Alois Dirnberger	GER III	Josef Hodl-Schlehofer Johann Mrakitsch Rudolf Wagner Friedrich Schieg Hubert Lodler	AUT II
1988 (m)		NOR	10-2		SUI		CAN
1988 (w)		CAN	7-5		SWE		NOR
1992 (m)		SUI	7-6		NOR		USA
1992 (w)		GER	9-2		NOR		CAN

Curling Stones

ICE HOCKEY

by John MacKinnon

The ice hockey tournament has been a centrepiece of the Olympic Winter Games since the sports festival was first convened, but the 1998 edition in Nagano can truly lay claim to being a piece of sporting history.

In Nagano, the Olympic men's ice hockey tournament will be a best-on-best tournament for the first time ever. In parallel, the best female hockey players from six participating countries will compete in the Olympic arena for the first time, just eight years after the inaugural International Ice Hockey Federation (IIHF) Women's World Hockey Championship, held in 1990 in Ottawa.

The men's tournament will mark the Olympic debut of the so-called "Dream Teams" involving the best professional hockey players in the world from all participating countries. Significantly, the National Hockey League (NHL) will take a recess for the duration of the final round of the Olympic hockey tournament, enabling its top players to join their respective national teams to play for the glory of country.

The top NHL pros have been permitted to play, in theory, since the 1988 Games in Calgary. But the point was largely moot since the NHL schedule had always been the ultimate barrier to entry for players earning their sporting living in North America. In effect, the best could not compete.

In recent years, a number of North American-based players have played in the Olympic Games — Peter Nedved for Canada in 1994 in Lillehammer, for example. But Nedved was only available for Team Canada that year because he and Vancouver Canucks, the team that held his rights at the time, had reached an impasse over a contract. This time around, only a personal choice or an injury could prevent a selected player from taking part.

In addition, the players will literally be in "mid-season form" at the Games. The 1996 World Cup of Hockey and its predecessor, the Canada Cup tournament, are also best-on-best events. But since they are held in September, before the NHL regular season begins, the fans do not see the players in peak form.

In Nagano, the galaxy of stars will truly dazzle. Jaromir Jagr from the Czech Republic, Zigmund Palffy from Slovakia, Peter Forsberg and Mats Sundin from Sweden, Pavel Bure and Sergei Fedorov from Russia, Mike Richter and Brian Leetch from the United States and Paul Kariya and Eric Lindros from Canada are all likely to compete in what could well be the most competitive, exciting hockey tournament ever held.

Competitive balance has not necessarily been a hallmark of the Olympic tournament. In the early years, Canada dominated, winning the first four tournaments and six of the first seven. The Canadians— for whom ice hockey is the national passion—dismissed their rivals with ridiculous ease despite sending club teams from the Canadian senior league rather than a representative national team composed of top professionals.

In 1924, Canada outscored its opponents 110–3 in five games. Harry (Moose) Watson poured 36 goals past rival goalies all by himself. Canada's dominance stopped abruptly following its gold medal victory in 1952. In 1956, the Soviet Union, which had studied the Canadian game and introduced some strategic changes, won its first gold medal, establishing itself as a legitimate hockey power.

Since that victory, a steady parade of Soviet hockey virtuosos— names such as Alexander Ragulin and Viacheslav Fetisov—have shone in Olympic competition, as the Soviet Union collected seven more gold medals after that first one in 1956. During the 1960s, '70s and '80s, the Russians dominated as the Canadians had in the 1920s, '30s and '40s.

The balance of hockey power in 1998 is such that any of six teams in the tournament has a solid chance to head home with gold. The teams that already have qualified for the final round include the usual medal candidates: Canada, Russia, the Czech Republic, Sweden, Finland and the United States of America.

Slovakia and Germany are the likeliest teams to emerge from the preliminary round, which also includes countries like Italy, France, Japan, Belarus, Austria and Kazakhstan, none of them a hockey power.

Countries did not need to name their team lists until December 1, 1997, but spectators can expect a number of key players to be wearing their countries' colours in the competition.

Among those carrying American hopes into the tournament will be feisty defenceman Chris Chelios, who helped Team USA defeat Canada in the inaugural World Cup of Hockey in September 1996.

Sweden's Peter Forsberg, who scored the spectacular gold medal-winning goal for his country against Canada in a dramatic shoot-out in 1994 in Lillehammer, will almost certainly be back to lead his teammates.

Finnish offensive magicians Teemu Selanne and Saku Koivu give their country a legitimate chance at a medal, while the hulking Lindors and swift, skilled Kariya are the capstone players for Canada. If goaltending is the key to Olympic success, then the Czech Republic, who will probably call on Dominik ("The Dominator") Hasek to backstop their team, should also be a contender.

In the women's tournament, there really are only three solid contenders for gold: top-seeded Canada, the USA and Finland. The other teams in the tournament—China, Sweden and Japan, the host nation— should not challenge seriously for a medal on paper.

The Chinese must be closely watched, however. That team, based in the Chinese city of Harbin, has trained as a unit for most of the last two years, plays an aggressive style of hockey and has improved steadily.

In the four IIHF Women's World Hockey Championship tournaments to date (1990,'92,'94 and '97) Canada, the USA and Finland have finished in that order on each occasion. This could well change at the Olympic Games. The gap separating the teams has all but evaporated, leaving the medal order in Nagano somewhat of a lottery. The teams will play a single-round robin, with the top two teams emerging to face off for the gold medal and the third and fourth-placed teams playing for the bronze medal.

Canada will be paced by its core of veterans: France St-Louis, Angela James, Judy Diduck, Geraldine Heaney and Stacy Wilson. Those five have been key members of all four of Canada's world championship teams. There is ample youth emerging, though, including 19 year-old Hayler Wickenheiser, a twice world champion despite her age, and Lori Dupuis and Jayna Hefford, both of whom won their first World Championship gold medals in April in Kitchener, Ontario.

The Americans, under head coach Ben Smith, have intensified their efforts. Smith, for example, was the first full-time head coach of a national women's team ever hired. She depends on an impressive array of American female hockey stars, such as forwards Cammi Granato, Sandra Whyte and Shelley Looney, along with defenders such as Kelly O'Leary and goaltender Erin Whitten.

Finland, meanwhile, has entrusted its medal fortunes to former national men's head coach, Rauno Korpi. The Finns bring impressive

Sweden celebrates 1994 win against the USA

The USA know they have the gold: 1980, Lake Placid

Ice Hockey : Sometimes an aggressive sport

talent to the tournament, including speedy forward Sari Krooks, forward Rikka Niemenen, their best all-round player, and goalie Tuula Puputti.

In contrast to the men's teams, who will have interrupted their professional seasons for two weeks to compete at the Games, the women will have interrupted their regular lives for a year or more in order to realize their dream. The Finns, Americans and Canadians, for example, all assembled in the autumn of 1996 to train full-time to prepare for the Games. The Canadians were obliged to take a year off from university or obtain a leave of absence from their regular jobs to join the national team.

The "Dream Team" tag doesn't fit the women's tournament, since virtually none of the players grew up daring to dream about competing at the Olympics as an ice hockey player. Now that women's hockey has crashed into the male bastion, expect the competition to be fierce indeed.

Background

The term "hockey" comes from the French *hocquet,* meaning a hooked stick. There is some evidence that indigenous North American peoples played a game similar to hockey on the ice in winter even before Christopher Columbus "discovered" the continent.

Several forms of ice hockey were played in Europe and North America prior to 1850. These included bandy and shinney. The first "modern-style" ice hockey match was played in Montreal in 1875. From that point onwards a number of clubs and associations were formed leading to the creation of an international federation for the sport, called the "Ligue Internationale de Hockey sur Glace (LIHG)", in Paris in 1908.

Existing Canadian rules were adopted as standard in 1911, fixing the match at three periods of 20 minutes. In 1912 the number of players was reduced from seven per team to six—still the case today.

Ice hockey first appeared in Olympic terms in 1920 when its first world championships ran alongside the Antwerp Olympic (Summer) Games. Four years later, it was part of the first Olympic Winter Games in Chamonix and has been on the programme ever since. Women's ice hockey, however, will make its Olympic debut in Nagano in 1998 following a decision taken by the IOC in Barcelona in 1992.

In 1948, following a political split in governing bodies for the sport in the USA, America turned up at the Olympic Winter Games in St Moritz with two teams—one representing the American Hockey

Association (AHA) and the other the Amateur Athletic Union. The former was affiliated to the international federation whilst the United States Olympic Committee (USOC) recognized only the latter because it felt that the AHA was commercially-sponsored.

An embarrassed IOC was furious with both the Swiss organizers and the international federation for allowing the situation to develop. The IOC proposed that no Olympic medals be awarded and that the tournament should simply be billed as a world championship. This was refused by the international federation who threatened to take all the teams away to Zurich to play. Eventually the team representing the AHA was allowed to play by the organizers. It finished fourth in a tournament won by Canada. Later the AHA team results were annulled — though, ironically, the official report still has them listed as fourth with no mention of the annulment.

Over the next three years, despite numerous meetings and proposed solutions, relations worsened between the IOC, who had decided that ice hockey would not be on the 1952 programme, and the "Ligue". In early 1951 ice hockey took a decision not to compete at future Games but the sport came back into the fold when an agreement was reached between the two factions in the USA in time for the Oslo Olympic Games. Norwegian IOC member Detlef Simonsen played a crucial role in the negotiations.

In Lausanne, in 1991, the IOC took a decision that all players — including those who were professionals in the National Hockey League (NHL) in North America — could participate in the Olympic Games. Although some professionals competed in Lillehammer, the big NHL stars will be on parade for the first time in Nagano. The NHL season begins in October and runs through until June. It will be broken in 1998 for the Games.

Canada won the first four Olympic ice hockey titles, including the 1920 Games. Remarkably, their run was interrupted by Great Britain. — hardly a modern-day ice hockey super-power. Britain had a team containing many British-born Canadians. They beat Canada 2–1 and even held the USA to a goal-less draw after overtime. Germany's team for the 1936 Games included Rudi Ball, a jew who played at the invitation of the authorities for his country, the hosts, in Garmisch-Partenkirchen. Many commentators saw this as a blatant propaganda exercise, caused by American pressure. Ball later emigrated to South Africa before the outbreak of war.

Canada, despite their proud Olympic tradition, refused to play in the 1972 Olympic Games in Sapporo. They objected to facing state-funded "amateurs" such as the Soviet Union at the Games. Eventually, the Soviet Union won the gold that year in a tournament which all rested on the last match against Czechoslovakia. The Soviets won by 5–2. Canada rejoined the Olympic fold in 1980.

Indeed, the Soviet Union dominated ice hockey from the 1960s onwards with two notable exceptions — both on American soil. In 1960 in Squaw Valley, a team of young American collegiate players took on the mighty Soviet defending champions in their third match of the Games and beat them by 3–2 in a desperately fought finish in front of a screamingly hysterical home crowd.

The Americans, already winners over Canada, then needed to beat Czechoslovakia in their final game — a team they had already beaten earlier in the group matches. In a remarkable gesture of sportsmanship the Soviet coach, Sologubov, gave the Americans a mid-match tip. He suggested that the players should take oxygen. They took his advice and turned the game round from a 3–4 deficit into a 9–4 win, taking the gold medal.

In 1980, the USA were again considered underdogs, having fielded a team of collegiate players once more. That they should win the tournament was wholly unexpected even though they had played a series of exhibition matches prior to the Games to build some kind of team spirit and strategy.

Despite being seeded seventh they emerged from the preliminary groups to take their place in the final round-robin group of four. Once there they faced the world's best team — the Soviet Union — who had won every Olympic ice hockey title since 1964. This was truly "David v Goliath", except that the young Americans refused to accept their supporting role. With just 12 minutes to go in the final period they drew level at 3–3. A frenetic and vocal home crowd cheered them on and they scored again with ten minutes remaining. American goal-keeper Jim Craig then faced a barrage of attacks from the Soviets — to no avail. The score remained 4–3 in favour of the Americans.

Only Finland now stood between the USA and gold. The Finns made life difficult but the Americans, carried on a wave of national euphoria, were the eventual winners by 4–2. Network television coverage of the Games kept the entire US population enthralled over the period of the Games and the winning team passed into the realms of "apple pie" sporting legends.

The Soviet Union goalkeeper for part of the 1980 encounter with the USA was Vladislav Tretiak. He won a record three golds and a silver between 1972 and 1984. David Christian was part of the 1980 US team — repeating the success of his father Bill who was a gold medallist for the USA in 1960.

Brothers Herbert, Hugh and Roger Plaxton as well as Joseph and Frank Sullivan were in the 1928 Canadian team. The 1948 Czech silver medal-winning team included Jaroslav Drobny who was later to go on to win the Wimbledon tennis men's singles title.

Dave Tomassoni, an Italian-born American playing for Italy in the 1984 tournament, turned to a team-mate as they were warming up for a match and said that he was sure he had just become a father. The match over, he phoned home in Minnesota to find out that he had been right—to the very minute.

In 1976 there was a three-way tie for third place between the USA, Germany and Finland. The bronze medal was awarded to Germany only after both goal average and goal difference had been taken into account. That same year, in the final, Czechoslovakia led Russia by 3–2 with five minutes to go. Russia hit back in the dying minutes with two more goals to take gold.

In the early editions of the Olympic Winter Games, ice hockey tournaments were played mainly outdoors. More recently, all matches have been played indoors. Canada often fielded a club team rather than a national team in some of those early Games.

Ice hockey has often been controversial at the Games, either for its aggressive play or for discussions over professional and amateur status. In 1976, Frantisek Pospisil of Czechoslovakia was also expelled from the Games for failing a random drugs test. His coach claimed that he had been given codeine for medical reasons as he was suffering a virus. However, the disqualification was permitted to begin only after Pospisil had competed against Finland. The Czech doctor was also disqualified.

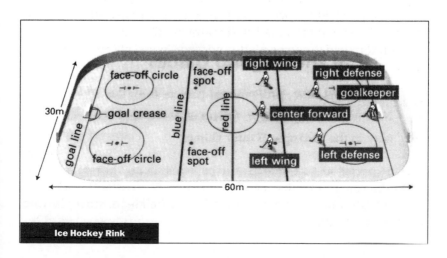

Ice Hockey Rink

Equipment

Ice hockey players use a stick to hit a hard rubber disk—called a puck.
The stick is 152cm (4ft 11.8in.) long and can be made of wood or metal
and its blade is covered with a special material to prevent the puck
from slipping. The puck itself is 2.54cm (1in.) thick and 7.62cm (3in.)
in diameter. It weighs between 156 and 170g (5.5 and 6 oz) and can
reach speeds of up to 160kmph (99mph).

The ice hockey rink is 60m by 30m surrounded by a wooden and
Perspex barrier to protect the spectators and delineate the playing
area. The barrier is curved around the corners and is 1.2m high. A
centre line divides the rink in half and two blue lines divide it into
equal thirds horizontally, creating three zones: defense, neutral and
attacking. There are four face-off circles and a centre circle. The goals,
which are set out from the backboards and placed on the goal-line,
consist of a framework with a net. They are 1.83m (6ft) wide, 1.22m
(4ft) high and 1.12m (3ft 8in.) deep.

Players wear head-guards and a series of protective pads
underneath their clothing, including those for the shoulders, knees
and elbows, as well as shin guards and large gloves. Their skates are
leather and lace up over the ankle. Ice hockey skates have a short
blade to allow for quick turns. They are 3mm (0.1in.) thick.

The goal-keeper wears additional protection, including complete
leg and body pads as well as a helmet and metal visor. Each goal-
keeper also has a blocker on one hand and a catcher on the other to
deal with the puck. The goal-keeper's stick has a longer blade than
that used for general play—39 instead of 32cm.

Rules and Regulations

The aim of ice hockey is to score more goals than the opposition. Six
players per team are allowed on court at any one time from a squad of
either 23 (for the men) or 20 (for the women). There is no limit to the
substitutions which can be made and teams normally field a goal-
keeper, two defense players and three attacking or forward players at
any one time during the game which lasts 60 minutes in three equal
20- minute periods, separated by two 15-minute intervals. Play can
take place behind the goal line as well as in the main court.

Play re-starts after a foul with a face-off from a face-off circle or
spot. Players can be sent off the ice (to a "sin-bin") for two, five or ten
minutes or can be suspended from the remainder of the game
depending on the seriousness of the offence.

Whilst the offending player is off the ice, their team must play one
short. However, the player may return to the ice during a two minute

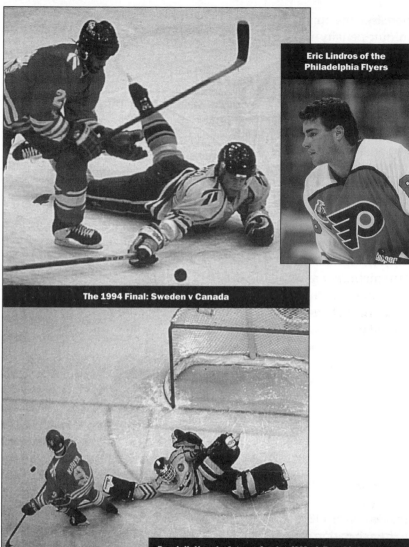

Eric Lindros of the
Philadelphia Flyers

The 1994 Final: Sweden v Canada

Dominik Hasek (Sabres) fends off Mark Recchi (Canadiens)

penalty if the opposition score a goal. This is not the case for a five minute penalty which must be served in full. When a team is playing with one player short it is said to be "on the penalty kill"—literally trying to kill the penalty time without surrendering a goal. During this time the opposition is said to be "on the power play".

There are some zonal rules. For instance, the puck may not be passed from within a team's defence zone directly across the centre line and to a team-mate on the other side. And a player is deemed to be offside if he or she travels before the puck into the attacking zone across the blue line from the neutral zone. Equally, the puck may not be sent directly from behind the centre line to beyond the opponent's goal line. This is called "icing" and is illegal.

Whilst ice-hockey has a reputation for being aggressive, there are strict rules governing the use of the stick and contact with other players. A player may not use the stick to strike, slash or swing at an opponent. Nor may they hook or trip an opponent with it. Players must not raise their stick above shoulder level.

A player cannot hold onto an opponent either with their stick or their hand. Elbowing an opponent is also disallowed as is any attempt to block or interfere with an opponent who does not have the puck.

One referee and two linesmen control the game. If the score is level after normal playing time, in the play-off and medal matches, two extra periods of five minutes each are played with the team which scores first winning. If the result is still a tie after these periods, a penalty shoot-out takes place to decide the winner.

Nagano Format

Six women's teams and 14 men's teams will take part in the 1998 Olympic Winter Games ice hockey tournaments, encompassing a maximum of 442 athletes (322 men and 120 women).

Each nation is permitted 23 per men's squad (20 players and three goal-keepers) and 20 per women's squad (18 players and two goal-keepers).

Teams have qualified for the Olympic Winter Games by a variety of routes. In the men's event, the top six nations in Pool A of the 1995 World championships qualified directly for the final round of the Olympic tournament. These are: Finland, Sweden, Canada, The Czech Republic, Russia, and the USA. The two teams placed seventh and eighth at that event—Italy and France—qualified directly for the preliminary rounds of the Olympic tournament alongside Japan as the host nation.

Other teams had to battle their way through Olympic qualification tournaments on a regional basis and, then, a final qualification tournament—all of which were held in 1997. These are: Austria, Slovakia and Kazakhstan joining Italy in Pool A; Germany, Japan and Belarus joining France in Pool B.

In Nagano, the preliminary rounds will be played on a round-robin basis with the top team in each group progressing to the final round of two round-robin groups C and D. Group C will consist of Finland, The Czech Republic, Russia and a qualifier. Group D will contain Sweden, Canada, the USA and a qualifier. After the pool games there will be cross-over quarter-finals, semi-finals and a final and a bronze medal play-off.

In the women's event, the top five nations at the 1997 world championships qualified directly for the Games alongside Japan as hosts. These are in order of seeding: Canada, the USA, Finland, China and Sweden with Japan as sixth seeds. The women's event will be a single round-robin group with the top two teams emerging to play the gold medal match and the third and fourth-placed teams playing for bronze.

Venue

Two stadia will be used to stage the 1998 Olympic Winter Games ice hockey tournament. The first is called the Big Hat and is located 1.5km south-east of Nagano. It gets its name from the shape of the roof. Inside, the stadium has an open ceiling of exposed steel frameworks. After the Games, it will become a multi-purpose arena. Care has been taken to make sure the stadium blends with the environment.

The second stadium is called "Aqua Wing" and is situated in Nagano Sports Park, in the Higashi Wada district of Nagano. Aqua Wing has a retractable roof. After the Games it will be converted to a swimming pool complex.

The Big Hat arena will host all the medal games as well as the majority of the men's pool games. All other elements of the competition will be played at the Aqua Wing.

A Sporting Legend

Harry Watson (Canada)

The early years of the Olympic Winter Games ice hockey tournament were characterized by utter domination by Canada who won six of the first seven tournaments.

In 1924, led by Harry (Moose) Watson, Canada, represented by the Toronto Granites, demolished the opposition, scoring 110 goals in five games while permitting their opponents only three. It was truly a case of "men versus boys" during the round robin portion of the Games as Canada defeated Czechoslovakia 30–0, Sweden 22–0 and Switzerland 33-0. The Watson-led Canadians scored 18 goals in the second period alone against the Swiss.

Watson, a left winger, born in Newfoundland and raised in Winnipeg and Toronto, finished the tournament with 36 goals, an Olympic record that still stands. True to the original spirit of Olympism, Watson never turned professional despite many attractive offers. Watson even turned down an offer from the Montreal Maroons of the National Hockey League who tried to woo him with a contract worth $30,000—or about six times what the average NHL pro was earning at that time.

A Sporting Legend

Anatoli Firsov (Soviet Union)

A left winger who stood out for both his technical and cerebral play, Firsov was a member of three Olympic gold medal-winning Soviet teams—1964, '68 and '72. He was the top scorer at the 1968 Games, collecting 16 points, including 12 goals in only seven games.

Drafted into the Soviet military in 1961, at the age of 20, Firsov, who had played bandy—a rudimentary version of hockey —as a youngster, joined the Central Red Army hockey team and became its star player. He was named to five straight all-star teams (1967– '71) at the annual world hockey championships.

Although Firsov was of average build, he was wiry and had tremendous stamina. He was perhaps the fittest Soviet player of his era because of his passion for training. So dedicated was Firsov to the sport of hockey and to his team-mates, he would invite his linemates on family vacations so he could maintain a hockey atmosphere in his few weeks away from the rink.

Sporting Legends

Anatoli Tarasov & Viktor Tikhonov (Soviet Union)

They were revered and reviled. They were described by some as hockey architects, while others regarded them as hockey autocrats. But there is no disputing the success of Anatoli Tarasov and Viktor Tikhonov who both presided over Soviet Union hockey dynasties in international competition.

The burly, outgoing Tarasov coached three gold medal winners: 1964, '68 and '72. He implemented a system that accented the counter-attack, positioning, stickhandling, discipline and year-round training. Between 1962 and '72, the Soviet Union won 12 from a possible 13 championships in world and Olympic ice hockey.

The dour-faced, taciturn Tikhonov took over the Soviet national team in 1977 and coached with an iron fist. But he got outstanding results—the team won Olympic gold in 1984, '88 and '92—and captured the world title in 11 of 13 years between 1978–'90. Tikhonov was not as successful in his relationship with his players, many of whom rebelled over his frequent rantings. The growing chasm between Tikhonov and his players contributed to his 1994 firing as the national team coach.

A Sporting Legend

Viacheslav Fetisov (Soviet Union)

Opposing forwards who cruised into the defensive zone of the Soviet national team in the 1980s did so at their own risk when Viacheslav Fetisov was on the ice. Fetisov combined toughness—he often infuriated opponents by brushing their face with his glove—and talent to become one of the most decorated hockey players in the country's history.

Fetisov was a member of two Olympic championships squads—in 1984 and '88. He was on seven world championships winning teams, was named European player of the year three times and a Soviet national league all-star nine times. He was so respected by his peers on the Central Red Army team from which most members of the national squad came—that he was named the captain of the club.

Fetisov was also an inspiration to a new generation of Russian hockey players. He was at the forefront of the battle by Soviet players to leave the mother country to play in the National Hockey League. Fetisov signed with the New Jersey Devils in 1989 and, last spring at the age of 39, he added another laurel by helping the Detroit Red Wings win the Stanley Cup.

Sporting Legends

The 1980 USA Olympic team

It will forever rank as one of the sport's geatest upsets. A United States team comprised of unheralded collegiate players defeating the vaunted Soviet hockey machine to open the medal round and then edging Finland for the gold at the 1980 Olympic Winter Games in Lake Placid, New York.

The Soviets had won five of six gold medals since entering the Olympic hockey competitions in 1956. Ironically, the Americans had broken the string with a win at Squaw Valley, California, at the 1960 Olympic Games. The 1980 squad, the youngest in American Olympic history, used the stellar 36-save goal-tending performance of Jim Craig to dethrone the powerful Soviets 4–3, before rallying from a 2–1 deficit with three third-period goals to beat Finland in the final.

Herb Brooks, the coach of the US team—ironically, he was the last player cut from the 1960 American squad—said youthful exuberance and a hunger to avenge a 10–3 pre-Olympic drubbing by the Soviets spurred the underdog Americans. More than a stunning upset, the US victory had political overtones, since it occurred shortly after the US was rocked by the hostage-taking crisis in Iran and The Soviet invasion of Afghanistan.

A Contemporary Heroine

Hayley Wickenheiser (Canada)

As a 15 year-old, Hayley Wickenheiser was nicknamed "high-chair Hayley" as she helped Canada's national women's team win the gold medal at the 1994 women's world hockey championships in Lake Placid, New York. That same year, the International Ice Hockey Federation officially added women's hockey to the Olympic Winter progamme for the Games in Nagano in 1998. Like many talented females, Wickenheiser grew up playing hockey on boys' teams where she excelled but also encountered hostility from resentful parents and coaches. "They thought I was taking a spot from a boy", she says.

There is certainly no resentment of Wickenheiser on Canada's national women's team which she helped win another gold medal in Kitchener, Ontario, at the 1997 women's world championships. Just 19, Wickenheiser is preparing to add an Olympic medal to her pair of world championship golds.

A Contemporary Hero
Chris Chelios (USA)

Chris Chelios is the first to admit that he plays the game with a mean streak which stems from a fiercely competitive nature and a loathing of defeat. More than one opponent has felt the sting of his body and stick checks or an errant elbow, just as referees have felt the sharpness of his tongue.

A member of the winning US team at the inaugural World Cup competition in 1996, Chelios played for the US Olympic team in 1984 at Sarajevo. But it was a brief experience as the Americans, who captured gold in 1980, failed to make the medal round.

An eight-time all-star in the National Hockey League, Chelios is a three-time winner of the Norris Trophy, awarded to the league's top defenseman. A member of the Stanley Cup-winning Montreal Canadiens in 1986, he has spent the last few seasons with the Chicago Blackhawks, where he continues to be, in the words of Tony Amonte, a former rival who is now a teammate: "the toughest defenseman in the league to play against".

A Contemporary Hero
Peter Forsberg (Sweden)

At the tender age of 23, Peter Forsberg is already a legend in international hockey competitions. He established a reputation in 1992 at the world junior championships with a record-shattering 31 points, including seven goals in a mere seven games.

Then, at the 1994 Olympic Games, Forsberg scored a spectacular goal in the tie-breaking shoot-out against Canada, as Sweden, who started playing Olympic hockey in 1920, won its first gold medal, an achievement which the Swedish government recognized by issuing a postage stamp of Forsberg scoring the game-winning goal.

Forsberg, who played for the MoDo team coached by his father Kent—now the Swedish national team coach—left Sweden in 1994 to pursue a career in the National Hockey League. A gifted scorer and playmaker who excels in all facets of the game, Forsberg helped the Colorado Avalanche team win the Stanley Cup in 1996 and is currently one of the NHL's top stars.

A Contemporary Hero
Sergei Fedorov (Russia)

Part of the wave of younger generation Russian players who came to North America and the National Hockey League at the start of the 1990s, Sergei Fedorov is arguably the most accomplished of the lot. In 1994, he became the first European-trained player, after scoring 56 goals and adding 64 assists. He has scored at least 30 goals in each of his six full NHL seasons.

A swift and powerful skater—a quality Fedorov says he acquired from vigorous 11-month training techniques which players went through in the Russian hockey system—Fedorov is also noted for his great versatility. Shifted to defense at one stage last season, he performed with distinction and, returning to his regular centre position, he was among the Detroit Red Wings' best players in the play-offs as the team ended a 42-year drought by winning the Stanley Cup.

Fedorov had already left for North America when Russia won its last Olympic hockey gold medal in 1992 but he was a member of that country's World Cup team in the fall of 1996.

A Contemporary Hero
Eric Lindros (Canada)

Although he will not turn 25 until after the 1998 Olympic Games, Eric Lindros is steeped in international hockey experience, having played with several Canadian teams at the world junior championships, world championships, Canada Cup and World Cup level.

Dubbed "the Next One", since he was earmarked while still a teenager as the National Hockey League superstar who would follow Wayne Gretzky. The square-jawed, battleship-strong Lindros spent much of the 1991-'92 season with Canada's national team, following his much-publicized refusal to sign with the NHL's Quebec Nordiques. His rights were later traded to the Philadelphia Flyers, with whom Lindros won the league's Most Valuable Player award in 1995.

Lindros, whose punishing style scatters opponents but also makes him vulnerable to injury, has won gold medals with Canadian world junior teams but also carries the stigma of a sixth-place finish—Canada's worst showing—with the 1992 world juniors. He contributed 11 points, including five goals in eight games, as Canada won a silver medal at the 1992 Olympic Games.

A Contemporary Hero
Paul Kariya (Canada)

Few players are as eager for the start of the 1998 Olympic hockey tournament than Paul Kariya. The flashy forward, whose peripheral vision and showy skating make him one of the most imaginative and exciting players on the National Hockey League, had his final shot blocked in the shoot-out at the 1994 Olympic Games. Sweden's Peter Fosberg scored on his attempt and Sweden snatched the gold medal from Canada.

The classy Kariya, whose overtime goal against the Czech Republic boosted Canada into the semi-finals of the 1994 Games was not depressed by his final -game setback. He has vowed "to work on my breakaway moves" for the 1998 Olympic Games.

A member of the NHL's Anaheim Mighty Ducks—which are owned by Disney Sports Enterprises—the 23 year-old Kariya certainly provides Disney-like entertainment. Not only is he one of the NHL's top scorers, he has earned awards for his gentlemanly conduct on the ice.

A Contemporary Hero
Zigmund Palffy (Slovakia)

Zigmund Palffy should be right at home at the 1998 Olympic Games. After all, he was the top scorer of the 1994 Games, collecting ten points, including three goals in eight games in Slovakia's first Olympic experience.

A former Czechoslovakian National League player, Palffy was not able to play for Czechoslovakia in the 1992 Olympic Games because of a shoulder injury. But a year earlier, he helped the country's junior team capture a bronze medal at the World Championships.

Described by his New York Islanders team-mate Darius Kasparaitis as "a very smart player who has unbelievable hands", Palffy has become one of the National Hockey League's top scorers through his ability to unleash lightning-quick wrist shots into the tiniest openings provided by opposing goal-tenders.

A Contemporary Hero

Dominik Hasek (Czech Republic)

If any goal-tender could almost single-handedly lift his country to Olympic gold in the hockey competition, it would probably be Dominik Hasek. It was the play of the man nicknamed "The Dominator" that turned the NHL's Buffalo Sabres into a surprise contender last season. Hasek won the Vezina Trophy as the NHL's top goal-tender for the third time in four years and he also became the first goal-tender to win the league's MVP Award since Jacques Plante in 1962.

Hasek, who was injured and unable to play for the Czech Republic in the World Cup tournament in the fall of 1996, is unconventional, both in goal-tending and clothing style. On the ice, he often flops around like a fish out of water. Off the ice, he has been known to war black socks with Bermuda shorts.

While he has garnered much publicity in North America for his stellar play, he also attracted much attention last year for his feuds with Buffalo coach, Ted Nolan, who was fired. He has been equally abrasive with the Buffalo media, a member of which he physically confronted after an unflattering article.

MEDALLISTS *(by nation)*

Country	Gold	Silver	Bronze	Total
URS/EUN	8	1	1	10
CAN	6	4	2	12
USA	2	6	1	9
SWE	1	2	4	7
GBR	1	-	1	2
CZE	-	4	4	8
FIN	-	1	1	2
GER/FRG	-	-	2	2
SUI	-	-	2	2

NAGANO SCHEDULE

Ice Hockey

Venue: B=Big Hat; A=Aqua Wing

Date	Round	Start	Finish	Venue
7 Feb	prelims (m)	16:00	18:30	A&B
		20:00	22:30	A&B
8 Feb	prelims (w)	12:00	14:30	B
		16:00	18:30	
		20:00	22:30	
	prelims (m)	14:00	16:30	A
		18:00	20:30	
9 Feb	prelims (w)	12:00	14:30	B
		16:00	18:30	
		20:00	22:30	
	prelims (m)	14:00	16:30	A
		18:00	20:30	
10 Feb	prelims (m)	14:00	16:30	A&B
		18:00	20:30	A&B
11 Feb	prelims (w)	12:00	14:30	B
		16:00	18:30	
		20:00	22:30	
12 Feb	prelims (m)	12:00	14:30	A
		16:00	18:30	
		20:00	22:30	
	prelims (w)	12:00	14:30	B
		16:00	18:30	
		20:00	22:30	
13 Feb	prelims (m)	14:45	17:15	A&B
		18:45	21:15	A&B
14 Feb	prelims (w)	12:00	14:30	B
		16:00	18:30	
		20:00	22:30	
	prelims (m)	14:45	17:15	A
		18:45	21:15	
15 Feb	prelims (m)	13:45	16:15	A
		18:45	21:15	
16 Feb	prelims (m)	13:45	16:15	A
		18:45	21:15	
		14:45	17:15	B
		18:45	21:15	
17 Feb	play-off (bronze) (w)	14:00	16:30	A
	FINAL (w)	18:00	20:30	
18 Feb	q/finals (m)	14:45	17:15	A&B
	q/finals (m)	18:45	21:15	A&B
20 Feb	s/finals (m)	14:45	17:15	A
		18:45	21:15	
21 Feb	play-off (bronze) (m)	15:15	17:45	A
22 Feb	FINAL (m)	13:45	16:15	A

Ice Hockey [Men]

Year	Gold	Country	Silver	Country	Bronze	Country
1920	Robert Benson	CAN	Raymond Bonney	USA	Karel Hartmann	CZE
	Walter Byron		Anthony Conroy		Karel Kotrba	
	Frank Fredrickson		Herbert Drury		Josef Loos	
	Christopher Fridfinnson		Edward Fitzgerald		Vilém Loos	
	Magnus Goodman		George Geran		Jan Palous	
	Haldor Halderson		Frank Goheen		Jan Peka	
	Konrad Johanneson		Joseph McCormick		Karel Pesek-Kada	
	Allan Woodman		Laurence McCormick		Josef Sroubek	
			Francis Synnott		Orakar Vindys	
			Leon Tuck		Karel Wälzer	
1924	Jack Cameron	CAN	Clarence Abel	USA	William Anderson	GBR
	Ernest Collett		Herbert Drury		Colin Carruthers	
	Albert McCaffrey		Alphonse Lacroix		Eric Carruthers	
	Harold McMunn		John Langley		George Clarkson	
	Duncan Munro		John Lyons		Ross Cuthbert	
	Beattie Ramsay		Justin McCarthy		George Holmes	
	Cyril Slater		Willard Rice		Hamilton Jukes	
	Reginald Smith		Irving Small		Edward Pitblado	
	Harry Watson		Francis Synnott		Blane Sexton	
1928	Charles Delahaye	CAN	Carl Abrahamsson	SWE	Giannin Andreossi	SUI
	Franklyn Fisher		Emil Bergman		Mezzi Andreossi	
	Louis Hudson		Gustaf Johansson		Robert Breiter	
	Herbert Plaxton		Henry Johansson		Louis Dufour	
	Hugh Plaxton		Nils Johansson		Charles Favel	
	Roger Plaxton		Ernst Karlberg		Albert Geronimi	
	John Primeau		Erik Larsson		Fritz Kraatz	
	Frank Sullivan		Bertil Linde		Arnold Martignoni	
	Joseph Sullivan		Wilhelm Pettersson		Helni Meng	
	Ross Taylor		Kurt Sukcsdorff		Anton Morosani	
	David Trotter		Birger Holmqvist		Luzius Ruedi	
					Luzius Ruedi	
1932	William Cockburn	CAN	Franklin Farrell	USA	Walter Leinweber	GER
	Stanley Wagner		Edward Frazier		Alfred Heinrich	
	Hugh Sutherland		Osborn Anderson		Erich Romer	
	Roy Hinkel		John Garrison		Rudi Ball	
	Walter Monson		Joseph Fitzgerald		Georg Strobl	
	Harold Simpson		Gerard Hallock		Erich Herker	
	George Garbutt		Robert Livingstone		Gustav Jaenecke	
	Norman Malloy		John Chase		Werner Korff	
	J Aliston Wise		Francis Nelson		Martin Schrottle	
	Victor Lindquist		John Bent		F Marquardt Slevogt	
	Romeo Rivers		John Cookman			
	Kennith Moore		Winthrop Palmer			
	Clifford Crowley		Douglas Everett			
	Albert Duncanson		Gordon Smith			
1936	James Foster	GBR	Francis Moore	CAN	Thomas Moone	USA
	Carl Erhardt		Arthur Nash		Francis Shaughnessy	
	Gordon Dailley		Herman Murray		Philip La Batte	
	James Borland		Walter Kitchen		Frank Stubbs	
	Robert Wyma		Raymond Milton		John Garrison	

Year	Gold	Country	Silver	Country	Bronze	Country
	Archibald Stinchcombe		David Neville		Paul Rowe	
	Edgar Brenchley		Kenneth Farmer-Horn		John Lax	
	John Coward		Hugh Farguharson		Gordon Smith	
	James Chappell		Maxwell Deacon		Eldridge Ross	
	Alexander Archer		Alexander Sinclair		Francis Spain	
	John Davey		William Thomson		August Kammer	
	John Kilpatrick		James Haggarty			
			Ralph St Germain			
1948	H Brooks	CAN	Vladimir Bouzek	CZE	H Baenninger	SUI
	Murray Dowey		Gustav Bubnik		Alfred Bieler	
	Bernard Dunster		Jaroslav Drobny		Heinrich Boller	
	R Forbes		Premysl Hajny		Ferdinand Cattini	
	A Gilpin		Zdenck Jarkovsky		Hans Cattini	
	Israel (Orval) Gravelle		V Kobrnov		Hans Dürst	
	Patrick Guzzo		Stanislav Konopasek		Walter Dürst	
	William Halder		Bohumil Modry		Emil Handschin	
	Thomas Hibberd		Misloslav Pokorny		Werner Lohrer	
	R King		Vaclav Rozinak		Heini Lohrer	
	Henri Laperrire		Miroslav Slama		Reto Perl	
	John Lecompte		Karel Stibor		Ulrich Poltera	
	J Leichnitz		Vilem Stovik		Gebhard Poltera	
	George Mara		Ladislav Trojak		Beat Rüedi	
	Albert Renaud		Josef Trousilek		Otto Schubiger	
	Reginald Schroeter		Oldrich Zabrodsky		Richard Torriani	
	Irving Taylor		Vladimir Zabrodsky		Hans Trepp	
1952	George Abel	CAN	Ruben Bjorkman	USA	Göte Amqvist	SWE
	John Davies		Leonard Ceglarski		Hans Andersson	
	Billie Dawe		Joseph Czarnota		Stig Andersson	
	Bruce Dickson		Richard Desmond		Åke Andersson	
	Donald Gauf		Andre Gambucci		Lars Björn	
	William Gibson		Clifford Harrison		Göte Blomqvist	
	Ralph Hansch		Gerald Kilmartin		Thord Flodqvist	
	Robrt Meyers		John Mulhern		Erik Johansson	
	David Miller		John Noah		Gösta Johansson	
	Eric Paterson		Arnold Oss		Rune Johansson	
	Thomas Pollock		Robert Rompre		Sven Johansson	
	Allan Purvis		James Sedin		Holger Nurmela	
	Gordon Robertson		Allen Van		Lars Pettersson	
	Louis Secco		Donald Whiston		Lars Svensson	
	Francis Sullivan		Kenneth Yackel		Sven Thunman	
	Robert Watt				Hans Öberg	
1956	Nikolai Puchkov	URS	Willard Ikola	USA	Denis Brodeur	CAN
	Grigori Mkrtchan		Donald Rigazio		Keith Woodall	
	Nikolai Sologubov		Richard Rodenhiser		Floyd Martin	
	Dimitri Ukolov		Daniel McKinnon		Howard Lee	
	Ivan Tregubov		Edward Sampson		Arthur Hurst	
	Genrikh Sidorenkov		John Matchefts		Jack McKenzie	
	Alfred Kuchevskiy		Richard Meredith		James Logan	
	Evgeni Babich		Richard Dougherty		Paul Knox	
	Viktor Shuvalov		Kenneth Purpur		Donald Rope	
	Vsavolod Bobrov		John Mayasich		Byrle Klinck	
	Yuri Krylov		William Cleary		Bill Colvin	
	Alexander Uvarov		Wellington Burtnett		Gerry Theberge	
	Valentin Kuzin		Wendell Anderson		Alfred Horne	

Year	Gold	Country	Silver	Country	Bronze	Country
	Yuri Pantjukhov		Eugene Campbell		Charles Brooker	
	Alexei Guryshev		Gordon Christian		George Scholes	
	Nikolai Khlystov		Weldon Olson		Robert White	
	Viktor Nikiforov		John Pettroske		Ken Laufman	
1960	John McCartan	USA	Harold Hurley	CAN	Nikolai Puchkov	URS
	John Kirrane		HaroldSinden		Nikolai Sologubov	
	John Mayasich		Maurice Benoit		Yuri Baulin	
	Paul Johnson		Kenneth Laufman		AlexanderAlmetov	
	Weldon Olson		Floyd Martin		Konstatin Loktev	
	Richard Rodenheiser		James Connelly		Venjamin Aleksandrov	
	Rodney Paavola		Robert Attersley		Alfred Kutchevski	
	Laurence Palmer		Jack Douglas		Stanislav Petukov	
	Thomas Williams		Fred Etcher		Viktor Priasjnikov	
	Roger Christian		Robert Forhan		Genrikh Sidorenkov	
	William Christian		Donald Head		Mikhail Bytchkov	
	Robert Cleary		Robert McKnight		Vladimir Grebennikov	
	William Cleary		Clifford Pennington		Evgeni Grosjev	
	Eugene Grazia		Donald Rope		Yuri Tsitsinov	
	Robert McVey		Joseph Rousseau		Viktor Jakusjev	
	Richard Meredith		George Samolenko		Evgeni Jerkin	
	Edwyn owen		Darryl Sly		Nikolai Karpov	
1964	Vanjamin Aleksandrov	URS	Folke Bengtsson	SWE	Jiri Kochta	CZE
	Alexander Almetov		Arne Carlsson		Oldrich Machac	
	Vitali Davidov		Patrik Carnback		Karel Masopust	
	Anatoli Firssov		Haris Dahllöf		Vladimir Nadrchal	
	Eduard Ivanov		Svante Granholm		Vaclav Nedomansky	
	Viktor Jakusjev		Henric Hedlund		Frantisek Paspisil	
	Viktor Konovalenko		Leif Henriksson		Frantisek Sevcik	
	Viktor Kuskin		Leif Holmqvist		Jan Suchy	
	Boris Zailsev		Nils Johansson		Vk(?)adimir Dzuritla	
	Oleg Zailsev		Tord Lunström		Josef Golonka	
	Konstantin Liklav		Lars-Gorän Nilsson		Jan Havel	
	Boris Majorov		Roger Olsson		Petr Hejma	
	Evgeni Majorov		Björn Palmqvist		Jiri Holik	
	Stanislav Petukov		Ulf Sandström ?		Josef Horesovsky	
	Alexander Ragulin		Roland Stoltz		Jan Hrbaty	
	Vjatjeslav Starsinov		Lennart Svedberg		Jaroslave Jirkovsky	
	Leonid Volkov		Haken Wickberg		Jan Klapac	
1968	Viktor Konovalenko	URS	Vladimir Nadrchal	CZE	Kenneth Broderick	CAN
	Viktor Zinger		Vk(?)adimir Durzila		Wayne Stephenson	
	Vitali Davydov		Oldrich Machac		Larry Johnston	
	Viktor Blinov		Jan Suchy		Paul Conlin	
	Igor Romichevskii		Josef Horesovsky		Brian Glennie	
	Viktor Kouzkine		Frantisek Pospichil		Terrence O'Malley	
	Oleg Zaitsev		Karel Masopust		John McKenzie	
	Alexander Ragouline		Jan Klapac		Ted Hargreaves	
	Boris Maiorov		Frantisek Sevcik		Raymond Cadieux	
	Yuri Moisseev		Jan Havel		Stephen Monteith	
	Anatoli Firsov		Jan Hrbaty		William McMillan	
	Vjatjeslav Starchinov		Vaclav Nedomansky		Francis Huck	
	Anatoli Ionov		Josef Golonka		Gary Dineen	
	Viktor Poloupanov		Petr Hejma		Daniel O'Shea	
	Vanjamin Alexandrov		Jiri Kochta		Herbert Pinder H	
	Evgeni Zimine		Jaroslav Jirik		Morris Mott	

Year	Gold	Country	Silver	Country	Bronze	Country
	Evgeni Michakov		Jiri Holik		Gerald Pinder	
	Vladimir Vykoulov		Josef Cerny		Roger Bourbonnais	
1972	Alexander Pachkov	URS	Vk(?)adimir Czurila	CZE	Leif Holmqvist	SWE
	Vladislav Tretiak		Jiri Holecek		Christer Abrahamsson	
	Vitali Davydov		Josef Horesovsky		Tommy Bergman	
	Vladimir Loutchenko		Oldrich Machac		Stig Östling	
	Viktor Kouzkine		Rudolf Tajcnar		Bert-Ola Nordlander	
	Alexander Ragouline		Frantisek Pospisil		Thommy Abrahamsson	
	Igor Romichevskii		Karel Vohralik		Lars-Eric Sjoberg	
	Gennadi Tsygankov		M Danek		Kjell-Rune Milton	
	Valeri Vassiliev		Vladimir Bednar		Kenneth Ekman	
	Yuri Blinov		Jaroslav Holik		Hakan Wickberg	
	Alexander Maltsev		Jiri Kochta		Tord Lundstrom	
	Anatoli Firssov		Vladimir Martinec		Stig-Göran Johansson	
	Evgeni Michakov		Richard Farda		Hans Hansson	
	Boris Mikhailov		Bohuslav Stastny		Lars-Göran Nilsson	
	Alexander Lakouchev		Vaclav Nedomansky		Mats Ahlberg	
	Evgeni Zimine		Josef Cerny		Mats Lindh	
	Vladimir Petrov		Jan Havel		Björn Palmqvist	
	Valeri Kharlamov		Eduard Novak		Inge Hammarstrom	
	Vladimir Vikoulov		Jiri Holik		Hakan Pettersson	
	Vladimir Chadrine		Ivan Hlinka		Hans Lindberg	
1976	Boris Aleksandrov	URS	Josef Augusta	CZE	Klaus Auhuber	GER
	Sergei Babinov		Jiri Bubla		Kgnaz Berndaner	
	Alexander Gusev		Milan Chalupa		Wolfgang Boos	
	Alexander Jakusjev		Jiri Crha		Lorenz Funk	
	Sergei Kapustin		Miroslav Dvorak		Martin Hinterstocker	
	Valeri Kharlamov		Bohuslav Eberman		Anton Kehle	
	Yuri Liapkin		Ivan Hlinka		Udo Keissling	
	Vladimir Lutchenko		Jiri Holecek		Walter Köberle	
	Alexander Maltsev		Jiri Holik		Ernst Köpf	
	Boris Mikhailov		Milan Kajki		Stefan Metz	
	Vladimir Petrov		Oldrich Machec		Rainer Philipp	
	Vladimir Shadrin		Vladimir Martinec		Franz Reindl	
	Viktor Shalimov		Eduard Novak		Alois Schloder	
	Viktor Shluktov		Jiri Novak		Rudolf Thanner	
	Viktor Sidelrukov		Milan Novy		Ferenc Vozar	
	Vladislav Tretjak		Frantisek Pospisil		Josef Völk	
	Gennadi Tsygankov		Jaroslav Pouzar		Erich Weisshaupt	
	Valeri Vassilev		Bohuslav Stastny			
1980	Steve Janaszak	USA	Vladimir Myshkln	URS	Pelle Lindbergh	SWE
	Jim Craig		Vladislav Tretjak		William Loefqvist	
	Kenneth Morrow		Viacheslav Fetisov		Tomas Jonsson	
	Michael Ramsey		Vasili Pervukhin		Sture Andersson	
	William Baker		Valeri Vasiliev		Ulf Weinstock	
	John O'Callahan		Alexei Kasatonov		Jan Eriksson	
	Bob Suter		Sergei Starikov		Tommy Samuelsson	
	David Silk		Zinetulla Biljaletdinov		Mats Waltin	
	Neal Broten		Vladimir Krutov		Thomas Eriksson	
	Mark Johnson		Alexander Maltsev		Per Lundqvist	
	Steven Christoff		Yuri Lebedev		Mats Aahlberg	
	Mark Wells		Boris Mikhailov		Haakan Eriksson	
	Mark Pavelich		Vladimir Petrov		Mats Naeslund	
	Eric Strobel		Valeri Kharlamov		Lennart Norberg	

Ice Hockey

Year	Gold	Country	Silver	Country	Bronze	Country
	Michael Eruzione		Helmut Balderis		Leif Holmgren	
	David Christian		Victor Zhlulktov		Bo Berglund	
	Robert McClanahan		Alexander Golikov		Dan Soederstroem	
	William Schneider		Sergei Makarov		Harald Luckner	
	Philip Verchota		Vladimir Golikov		Lars Mohlin	
	John Harrington		Alexander Skvortsov			
1984	Zenetula Biljaletdinov	URS	Jaroslav Benak	CZE	Per-Erik Eklund	SWE
	Nikolai Drosdetski		Mojmir Bozik		Thom Eklund	
	Viacheslav Fetisov		Jiri Dotezal		Bo Ericson	
	Alexander Gerasimov		Oto Hascak		Hakan Erikson	
	Alexei Kasatonov		Dominik Hasek		Peter Gradin	
	Andrei Khomutor		Miloslav Horava		Mats Hesel	
	Alexander Kasjevnikov		Jiri Hrdina		Michael Hjälm	
	Vladimir Kavin		Jiri Lala		Göran Lindblom	
	Vladimir Kutov		Igor Liba		Tommy Mörth	
	Sergei Makarov		Vincent Lukac		Hakan Nordin	
	Vladimir Mysjkin		Pavel Richter		Rolf Ridderwall	
	Vasili Pervukin		Vladimir Rusica		Thomas Rundqvist	
	Sergei Shepelev		Darius Rusnak		Thomas Sandström	
	Alexander Skvortsov		Jaromir Sindel		Hakan Södergren	
	Sergei Starikov		Radoslav Svoboda		Mats Thelin	
	Igor Stelnov		Eduard Uvira		Göte Wältin	
	Vladislav Tretjak				Thomas Ahlén	
	Viktor Tumenev					
	Jens Öhling					
	Mikhail Vassiliev					
1988	Ilja Biakin	URS	Timo Blomqvist	FIN	Mikael Andersson	SWE
	Viacheslav Bykov		Kari Eloranta		Peter Andersson	
	Viacheslav Fetisov		Raimo Helminen		Jonas Bergkvist	
	Alexei Gusarov		Iiro Järvi		Bo Berglund	
	Sergei Jasjin		Esa Keskinen		Thom Eklund	
	Valeri Kamenski		Erkkl Lalne		Anders Eldebrink	
	Alexei Kasatonov		Kari Laitinen		Peter Eriksson	
	Andrei Khomutov		Erkki Lehtonen		Thomas Eriksson	
	Alexander Kosjevnikov		Jyrkki Lumme		Michael Hjälm	
	Igor Kravtchuk		Reijo Mikkolainen		Lars Ivarsson	
	Vladimir Krutov		Jarmo Myllys		Mikael Johansson	
	Igor Larionov		Teppo Numinnen		Lars Karlsson	
	Andrei Lomakin		Janne Ojanen		Mats Kihlström	
	Sergei Makarov		Arto Rustanen		Peter Lindmark	
	Alexander Mogitny		Reijo Ruotsalainen		Lars Molin	
	Sergei Mylnikov		Simo Saarinen		Lars-Gunnar Pettersson	
	Anatoli Semjanov		Kari Suikkanen		Thomas Rundqvist	
	Sergei Starikov		Timo Susi		Tommy Samuelsson	
	Igor Stelnov		Jukka Tammi		Ulf Sandström	
	Alexander Svetlov		Jari Torkki		Hakan Södergren	
	Alexander Tchernych		Pekka Tuomisto		Peter Aslin	
			Jukka Virtanen		Jens Öhling	
1992	Sergei Bautin	EUN	David Archibald	CAN	Patrick Auguste	CZE
	Igor Boldin		Todd Brost		Petr Briza	
	Nikolai Bortchevski		Sean Burke		Milaslav Horava	
	Viacheslav Butsajev		Kevin Dahl		Petr Hrbek	
	Viacheslav Bykov		Curtis Giles		Otakar Janecky	
	Evgeni Davidov		David Hannan		Tomas Jelinck	

Year	Gold	Country	Silver	Country	Bronze	Country
	Alexei Jamnov		Gordon Hynes		Drahomir Kadlec	
	Dmitri Jusjkievitch		Fabian Joseph		Kamil Kastak	
	Darus Kasparaitis		Joe Juneau		Robert Lang	
	Yuri Khmylov		Trevor Kidd		Igor Liba	
	Andrei Khomutov		Patrick Lebeau		Ladislav Lubina	
	Andrei Kovalenko		Christopher Lindberg		Frantisek Prochazka	
	Alexei Kovalev		Eric Lindros		Petr Rosol	
	Igor Kravtchuk		Kent Manderville		Bedrich Scerban	
	Vladimir Malakov		Adrian Plasvic		Jiri Slegr	
	Dimitri Mironov		Daniel Ratushmy		Richard Smehlik	
	Sergei Petrenko		Bradley Schlegel		Robert Svetela	
	Vitali Prokorov		Wallace Schreiber		Oldrich Svoboda	
	Alexei Shitnik		Randolph Smith		Radek Toupal	
	Mikhail Shtalenkov		David Tippett		Peter Veselovsky	
	Andrei Trefilov		Brian Tutt		Richard Zemlicka	
	Sergei Zubov		Jason Woolley			
1994	Haken Algotsson	SWE	Corey Hirsch	CAN	Pasi Kuivalainen	FIN
	Mikael Sundloev		Manny Legace		Jukka Tammi	
	Tommy Salo		Allain Roy		Jarmo Myllys	
	Tomas Jonsson		Adrian Aucoin		Marko Kiprusov	
	Christian Due-Boje		Derek Mayer		Timo Jutila	
	Leif Rohlin		Werenka Brad		Pasi Sormunen	
	Magnus Svensson		Ken Lovsin		Janne Laukkanen	
	Fredrik Stillman		Mark Asley		Hannu Virta	
	Kenny Joensson		David Harlock		Mika Stroemberg	
	Roger Johansson		Chris Therien		Janne Ojanen	
	Patrik Juhlin		Bradley Schlegel		Es Keskinen	
	Roger Hansson		Todd Hlushko		Saku Koivu	
	Häkan Loob		Fabian Joseph		Marko Palo	
	Stefan Oernskog		Paul Kariya		Raimo Helminen	
	Niklas Eriksson		Dwayne Norris		Mika Alatalo	
	Daniel Rydmark		Greg Johnson		Ville Peltonen	
	Jonas Bergkvist		Brian Savage		Jere Lehtinen	
	Joergan Joensson		Wallace Schreiber		Sami Kapanen	
	Peter Forsberg		Todd Warriner		Tero Lehterae	
	Charles Berglund		Greg Parks		Petri Varis	
	Andreas Dackell		Jean Roy		Mika Nieminen	
	Mats Naeslund		Christopher Kontos		Mikko Maekelae	
	Patric Kjellberg		Peter Nedved			

LUGE

Stars to Watch
Germany are strong medal contenders

by Harro Esmarch

In Nagano, competition for gold, silver and bronze medals in the luge events will be tougher than ever before. In all three disciplines — men's and women's singles and men's doubles — there are a large number of established medal contenders. But, thrillingly, there are also a number of athletes who made their mark for the first time last season. This latter group could create a few upsets on the Nagano track.

Germany, Italy and Austria will all come to Japan with potential gold medallists in the women's event. Susi Erdmann of Germany is the reigning world champion (adding to the titles she won in 1989 and '91) and twice winner of both the world cup and the European championships. She is also no stranger to Olympic competition having won a silver in 1994 and a bronze in 1992. Her compatriots Jana Bode and Sylke Otto are also tipped for medals. Bode won the world and European titles in 1996 and the world cup in the 1995/'96 season. Otto was the world cup winner in the previous season.

However, it is Italy's Gerda Weissensteiner who is the reigning Olympic champion — a title she won with a combined time of 3:15.517 in Lillehammer. Weissensteiner won the world title a year before the Games and the European title in the same year.

Austria's Angelika Neuner was the Olympic silver medallist in 1992 but her team-mate, Andrea Tagwerker, the 1994 Olympic bronze medallist, has shown the most recent form, winning the world cup in the pre-Olympic season.

Germany has dominated recent Olympic Games in the men's singles. Jens Mueller won the title in 1988 with Georg Hackl second. Hackl then took over the mantle by winning the Olympic gold in both

1992 and '94. Twice European champion and twice world cup winner, Hackl is the reigning world champion — an event he also won in 1989 and '90.

Austria could provide the main threat to German dominance. Markus Prock was Olympic silver medallist in both Albertville (1992) and Lillehammer (1994). In 1987 and '96 he won the world championship title and has won the world cup eight times. Italy, meanwhile, have Armin Zoeggeler who was world champion in 1995 and an Olympic bronze medallist in 1994. The only North American candidate for medals must be American Wendel Suckow, a previous world champion who was fifth in Lillehammer.

Italy are the defending champions in the luge men's doubles events through Kurt Brugger and Wilfried Huber. Yet Austria are the reigning world champions through Tobias and Markus Scheigl. This pairing also won the 1996 world title. Americans Chris Thorpe and Gordy Sheer were world cup winners in the 1996/'97 season. And America also have the promising duo of Chris Niccum and Matt McClain who were world junior champions in 1995/'96 and '97. Germany, inevitably, are medal contenders. Stefan Krausse and Jan Behrendt won the Olympic title in 1992 and were bronze medallists in 1994 as well as winning the world title in 1989, '91, '93 and '95. Yves Mankel and Thomas Rudolph were Olympic silver medallists in 1992.

Background

The modern version of luge can trace its origins back to the pastime of tobogganing down hills. In the late nineteenth century, participants began to race down icy tracks and roads. The first international sledge sport competition took place in 1883 in Switzerland and, from then on, various types of sled were developed. The first European championships were in 1914 — for men only. Women took part from 1928 onwards.

The sport of skeleton — a precursor to Olympic lugeing in which the sled is ridden head first in a prone position — appeared on the Olympic programme in 1928 and '48. In 1935 a special luge section of the FIBT (International Bobsleigh and Tobogganing Federation) was formed. However, this did not reflect the growing popularity of the sport and, in 1957, the International Luge Federation (FIL) was created. In 1955 the first world championships took place in Norway. The decision to add luge to the Olympic programme was taken at an IOC meeting in Athens in 1961.

Luge made its Olympic debut in 1964 on the track at Igls, Innsbruck, and has remained on the programme ever since.

Competitors propel the luge forward at the start in a sitting position and then lie back once they have got up speed. Lifting their head would cause wind drag in this sport where speed is of the essence. There were concerns, originally, that luge should not be added to the Olympic programme because it was considered too dangerous. Indeed, just prior to the 1964 Games, a British luger was killed on a training run on the Olympic course. However, the sport has strenuous safety procedures and regulations.

Over the years there have been several changes in technology, many of them driven by the former East Germany. In 1972 they were the first to use a plastic seat, rather than the previous webbing. And, in 1976, they did away with the steering straps and guided the sled down the track simply by shifting their weight at the shoulder and feet, putting pressure on the curved front end of the runners with their calf muscles. — a technique still employed by top lugers today.

Artificially-banked curves were added to tracks in the mid-1970s. Previously, luge and bobsleigh competitions had taken place on tracks made purely of natural ice. Since that time, all Olympic tracks have followed suit. There are 13 tracks world-wide. Nagano's "spiral" has a unique feature. It has two climbing stretches. At the 1997 world cup final, in February in Nagano, the fastest man (course length 1,326m drop 114m) achieved around 130kmph.

Many of the all-time luge "greats" came from the former East Germany. There, the intensive development of luge athletes started at an earlier age and successful lugers were rewarded with secure employment — often in the army.

East Germany were involved in luge controversy, however, in 1968. Their three women finished in gold, silver and fourth positions but were later disqualified. Officials inspecting their sleds after the races decided they had heated the runners to give them an unfair advantage.

In 1972, the East Germans secretly developed radically-new designs for their sleds and won eight of the nine luge medals on offer. Innsbruck, in 1976, saw similar scenes — this time involving West Germany. They arrived with new sleds and egg-shaped aerodynamic helmets. Several nations protested the new designs unsuccessfully.

At the 1984 Sarajevo Games, George Tucker of Puerto Rico competed in the luge events. In preparation for the Games he had competed several times internationally but had never finished a single run. On the way to the airport to travel to the Games he crashed his girlfriend's car and, in pre-Games training, he crashed his sled once more and almost missed the opening ceremony because he was repairing it. Astoundingly, once competition began he managed to complete runs one and two without a spill.

Sarajevo's men's and women's singles winners were Paul Hildgartner of Italy and Steffi Martin of East Germany. They were both former track and field athletes.

At the 1968 Games in Grenoble, organizers had severe problems with the weather. Eventually, the men's and women's events were decided over three runs instead of four. One of the Italian women's team had a serious accident prior to the Games, breaking her pelvis and elbow after a crash.

Georg Hackl, of Germany, and Thomas Koehler of the former East Germany have both won two luge golds. Hackl also won a silver in 1988 and Koehler silvers in 1964 and '68. Steffi Walter-Martin is the most successful woman. The German won golds in 1984 and 1988.

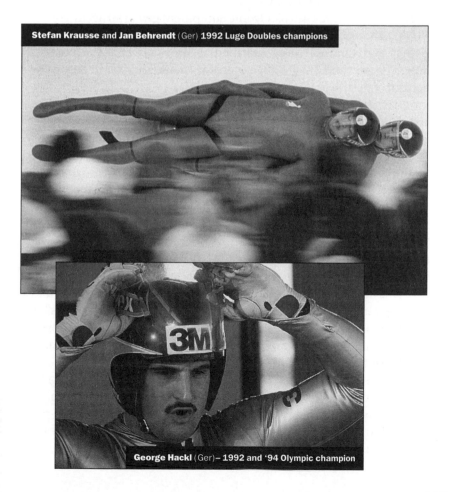

Stefan Krausse and **Jan Behrendt** (Ger) 1992 Luge Doubles champions

George Hackl (Ger)– 1992 and '94 Olympic champion

Equipment

A luge is a sled set on two runners which are rounded at the front ends and is not more than 550mm (1ft10in.) wide. A pod seat is set on a bridge between the two runners. This can be graduated for use in the doubles event. A luge must not weigh more than 23kg (50.7lbs) for the singles event and 27kg (59.5lbs) for doubles. Modern sleds generally have steel runners, steel or titanium bridges and carbon fibre shells.

Competitors wear aerodynamic clothing and specially-designed and reinforced shoes to protect their ankles and feet. The suits must be of textile fabrics and must not be plasticized or otherwise sealed. Competitors can wear some protective padding as long as it is not more than 10mm (0.4in.) thick. They can also wear specially-designed belts carrying weights (see below). At the start they use spiked gloves to propel themselves forward. A safety helmet is mandatory. This has a Perspex visor which fits down over the chin. Competitors must also wear a bib with their race number.

Races are timed with electronic equipment giving an accuracy within a thousandth of a second. This equipment is also capable of giving a start time and three intermediate times as well as the finish time. The start and finish light barriers are marked in colour across the bottom of the track.

Over the last three decades, luge has taken place on the same tracks as bobsleigh events. These are artificially refrigerated and have a series of curves and straights to test a luger's skill in finding the best trajectory. The tracks are frozen using either a new-style freezing agent, developed for the Nagano track, or ammonia which is fed through pipes set in the ice. Each track has a number of safety barriers which guide the sled back into the track in the event of it flying to the top wall at any time.

Rules and Regulations

In Olympic competition there are four runs in each of the men's and women's singles — rather than two runs as in world cup races — and two runs in the doubles event. In the singles events, competition takes place over two days with two runs on each day. Both doubles runs take place on the same day. The winner is the luger (or pair) who achieves the fastest aggregate time over the runs. Under FIL rules, five training runs must be offered before competition begins.

A competitor must start and finish in contact with the sled. Any luger who crashes may re-start and continue to the end of the run. However, with winning margins sometimes measured in mere hundredths of a second, any crash would preclude that athlete from winning a medal.

In the doubles event, the lugers effectively lie on top of each other with the heavier of the two at the front. A strap secures the front luger to the sled.

Start order for the singles events is drawn by lot within seeded groups. The top twelve lugers, according to world cup rankings, are put in the leading group and race off in descending order. They are followed by a group ranked from 12 to 24. On the third run lugers go down the course in descending order of their placing after the first two runs — i.e from first through to last place. For the final run the top 15 go first in ascending order from 15 to 1, followed by the remaining lugers in descending order.

Starting order for the doubles first run is the same as that for singles whilst the second run is based on the same format as the final run in singles.

At the start of each run the temperature of the runners is taken to ensure that they have not been heated. And, at the end of each run, the athlete and sled are weighed. Each athlete is also weighed prior to the competition. On a set scale, according to that pre-race body weight, athletes are allowed to wear additional weights: up to 10kg (22lbs) for women, 13kg (28.5lbs) for men and 10kg (22lbs) for a doubles pair. Their racing clothing must not weigh more than 4kg (9lbs). There are no limits on a competitor's own body weight.

A luge course must be at least 1000m (0.6 miles) long for men and 800m (0.5 miles) for women and doubles. There are different start houses for the two. At each start point there is a flat area of ice where the athletes prepare to race. This must be at least 20m (65ft 7in.) long. At the start, athletes propel themselves forward using handles and then "paddle" the ice with spiked gloves to gain momentum over a 5m (16ft 5in.) long section of the ice before the descent begins.

Only one sled is allowed in the track at any one time. The start is controlled by red and green lights and competitors in singles must start within 30 seconds (45 seconds for doubles) of the starter announcing that the "track is clear".

Any disputes over rules are handled by the race jury which is composed of three members. A technical delegate is also appointed by the FIL with supervisory and inspection duties.

Nagano Format

110 athletes will take part in the 1998 Olympic Winter Games luge competition: 82 men, including doubles, and 28 women. A maximum of three men, three women and two doubles teams are permitted (10 athletes maximum) per nation.

Each athlete will have qualified for Nagano by participating in at least one FIL sanctioned competition — European championships or world cup — during the Olympic season and have finished within 7% of the time recorded by the first-placed athlete on the official training runs for that event. In exceptional circumstances, six athletes may have qualified without reaching these standards if their continent would not otherwise be represented. All entries must be ratified by the relevant National Olympic Committee who may also have imposed stricter standards of their own.

Venue

Luge at the 1998 Olympic Winter Games will take place on Nagano's famous "Spiral" track. This is based in the foothills of Mount Iizuna in the Asakawa district, north-east of the city. It is unique because it has two uphill stretches. The first, coming out of corner seven, rises 1.9m (6ft 2in.) over 50m (164ft) and the second, more dramatically coming out of corner 11, rises 12m (39ft 4in.) over a distance of 123m (403ft 6in.). This makes the course more demanding as lugers cannot depend on acceleration in the lower stretches to make up for any errors in the top section. The track is over 1326m (0.8 miles) long (for the men) with a drop of 114m (374ft) and has been constructed on the north-eastern facing slopes of the mountain.

Nagano spiral track

A Sporting Legend
Steffi Walter-Martin (GDR)

Steffi Walter-Martin led the luge all time greats list for two decades after winning Olympic gold both in Sarajevo (1984) and Calgary (1988). She was also twice world champion, winning in 1983 in Lake Placid and 1985 in Oberhof, Germany. Walter-Martin was born in Lauter in Saxony and competed for the sports club "Traktor Oberwiesenthal" from 1976 to'88. Married to a teacher, Gernot Walter, she lives in Grossdubrau in Saxony and is now a mother of three. Ironically, neither Sebastian, aged 12, nor Sabrina, aged eight, are interested in the luge and it is too early to decipher whether Simon, aged two, will follow in their mother's footsteps.

A Comtemporary Hero
Georg Hackl (GER)

Georg Hackl, born in 1966, comes from Bischofswiesen near Berchtesgarden in Bavaria. The most successful German Luger, Hackl started with the Berchtesgarden Luge Club in 1977. His gold medals from Albertville in 1992 and Lillehammer in 1994 and a silver from Calgary in 1988, have already put him at the top of the all time greats.

Hackl was world champion at Winterburg, West Germany, in 1989, Calgary in 1990 and Igls, Austria in 1997. Twice European champion, Hackl won the 1989/'90 world cup and has no fewer than ten national titles to his name.

He still lives with his partner, Margrit, in the place where has was born, Bischofswiesen, in a house he built himself. A qualified metal worker, he is also a DIY enthusiast and has even made his own sled. As a soldier, he served as a sergeant-major in the sport development group of 232 battalion in Bischofswiesen-Strub

Sporting Legends
Hans Rinn and Norbert Hahn (GDR)

The luge doubles team of Hans Rinn and Norbert Hahn won Olympic gold for East Germany in 1976 in Insbruck and 1980 in Lake Placid. The pair, who in 1998 will have already spent 18 years at the top of the all-time rankings, were also world champions in 1977 and four times European champions.

Rinn was born in 1953 in Langewiesen and was an office machine and data processing technician by trade. From 1967 to 1983, he competed for the 'ASK Vorwarts Oberhof' club. Today he lives with his wife Carmen, a doctor's assistant, and their son Toni (14) and daughter Hanni (10) in Ilmenau, near Thuringen. Since 1990, Hans Rinn and two colleagues, have manufactured plastic moulds for indoor and outdoor swimming pools in neighbouring Wimbach. He has also developed a "bob-on-wheels" for summer use.

Rinn was also a successful individual luger. He was world champion in 1973 in Oberhof and in 1977 in Igls as well as winning the European championships title three times.

Hahn, meanwhile, was Rinn's "backman". He was born in 1964 in Elbingerodem but grew up in Wermigode. A qualified sports teacher, he also competed for the DDR Club 'ASK Vorwarts Oberhof'

It was during his time as a student that he met his wife Doris, a former long distance runner. He now lives with her in Oberhof. Both his son Mike (23) and daughter Nicole (16) were enthusiastic lugers until a few years ago. Today Hahn is employed by the Bob- und Schlittensportverband (DBSV) (German Bob and Luge Association) and looks after the national team as well as coaching technique.

Gerda Weissensteiner Italy's reigning Olympic women's champion

Luge

NAGANO SCHEDULE

Venue: Spiral

Date	Description	Start	Finish
8 Feb	Single (m)	14:00	16:30
9 Feb	Single (m)	14:00	16:30
10 Feb	Single (w)	14:00	16:00
11 Feb	Single (w)	14:00	16:00
13 Feb	Double (m)	14:00	16:00

MEDALLISTS *(by nation)*

Including skeleton 1928 & 1948

Country	Gold		Silver		Bronze		Overall
	m	w	m	w	m	w	total
GDR	10	5	4	6	5	3	33
ITA	3+1*	2	3	-	3	-	12
AUT	2	1	4	1	3	2	13
GER	3	-	1	1	1	1	7
FRG	1	-	3	1	4	2	11
URS	-	1	2	-	2	1	6
USA	1*	-	2*	-	-	-	3*
GBR	-	-	-	-	2*	-	2

* Skeleton

Luge [Men]

Year	Gold	Country	Time	Silver	Country	Time	Bronze	Country	Time
Single									
1964	Thomas Koehler	GER	3:26.77	Klaus Bonsack	GER	3:27.04	Hans Plenk	GER	3:30.15
1968	Manfred Schmid	AUT	2:52.48	Thomas Koehler	GDR	2:52..66	Klaus Bonsack	GDR	2:53.33
1972	Wolfgang Scheidel	GDR	3:27.58	Harald Ehrig	GDR	3:28.39	Wolfram Fiedler	GDR	3:28.73
1976	Detlef Gunther	GDR	3:27.688	Josef Fendt	FRG	3:26.196	Hans Rinn	GDR	3:28.574
1980	Bernhard Glass	GDR	2:54.796	Paul Hildgartner	ITA	2:55.372	Anton Winkler	FRG	2:56.545
1984	Paul Hildgartner	ITA	3:04.258	Sergei Danilin	URS	3:04.962	Valeri Doudin	URS	3:05.012
1988	Jens Mueller	GDR	3:05.548	Georg Hackl	FRG	3:05 916	Yuri Khartchenko	URS	3:06.274
1992	Georg Hackl	GER	3:02.363	Markus Prock	AUT	3:02.669	Markus Schmidt	AUT	3:02.942
1994	Georg Hackl	GER	3:21.571	Markus Prock	AUT	3:21.584	Armin Zoeggler	ITA	3:21.833
Double									
1964	Josef Feistmantl Manfred Stengl	AUT	1:41.62	Reinhold Senn Helmut Thaler	AUT	1:41.91	Walter Aussendorfer Sigisfredo Mair	ITA	1:42.87
1968	Klaus Bonsack Thomas Koehler	GDR	1:35.85	Manfred Schmid Ewald Walch	AUT	1:36.34	Wolfgang Winkler Fritz Nachmann	FRG	1:37.29
1972	Paul Hildgartner Walter Plaikner	ITA	1:28.35	Horst Hornlein Reinhard Bredow	GER	1:28.35	Wolfram Fiedler Klaus-Michael Bonsack	GDR	1:29.16
1976	Hans Rinn Norbert Hahn	GDR	1:25.604	Hans Brandner Balthasar Schwarm	GER	1:25.889	Rudolf Schmid Franz Schachner	AUT	1:25.919
1980	Hans Rinn Norbert Hahn	GDR	1:19.331	Peter Gschnitzer Karl Brunner	ITA	1:19.606	Georg Fluckinger Karl Schrott	AUT	1:19.795
1984	Hans Stangassinger Franz Wembacher	FRG	1:23.620	Evgeni Belooussov Alexander Belyakov	URS	1:23.660	Jörg Hoffmann Jochen Pietzsch	GDR	1:23.887
1988	Joerg Hoffmann Jochen Pietzsch	GDR	1:31.940	Stefan Krausse Jan Behrendt	GDR	1:32.039	Thomas Schwab Wolfgang Staudinger	FRG	1:32.274
1992	Stefan Krausse Jan Behrendt	GER	1:32.053	Yves Mankel Thomas Rudolph	GER	1:32.239	Hansjorg Raffl Norbert Hubert	ITA	1:32.298
1994	Kurt Brugger Wilfried Huber	ITA	1:36.720	Hansjoerg Raffl Norbert Huber	ITA	1:36.769	Stefan Krausse Jan Behrendt	GER	1:36.945

Luge [Women]

Year	Gold	Country	Time	Silver	Country	Time	Bronze	Country	Time
Single									
1964	Ortrun Enderlein	GER	3:24.67	Ilse Geisler	GER	3:27.42	Helene Thurner	AUT	3:29.06
1968	Erica Lechner	ITA	2:28.66	Christ Schmuck	GER	2:29.37	Angelika Duenhaupt	FRG	2:29.56
1972	Anna-Maria Muller	GDR	2:59.18	Ute Rührold	GER	2:59.49	Margit Schumann	GDR	2:59.54
1976	Margit Schumann	GDR	2:50.621	Ute Rührold	GER	2:50..846	Elisabeth Demleitner	FRG	2:51.056
1980	Vera Zozulia	URS	2:36.537	Melitta Sollmann	GDR	2:37.657	Ingrida Amantova	URS	2:37.817
1984	Steffi Martin	GDR	2:46.57	Bettina Schmidt	GDR	2:46.873	U Weiss	GDR	2:47.248
1988	Steffi Walter-Martin	GDR	3:03.973	Ute Oberhoffner	GDR	3:04.105	Cerstin Schmidt	GDR	3:04.181
1992	Doris Neuner	AUT	3:06.696	Angelika Neuner	AUT	3:06 769	Susi Erdmann	GER	3:07.115
1994	Gerda Weissensteiner	ITA	3:15.517	Susi Erdmann	GER	3:16.276	Andrea Tagwerker	AUT	3:16.652

FIGURE SKATING

Stars to Watch
Teenage Titans

by Debbie Becker

The most-watched event of the 1998 Olympic Winter Games is likely to result in two American teenagers skating for the gold medal in women's figure skating. Michelle Kwan and Tara Lipinski are clearly the best in the world. Kwan is a 1996 world champion, Lipinski won the title in 1997. But what of the others? Who could unseat them?

In a sport where one fall can end a lifetime of dreams, the world rankings include several women ready to step to the top of the podium should Kwan or Lipinski falter. That group includes another American skater, Nicole Bobek, the 1995 US champion and world bronze medallist. A back injury last season left her unable to climb a flight of stairs but, by the 1997 world championships, Bobek was regaining her championship form. Then, a day before the women's competition began, her coach Carlo Fassi died from a heart attack.

Bobek was distraught. Her grief left her unable to show the form she had worked so hard to regain. She finished 13th overall. "I know I have to prove to a lot of people that I'm not out of the sport", said Bobek. "There have been a lot of questions: 'Where is Nicole?' Skating is my way of saying, 'Hey, don't forget about me, I'm still here'." Bobek is training with Fassi's widow, Christa, in Lake Arrowhead, California.

France's Vanessa Gusmeroli was third at the 1997 worlds, followed by Russia's Irina Slutskaya and Maria Butyrskaya. France's Laetitia Hubert was sixth. Gusmeroli, who competed in both figure skating and water skiing as a child, picked figure skating when the federations asked her to choose between the two sports when she was 13. Slutskaya, the 1996 world bronze medallist, underwent 45 minutes of physiotherapy before she competed at the event. Four hours before the long programme, she had crashed into the boards back-first.

Besides the drama of the Kwan-Lipinski duel, there will be great interest in the performance of China's Chen Lu. Chen, the 1995 world champion, withdrew from the 1997 world championships because of continuing problems with a stress fracture in her right foot. She could barely land a triple jump and appeared so unlike the champion she once was. Chen has also had problems with her coach, Li Mingzhu, and with the Chinese federation that insisted the two work together.

France's Surya Bonaly has allegedly also had difficulties with her federation who left her at home during the 1997 world championships because federation officials said other skaters were healthier and better prepared to compete. For Bonaly, an erratic yet athletic skater, that omission meant a missed, valued showing before the judges the year before the Olympic Games. Bonaly, a three-times world silver medallist is among the best jumpers in the world.

The number of entries in each category (ladies', men's, pairs and dance) will be decided by the overall performance of the entire team at the previous world championships under new International Skating Union (ISU) rules. Previously, the number of entries was determined by the finishing position of just the best skater. This change means that two dominant countries in the sport will each only send two men to the Nagano Games—Russia and the USA—making selection difficult.

In the men's event, Russia's Alexei Urmanov, Ilia Kulik and Alexei Yagudin are all capable of dislodging Todd Eldredge of the USA and Canada's Elvis Stojko from the top of the world standings. Ukraine's Viacheslav Zagorodniuk was fourth at last year's worlds. Eldredge won the 1996 world title, Stojko beat him last year with Yagudin placing third.

Urmanov, the 1994 Olympic champion, withdrew from the 1997 world championships with a groin injury. Under the new ISU rules, that cost Russia its third spot in the Nagano Olympic Games. Russian coach Alexei Mishin gave Urmanov three injections for the pain in the five hours before he was to skate but he still could not land a jump. Since his 1994 gold medal, Urmanov—who always competes in his trademark gloves—has yet to reach the top of the podium again. He says it is very difficult to stay no. 1: "The men's competition changes every week. You can't make a mistake, not on the jumps, not in the steps. If you miss one jump, you lose".

Kulik, second in the 1996 worlds and fifth last year, trains in Marlboro, Massachusetts. The lanky teenager is among the sport's most gifted jumpers. To win, though, he must skate two programmes in the Games without error. China's Guo Zengxin made history at the

Tara Lipinski (USA)

Elvis Stojko (CAN)

Michelle Kwan (USA)

Ilia Kulik (RUS)

1997 worlds by landing two "quads" (a jump with four rotations) in one programme. Latvia's Konsantin Kostin also landed a quad. A notable absence, though, was Philippe Candeloro of France who is struggling with a foot injury. If he is healthy, Candeloro—the 1995 world bronze medallist—will be a factor.

Michael Weiss, of the USA, was seventh at 1997 worlds. A month earlier at the US championships, Weiss landed what many believed to be a successful quad. That was something no American skater had ever accomplished in competition. However, a replay showed his second foot touched on the landing, invalidating the jump.

Weiss, who played football and ice hockey growing up, bench presses 300lbs (136kg) and believes the weight training helps his ability to jump: "A lot of people don't realize how physically demanding figure skating is. A long programme (4.5 minutes) is the most difficult thing I've ever done in sports".

The Olympic Games could well turn into a quad jumping contest. Stojko has initiated the challenge. Last season, he became the first skater to complete the quad-triple jump combination in competition. Eldredge spent the off-season working on his quad. However, he hopes that artistry does not become lost in the race to match jump-for-jump: "I don't think one jump makes a programme. Each jump only takes a second. A long programme takes 4.5 minutes. That's a lot of time to fill up. You have to look at the spins, the speed, a lot of things".

The likely outcome of the pairs competition is more open. If the 1997 world championships are an accurate predictor, the top teams include: gold medallists Mandy Wotzel and Ingo Steuer, from Germany, Marina Eltsova and Andrei Bushkov, of Russia, and Oksana Kazakova and Artur Dmitriev, also of Russia. Dmitriev won Olympic gold and silver medals with former partner Natalia Mishkutenok.

American pairs captured the next two spots with US champions Kyoko Ina and Jason Dungjen in fourth, and Jenni Meno and Todd Sand in fifth. Meno and Sand are twice former world bronze medallists but struggled in both the 1997 US and world championships.

In the steady world of dance, where changes come incrementally over the years, the Russian teams of Oksana Grichtchuk and Evgeni Platov and Anzhelika Krylova and Oleg Ovsiannikov will vie for the gold medal. Grichtchuk and Platov have won virtually every major competition in the last four years, including the 1994 Olympic gold medal. The original dance portion in the Nagano Games will be skated to a jive rhythm, and vocals will be permitted for the first time.

Krylova, world silver medallist in 1997, holds out hope of unseating Grichtchuk and Platov. "We want this, really want this. We are trying everything for this".

Background

Mankind first developed skates as a means of transport across frozen lakes and waterways. Early skates were made of polished bone, wood and, then, metal. The arrival of iron-bladed skates is recorded in Holland as early as 1250. The Dutch were the pioneers, too, of competitive racing on skates. Yet figure skating owes some of its development and popularization to the British.

The first international figure skating competition was held in the 1880s and in 1892 the ISU (International Skating Union which was then called the Union Internationale de Patinage) was formed, making this body the oldest international winter sports federation.

Figure skating is also remarkable in that it made its Olympic debut as a "summer" sport, appearing on the programme of the Olympic Games of London in 1908 and Antwerp in 1920. The sport then became part of the first Olympic Winter Games in 1924 in Chamonix and has remained on the programme ever since where it is the only sport to have mixed competitions. Ice dance was added in 1976.

Over the years there were many critics of skaters using their Olympic medals merely as a springboard to a professional career. However, the rules were altered prior to the 1994 Olympic Winter Games to allow a one-time re-entry into the Games, under certain conditions, of skaters who had previously turned professional.

It has also been easy for the role of judges to be criticized, particularly when the analysis can appear subjective. Over twenty years ago, the minutes of an IOC Programme Commission meeting recommended that the ISU "should develop a method permitting its figure skating judging to be improved".

Many changes have since taken place to the sport. These included a re-weighting of the value given to the compulsory figures (before they were abolished) so that skaters could not win gold based mainly on their "figures" marks rather than the free programme.

Figure skating has produced many of the superstars of the Olympic Winter Games. None more so than Norwegian Sonja Henie. In 1924, aged just 11, she made her Olympic debut finishing in eighth place. Four years later, at 15, she returned to win her first of three consecutive golds at the Games of St Moritz, Lake Placid and Garmisch-Partenkirchen.

Henie was inspired by the Russian ballerinas Tamara Karsavina and Anna Pavlova—the former even came to Henie's home to work with her in training. Henie's methods and style sparked a revolution in skating. Her three Olympic golds and ten world championship titles meant that she transcended her own sport. A successful post-competitive cinema career at home and in the USA meant that she was the first female sports star to become a multi-millionaire. Sonja Henie died of leukemia aged 57.

Only Ulrich Salchow, the 1908 Olympic champion, has won as many world titles (10) as Henie. He also gave his name to one of the most popular jumps. Gillis Grafström of Sweden and Irina Rodnina, a Russian pairs skater, are the only other skaters to have won three golds.

In 1984 in Sarajevo, Britain's Jayne Torvill and Christopher Dean scored a maximum of nine sixes for artistic impression with a further three sixes for technical merit for their ice dance interpretation of Ravel's "Bolero"—a performance which was a dramatic departure from previous ice dance style. This level of scoring has not been bettered at any other Games.

Torvill and Dean's innovations were copied by many other couples in the intervening years but the ISU's Technical Dance Committee decided after 1992 to bring the sport back to its origins with strict new rules. These had their lighter moments as they forbade, amongst other things, "the men to wear tights" and "the lady not wearing a skirt"!

American brothers David and Hayes Allen Jenkins were both successful figure skaters. They each won Olympic gold, Hayes Allen in 1956 and David in 1960. David also won Olympic bronze in 1956. The 1956 women's figure skating winner, Tenley Albright, also of the USA, badly slashed her foot with a skate blade just weeks before the Games and had to undergo surgery to allow her to compete. After the Games, Albright went on to become a surgeon herself.

Another American, Richard (Dick) Button who won the men's individual title in both 1948 and 1952 was famous for introducing new moves at the Games. For his 1948 title it was a double axel and in 1952 it was a triple loop—the first man to complete a triple jump of any type in Olympic competition.

The most extraordinary skating soap-opera style scenes, however, took place in 1994 and involved two American medal contenders, Nancy Kerrigan and Tonya Harding. At a pre-selection event in the USA, Kerrigan received knee injuries after being attacked by a man wielding an iron bar. Rumours abounded that the perpetrator was linked with the Harding camp. Nothing was proven in advance and

Oksana Grichtchuk and Evgeni Platov (URS)

Irina Rodnina and Alexander Zaitsev (URS)

Sonja Henie (NOR)

the rivals travelled to Lillehammer to compete followed by a huge swarm of journalists—some of whom were there to report on the media circus.

Harding, cast as the villain, produced a poor technical progamme and was left skating for pride—and in tears—to finish in eighth place after the free programme. Squeaky clean Kerrigan kept the script dripping with drama by skating a flawless technical programme to lead going into the free programme. Only world champion Oksana Baiul skating next to last could put an end to the dream by five judges' votes to four over Kerrigan, who won silver.

Once back in the USA, Kerrigan is reputed to have made a fortune in endorsements and contracts whilst Harding was doing community service—the case against her camp having eventually been proven.

Ekaterina Gordeeva and Sergei Grinkov of Russia, the charismatic and volatile pairs skaters, who had done so much to set competition alight in Calgary in 1988 returned to Olympic skating in 1994 to win back their title. The husband and wife team, who seemed so blessed with talent, however, were about to be struck with tragedy. Two years later, Grinkov, still in his twenties, suffered a massive heart-attack whilst training and died.

Irina Rodnina, of the Soviet Union, was the winner of three Olympic pairs golds—two with eventual husband Alexander Zaitsev and the first with Alexei Ulanov. Ulanov caused a sensation prior to their victory in 1972 by starting a romantic affair—after an on-off romance with Rodnina—with the second-ranked Soviet couple's Ludmila Smirnova. Tensions were unusually high during competition which ended with Rodnina in tears. The Soviet pairing with their exciting, new holds and jumps succeeded their elegant compatriots Ludmila Belusova and Oleg Protopopov (winners in both 1964 and '68) as Olympic champions.

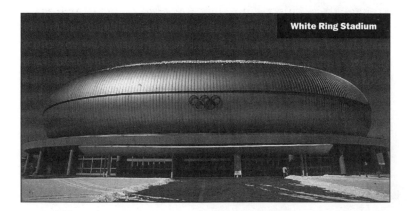

White Ring Stadium

Equipment

Figure skating blades are made of high carbon steel which is hardened and tempered for strength and reliability. The blades are 3.175mm (1/8in.) wide and are concave so that movements can be executed on different edges. This, combined with the curvature of blade unlike those used for ice hockey, allows the skater to turn and spin with greater ease. The front of the blade also has a toe pick with a serrated edge which is used in jumps and spins.

Skaters protect their blades with plastic or rubber guards when they are off the ice as it is important to keep the edges sharp. Skating boots are made of leather and come up over the ankle. They have reinforced arches and heel supports and are carefully and individually fitted.

The skating rink for figure skating is 30m x 60m (98ft x 197ft) and the ice has no markings.

Rules and Regulations

There are four figure skating events: men's and ladies' singles; pairs and ice dance. Skaters in the first three events perform both a short programme and a free programme. There is no longer a "compulsory figures" section. This was dropped prior to the 1992 Olympic Winter Games.

The short programme consists of eight required elements including jumps, jump combinations, spins, spin combinations, step sequences and, in the case of the pairs, two different lifts. A skater's short programme must not exceed two minutes and 40 seconds but can be shorter if all the elements have been executed.

33.3% of the total marks are awarded to the short programme. Two marks are awarded to a skater by each of the nine judges. The first is for required elements and the second is for presentation. In the case of a tie between skaters, the first mark prevails. In marking the required elements, the judges must take into account areas such as the difficulty of each step sequence, the length, height and technique of the jumps, smoothness of lifts, unison, and the strength, duration and control of spins as well as conformity with the character and rhythm of the music. Marks are deducted for errors in executing the required elements from the first mark only.

The free programme counts for 66.7% of the overall marks with a duration of four minutes for the ladies and four and a half minutes for men and pairs. Skaters must finish within plus or minus ten seconds of the required time. Judges look for a well-balanced overall free programme for which skaters are awarded two marks.

The first, for technical merit, takes into account the difficulty of the performance—its variety, cleanness, sureness and speed. The second, for presentation, examines a performance for its harmonious composition and conformity to music. It also considers speed variation, use of the ice surface, easy movement, carriage and style as well as expression and unison. The latter is a particularly important element in the marking of pairs skating.

In the case of a tie between skaters after the free programme, the second mark prevails.

Ice dancing has many steps which are akin to ballroom dancing. The ice dance competition consists of two compulsory dances, the original dance and the free dance. Skaters are warned in advance of the two compulsory dances. Each dance counts for 10% of the skaters' total score and two sets of marks are awarded for technique and timing and expression. Deductions are made for falls or interruptions. The second part of the competition is the original dance to a prescribed rhythm and tempo. This will count for 30% of the marks, judged according to composition and presentation, and lasts for no more than two minutes, plus or minus ten seconds.

Skaters are warned in advance of the dances chosen for the compulsory and original dances. In Nagano these will be selected from four possibilities: golden waltz, quickstep, silver samba or Argentine tango.

Skaters' free dance programmes last for four minutes, plus or minus ten seconds, counting for 50% of the overall score. Marks are given for technical merit and presentation with the latter prevailing in the event of a tie. Amongst other elements the judges must evaluate difficulty and variety of steps, turns and movements, correct timing, harmonious choreography, style and unison. Deductions are made for violation of the rules under both categories of mark.

In each competition—men's and ladies' singles, pairs and ice dance—the judges can award up to six for each mark. Six represents perfection whilst zero is given if a skater does not skate at all. These marks are only of value in relation to the marks awarded by a judge to other skaters. It is the ranking of skaters which is important. Therefore, the skater with the highest marks from a particular judge receives a first place from that judge for that particular section.

To determine the result in each part of the competition, the competitor placed first by the absolute majority of the judges is first and all other skaters are ranked below according to their majorities for the subsequent places. Then each skater's placement is multiplied by a pre-determined factor for each section and the final result is calculated by adding the factored placements for each section of the event, making the skater with the lowest factored placement first, the second lowest, second, and so on.

There are six different types of jump in figure skating. The axel is the easiest to recognize as it is the only jump where the skater takes off going forwards. It is, therefore, the most difficult to complete as it has an extra half-rotation in the air. The number of rotations completed for each type of jump make it a double, triple or quadruple version. "Combinations" occur where one jump is immediately followed by another, the second jump taking off from the leg on which the first was landed.

In the Lutz, skaters rotate counter clockwise taking off backwards using the toe pick to vault from one leg extended behind them. A similar take off is used for the flip except that skaters enter the jump on the inside rather than outside edge of their skates.

To execute a "loop" jump, skaters enter the jump backwards with slightly bent legs and use the left toe pick to take off from the right leg before rotating and landing. The main characteristic, meanwhile, of the Salchow jump is that skaters swing from backwards to forwards and then pause before jumping, rotating and landing on the opposite foot.

Nagano Format

30 skaters take part in each of the men's and ladies' singles, 20 couples in the pairs event and 24 ice dance pairs. Only skaters who were aged 15 or over on July 1, 1997, can compete except for those under that age who had previously competed in a world championship. Unlike previous Games, the number of competitors that each nation can enter per event was determined by the finishing position of their entire team at the 1997 world championships—rather than the finishing position of their top-ranked individual. This has left some of the top nations with two rather than the expected three competitors in some events. Each nation has filled its quota of skaters from its own selection trials and procedures and from a final special trial in Vienna in autumn 1997.

Venue

Figure skating will take place in the "White Ring", Mashima, which is in the south-east sector of Nagano City. Its round and gently sloping roof means that the building has been likened to a water droplet. The venue will also play host to short-track speed skating during the 1998 Olympic Winter Games.

A Contemporary Heroine

Michelle Kwan (USA)

Winner of the 1996 world championships, aged 15, Michelle Kwan experienced growing pains, quite literally, in the final months of the 1997 season. Before the 1997 US championships she had a remarkable record, having won ten of her last 11 competitions. However, she lost her US title when she fell twice and Tara Lipinski skated perfectly. She lost again to Lipinski in the Champions Series final and once more at the world championships. Kwan was fourth in the short programme at those worlds but won the long programme, worth 66%, almost beating Lipinski for the overall title. France's Vanessa Gusmeroli won the bronze.

At the time Kwan was going through puberty, a stage of life that can ruin the careers of young women in gymnastics and figure skating. As Kwan, 5ft 4in. (162.5cm), 102lbs (46.3 kg), explained: "Even if your body is a little bit different, it throws you off. Even if you gain one pound, it makes you jump lopsided. In practice sometimes when something is off I'll ask myself, 'What's wrong with me? Am I thinking too much'?"

It was just as the world championships were concluding that Kwan found the mindset that makes her perhaps the best skater in the world. "It's been a difficult year for me," she said, "but I thought of Scott Hamilton (a top skater diagnosed with cancer) and that really put things in perspective. We're just competing. This is nothing. I said, 'OK let's have fun.' I stepped on the ice and let myself fly."

Kwan's life is far different from that of a typical teenager. She spends four hours a day on the ice and is tutored instead of attending school. Her world title in 1996 earned Kwan an estimated $1 million annual income. An Olympic gold medal, though, is the jackpot, worth $10 million. Last year, Kwan bought a burnt gold Jeep Grand Cherokee after passing her driver's test on the second try (she missed a three-point turn in the first time round). She listens to Tracy Chapman and Natalie Merchant and loves to shop.

But what she would love more than anything else is a gold medal. The biggest question at the Nagano Olympic figure skating venue will be if Kwan's experience and maturity is enough to hold off Tara Lipinski's incredible jumping ability.

A Contemporary Heroine

Tara Lipinski (USA)

Tara Lipinski became world figure skating champion in 1997. At 4ft 8.5in. (143.5cm) and 75 lbs (34kg), she was smaller even than the flower girls who scooped up the stuffed animals and bouquets tossed on the ice after her victory. And, only 14, she became the sport's youngest ever world champion, younger by one month than legendary 1927 winner Sonja Henie, of Norway. "I never expected it," said Lipinski who is coached by Frank Carroll and who was 15th the year before. "It was a big shock, but I love it".

Expecting a difficult challenge from Michelle Kwan for the gold medal, Lipinski had spent the winter working on jumps no other woman can currently perform. No woman has ever performed the quad, and the triple axel has only been landed by Tonya Harding and Midori Ito.

After her US title, Lipinski met with David Letterman, one of America's top chat show hosts, and did the round of network morning shows. She got a raincheck from Oprah Winfrey, another top show host, after getting anxious to return to practice.

Lipinski has had plenty of podium training. When she was two years old watching the Summer Olympic Games, she turned a Tupperware bowl upside down, stood on it and pretended she was the champion. Lipinski only lost her last baby molar tooth at the 1997 US national championships. She gets her driver's permit in 1998. "I think she'll just be happy if she can reach the pedals," says her agent Mike Burg.

Lipinski and her mother, Pat, moved to Bloomfield Hills, Michigan, three years ago. She started skating at Houston's Galleria Mall at 4.30 am each day. In the winter, she had to dodge a Christmas tree erected at centre ice each holiday. Lipinski wears a gold necklace with three pendants. One is a St Theresa medal, another is a skate and the third says: "Short but Good". In her bedroom in Bloomfield Hills Lipinski has something she calls her "dream jar". Asked what it contains, Lipinski says: "I can't tell you, because then it won't happen".

A Contemporary Hero

Todd Eldredge (USA)

When Todd Eldredge was a young boy growing up in Chatham, Massachusetts, he would rise early, stand by his parents' bed in his pyjamas, clutch his tiny black skates and ask when they could go to the skating rink. Eldredge's early devotion to the sport has paid off. He is a four-times US champion and in 1996 became world champion before losing his title to Canada's Elvis Stojko a year later.

In one of the sport's most touching moments, after being awarded his world championship gold medal, Eldredge skated across the ice and placed the medal over his mother's head. His parents had made the ultimate sacrifice, agreeing to send their son away early in his life to pursue his Olympic dream. They mortgaged their home three times to pay Eldredge's skating expenses. The sea-sick son of a fisherman, Eldredge knew his life would be on the ice. With his world championship title in '96, Eldredge thanked his parents in another way—he paid off their mortgage.

A steady, consistent performer who worked on his quad all winter, Eldredge is high on the short list of those favoured to win gold in Nagano. He has the total package: the jumps; the spins; the artistry; everything required of an Olympic champion. It is all a far cry from Eldredge's first skating outing when he hung onto the railing and would not let go.

Eldredge had an uncharacteristic fall in the long programme at the 1997 world championships that cost him the title. These Olympic Games are likely to be his last. "The Olympics is what it's all about", says Eldredge. "This is what I've dreamed of".

Eldredge learned a great lesson when he placed second to Rudy Galindo in the US championships in 1996. He had spent too much time on performances and not enough on practice. It is a mistake he is unlikely to repeat as he prepares for the Nagano Games. He wants the ultimate reward.

A Contemporary Hero

Elvis Stojko (CAN)

Growing up a diminutive figure skater named Elvis, in a country where ice hockey is revered, is a tough way to survive childhood. Canada's Elvis Stojko remembers the taunts about competing in a "girl's sport" as well as those about being perhaps the only person in his country named after Elvis Presley.

When their son was born on March 22, 1972, in Newmarket, Ontario, Stojko's Hungarian-Slovenian parents knew immediately that he was special. "That's why we named him Elvis", they said.

A three-times world champion and Olympic silver medallist, Stojko thrilled the crowds at the 1997 world championships in Lausanne, Switzerland, with his amazing jumping ability. He has perfected the quad and brought the sport to an entirely different level of difficulty. Still, he has his critics, who say his jumping ability comes at the expense of artistry.

Stojko, the first person in history to land a quadruple toe-triple toe (loop) in combination in competition, says he is sticking to what works for him: "I have a harder, more powerful style but I still have finesse. I don't know what else they want to be honest. The quality of the edges is there, the quality of motion is there, all the lines are there, the footwork is there, the jumps are there. I know what I can do. I won't allow anyone to tell me what to do because then you aren't an artist. Whoever puts it together, makes it".

"The gold medal pushes you to the limits. Risk is everything. I never want to back off. If you never fall down, you don't know how fast you can get back up and handle it".

A national treasure in Canada, Stojko, 5ft 7in. (170cm) and a martial arts expert, believes this is the year he will return home with an Olympic gold medal. He is planning on being around until he does. It might not be that long a wait.

A Sporting Legend

Sonja Henie (NOR)

Sonja Henie was a star in every conceivable sense. She remains the only female skater ever to win gold medals in three consecutive Olympic Games (1928, 1932, and 1936).

Born in Oslo, Norway, in 1912, Henie competed in her first Games as an 11 year-old in 1924 in Chamonix. She won the first of ten world championships titles at 14 and the following year won her first Olympic gold.

Under the direction of her father Wilhelm, Henie captured the unique combination of grace and strength to give her a look that was revolutionary. She delighted in bucking fashion trends and began wearing short dresses in competition. Henie drew criticism, though, for saluting Hitler in the 1936 Olympic Games in Germany.

After the 1936 Games in Germany, Henie began another high profile career in movies and ice shows that earned her millions. Henie, who became an American citizen in 1941, died of leukemia in 1969 at 57. Her image remains synonymous with the glamour and intrigue that is figure skating.

A Sporting Legend

Carol Heiss Jenkins (USA)

Heiss Jenkins is a four-times US champion (1957–'60), five-times world champion (1956–'60), an Olympic silver medallist (1956) and Olympic gold medallist (1960).

After winning the silver medal, aged 16, in the Cortina Games, Heiss Jenkins promised her mother, who was dying of cancer, that she would one day win the gold. She did it four years later in Squaw Valley, winning the first-place votes of all nine judges. "It was then I knew that dreams do come true", said Heiss Jenkins.

In 1961, the year after Heiss Jenkins retired, the entire US delegation was killed in a plane crash on the way to the world championships in Prague.

Heiss Jenkins grew up the daughter of German immigrants living in Queens, New York. She commuted by subway to practise at Madison Square Garden. After her amateur career, Heiss Jenkins married Olympic gold medallist Hayes Allen Jenkins and raised three children. She returned to the sport as a coach and teaches skaters from those as young as five years old to those who are Olympic hopefuls.

A Sporting Legend
Peggy Fleming (USA)

Fleming was a ballerina on ice. Her beauty, grace and delicate style earned her the Olympic gold medal in 1968. She was the only US competitor in the Grenoble Games to win. "I felt an enormous burden of responsibility not to let myself or my country down," said Fleming, who was so nervous before the event that she could not eat.

Fleming's victory helped bring a sense of healing to American figure skating. In 1961, Fleming's coach Will Kipp and the entire US team perished in a plane crash. Without its top athletes and coaches, the US programme struggled for years. Fleming's victory re-established an American presence in the elite ranks.

Fleming grew up in San Jose, one of four daughters of Albert and Doris Fleming. Doris designed and sewed all of her daughter's costumes to save the family much-needed money. Today, Fleming, a mother of two sons herself, continues in the sport as a TV analyst.

A Sporting Legend
Dorothy Hamill (USA)

Hamill's first pair of skates were her brother's hand-me-downs. She had to stuff socks in the toes to make them fit.

Her ignoble start in the sport, however, was not evident one chilly night in 1976 in Innsbruck when Hamill won the Olympic gold medal. She slept with her medal that night. Her victory also had an unusual spin-off. It inspired women all over the USA to get a "wedge cut" hairdo. A haircut was easy to copy, not so, was Hamill's trademark "Hamill Camel" spin.

Several weeks later, Hamill became the first American since Peggy Fleming in 1968 to win the US championship, the Olympic gold medal and the world championship in the same year. Hamill's world title came on Friday, the 13th. She wore a gold four-leaf clover for good luck.

To this day, Hamill remains among the favourites in the sport. When 1992 Olympic gold medallist Kristi Yamaguchi was a little girl, her favourite toy was a Dorothy Hamill doll. Backstage at the Albertville Olympic Games, it was Hamill who wished Yamaguchi well before she took the ice.

A Sporting Legend

Scott Hamilton (USA)

Hamilton, one of skating's most loved champions, has always joked that he skates for all the short, bald guys in the world.

In 1984, he won the Olympic gold medal, becoming the first American male champion in 24 years. He placed second to Canada's Brian Orser in the short and long programmes but won the gold medal based on his large lead in the compulsories. "Maybe it wasn't pretty", said Hamilton. "But I did it".

It was a remarkable victory considering what he had overcome as a child. The adopted son of two professors in Bowling Green, Ohio, Hamilton stopped growing when he was three. Doctors did not believe he would survive past the third grade at school. Misdiagnosed early on, Hamilton would never grow beyond 5ft 3.5in. (161cm), 120lbs (54.5kg) as an adult. It turned out that he had a malabsorption problem. Doctors suggested exercise, including skating, and special diets.

The first time Hamilton laced on skates, aged three, he crashed and hit his head. He did not put on another pair for six years. The delay did not hurt. Hamilton went on to win four consecutive US and world championships. He was elected by his team-mates to carry the US flag at the Lake Placid Olympic opening ceremonies in 1984.

His small stature did not hurt his career. In fact, Hamilton said the ice was a great equalizer. "It didn't require that you be tall", he said. "It's a matter of ability and determination".

Following his amateur career, Hamilton became a crowd favourite on the "Discover Stars on Ice" tour and thrilled audiences with his trademark back flip and fancy footwork. He also continued winning, this time as a professional. Hamilton was forced to quit touring in March of 1997, aged 38, after being diagnosed with testicular cancer. He remains upbeat and joked early on about losing his thinning hair to chemotherapy. "The only disability in life is a bad attitude", says Hamilton.

A Sporting Legend

Brian Boitano (USA)

The 1988 Olympic Games featured the "Battle of the Brians" — Boitano of the USA and Orser of Canada. Orser was the 1987 world champion and silver medallist at the 1984 Sarajevo Olympic Games. Boitano was the 1986 world champion who had finished fifth in the '84 Games. The two had met ten times before in competition, with Orser leading 7–3.

Based on judges' suggestions, Boitano and Linda Leaver, his coach for 16 years, had scrapped his Olympic programme just months before the competition and begun anew. It was a risky move but necessary to put Boitano in position to win the gold.

Boitano took the ice before Orser, skating to near-perfection. It was a rare and defining performance under such pressure. One which transcended figure skating to rank alongside many other great Olympic moments. Orser, skating last, nearly missed a triple flip jump and late in his programme did a double axel instead of a triple. Boitano won five judges to four. "It was like the angels lifted me off the ice", said Boitano, the grandson of Italian immigrants. "It was a dream come true. It made my whole life".

Despite the great hype over "The Battle of the Brians", the two skaters were actually good friends and Boitano later said he almost felt guilty about winning the gold medal. Boitano went on to fight to gain entry into the 1994 Games in Lillehammer even though he had turned professional five years earlier. Given the chance and despite his intense preparations, Boitano stumbled in the short programme and placed sixth overall.

Boitano, the first skater to complete all six triple jumps in one competition, was always a risk-taker, never fearful to try anything new. He began the sport at eight years old, trading in his roller skates for figure skates. "He was the first one on the ice, the last off, the hardest worker, a daredevil," said Leaver, who continues to coach Boitano in a professional career where he continued to make headlines on the World Tour.

Sporting Legends

Ekaterina Gordeeva and Sergei Grinkov (URS)

It was impossible not to be moved by the magic of this Russian pairs team that won two Olympic gold medals. Skating partners for 15 years, married for four and a half of those, the union was shattered in November, 1995, when Grinkov died from a heart attack. Gordeeva was at his side when he took his last breath in Lake Placid, New York. He was 28.

Back home in Simsbury, Connecticut, the couple's three-year old daughter Daria, too young to understand, skated around the rink, blissfully unaware of the tragedy.

Considered to be among the greatest pairs teams of all time, the couple was known simply as "G & G". They were paired up when she was 11 and he was 14. "We matched perfectly from the very start," said Gordeeva. Winners of the Olympic gold medal in 1988, the couple re-instated as amateurs for the 1994 season. For their comeback, they skated to Beethoven's "Moonlight Sonata". Their unison on ice was uncanny.

"I remember everything," wrote Gordeeva in her bestseller "My Sergei". "You cannot describe the four minutes of skating in words, but I was aware of every movement that I was making, conscious of the meaning behind these movements and conscious of what Sergei was doing. It is a clarity that one so seldom finds elsewhere in life, a clarity any athlete can relate to, moments in time that we remember the rest of our lives. I believe it is why we compete."

Following Grinkov's death, Gordeeva skated alone in an emotional tribute to her husband. She continues to tour, only now she is alone on the ice. She says it is still a strange feeling, to be without his strong hands, throwing, twisting and catching her in perfect symmetry.

"Time, I have learned, is a doctor", said Gordeeva. "I am finding that the good days increasingly outnumber the bad ones".

Sporting Legends

Jayne Torvill and Christopher Dean (GBR)

Few skaters have revolutionized their particular event as dramatically as did ex-policeman Christopher Dean and his partner, Jayne Torvill, at the 1984 Sarajevo Olympic Games.

Already twice European champions, Torvill and Dean scored an unparalleled six perfect sixes for artistic impression and a further three for technical merit in winning the 1984 Olympic ice dance gold. Their free dance programme, skated to Ravel's Bolero, was a themed love story and totally different in content and style to previous ice dance programmes. The dance ended with the fated lovers falling to the ground, drawing gasps of appreciation and amazement. Many subsequent skaters copied their innovative style and choreography.

1984 Olympic gold was followed by the world title a month later in Canada. Torvill and Dean were also world champions in 1981, '82 and '83. After their 1984 world championships win, they toured in their own professional show. But the lure of another Olympic gold remained and "T&D", as the fans called them, reverted to amateur status. They won a sixth British championships title in 1993 and went on, somewhat controversially, to take European gold in early 1994.

In Lillehammer, at the Olympic Games, they duelled with two top Russian pairings throughout the early stages. An inauspicious start in the compulsory dance was salvaged by a brilliant Rhumba in the original dance section. Their free programme drew an ecstatic reaction from the crowd. But not the judges. Oksana Grichtchuk and Evgeni Platov took the gold, Torvill and Dean won bronze and returned to the ranks of the professionals.

A Sporting Legend
Irina Rodnina (URS)

Irina Rodnina was Olympic figure skating pairs gold medallist at three successive Games in 1972, '76 and '80. She took her first title with Alexei Ulanov and achieved her two subsequent successes with Alexander Zaitsev whom she later married.

Rodnina's style was youthful and energetic. Her programmes were packed with jumps and innovations. By 1978 she had won ten world championships. This record, plus her three Olympic golds, equalled the achievements of legendary Norwegian, Sonja Henie.

Drama surrounded Rodnina's first Olympic gold. Spurned by Rodnina, Ulanov had set up a relationship with another Soviet pairs skater, Ludmila Smirnova. Rodnina may have won gold but she ended in tears as she left the ice. Ulanov later married Smirnova.

MEDALLISTS *(by nation)*

Country	Gold	Silver	Bronze	Total
USA	11	12	14	37
URS	10	9	5	24
AUT	7	9	4	20
SWE	5	3	2	10
SWE	5	3	2	10
GBR	5	2	6	13
GER	4	4	1	9
RUS	4	2	-	6
GDR	3	3	4	10
GDR	3	3	4	10
NOR	3	2	1	6
RUS	3	2	-	5
EUN	3	1	1	5
CAN	2	6	9	17
FRA	2	2	5	9
NED	1	2	-	3
CZE	1	1	3	5
FIN	1	1	-	2
BEL	1	-	1	2
UKR	1	-	-	1
HUN	-	2	4	6
SUI	-	1	1	2
JPN	-	1	-	1
FRG	-	-	1	1
CHN	-	-	1	1

NAGANO SCHEDULE

Figure Skating

Venue: White Ring

Date	Description	Round	Start	Finish
8 Feb	Short Programme (prs)		20:00	22:30
10 Feb	Free Skating (prs)	FINAL	20:00	22:15
12 Feb	Short Programme (m)		19:00	22:30
13 Feb	Compulsory Dance		19:00	22:15
14 Feb	Free Skating (m)	FINAL	19:00	22:45
15 Feb	Original Dance		19:00	23:00
16 Feb	Free Dance	FINAL	19:00	23:00
18 Feb	Short Programme (w)		19:00	22:30
20 Feb	Free Skating (w)	FINAL	19:00	22:30
21 Feb	Exhibition		15:00	17:00

Figure Skating [Men]

MEDALLISTS

Year	Gold	Country	Points	Silver	Country	Points	Bronze	Country	Points
Special Figures									
1908	Nikolai Panin	URS		Arthur Cumming	GBR		Geoffrey Hall-Say	GBR	

Year	Gold	Country	Points	Silver	Country	Points	Bronze	Country	Points
1908*	Ulrich Salchow	SWE		Rickard Johansson	SWE		Pér Thoren	SWE	
1920*	Gillis Grafström	SWE		Andreas Krogh	NOR		Martin Stixrud	NOR	
1924	Gillis Grafström	SWE	2737.2	Willy Böckl	AUT	2518.75	Georges Gautschi	SUI	2233.5
1928	Gillis Grafström	SWE	2698.25	Willy Böckl	AUT	2682.5	Robert van Zeebroeck	BEL	2578.75
1932	Karl Schäfer	AUT	2602	Gillis Grafström	SWE	2514.5	Montgomery Wilson	CAN	2448.3
1936	Karl Schäfer	AUT	422.7	Ernst Baier	GER	400.8	Felix Kaspar	AUT	400.1
1948†	Richard Button	USA	994.7	Hans Gerschwiler	SUI	965.1	Edi Rada	AUT	941
1948‡	Richard Button	USA	191.177	Hans Gerschwiler	SUI	181.122	Edi Rada	AUT	178.133
1952	Richard Button	USA	1730.3	Helmut Seibt	AUT	1621.3	James Grogan	USA	1627.4
1956	Hayes Jenkins	USA	166.43	Ronald Robertson	USA	165.79	David Jenkins	USA	162.82
1960	David Jenkins	USA	161.3	Karol Divin	CZE	158.2	Donald Jackson	CAN	156.7
1964	Manfred Schnelldorfer	GER	1916.9	Alain Calmat	FRA	1876.5	Scott Allen	USA	1873.6
1968	Wolfgang Schwarz	AUT	1904.1	Timothy Wood	USA	1891.6	Patrick Pera	FRA	1864.5
1972	Ondrej Nepela	CZE	2739.1	S Tchetveroukhin	URS	2672.4	Patrick Pera	FRA	2653.1
1976	John Curry	GBR	192.74	Vladimir Kovalev	URS	187.64	Toller Cranston	CAN	187.38
1980	Robin Cousins	GBR	189.48	Jan Hoffmann	GDR	189.72	Charles Tickner	USA	187.06
1984	Scott Hamilton	USA	3.4	Brian Orser	CAN	5.6	Jozef Sabovtchik	CZE	7.4
1988	Brian Boitano	USA	3.0	Brian Orser	CAN	4.2	Viktor Petrenko	URS	7.8
1992	Viktor Petrenko	EUN	1.5	Paul Wylie	USA	3.5	Petr Barna	CZE	4
1994	Alexei Urmanov	URS	1.5	Elvis Stojko	CAN	3	Philippe Candeloro	FRA	6.5

Figure Skating [Women]

MEDALLISTS

Year	Gold	Country	Points	Silver	Country	Points	Bronze	Country	Points
1908*	Florence Syers	GBR		Elsa Rendschmidt	GER		Dorothy Greenhough Smith	GBR	
1920*	Magda Julien	SWE		Svea Noren	SWE		Theresa Weld	USA	
1924	Herma Plank-Szabo	AUS	2094.25	Beatrix Loughran	USA	1959	Ethel Muckelt	GBR	1750.5
1928	Sonja Henie	NOR	2452.25	Fritzi Burger	AUT	2248.5	Beatrix Loughran	USA	2254.5
1932	Sonja Henie	NOR	2302.5	Fritzi Burger	AUT	2167.1	Maribel Vinson	USA	2158.5
1936	Sonja Henie	NOR	424.5	Cecilia Colledge	GBR	418.1	Vivi-Anne Hulten	SWE	394.7
1948	Barbara Scott	CAN	163.077	Eva Pavlik	AUT	157.588	Jeanette Altwegg	GBR	156.166
1952	Jeanette Altwegg	GBR	1455.8	Tenley Albright	USA	1432.2	Jacqueline du Bief	FRA	1422
1956	Tenley Albright	USA	169.67	Carol Heiss	USA	168.02	Ingrid Wendl	AUT	159.44
1960	Carol Heiss	USA	169.5	Sjoukje Dijkstra	NED	156.9	Barbara Roles	USA	157.8
1964	Sjoukje Dijkstra	NED	2018.5	Regine Heitzer	AUT	1945.5	Petra Burka	CAN	1940
1968	Peggy Fleming	USA	1970.5	Gabriele Seyfert	GDR	1882.3	Hana Maskova	CZE	1828.8
1972	Beatrix Schuba	AUT	2751.5	Karen Magnussen	CAN	2673.2	Janet Lynn	USA	2663.1
1976	Dorothy Hamill	USA	193.8	Dianne De Leeuw	NED	190.24	Christine Errath	GDR	188.16
1980	Anett Potzsch	GDR	189	Linda Fratianne	USA	188.3	Dagmar Lupz	FRG	188.04
1984	Katarina Witt	GDR	3.2	Rosalyn Sumners	USA	4.6	Kira Ivanova	URS	9.2
1988	Katarina Witt	GDR	1.4	Elizabeth Manley	CAN	2.8	Debra Thomas	USA	4.2
1992	Kristi Yamaguchi	USA	1.5	Midori Ito	JPN	4	Nancy Kerrigan	USA	4
1994	Oksana Baiul	UKR	2	Nancy Kerrigan	USA	2.5	Chen Lu	CHN	5

*(part of summer Games)   † (compulsory)   ‡ (freestyle)

Figure Skating [Pairs]

Year	Gold	Country	Points	Silver	Country	Points	Bronze	Country	Points
1908	Anna Hübler Heinrich Burger	GER		Phyllis Johnson James Johnson	GBR		Florence Syers Edgar Syers	GBR	
1920	Ludovika Jakobsson Walter Jakobsson	FIN	80.75	Alexia Bryn Yngvar Bryn	NOR	72.75	Phyllis Johnson Basil Williams	GBR	66.25
1924	Helena Engelmann Alfred Burger	AUT	74.5	Ludovika Jakobsson Walter jakobsson	FIN	71.75	Andrée Joly Pierre Brunet	FRA	69.25
1928	Andrei Joly Pierre Brunet	FRA	100.5	Lilly Scholz Otto Kaiser	AUS	99.25	Melitta Brunner Sherwin Badger	AUS	93.25
1932	Andree Brunet Claude Brunet	FRA	76.7	Beatrix Loughran Sherwin Badger	USA	77.5	Emilia Rotter László Szollás	HUN	76.4
1936	Maxie Herber Ernst Baier	GER	11.5	Ilse Pausin Erik Pausin	AUS	11.4	Emilia Rotter László Szollás	HUN	10.8
1948	Micheline Lannoy Pierre Baugniet	BEL	11.227	Andrea Kekessy Ede Kiraly	HUN	11.109	Suzanne Morrow Wallace Diestelmleyer	CAN	11
1952	Ria Falk Paul Falk	GER	102.4	Karol Kennedy Michael Kennedy	USA	100.6	Marianna Nagy Laszlo Nagy	HUN	97.4
1956	Elisabeth Schwarz Kurt Oppelt	AUS	11.31	Frances Dafoe Norris Bowden	CAN	11.32	Marianna Nagy Franz Nagy	HUN	11.03
1960	Barbara Wagner Robert Paul	CAN	80.4	Marika Kilius Hans Baumler	GER	76.8	Nancy Ludington Ronald Ludington	USA	76.2
1964	Ludmila Belousova Oleg Protopopov	URS	104.4	Marika Kilius Hans-Jurgen Bäumler	GER	103.6	Debbi Wilkes Guy Revell	CAN	98.5
1968	Ludmila Beloussova Oleg Protopopov	URS	315.2	Tatiana Joukchesternava Alexander Gorelik	URS	312.3	Margot Glocksahuber Wolfgang Danne	FRG	304.4
1972	Irina Rodnina Alexei Oulanov	URS	420.4	Ludmila Smirnova Andrei Souraikin	URS	419.4	Manuela Gross Uwe Kagelmann	GDR	411.8
1976	Irina Rodnina Alexander Zaitsev	URS	140.54	Romy Kermer Rolf Österreich	GDR	136.35	Manuela Gross Uwe Kaagelmann	GDR	134.57
1980	Irina Rodnina Alexander Zaitsev	URS	147.26	Marina Cherkosova Sergei Shakrai	URS	143.8	Manuela Mager Uwe Bewersdorff	GDR	140.52
1984	Elena Valova Oleg Vassilliev	URS	1.4	Kitty Carruthrs Peter Carruthers	USA	2.8	Larissa Selezneva Oleg Makarov	URS	3.8
1988	Ekaterina Gordeeva Sergei Grinkov	URS	1.4	Elena Valova Oleg Vassiliev	URS	2.8	Jill Watson Peter Oppegard	USA	4.2
1992	Natalia Michkouteniko Artur Dmitriev	EUN	1.5	Elena Betchke Denis Petrov	EUN	3	Isabelle Brasseur Lloyd Eisler	CAN	4.5
1994	Ekaterina Gordeeva Sergei Grinkov	URS	1.5	Natalia Mishkutenok Artur Dmitriev	URS	3	Isabelle Brasseur Lloyd Eisler	CAN	4.5

ICE DANCE

Year	Gold	Country	Points	Silver	Country	Points	Bronze	Country	Points
1976	Ludmila Pakhomova Alexander Gorshkov	URS	209.92	Irina Moiseeva Andrei Minenkov	URS	204.88	Natalia Linichuk James Millns	USA	202.64
1980	Natalia Linichuk Gannadi Karponosov	URS	205.48	Krisztina Regoczy Andras Sallay	HUN	204.52	Irina Moiseeva Andrei Minenkov	URS	201.86
1984	Jayne Torvill Christopher Dean	GBR	2	Natalia Bestemyanova Andrei Boukin	URS	4	Marina Klimova Sergei Ponomarenko	URS	7
1988	Natalia Bestemyanova Andrei Boukin	URS	2	Marina Klimova Sergei Ponomarenko	URS	4	Tracy Wilson Robert McCall	CAN	6
1992	Marina Klimova Sergei Ponomarenko	EUN	2	Isabelle Duchesnay-Dean Paul Duchesnay	FRA	4.4	Maia Usova Alexander Zhulin	EUN	5.6
1994	Oksana Grichtchuk Evgeni Platov	URS	3.4	Maya Usova Alexander Zhulin	URS	3.8	Jayne Torvill Christopher Dean	GBR	4.8

LONG TRACK: SPEED SKATING

Olympics with slapskates

by Mette Bugge

Last season was a break-through for a "new" type of skates called "slapskates". Some called it a revolution, even though slapskates had been in existence for more than fifteen years. Their true pioneers were 11 Dutch junior international skaters and their coaches Erik van Kordelaar and Dick de Bles. But the top skaters had remained sceptical until three Dutch senior female skaters (de Jong, de Loor and Zijlstra) used the skates in the 1996/'97 season with great success.

In Nagano these slapskates will be introduced to an Olympic audience for the first time. They offer a new pattern of coordination, allowing for a longer push with a powerful ankle extension.

Adne Søndrål from Norway, therefore, might have been the last world champion on old-style skates. He was too afraid to change skates last season, even if the other top male and female speedskaters, one after the other, became convinced that slapskates really improved performance.

Søndrål, however, was injured before Christmas and when he started at the world championships in Warsaw in March 1997 he hoped the old skates would be good enough. They were. For the first time in his career, 25 year-old Søndrål was a winner when it came to a major championships.

The "veteran" who had already won Olympic 1500m silver in Albertville in 1992 at the age of 17 (followed by nothing for his troubles at the 1994 Games), will use slapskates in Nagano. This will be his last season, whatever happens. He is the father of a little son and wants more time with his family. "Life is more than sport", he said.

But Søndrål, born in 1971, is one of the favourites at both 1000m and 1500m and hopes Norway can feature amongst the gold medallists again. In 1994 his countryman Johann Olav Koss won three golds but he has since retired. At 1500m, skaters such as Rintje Ritsma (Holland), Ids Postma, Neal Marshall of Canada, CK Boutiette and the Japanese, Noake and Shirahata, will fight Søndrål hard for gold.

Last season several new people featured highly in the rankings, mainly because of slapskates. Bob de Jong, world champion as a junior in 1995, was impressive with new skates in the world cup race in Italy, in January 1997. He beat his nearest opponent Bart Veldkamp, of the Netherlands, at 10,000m by more than 20 seconds. His race time of 13:51.56 is one of the best outdoors ever.

"There is no doubt that these skates will make a revolution in speedskating. I guess it takes some time to get used to them. Therefore, I will wait to use them in the Olympic season", said the Norwegian skater, Kjell Storelid, twice Olympic silver medallist in '94.

The young Dutch girl, Tonny de Jong, took a long step forward in her career when she tried out the slapskates from the start of the 1996/'97 season. She won the world cup at the longer distances and is tipped to win the 1500m, 3000m and 5000m in Nagano.

Germany's Gunda Niemann will, of course, also go for gold. She is eight years older than de Jong and commensurately more experienced. At 1500m Anni Friesinger, Marianne Timmer and Annamarie Thomas of Holland will try to be golden girls. At the longer distances Niemann, Claudia Pechstein (Germany), Annie Friesinger and Tonny de Jong will fight for medals.

By the end of last season speedskaters from nearly every leading country were trying the new skates. Dutchman, Rintje Ritsma, at first a little wary, dropped his old skates and got back to winning ways. In Warsaw, in March, he showed the world that he could handle the new technique.

When it comes to the longer distances (5000m/10,000m) Ritsma, Bob de Jong, Gianne Romme, Ids Postma, Kjell Storelid (Norway), Frank Dittrich (Germany) and Bart Veldkamp (Holland) all have the capacity to win.

In the longer women's events there is a rising star, the young Kirsten Holum from the USA. She is a speedskater to watch. Kirsten was a world junior champion last season and comes from a family with the sport in its veins. Her mother, Dianne, has several Olympic medals including a gold from Sapporo in 1972. Dianne was later known as the coach of Eric Heiden, the American speedskater who won five Olympic golds.

Competition in the men's and women's sprint will be very tough. A lot is expected from the Japanese Manabu Horii, Yasunori Miyabe and

Hiroyasu Shimizu. Russia's twice world sprint champion, Sergei Klevchenya, American youngster Casey Fitz Randolph and Norwegian veterans Roger Strøm and Grunde Njøs all want to be on the medal list.

American, Chris Witty, the 1996 world sprint champion, Dutchwoman Marianne Timmer, the 1997 1000m world champion, Franzizka Schenk from Germany, Xue Ruihong, the 1997 500m world champion and Japan's Okazaki Shimazaki are all female sprinters with good track records going into Nagano.

Sprinting itself also has a different format in Nagano. For the first time in Olympic history the sprinters will race the 500m twice instead of once so that each racer gets both the inner and outer last bend. The overall time is then used to determine the winner.

Background

As already mentioned in the figure skating section the history of skating goes back centuries and developed from mankind's need to travel along frozen waterways, canals and lakes. Early skates were made of polished bone, wood and then metal. The use of iron-bladed skates was recorded in Holland as early as 1250.

Indeed Holland is considered the cradle of competitive speed skating. Throughout the nineteenth century, clubs formed in Holland and in other parts of Europe. In July 1892, the Dutch skating association invited all interested nations to a congress from which emerged the "Union Internationale de Patinage (UIP)", now called the International Skating Union (ISU).

Long track speed skating—known colloquially in current skating circles as "speed" to distinguish it from "short track"—made its Olympic Winter Games debut at the inaugural edition in Chamonix in 1924. It has remained on the programme ever since. However, all the early events—500, 1500, 5000 and 10,000m—were for men.

At the first Games, there was also an event called the "four distances". This was a sort of skating "omnium". No additional competition was involved, the title simply went to the skater with the best overall results from the other events. The "four distances" was dropped after the Chamonix Games. A men's 1000m was added in 1976 otherwise the long track programme has remained static.

Women, meanwhile, were causing the Games authorities a few headaches. The ISU wanted them to take part. The IOC seemed not to. Four events for women were finally added to the programme in 1960 — at 500, 1000, 1500, and 3000m—but only after a series of debates. A 5000m for women was added in 1988. As early as 1936, the ISU

President recorded his regret that speed skating events for women were not part of the programme of the Games in Garmisch-Partenkirchen. Many National Olympic Committees voiced their support for the inclusion of women at the 1939 IOC session and a vote was taken which ended in favour of inclusion.

However, world war intervened and, in 1953, an IOC Session carried over the ISU's continuing demand for women's events until the next year's meeting. There, the inclusion of women was rejected after a vote. The same happened in 1955 at the Session where the motion failed to get the required two-thirds majority of votes. Finally, in Melbourne in 1956, the ISU achieved its goal and women's speed skating was added to the programme for the Squaw Valley Games.

In 1932 controversy struck speed skating at the Lake Placid, USA, Games when a mass start was used for the only time in Olympic history—rather than the conventional pairings (see rules below). This kind of start was widely-practised in America and Canada and gave the "home skaters" a great advantage over their European counterparts. Indeed some of the top Europeans refused to participate, only discovering the format on arrival in Lake Placid.

The Finn, Clas Thunberg, was the hero of the very early Olympic Winter Games winning five golds in 1924 and 1928. Speed skating has a history of producing Olympic multi-gold medal winners. Perhaps the most famous of these was Eric Heiden who won all five distances at the 1980 Lake Placid Games. The American 21 year-old became an overnight national hero. Heiden's dedication to pre-Games training was unparalleled. After his victories he admitted that his motivation had been to make people in the USA pay attention to this otherwise unheralded sport.

In 1972 it was the turn of Ard Schenk of Holland to be crowned "King of the Games". He won three golds and set two Olympic records. Lillehammer, 1994, meanwhile, became the territory of "Koss the Boss". Norwegian skater Johann Olav Koss, already a gold medallist from 1992, delighted his home crowd by winning three golds and setting three world records in the dramatic Viking long-ship hall in Hamar.

Afterwards, he donated his first gold medal bonus of around £32,000 (US$53,400) (a Norwegian organization called "Olympia-toppen" reward their athletes post-Games with bonuses depending on results achieved) to Olympic Aid for Sarajevo, the war-torn 1984 Olympic Winter Games host city. Only Koss, the archetypal "boy next door", was surprised when lucrative advertising and Hollywood deals arrived on the coat-tails of his success and the media exposure brought by his gift.

Lillehammer still had some further heart strings to pull. The American, Dan Jansen, had been part of his nation's Olympic team since Sarajevo in 1984 when, as a 19 year-old, he finished fourth in the 500m. He went to Calgary in 1988 as favourite for gold in the shorter distances. However, just hours before he was due to skate he was told that his sister had died of leukemia. Jansen, unable to concentrate, fell in his first race—and then fell again. He left Calgary empty-handed

Again one of the 500m favourites in 1992, Jansen did not perform to his best and finished fourth. Lillehammer was a last chance for the man who had dominated his sport outside of the Games setting a hatful of world records—including one just two weeks before the 1994 opening ceremony in the 500m. However, in the same event in Lillehammer, with 200m to go Jansen's right blade slipped and he stuttered, losing vital fractions of a second. He finished eighth.

Only the 1000m remained. This was not his speciality. Yet the local crowd knew they were about to witness something special when Jansen was ahead of world record pace at 600m. In a true Olympic fairytale, he went on to win and take the record in 1:12.43

Similar fortune smiled on Sweden's Thomas Gustafson in 1984. He came off the ice after his 5000m performance believing he was not a medallist. So he went to watch the figure skating with a young female companion. On his return, he discovered that he had won gold by just two-hundredths of a second—half the length of a skate blade. Gustafson re-visited the Olympic arena in 1988 and won two more golds. Between the Games he had been burdened by knee surgery, serious illness and the death of his father.

Speed skating has also brought some multi-medal female competitors to the eyes of the world. These include Lydia Skoblikova of the Soviet Union who took all four titles in 1964 and the legendary Karin Enke (later Enke-Kania), of the former East Germany, who won a total of eight medals—three golds, four silvers and a bronze from 1980 to '88. Enke was a converted figure skater. "I gave up figure skating because I didn't like.....the acting, the playing to the audience, the starring role", she said.

American Bonnie Blair became one of the most successful women speedskaters of all time in 1994 when she won the 500m for the third successive Games. Blair's other medals included 1992 and 1994 1000m gold and a 1988 1000m bronze.

Yvonne van Gennip was the discovery of the 1988 Olympic Winter Games. The Dutchwoman won three golds despite needing surgery to her right foot two months before the Games. Christa Rothenburger of the former East Germany has a special place in Olympic history. She won 1000m gold at speed skating in Calgary. Seven months later she competed at the Games of the XXIV Olympiad in Seoul, South Korea, where she won a cycling silver medal.

Early Games speed skating competitions were held outdoors and tales abound of races run in adverse weather conditions. Much to the annoyance of the Americans who were winning at the time, the 1928 10,000m event was wiped out by the weather mid-competition. The1952 Games report describes skaters in the 1500m having to skate into a headwind and heavy snowfall.

As recently as 1976, Jan Egil Storholt of Norway won the 1500m title—on his 27th birthday—despite a gale force wind. Seven other skaters managed to better the previous Olympic record in the same race. Another Norwegian, Knut Johannesen, made speed skating history by winning the 10,000m in 1960 in a time of 15:46.6. He became the first man to break the sixteen minute barrier at the distance.

At the 1968 Grenoble Games, the ice for the long-track events was made from de-mineralized water as it was considered to make the track faster. Five Olympic records were broken during the Games. However, unlike previous and future Games the speed-skating titles went to a variety of different competitors.

Johann Olav Koss (NOR)

Equipment

Skaters wear gloves and tight-fitting, all-in-one aerodynamic suits with an integral hood. The clothing is designed to offer the least possible wind drag. The skater starting in the outside lane wears a red armband and the skater starting in the inside lane wears a white armband.

Speed skates have long, straight blades—longer than their figure skating and ice hockey counterparts—reaching up to 46cm (18in.) long. The boot does not come up over the ankle, allowing flexibility of movement. The blade is only 1mm (0.04in.) thick.

The new slapskates are revolutionary because the heel on the boot is not fastened to the blade which permits the blade to remain on the ice longer during a stroke, creating an increased thrust. When the foot is lifted from the ice, the heel retracts by the action of a spring, "closing" the gap.

A speed skating track is a 400m oval. The home straight is 111.43m long (365ft 7in.) and the finish line is in the centre of the home straight for the 1000m. For every other race it is at the end of the straight. Each curve has a radius of 26m (85ft 3in.). The beginning and end of the back straight are clearly marked so that a skater is aware of the area in which the lane changeover must take place.

Rules and Regulations

Competitors skate counter-clockwise around an oval track which is 400m long. They skate in pairs and change lanes once each lap in the back straight so that they both travel an equal distance. Skaters in the outer lane have right of way at the cross-over. It is considered an offence to obstruct another skater, leading to disqualification. If a collision takes place at the changeover, the skater on the inside lane is deemed responsible except in cases of clear obstruction.

The object is to skate the fastest time possible. A race is only decided once all the skaters have completed the race. Therefore, for instance, in a race with 32 skaters there will be 16 "heats".

For the first time in Nagano, each skater will skate the 500m race twice rather than once and the winner will be decided on the fastest total time. The change has been made to allow both skaters optimum conditions. Each will now skate once in the inner lane and once in the outer lane so that neither has an advantage due to the slight differences in distance and centrifugal force.

Speed skaters have extremely powerful legs to gain maximum push but they also use their arms to great effect and must lean inwards on the bends to combat the centrifugal force which would otherwise push them outwards.

Nagano Format

There will be ten long track speed skating events at the 1998 Olympic Winter Games—the 500, 1000, 1500, and 5000m for both men and women together with the 10,000m for men only and the 3000m for women only.

A maximum of ten women and ten men are permitted per nation. Up to four competitors per nation may enter each of the 500, 1000 and 1500m for both sexes.

And a maximum of three per nation may enter the men's 5000 and 10,000m as well as the women's 3000 and 5000m.

All skaters must have achieved qualifying times laid down by the ISU at any of the following: world championships, world cup competitions, international competitions or matches or a national championships in the preceding season. They will also have been nominated to the places won by their National Olympic Committee. Some nations may lay down stricter guidelines for their own competitors than those set by the ISU.

No more than 32 entrants are permitted to skate in each of the men's 5000m and the women's 3000m and no more than 16 in each of the women's 5000m and the men's 10,000m. Extra qualification criteria have been established if more than that number become eligible.

Venue

The 1998 Olympic Winter Games speed skating venue has been dubbed the "M-Wave". It is located in the Asahi and Maejima districts of Nagano city. The name comes from the design of the roof which looks like a giant "M" against the backdrop of the Japanese Alps. The river Chikuma flows nearby. This arena's ice track is 15m wide.

A Sporting Legend
Eric Heiden (USA)

There has never been a more impressive Olympic Winter Games athlete. Eric Heiden, born in 1958, won all five speed skating gold medals in Lake Placid in 1980.

Heiden, from Madison, Wisconsin, came from a sporting family. His sister Beth, a year younger than him, was also a brilliant sportswoman who was a world champion in both speed skating (1979) and cycling (1980).

Eric, born to be an athlete, caused a revolution in speed skating. He introduced new training methods. His career was amazing. At the age of 17, in 1976, he made his Olympic debut, finishing 7th at 1500m. It was in Lake Placid that he was truly outstanding, not only by winning all 5 distances, but also defeating his main opponents man-to-man in three of the distances. He dominated the sport from 1977 to 1980. Then he dropped out.

By that time he had won nine world championship titles in sprint and all-round, two of them as a junior and the others at senior level. He won 28 out of 40 possible distances in the ten world championships in which he participated. He set eight world records. Later, Heiden became a professional cyclist.

A Sporting Legend
Yvonne van Gennip (Holland)

Yvonne van Gennip, born in 1964, and from Harlem, Holland, over-shadowed the East German favourites in Calgary in 1988 when she won gold at two distances: 1500m and 3000m. She also broke the world record at 3000m under the dome of Calgary's super-fast Oval.

The Dutchwoman was the discovery of the Games. Having been injured for most of the preceding season, including the need for ankle surgery, she came to Calgary as a dark horse, rather than a favourite.

Before winning Calgary gold, van Gennip's international break-through came with 1981 world junior championships bronze. She also competed at the 1984 Olympic Games coming fifth at 3000m.

"I went to church last Sunday and found the inspiration to

win", said the, then, 23 year-old van Gennip after her first Olympic gold medal at 3000m.

The Dutch woman ended her Olympic odyssey in Albertville in 1992, where she finished sixth at 3000m.

A Sporting Legend

Johann Olav Koss (Norway)

Johann Olav Koss, born in 1968, was the outstanding heroic figure of the Olympic Winter Games in Norway in 1994. They dubbed him "Koss the Boss". In Hamar's beautiful Vikingship-arena the 25 year-old Norwegian won three Olympic speed skating gold medals at 1500m, 5000m and 10,000m. Each time he set a world record.

Perhaps more sensationally at the time, however, Koss gave away the medal bonus of 225,000 Norwegian Kroner (£32,000/US$53,440), due to him from the National Olympic Committee after his second gold, to Olympic Aid. It put a focus on the aid programme, speeding up contributions. Koss became celebrated for his generosity by the worldwide media. Sports journalists from 118 countries elected him as the world's greatest athlete in 1994, with tennis player Pete Sampras and cyclist Miguel Indurain behind him in the poll.

Johann Olav Koss came from Lørenskog, just outside Oslo. He made his Olympic debut in Albertville 1992, two years after his international breakthrough as a world all-round champion. He came home from France with one gold (1500m) and a silver (10,000m)

Koss was also world champion, all-round, in 1990, 1992 and 1994. He gave up speed skating after the 1994 season, to finish his medical studies and to promote the Olympic aid programme.

A Sporting Legend

Bonnie Blair (USA)

Bonnie Blair, born in 1964 and from Urbana-Champaigns, Illinois, USA, is one of the greatest names in Olympic winter history. The sprinter won five Olympic golds and one bronze in three different Olympic Games. No other American winter athlete, in any sport, has had such a long and impressive Olympic career.

Blair first struck gold in Calgary in 1988 when she was the fastest woman at the shortest distance (500m). Her time (39.10) was a world record. At the same Games she won a bronze at 1000m.

Four years later, in Albertville, Blair was the best at both sprint distances—a feat she repeated at the Lillehammer Games of 1994. She is the only speed skater in history to win the same distance (500m) at three Olympic Games in a row. The American sports magazine, "Sports Illustrated", elected her their female athlete of the year in 1994.

Blair also won 3 world championship sprints (1989, 1994, 1995). The last of these came at the rink in her home city. The American was the first woman in history to skate under 39 seconds for 500m. In March 1994, she clocked 38.99 in Calgary's Olympic Oval.

Amazingly, Bonnie Blair started her skating career in the sport's short track discipline, earning a world championship title in 1985. Short track speed skating was not added to the Olympic programme until 1992.

A Contemporary Hero

Manabu Horii (Japan)

The Japanese sprinter, Manabu Horii, born in 1972 in Muroran, can justifiably claim to be at the Formula One end of speed skating. He was the first man to break 1:12.00 for the 1000m. His rival to the tag of "fastest skater on earth" is his countryman, the 500m world record holder, Hiroyasu Shimizu.

Horii's 1:11.67 for the 1000m was set in Calgary at the end of the 1996/'97 season. It broke Yasaunori Miyabe's two year-old world record of 1:12.37.

Horii was a soccer player but changed to speed skating as a junior. Just 76kg (11st 13.5lbs) he took a bronze medal in the 1994 Olympic Games and must now be a medal favourite on home territory.

Last season Horii showed strength of character in the face of adversity, even if he was also unlucky. As a favourite in the world championships for sprinters, in the Norwegian Vikingship-arena at Hamar, he fell on the first of the 500m races ruining his chances of the championship title but went on to win the three remaining distances.

In Warsaw, last March, he got his revenge with a win in the 500m at the world championships for single distances, giving him his inspiration for Nagano.

Horii, who made his debut in the world championships in 1993, is part of a strong Japanese squad who specialize in sprints and must be strong contenders in Nagano.

A Contemporary Heroine

Gunda Niemann (Germany)

Gunda Niemann, born in 1966 in Sonderhausen, Germany, is one of the most successful female speed skaters of the last decade. Since she made her international debut in the European championships, with a silver in 1988, she has been European champion seven times and the world's best all-rounder in 1991, '92, '93, '95, '96 and '97.

In Nagano she will be 31. But she is still a skater to watch. Last season she ended up world champion again, both in the all-round event in Nagano and at 1500m, 3000m and 5000m in the world championships for single distances in Warsaw.

Niemann's Olympic career started in Calgary in 1988. There she was seventh, twice. Four years later she won two golds and a silver in Albertville. Her greatest disappointment came in the Games of Lillehammer (1994). She was expected to win three gold medals, but ended up with just a silver (5000m) and a bronze (1500m). Nagano will be the end of her Olympic career...with how many golds?

A Contemporary Hero

Rintje Ritsma (Holland)

"Tarzan, Apollo, Superman, The Flying Dutchman". Holland's Rintje Ritsma has been given many nicknames. Born in 1970, Ritsma was the world's best all-round speed skater last season, with the leading results at 1500m, 5000m and 10,000m. The Dutchman made his Olympic debut in Albertville and almost took a medal, finishing 4th in the 1500m.

In the 1994/'95 season he was the world's best all-rounder, with a title in both the European and world championships. Then Ritsma cut his links with the national team. He wanted to go his own way and did not get any further financial support from the Dutch speed skating federation. He brought in his own sponsors and proved himself by successfully defending his international titles the following season.

Last winter Ritsma failed to win the European and world championship title but, at the end of the season, he was again, unbeatable, winning the world championship (for single distances) title with a huge margin in both the 1500m and 5000m.

Ritsma was the first speed skater in the world to go under 1:52 at 1500m. That happened in Hamar, Norway, at the European championships in January 1994, with a world record of 1:51.60. The time annihilated André Hoffmann's record from the Calgary Games 1988.

In Lillehammer at the 1996 Olympic Games, Johann Olav Koss denied him the 1500m gold but he won bronze at 5000m. In Nagano, he has vowed to do better.

Gunda Niemann (GER) (left) and
Tonny de Jong (NED)

Eric Heiden (USA)

NAGANO SCHEDULE

Long track speed skating

Venue: M-Wave

Date	Description	Start	Finish
8 Feb	5000m (m)	15:00	18:00
9 Feb	500m (m)	16:30	17:30
10 Feb	500m (m)	16:30	17:30
11 Feb	3000m (w)	15:00	17:30
12 Feb	1500m (m)	15:00	16:45
13 Feb	500m (w)	16:30	17:30
14 Feb	500m (w)	16:30	17:30
15 Feb	1000 (m)	15:00	16:30
16 Feb	1500 (w)	15:00	16:30
17 Feb	10,000m (m)	15:00	17:45
19 Feb	1000m (w)	15:00	16:30
20 Feb	5000m (w)	15:00	17:15

MEDALLISTS *(by nation)*

Country	Gold		Silver		Bronze		Overall
	m	w	m	w	m	w	total
NOR	24	1	29	-	23	1	78
USA	14	8	7	8	3	6	46
URS	11	12	10	7	8	10	58
SWE	7	-	3	-	5	-	15
NED	6	7	13	4	13	4	47
FIN	6	1	6	2	7	2	24
GDR	3	6	1	1	12	7	30
FRG	2	1	-	-	-	-	3
CAN	2	-	2	2	6	-	12
GER	1	5	-	6	-	6	18
RUS	1	1	1	1	1	1	5
AUT	-	1	1	1	2	1	6
JPN	-	-	2	-	5	2	9
KOR	-	-	1	-	-	-	1
BLR	-	-	1	-	-	-	1
CHN	-	-	-	2	-	1	3
POL	-	-	-	1	-	1	2
PRK	-	-	-	1	-	-	1

Bonnie Blair (USA)

MEDALLISTS   Long track speed skating [Men]

Year	Gold	Country	Time	Silver	Country	Time	Bronze	Country	Time
500m									
1924	Charles Jewtraw	USA	44	Oskar Olsen	NOR	44.2	Roald Larsen	NOR	44.8
							Clas Thunberg	FIN	
1928	Bernt Evensen	NOR	43.4				Roald Larsen	NOR	43.6
	Arnold Thunberg	FIN	43.4						
1932	John Shea	USA	43.4	Bernt Evensen	NOR		Alexander Hurd	CAN	
1936	Ivar Bailangrud	NOR	43.4	Georg Krog	NOR	43.5	Leo Freisinger	USA	44
1948	Finn Helgesen	NOR	43.1	Kenneth Barthelomew	USA	43.2			
				Thomas Byberg	NOR	43.2			
				Robert Fitzgerald	USA	43.2			
1952	Kenneth Henry	USA	43.2	Donal McDermott	USA	43.9	Arne Johansen	NOR	44
1956	Evgeni Grishin	URS	40.2	Rafael Gratch	URS	40.8	Alv Gjestvang	NOR	41
1960	EvgeniGrishin	URS	40.2	William Disney	USA	40.3	Rafael Grach	URS	40.4
1964	Richard McDermott	USA	40.1	Evgeni Grishin	URS	40.6			
				Vladimir Orlov	URS	40.6			
				Alv Gjestvang	NOR	40.6			
1968	Erhard Keller	FRG	40.3	Magne Thomassen	NOR	40.5			
				Richard McDermott	USA	40.5			
1972	Erhard Keller	FRG	39.44	Hasse Borjes	SWE	39.69	Valeri Mouratov	URS	39.8
1976	Evgeni Kulikov	URS	39.17	Valeri Murtov	URS	39.25	Daniel Immerfall	USA	39.54
1980	Eric Heiden	USA	38.03	Evgeni Kulikov	URS	38.37	Lieuwe De Boer	NED	38.48
1984	Sergei Fokitchev	URS	38.19	Yoshiniro Kitazawa	JPN	38.3	Gaetan Boucher	CAN	38.39
1988	Jens Mey	GDR	36.45	Jan Ykema	NED	36.76	Akira Kuroiwa	JPN	36.77
1992	Uwe-Jens Mey	GER	37.14	Toshiyuki Kuroiwa	JPN	37.18	Junichi Inoue	JPN	37.26
1994	Alexander Golubev	URS	36.33	Sergei Klevchenya	URS	36.39	Manabu Horii	JPN	36.53
1000m									
1976	Peter Muller	USA	01:19.3	Jorn Didriksen	NOR	01:20.4	Valeri Muratov	URS	01:20.6
1980	Eric Heiden	USA	01:15.2	Gaetan Boucher	CAN	01:16.7	Frode Roenning	NOR	01:16.9
1984	Gaetan Boucher	CAN	01:15.8	Sergei Khlebnikov	URS	01:16.6	Kai Engelstad	NOR	01:16.8
1988	Nikkolai Gouliaev	URS	01:13.0	Jens-Uwe Mey	GDR	01:13.1	Igor Gelezovsky	URS	01:13.2
1992	Olaf Zinke	GER	01:14.8	Kim Yoon Man	KOR	01:14.9	Yukinori Miyabe	JPN	01:14.9
1994	Daniel Jansen	USA	01:12.4	Igor Zhelezovsky	BLR	01:12.7	Sergei Klevchenya	URS	01:12.9
1500m									
1924	Clas Thunberg	FIN	02:20.8	Roald Larsen	NOR	02:22.0	Sigurd Moen	NOR	02:25.6
1928	Arnold Thunberg	FIN	02:21.1	Bernt Evensen	NOR	02:21.9	Ivar Ballangrud	NOR	02:22.6
1932	John Shea	USA	02:57.5	Alexander Hurd	CAN		William Logan	CAN	
1936	Charles Mathisen	NOR	02:19.2	Ivar Ballangrud	NOR	02:20.2	Birger Vasenius	FIN	02:20.9
1948	Sverre Farstad	NOR	02:17.6	Ake Seyffarth	SWE	02:18.1	Odd Lundberg	NOR	02:18.9
1952	Hjalmar Andersen	NOR	02:20.4	Willem van der Voort	NED	02:20.6	Roald Aas	NOR	02:21.6
1956	Evgeni Grishin	URS	02:08.6				Toivo Salonen	FIN	02:09.4
	Yuri Mikailov	URS							
1960	Roald Aas	NOR	02:10.4				Boris Stenin	URS	02:11.5
	Evgeni Grishin	URS							
1964	Ants Antson	URS	02:10.3	Cornelis Verkerk	NED	02:10.6	Villy Haugen	NOR	02:11.2
1968	Cornelis Verkerk	NED	02:03.4	Ard Schenk	NED	02:05.0			
				Ivar Eriksen	NOR				
1972	Ard Schenk	NED	02:03.0	Roar Grönvold	NOR	02:04.3	Goran Claesson	SWE	02:05.9
1976	Jan Storholt	NOR	01:59.4	Yuri Kondakov	URS	02:00.0	Hans van Halden	NED	02:00.9

Skating: Long Track Speed

Year	Gold	Country	Time	Silver	Country	Time	Bronze	Country	Time
1980	Eric Heiden	USA	01:55.4	Kai Stenshjemmet	NOR	01:56.8	Terje Andersen	NOR	01:56.9
1984	Gaetan Boucher	CAN	01:58.4	Sergei Khlebnikov	URS	01:58.9	Oleg Bogiev	URS	01:58.9
1988	Andre Hoffmann	GDR	01:52.1	Eric Flaim	USA	01:52.1	Michael Hadschieff	AUT	01:52.3
1992	Johann Koss	NOR	01:54.8	Adne Søndrål	NOR	01:54.8	Leo Visser	NED	01:54.9
1994	Johann Koss	NOR	01:51.3	Rintje Ritsma	NED	01:52.0	Falko Zandstra	NED	01:52.4

5000m

Year	Gold	Country	Time	Silver	Country	Time	Bronze	Country	Time
1924	Clas Thunberg	FIN	08:39.0	Julius Skutnabb	FIN	08:48.4	Roald Larsen	NOR	08:50.2
1928	Ivar Ballangrud	NOR	08:50.5	Julius Skutnabb	FIN	08:59.1	Bernt Evensen	NOR	09:01.1
1932	Irving Jaffee	USA	09:40.8	Edward Murphy	USA		William Logan	CAN	
1936	Ivar Ballangrud	NOR	08:19.6	Birger Vasenius	FIN	08:23.3	Antro Ojala	FIN	08:30.1
1948	Reidar Liaklev	NOR	08:29.4	Odd Lundberg	NOR	08:32.7	Hedlund	SWE	08:34.8
1952	Hjalmar Andersen	NOR	08:10.6	Kees Broekman	NED	08:21.6	Sverre Haugli	NOR	08:22.4
1956	Boris Schilkov	URS	07:48.7	Sigvard Ericsson	SWE	07:56.7	Oleg Gontcharenko	URS	07:57.5
1960	Viktor Kosichkin	URS	07:51.3	Knut Johannesen	NOR	08:00.8	Jan Pesman	NED	08:05.1
1964	Knut Johannesen	NOR	07:38.4	Per Moe	NOR	07:38.6	Fred Maier	NOR	07:42.0
1968	Anton Maier	NOR	07:22.4	Cornelis Verkerk	NED	07:23.2	Petrus Nottet	NED	07:25.5
1972	Ard Schenk	NED	07:23.6	Roar Grönvold	NOR	07:28.2	Sten Stensen	NOR	07:33.4
1976	Sten Stensen	NOR	07:24.5	Piet Kleine	NED	07:26.5	Hans van Helden	NED	07:26.5
1980	Eric Heiden	USA	07:02.3	Kai Stenshjemmet	NOR	07:03.3	Tom Oxholm	NOR	07:05.6
1984	Sven Gustafson	SWE	07:12.3	Igor Malkov	URS	07:12.3	Rene Schoefisch	GDR	07:17.5
1988	Tomas Gustafson	SWE	06:44.6	Leo Visser	NED	06:45.0	Gerard Kemkers	NED	06:45.9
1992	Geir Karlstad	NOR	07:00.0	Falco Zandstra	NED	07:02.3	Leo Visser	NED	07:05.0
1994	Johann Koss	NOR	06:35.0	Kjell Storelid	NOR	06:42.7	Rintje Ritsma	NED	06:43.9

10,000m

Year	Gold	Country	Time	Silver	Country	Time	Bronze	Country	Time
1924	Julius Skutnabb	FIN	18:04.8	Clas Thunberg	FIN	18:07.8	Roald Larsen	NOR	18:12.2
1928	Irving Jaffee	USA	18:36.5	Bernt Evensen	NOR	18:36.6	Polacsek	AUT	20:00.9
1932	Irving Jaffee	USA	19:13.6	Ivar Ballangrud	NOR		Frank Stack	CAN	
1936	Ivar Ballangrud	NOR	17:24.3	Birger Vasenius	FIN	17:28.2	Max Stiepl	AUT	17:30.0
1948	Ake Seyffarth	SWE	17:26.3	Lauri Parkinen	FIN	17:36.0	Lammio	FIN	17:42.7
1952	Hjalmar Andersen	NOR	16:45.8	Kees Broekman	NED	17:10.6	Carl-Erik Asplund	SWE	17:16.6
1956	Sigvard Ericsson	SWE	16:35.9	Knut Johannesen	NOR	16:36.9	Oleg Gontcharenko	URS	16:42.3
1960	Knut Johannesen	NOR	15:46.4	Viktor Kosichkin	URS	15:49.2	Kjell Backman	SWE	16:14.2
1964	Jonny Nilsson	SWE	15:50.1	Fred Maier	NOR	16:06.0	Knut Johannesen	NOR	16:06.3
1968	Johnny Hoeglin	SWE	15:23.6	Anton Maier	NOR	15:23.9	Oerjan Sandler	SWE	15:31.8
1972	Ard Schenk	NED	15:01.4	Cornelius Verkerk	NED	15:04.7	Sten Stensen	NOR	15:07.1
1976	Piet Kleine	NED	14:50.6	Sten Stensen	NOR	14:53.3	Hans van Helden	NED	15:02.0
1980	Eric Heiden	USA	14:28.1	Piet Kleine	NED	14:36.0	Tom Oxholm	NOR	14:36.6
1984	Igor Malkov	URS	14:39.9	Sven Gustafson	SWE	14:40.0	Rene Schoefisch	GDR	14:46.9
1988	Tomas Gustafson	SWE	13:48.2	Michael Hadschieff	AUT	13:56.1	Leo Visser	NED	14:00.6
1992	Bart Beldkamp	NED	14:12.1	Johann Koss	NOR	14:14.6	Geir Karlstad	NOR	14:18.1
1994	Johann Koss	NOR	13:30.6	Kjell Storelid	NOR	13:49.2	Bart Veldkamp	NED	13:56.7

4 races

Year	Gold	Country	Time	Silver	Country	Time	Bronze	Country	Time
1924	Clas Thunberg	FIN	5.5pts	Roald Larsen	NOR	9.5pt	Julius Sksutnabb	FIN	11pts

MEDALLISTS Long track speed skating [Women]

Year	Gold	Country	Time	Silver	Country	Time	Bronze	Country	Time
500m									
1932*	Jean Wilson	CAN	58	Elizabeth Dubois	USA		Kit Klein	USA	
1936-1960		not held							
1964	Lidya Skoblikova	URS	45	Irina Yegorova	URS	45.4	Tatiana Sidorova	URS	45.5
1968	Ludmila Titova	URS	46.1	Mary Meyers	USA	46.3	Dianne Holum	USA	46.3
1972	Anne Henning	USA	43.33	Vera Krasnova	URS	44.01	Ludmila Titova	URS	44.45
1976	Sheila Young	USA	42.76	Cathy Priestner	CAN	43.12	Titiana Averina	URS	43.17
1980	Karin Enke-Kania	GDR	41.78	Leah Mueller	USA	42.26	Natalia Petruseva	URS	42.42
1984	Shrista Rothenburger	GDR	42.02	Karin Enke-Kania	GDR	41.28	Natalia Chive	URS	41.5
1988	Bonnie Blair	USA	39.1	Christa Rothenburger	GDR	39.12	Karin Enke-Kania	GDR	39.24
1992	Bonnie Blair	USA	40.33	Qiaoabo Ye	CHN	40.51	Christa Luding	GER	40.57
1994	Bonnie Blair	USA	39.25	Susan Auch	CAN	39.61	Franziska Schenk	GER	39.7
1000m									
1932*	Elizabeth Dubois	USA	02:04.0	Hattie Donaldson	CAN		Dorothy Franey	USA	
1936-1960		not held							
1964	Lidya Skoblikova	URS	01:33.2	Irina Yegorova	URS	01:34.3	Kaija Mustonen	FIN	01:34.8
1968	Carolina Geijssen	NED	01:32.6	Ludmila Titova	URS	01:32.9	Dianne Holum	USA	01:33.4
1972	Monika Pflug	FRG	01:31.4	Aatje Deelstra	NED	01:31.6	Anne Henning	USA	01:31.6
1976	Tatiana Averina	URS	01:28.4	Leah Poulos	USA	01:28.6	Sheila Young	USA	01:29.1
1980	Natalia Petruseva	URS	01:24.1	Leah Mueller	USA	01:25.4	Silvia Albrecht	GDR	01:26.5
1984	Karin Enke-Kania	GDR	01:21.6	Andra Schoene	GDR	01:22.8	Natalia Petrousseva	URS	01:23.2
1988	Christa Rothenburger	GDR	01:17.6	Karin Enke-Kania	GDR	01:17.7	Bonnie Blair	USA	01:18.3
1992	Bonnie Blair	USA	01:21.9	Qiaoabo Ye	CHN	01:21.9	Monique Garbrecht	GER	01:22.1
1994	Bonnie Blair	USA	01:18.7	Anke Baier	GER	01:20.1	Ye Qiaobo	CHN	01:20.2
1500m									
1932*	Kit Klein	USA	03:06.0	Jean Wilson	CAN		Helen Bina	USA	
1936-1960		not held							
1960	Lidya Skoblikova	URS	02:25.2	Elwira Seroczynska	POL	02:25.7	Helena Pilejczyk	POL	02:27.1
1964	Lidya Skoblikova	URS	02:22.6	Kaija Mustonen	FIN	02:25.5	Berta Kolokoltseva	URS	02:27.1
1968	Kaija Mustonen	FIN	02:22.4	Carolina Geijssen	NED	02:22.7	Christina Kaiser	NED	02:24.5
1972	Dianne Holum	USA	02:20.9	Stein Kaiser	NED	02:21.0	Aatje Deelstra	NED	02:22.1
1976	Galina Stepanskaya	URS	02:16.6	Sheila Young	USA	02:17.1	Tatiana Averina	URS	02:18.0
1980	Annie Borckink	NED	02:11.0	Ria Visser	NED	02:12.4	Sabine Becker	GDR	02:12.4
1984	Karin Enke-Kania	GDR	02:03.4	Andrea Schoene	GDR	02:05.3	Natalia Petrousseva	URS	02:05.8
1988	Yvonne van Gennip	NED	02:00.7	Karin Enke-Kania	GDR	02:00.8	Andrea Ehrig	GDR	02:01.5
1992	Jacqueline Boernere	GER	02:05.9	Gunda Niemann	GER	02:05.9	Seiko Hashimoto	JPN	02:06.9
1994	Emese Hunyady	AUT	02:02.2	Svetlana Fedotkina	URS	02:02.7	Gunda Niemann	GER	02:03.4
3000m									
1960	Lidya Skoblikova	URS	05:14.3	Valentina Stenina	URS	05:16.9	Eevi Huttunen	FIN	05:21.0
1964	Lidya Skoblikova	URS	05:14.9	Valentina Stenina	URS	05:18.5	Pil Hwa Kan	KOR	05:18.5
1968	Johanna Schut	NED	04:56.2	Kaija Mustonen	FIN	05:01.0	Christina Kaiser	NED	05:01.3
1972	Stein Kaiser	NED	04:52.1	Dianne Holum	USA	04:58.7	Aatje Deelstra	NED	04:59.9
1976	Tatiana Averina	URS	04:45.2	Andrea Mitscherlich	GDR	04:45.2	Lisbeti Korsmo	NOR	04:45.2
1980	Bjoerg Jensen	NOR	04:32.1	Sabine Becker	GDR	04:32.8	Beth Heiden	USA	04:33.8

*(Demo)

Skating: Long Track Speed

Year	Gold	Country	Time	Silver	Country	Time	Bronze	Country	Time
1984	Andrea Schoene	GDR	04:24.8	Karin Enke-Kania	GDR	04:26.3	Gabie Schoenbrunn	GDR	04:33.1
1988	Yvonne van Gennip	NED	04:11.9	Andrea Ehrig	GDR	04:12.1	Gabi Zange	GDR	4;16.92
1992	Gunda Niemann	GER	04:19.9	Heike Warnicke	GER	04:22.9	Emese Hunyady	AUT	04:24.6
1994	Svetlana Bazhanova	URS	04:17.4	Emese Hunyady	AUT	04:18.1	Claudia Pechstein	GER	04:18.3

5000m

Year	Gold	Country	Time	Silver	Country	Time	Bronze	Country	Time
1988	Yvonne van Gennip	NED	07:14.1	Anrea Ehrig	GDR	07:17.1	Gabi Zange	GDR	07:21.6
1992	Gunda Miemann	GER	07:31.6	Heike Warnicke	GER	07:37.6	Claudia Pechstein	GER	07:39.8
1994	Claudia Pechstein	GER	07:14.4	Gunda Niemann	GER	07:14.9	Hiromi Yamamoto	JPN	07:19.7

CURRENT OLYMPIC RECORD HOLDERS

Event	Name	Country	Time	Games	Year
Long track [Men]					
500m	Alexander Golubev	URS	36.33	Lillehammer	1994
1000m	Daniel Jansen	USA	1:12.43	Lillehammer	1994
1500m	Johann Koss	NOR	1:51.29	Lillehammer	1994
5000m	Johann Koss	NOR	6:34.96	Lillehammer	1994
10,000m	Johann Koss	NOR	13:30.55	Lillehammer	1994
Long track [Women]					
500m	Bonnie Blair	USA	39.10	Calgary	1988
1000m	Christa Rothenburger	GDR	1:17.65	Calgary	1988
1500m	Yvonne van Gennip	NED	2:00.68	Calgary	1988
3000m	Yvonne van Gennip	NED	4:11.94	Calgary	1988
5000m	Yvonne van Gennip	NED	7:14.13	Calgary	1988

Ids Postma (NED)

SHORT TRACK SPEED SKATING

A thrilling unpredictability

by Dick Kiers

Short track is probably one of the most unpredictable sports in the Olympic Winter Games. This sport is an exciting combination of tactics, skills and, not least, luck. The track is only 111m long, the bends are tight and every skater is looking for the ideal position. Accidents can happen very quickly and easily. The risk of falling is never far from the skaters' minds.

This also means that a championships rarely concludes without major surprises, although the men and women from the Republic of Korea (South Korea) are often in front. In this Asian country, short track is extremely popular. Its training facilities are the best in the world and, because Nagano is close at hand, many Korean fans are expected to watch the competition live lending their own brand of enthusiasm to the occasion.

"Training, training and once more training, that is the only reason behind our success", superstar Chun Lee Kyung said in an Olympic press conference in 1994. "We do not have any secrets. All year the Koreans are together in a training camp near Seoul for sessions of six hours a day. Except on Sundays when three hours are supposed to be enough."

The Koreans, who were merely interested spectators when short track was introduced as an exhibition sport in Calgary 1988, will therefore be the ones to beat a decade later in Nagano. Chun Lee Kyung is a three-times world champion in the women's event. In March she had to share the title with Yang Yang from China. Yang Yang-"A" that is, because there are two top competitors with the same name. The other, Yang Yang-"S", might also come to the 1998 Olympic Games.

The last world championships were a good test case for the Olympic Winter Games. The skaters all reacted with enthusiasm to conditions at the White Ring in downtown Nagano. In front of a good crowd, Yang Yang won the finals of the 500m and 1000m, the Olympic distances. Chun Lee Kyung was the fastest skater at 1500m and 3000m. In the final ranking the bronze medal went to Won Hyekyung, also of Korea.

Her compatriot Kim Dong Sun clinched the men's overall title. The result was spectacular because the 17 year-old had only just won the world junior title, in January in the USA. Canadian star Marc Gagnon, three-times world champion in the 1990s, had to settle for silver, Saturo Terao of Japan and Derrick Campbell of Canada got the bronze.

In Nagano, Kim won the 1000m and 3000m races whilst the 500m and 1500m went to Canada through Campbell and Gagnon respectively. A week later, the world team championships took place in Seoul. Both titles were won by the home country, Korea, an indication of their Olympic ambitions.

Unfortunately, one major short-tracker will not be skating in Nagano. Orazio Fagone, a member of the Italian relay team which won the Olympic title at 5000m in Lillehammer, had a motorcycle accident in Italy on May 30th, 1997. Fagone was seriously hurt and surgeons had to amputate one of his legs. It was a major blow for the Italian team, which also has very skilful short-trackers in Mirko Vuillermin, Fabio Carta and Michele Antonioli. The Italian men's team represents one of the best European chances of Olympic success.

Background

The juxtaposition of speed and potential spills makes this one of the most thrilling of all Olympic Winter Games sports. It is one of few events in the Games during which competitors race directly against each other rather than against the clock.

Races take place around an oval track designed to fit inside an average ice rink. The bends are tight and "short-trackers" skate close together counter-clockwise jockeying for position in "pack style" and trying to cover any attempted breaks. In such circumstances the odd clash and tumble are inevitable.

Short track was introduced to the Olympic Winter Games programme in 1992. It had been a demonstration sport in 1988 when Great Britain's Wilf O'Reilly won two golds. O'Reilly, of Irish and West Indian descent, hailed from the central, industrial British city of Birmingham—an unlikely breeding ground for Winter sports champions.

Winner of the 1991 world championships, O'Reilly came to Albertville in 1992 as a heavy pre-Games favourite. The hopes of his infrequent winter gold-winning nation were pinned on his back. Perhaps the weight was too much and the inaugural 1000m gold went to Kim Ki Hoon of South Korea. His nation also won the men's 5000m relay.

Two years later, just weeks before the 1994 Games in Lillehammer, tragedy of a more significant nature visited O'Reilly when his girlfriend Monique Velzeboer of Holland, herself a short track world-class skater, was paralysed in a training accident.

The couple debated whether O'Reilly should go to the Games. Finally deciding to compete, O'Reilly was visited by double misfortune when in both the 500m and 1000m his skate blades were damaged in first round clashes ruling him out of further competition and dashing his hope of Olympic medals. Perhaps, as coach to the Dutch team in 1998, he will savour victory if only second-hand.

Kim Ki Hoon was again in devastating form in Lillehammer successfully defending his 1000m title. In that race Great Britain's Nicky Gooch crossed the line in silver medal position but was later disqualified, judged to have fouled Derrick Campbell of Canada who fell. In a bizarre twist, world champion Marc Gagnon of Canada was, therefore, awarded the 1000m bronze for winning the "B" Final.

South Korea went on to win 500m men's gold through Chae Ji Hoon, women's 1000m gold through Chun Lee Kyung as well as the women's relay. Only Italy, in the men's relay, and Cathy Turner, of the USA, in the women's 500m individual race, broke the South Korean grip.

Controversy, however, surrounded Turner's win. China's Zhang Yanmei was so incensed at the manner in which the eventual women's 500m gold medallist had escaped disqualification in an earlier incident that she refused to remain on the podium during the medal ceremony once she had received her own silver medal. She threw her medallists' bouquet on the floor in disgust and stomped away.

Equipment

Short-trackers wear the same aerodynamic all-in-one suits as their long track counterparts minus the hood. They must wear helmets, gloves and knee and shin guards to prevent an injury if they fall. In addition, the knee and shin guards afford protection from other skaters' blades.

Skates are custom-made from moulds of a short-tracker's feet to allow for a perfect fit. The skate blade can be adjusted to the position which suits their style of skating best. It is set high and straight, rather than the curved version used in figure skating, and slightly off-centre to help negotiate the bends.

The track itself is 111.12m (364ft 7in.) long with tight bends. Seven plastic cones are used as track markers around each bend. These are put back in place at the end of each race if they have been disturbed and water is poured on the ice to repair any ruts which may have been made. There are no other lane markings elsewhere on the rink. Padded safety mats surround the edge of the rink to protect skaters who may fly off the track and into the barriers after a crash.

Rules and Regulations

There are six events on the 1998 Olympic Winter Games short track speed skating programme: men's and women's 500m and 1000m; women's 3000m and men's 5000m relay. In each event there will be preliminary rounds, semi-finals and finals.

Skaters are drawn in groups of four to skate. The top two proceed to the later rounds.

Race results often depend on tactical skill as well as skating speed. Skaters normally overtake each other on the outside but may do so on the inside if the opportunity arises and if the move does not hamper the lead skater. Skaters are disqualified if they cross over the plastic lane markers on the bends. However, skaters try and judge their speed so as to cling tightly to the inside of the bends to avoid being overtaken. They may also put their hand down to the ice to help steady themselves whilst negotiating the bends.

There is an overall referee for each race as well as two assistant referees with responsibility for each bend. They adjudicate on any incidents. A skater is disqualified if he or she is judged to have pushed or otherwise interfered with the progress of another skater.

The officials may re-start a race if an incident occurs before the first bend. A race starts with each of the skaters lining up in a ready position along the width of the start line and then racing to gain position on the first bend. Two false starts result in disqualification.

For relay races each team consists of four racers. A team can make changeovers between skaters at any stage of the race and on any part of the track except the last two laps which must be completed by one skater. These flexible rules make the event one of the most exciting within the sport.

More seasoned spectators are able to anticipate when a team is going to make a change because a team member will begin to pick up speed on the inner zone before coming into the track at the appropriate moment and receiving a push from his or her departing compatriot to keep the race momentum going. Sometimes one team is able to build up a lead. However, there are often extremely close finishes.

Each 500m race is 4.5 laps of the track. A 1000m race is nine laps, a 3000m relay is 27 laps and a 5000m relay is 45 laps of the track. Just as in track and field athletics or cycling, skaters often tuck behind the leading skater to benefit from the sheltered air pocket — a technique called "drafting" — before moving out during the last stage of a race to try and overtake with a sprint finish. At other times, the lead can change from one moment to the next.

Nagano Format

Each nation is permitted to enter a maximum of six male and six female short track speed skaters for the 1998 Olympic Winter Games provided they are suitably qualified. For each individual event, a maximum of three per nation are allowed, up to a total of 32 racers.

An Oympic qualifying tournament in November 1997 set the pattern for entry. Any nation who had two competitors finishing in the top 20 won Olympic places for four skaters of which three could participate in any one individual event. Those with one skater within the top 20 qualified for three competitors (two per individual event), and those outside the top 20 qualified for two competitors (one per individual event).

Eight teams, including the host nation, also qualified for the relay events as a result of the tournament. Those skaters in the individual events also have to form part of these relay teams.

Venue

The 1998 Olympic Winter Games short track speed skating events will take place in the "White Ring" skating arena which is in the Mashima district of Nagano City. The White Ring is also playing host to the figure skating competition. In exterior design, the venue is supposed to portray a water droplet. The rink itself is 30 x 60m (98ft x 197ft). After the Games the ice will be removed and a wooden floor laid to convert the venue into a gymnasium.

A Sporting Legend

Wilfred O'Reilly (Great Britain)

Wilfred, alias "Willy", alias "Wilf", O'Reilly was for many years one of the few black skaters on the international scene. As a participant, he was very successful for Great Britain winning two demonstration golds at the 1988 Olympic Winter Games in Calgary as well as the 1991 individual world title in Sydney. Now he is coach to the Dutch national team. He lives with Monique Velzeboer, herself a former top Dutch skater. Velzeboer had a serious training accident in December 1993 in Font Romeu which left her paralysed and in a wheelchair.

O'Reilly took part in the Games of Albertville in 1992 (5th in the 1000m) and Lillehammer, 1994, where he suffered a crash and a broken skate. As a member of ice club "Mohawks Solihull" the skater from Birmingham won the 1992 European title. Now he is very anxious to find out how well the leading Dutch skaters can perform. Ellen Wiegers and Dave Versteeg are the top skaters in his squad.

A Sporting Legend

Cathy Turner (United States)

Cathy Turner had two passions in life, short track speed skating and Country & Western music. In sport she twice won the Olympic 500m title, in both 1992 and 1994. Turner always had the reputation of being a very aggressive skater and on the latter occasion, in Hamar's Amfi-theatre, she went momentarily in fear of the jury's decision. China's Zhang Yanmei felt she had been troubled by Turner, but her coach's protest was not accepted.

Cathy Turner was also successful in music. She sang under the name of Nikki Newland in the Spyro Gyra-band, toured the United States, and was active in producing commercials. As a song writer she was responsible for hits like "Sexy Kinky Tomboy". Turner described herself as a "roughneck" and "tomboy", both in skating and in normal life.

Wilf O'Reilly (GBR) won two demonstration golds in 1988

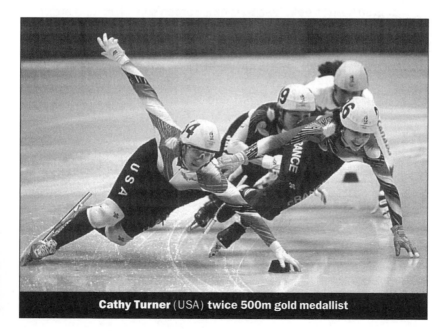

Cathy Turner (USA) twice 500m gold medallist

A Contemporary Hero

Marc Gagnon (Canada)

Pony tails are remarkably popular in the world of short track speed skating. Marc Gagnon is one of this long-haired species. The French-speaking Canadian who comes from Montreal has a specific style of short track speed skating. Physical strength and aggressive attacking are the key elements to his successes. Sometimes he has to pay for that wild-west style through falls but he often manages to stay up and storm to the finish line in first place.

Gagnon won the world title in 1993, '94 and '96. In 1993 his brother Sylvain finished second. In 1995 and '97 Marc Gagnon, was second behind Korean rivals Chae Ji Hoon and Kim Dong Sung. In 1995, in the cavern hall of the small Norwegian village of Gjövik, Gagnon fell at two out of four distances, but still got the silver medal.

A Contemporary Hero

Chun Lee Kyung (Republic of Korea)

It is so hard to get close to them! Korean short-trackers are very difficult to approach whether on-ice for their competitors or off-ice for interested journalists. Chun Lee Kyung is a typical example. The 21 year-old from Seoul was very successful, winning three world titles in a row. Yet at every press conference, the champion simply thanked her trainers and her parents at home. And that was it.

The diminutive 1.60m (5ft 3in.) and 54kg (8st 7lbs) Chun lets her skates speak for her - in an impressive way. Chun is a miracle on skates, her overtaking manoeuvres are a delight to watch if you are a neutral spectator. It does not seem to cost her any energy at all. And if Chun sets the best start of the field, you know she is going to win. Her rivals can only watch the back of her yellow and blue suit.

Speed skating — short track

Venue: White Ring

Date	Description	Round	Start	Finish
17-Feb	10,000m (m)	Q/fying & FINAL	19:00	22:30
	3000m relay (w)	s/final & FINAL	19:00	22:30
19-Feb	500m (w)	Q/fying & FINAL	19:00	22:30
	500m (m)	Q/fying	19:00	22:30
	5000m relay (m)	s/final	19:00	22:30
21-Feb	1000m (w)	Q/fying & FINAL	19:00	22:30
	500m (m)	FINAL	19:00	22:30
	5000m relay (m)	FINAL	19:00	22:30

MEDALLISTS *(by nation)*

Country	Gold		Silver		Bronze		Overall
	m	w	m	w	m	w	total
KOR	4	2	1	-	1	1	9
USA	-	2	1	1	-	2	6
CAN	-	1	2	3	1	-	7
ITA	1	-	1	-	-	-	2
CHN	-	-	-	1	-	-	1
GBR	-	-	-	-	1	-	1
AUS	-	-	-	-	1	-	1
JPN	-	-	-	-	1	-	1
PRK	-	-	-	-	-	1	1
EUN	-	-	-	-	-	1	1

MEDALLISTS Short track speed skating [Men]

Year	Gold	Country	Time	Silver	Country	Time	Bronze	Country	Time
500m									
1994	Chae Ji Hoon	KOR	43.45	Mirko Vuillermin	ITA	43.47	Nicholas Gooch	GBR	43.68
1000m									
1992	Kim Ki Hoon	KOR		Frederic Blackburn	CAN		Lee Joon Ho		
1994	Kim Ki Hoon	KOR	1:34.57	Chae Ji Hoon	KOR	1:34.92	Marc Gagnon	CAN	1:33.03
5000m relay									
1994	Maurizio Carnino	ITA	7:11.74	Randall Bartz	USA	7:13.37	Steven Bradbury	AUS	7:13.68
	Diego Cattani			John Coyle			Kieran Hansen		
	Hugo Herrnhof			Eric Flaim			Andrew Murtha		
	Mirko Vuillermin			Andrew Gabel			Richard Nizielski		

MEDALLISTS Short track speed skating [Women]

Year	Gold	Country	Time	Silver	Country	Time	Bronze	Country	Time
500m									
1992	Cathy Turner	USA		Li Yan	CHN		Ok Sil Hwang	PRK	
1994	Cathy Turner	USA	45.98	Zhang Yanmei	CHN	46.44	Amy Peterson	USA	46.76
1000m									
1994	Chun Lee Kyung	KOR	1:36.87	Nathalie Lambert	CAN	1:36.97	Kim So Hee	KOR	1:37.09
3000m relay									
1994	Chun Lee Kyung	KOR	4:26.64	Christine-Isabel Boudrias	CAN	4:32.04	Karen Cashman	USA	4:39.34
	Kim So Hee			Isabelle Charest			Amy Peterson		
	Kim Yoon Mi			Sylvie Daigle			Cathy Turner		
	Wom Hye Kyung			Nathalie Lambert			Nicole Ziegelmeyer		

CURRENT OLYMPIC RECORD HOLDERS

Event	Name	Country	Time	Games	Year
Short track [Men]					
500	Chae Ji Hoon	KOR	43.45	Lillehammer	1994
1000m	Kim Ki Hoon	KOR	1:30.76	Albertville	1992
5000m relay	Maurizio Carnino	ITA	7:11.74	Lillehammer	1994
	Orazio Fagone				
	Hugo Herrnhof				
	Mirko Vuillermin				
Short track [Women]					
500m	Cathy Turner	USA	45.98	Lillehammer	1994
1000m	Chun Lee Kyung	KOR	1:36.87	Lillehammer	1994
3000m relay	Chun Lee Kyung	KOR	4:26.94	Lillehammer	1994
	Kim So Hee				
	Kim Yoon Mi				
	Won HyeKung				

ALPINE SKIING

Stars to Watch
Ski time is show time

by Joseph Metzger

Nagano should be relieved. Alpine skiing will not lack its biggest attraction otherwise known as "Tomba-mania". Alberto Tomba, the legendary and sometimes controversial but always mercurial 31 year-old son of an Italian millionaire from San Lazzaro di Savena (a suburbian village of Bologna), has said that he wants to chase a fourth Olympic title.

For him it would be the first since edging out five times overall World Cup winner, Marc Girardelli, the Austrian-born all-rounder who now skis for Luxembourg, in a breath-taking battle on the slopes of the giant slalom event in Val D'Isere in 1992. The Italian, famous throughout the world, is willing to turn back the clock despite a rather sloppy pre-Olympic season which yielded him only one race win and a world championship slalom bronze. Yet, time after time, when Tomba seems over the hill he has hit back strongly.

In Sierra Nevada, at the 1996 world championships, he won his first-ever world title despite arguments over some controversial comments which he made about the venue. It was an indication that nobody currently handles pressure better than Tomba. Nobody lives up to expectations in quite the same way, either. He is constantly protrayed as a "bon-viveur" who even uses his playboy lifestyle to get into the right frame of mind to race. A girl here, there a glass or two of red wine. Inside the desire still burns, boosting his ambitions to get back to the kind of peak which gave him two golds in Calgary and another in Albertville.

"Tomba la Bomba", as his fans know him, however, has strong challengers in the slalom event. These include the Austrians who can hardly wait to make up for their 1997 losses in Sestriere at the world championships. They entered the event as heavy favourites but left empty-handed, either freezing under the pressure or through injury. These included Thomas Sykora, who won five consecutive races before Sestriere but suffered a heavy pre-event fall in Kitzbuehel, Mario Reiter and Thomas Stangassinger.

Skykora, nephew of the former pentathlon world record holder and current deputy governor of Lower Austria, Liese Prokop, found some compensation taking the world cup slalom trophy in Vail, Colorado, but still has to win a medal. "If I am fit, I am going to win again", said Sykora. Many experts rate him, and Frenchman Sebastian Amiez, the Sestriere runner-up, more highly than current world champion Tom Stiansen from Norway. Stiansen is best known as a dark horse, cold-blooded and always at his best in moments when the big stars falter.

Swiss skier Michael von Gruenigen is calm introverted, softly-spoken and a family man from the village of Einiedeln. Many title chances had slipped through his hands before he was crowned the undisputed king of giant slalom by taking the world title in Sestriere. It was an outstanding performance—one which left the rest trailing— even Tomba. Von Gruenigen gave them all a lesson in skiing so smoothly that he appeared to be running on rails.

It was ironic, then, that this quiet man should attack Tomba's sportsmanship by claiming that the Italian with the media-magnetic personality had deliberately missed a lot of world cup races to save himself for the big occasion. Tomba countered by calling the Swiss an "excellent skier but boring anti-star". The two have since come to a truce, a sort of gentleman's agreement.

Tomba, von Gruenigen and Norway's Olympic and world champions, Kjetil Andre Aamodt and Lasse Kjus, all belong to the establishment challenge. Yet a group of young lions is also hungry for Nagano success. They are willing to take any risk at any time— gamblers on a small roof.

They are headed by two Austrians. The first is Josef "Pepi" Strobl who made history as the youngest downhill winner ever when he stole victory from Luc Alphand at Val D'Isere in December 1995. Andreas Schifferer is the other. He came close to retiring after a near-fatal fall on the famous Streif course in Kitzbuehel. Schifferer has since had a long lay-off and many psychotherapy sessions and was able to shrug off bad memories to take a giant slalom bronze at the 1997 worlds followed by the world cup final title in Vail.

Another Italian could also create headlines. Matteo Nana is considered to be the new Tomba—and not just by the "Tifosi". Local

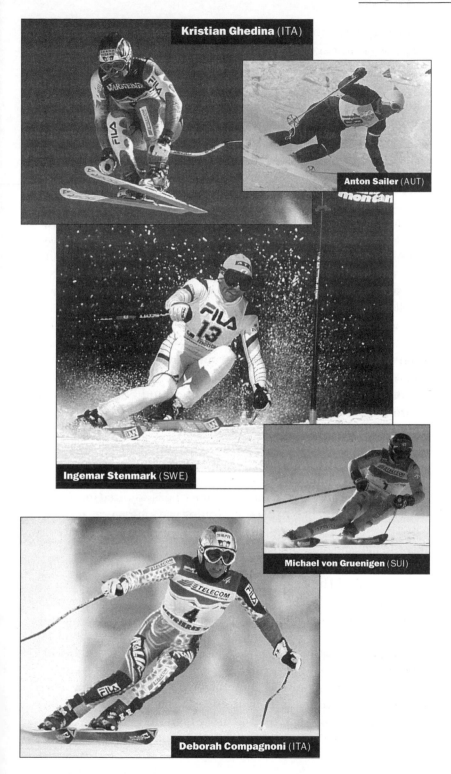

Kristian Ghedina (ITA)

Anton Sailer (AUT)

Ingemar Stenmark (SWE)

Michael von Gruenigen (SUI)

Deborah Compagnoni (ITA)

crowds, however, will concentrate on the fortunes of Kimura of Japan who is a versatile slalom racer with a track record which includes several top ten placings in world cup races. The pressure will be on him to see whether he can emulate Chiharu Igaya's runner-up position to Toni Sailer in Cortina in 1956.

The downhill, the blue riband of Alpine skiing, is an entirely different story in 1998. It will be raced in Hakuba where recreational skiers can swing gently down the upper slopes but where the Games Organizing Committee has been refused permission to build a start house due to environmental considerations. The course, therefore, has been cut to a race time of approximately 1 minute, 35 seconds.

"It is a shame", says Patrick Ortleib, the 1992 Olympic and 1996 world champion. "But it is better to have a short race than no race at all".

Whilst the course may be short, it is demanding. It has difficult bends, long jumps and flats. It requires all-round ability and favours experienced downhillers who need to adjust quickly to changing conditions either by instinct or analysis—with style or with last second adjustments.

The question remains as to who will manage the task the best. There are doubts that it will be three-times overall world cup downhill winner Luc Alphand of France. He may drop out. "In one race", he explained, "everything can be ruined in one hundredth of a second, everything which you have built up over a long period. Is it worth the time you sacrifice and the energy you put in?".

Twice world super-G champion, Atle Skaardal of Norway, is also in doubt after two bouts of knee surgery. That leaves the door wide open to a group of contenders including Kristian Ghedina of Cortina in Italy. He is an amusing character and one who is admired for the will-power which brought him back to winning ways after a car accident. Ghedina was in a coma and fought for his life before getting back on skis and fighting to re-build his career. He succeeded in both senses, winning world championships silver in 1996 and bronze in 1997. Gold in Nagano would be a fairytale ending.

Perhaps, though, the man to beat could be Austrian Fritz Strobl, a 25 year-old from Gerlamoos, Carinthia. He had been written off after an unlucky series of injuries and missed seasons but roared back to form by winning at Val D'Isere in 1996 and at prestigious Kitzbuehel. Strobl is a threat to the best as is another Austrian, Werner Franz. Franz, until now a perennial runner-up, would like to turn the tide on Switzerland's world champion Bruno Kernen who won in Sestriere in a race in which Franz crashed and broke his arm.

Olympic races are more special than any others. One day, one race, changing conditions, different propositions. In Nagano, anything could happen. An under-dog may have his day, especially from amongst the North Americans, just as Tommy Moe and Bill Johnson did in 1994 and 1984 respectively.

Moe's Lillehammer victory is fresh in the memory as is the similar success of Hilary Lindh who has quit racing with a world downhill gold medal around her neck. While Lindh has chosen retirement her American team-mate and 1994 Olympic downhill silver medallist Picabo Street is aiming for a comeback after being ruled out of the whole pre-Olympic season by a bad fall in its opening downhill race.

Herwig Demschar, coach to the US team, says that Street will be as strong as ever—ready to shine, as usual, in high-speed events. She is rare amongst the top female skiers because, in contrast to the men's tour, a large number of them compete in at least three of the four alpine disciplines rather than specializing.

Two of the top racers are a testament to this versatility. Reigning Olympic downhill champion, Katja Seizinger, a millionaire's daughter from Heidelberg, Germany, first climbed to the top in downhill and Super G before also winning major medals in the giant slalom and slalom. Powerfully-built Swede and world champion, Pernilla Wiberg, did it the other way round. With Olympic golds to her credit from Albertville and Lillehammer, Wiberg won downhill bronze at the 1997 worlds in Sestriere. At home, Wiberg doubles as a pop star playing to packed live audiences and with CDs in the charts. In commercial and sporting terms, she is a born winner.

In contrast to Wiberg, Italy's Deborah Compagnoni, shuns the limelight. This shy daughter of small-hotel owners, in Santa Caterina, was Olympic super-G champion in 1992 and has been the outstanding giant slalom racer since 1994 as well as winning the world slalom title in 1997.

She is famous for her stylish skiing and her ability to find the quickest line between gates—the latter giving her a touch of Tomba but without his personality. Indeed, Compagnoni has learnt a lot from practice sessions with Tomba early in her career. She might be female from top to toe but she skis in a male style.

So does Isolde Kostner from Ortisei, Val Gardena, who is a daredevil, downhill skier and one who has matured and improved technically over the years in giant slalom and super-G where she won back to back world championship titles. Kostner has a major chance of Nagano success.

Meanwhile, the Austrians are still struggling with the tragic death of Ulrike Maier in 1994 as well as a change in generations. Anita

Wachter, ageing 1988 Olympic combined champion, who has been plagued by illness, may have run out of steam. Elfi Eder, 1996 slalom world cup winner and 1994 Olympic silver medallist, has fallen out with her coaches and may even switch federations.

Yet the Austrians may have new cards to play such as 1997 world combined champion Renate Goetschl. The combined is a classical Alpine competition linking the downhill and slalom which are raced within hours of each other and finishing under floodlights. In Sestriere, it turned out to be a thriller with the last skier going for gold. This format will be adopted for the first time in Nagano. Ski-time will be show-time, even at the Olympic Games. Ask Tomba.....

Background

In Sweden, geologists have found fragments of ancient skis dating back 4000 years and in a northern Russian cave there are 2000 year-old murals representing skiing. Old Scandinavian legends are full of daring tales of skiing adventures.

Man used this form of transport to travel cross deep snow long before skiing became a competitive sport. The first competitions took place in Norway, around the Oslo area, in the 1850s. By the 1870s the Alpine regions had been touched by the same developments. The first ski club was formed in Switzerland in 1893.

At an IOC congress in 1910 the idea of forming an international ski federation was discussed and the Commission Internationale de Ski (CIS) emerged to help guide the sport over the next fourteen years. And the following year the first international skiing rules were adopted. As early as 1914 a proposal was put forward during the Christiania IOC Congress that ski events should be included in the Olympic Games. No approval was given for the idea at the time. Ten years later, at the IOC congress held in Chamonix, at the inaugural Olympic Winter Games, a founding congress of the Federation Internationale de Ski (FIS) took place. The FIS took over where the CIS had begun.

Although skiing featured in the Chamonix Games the debate over the sport's Olympic inclusion still raged. As late as 1926 Finland and Norway continued to vote against Olympic skiing at an IOC Congress in Lahti. The Nordic countries were sensitive to the fact that Olympic skiing might detract from their own well-established international competitions.

Cross-country skiing and ski jumping have been a part of the Olympic Winter Games since their inception in 1924. However, Alpine skiing did not appear on the progamme until 1936 when the "Alpine combined" for men and women was the only event. This was dropped eight years later and only reappeared in 1988 alongside the inaugural inclusion of the super-G. The first Olympic downhills and slaloms were added in 1948 and the giant slalom in 1952.

In 1935 the IOC took a decision that ski instructors would not be permitted to compete at the Games because they, in effect, earned money from the sport and were not true amateurs. This led to a protracted row between FIS and the IOC. The skiing authorities informed the IOC in 1936 that unless their own international rules were adopted for the 1940 Games—i.e. allowing entry to ski instructors—that skiing would withdraw from the Olympic Movement.

This was a precusor for a series of clashes between skiing and the IOC over professionalism in a sport which relied heavily on commercial resorts and ski manufacturers. One of the better-publicized clashes came when the top Austrian Karl Schranz was barred from competing in 1972 on the grounds that he had allowed his image to appear in advertising.

Back in 1938, however, the IOC was faced with a considerable dilemma. Should they cancel the 1940 Games, should they go ahead with them minus skiing? Eventually, the IOC took the decision to celebrate the Games in Sapporo, Japan, in 1940 but without any skiing events.

Fortunately, in one sense, world war interrupted negotiations. In 1946 17 nations at a FIS conference stated their desire to take part in the 1948 Olympic Winter Games and two representatives were chosen to try and close the gap between FIS and the IOC. A compromise was found whereby FIS rules would apply to the Games but that the nations affiliated to FIS would not send any competitors to the Games who may infringe the spirit of the Olympic Charter.

Relations between FIS and the IOC then experienced a quieter period until 1972 and the Schranz affair. At the IOC Session in Munich later that year the IOC President, Avery Brundage, a long-time critic of alpine skiing, was severe in his condemnation of Alpine skiing and its professionalism and wanted the discipline deleted from the Olympic programme. History shows that he did not succeed. Subsequently, the Olympic Movement, via its constituent international federations, has significantly altered its rules on professional and amateur status.

Outside of sporting politics, Alpine skiing is one of the most prestigious and exciting sections of the Olympic Winter Games programme. It has produced many of the Games' stars and stories.

American twins Phil and Steve Mahre won Olympic slalom gold

and silver respectively in Sarajevo in 1984. Phil had also won Olympic silver in the same event four years previously despite having smashed his ankle so badly in 1979 that it needed several screws and a metal plate to repair it.

The 1984 Games also provided a dramatic downhill winner in the shape of the previous, virtual-unkown, Bill Johnson of America. "All I have to do is come down, be decent , be aggressive and I'll win", he said before the race. Few, on the strength of just one world cup win, were in a position to believe the 23 year-old from the surfing rather than skiing state of California. Even fewer might have backed his compatriot Tommy Moe who came from nowhere to win the Olympic downhill a decade later in Lillehammer.

Whilst Moe and Johnson were underdogs from a superpower, tiny Liechtenstein gave the USA-based Games a touch of colour in 1980 in Lake Placid. Diminutive Hanni Wenzel won her country's first Olympic gold medals—in the slalom and giant slalom—as well as a silver in the downhill. Her brother, Andreas, was a silver medallist in the men's giant slalom of that year, making them the first brother and sister combination to win Alpine medals at the same Games.

Similar "family" history was made by Marielle and Christine Goitschel of France in 1964. They were the first sisters to win gold medals at the same Games. Christine won the slalom and Marielle, the giant slalom. Marielle went on to win the slalom gold in 1968 in Grenoble.

In Grenoble, too, the host nation's Jean Claude Killy joined triple gold winner Toni Sailer, of Austria, from 1956 by taking a clean sweep of the men's alpine gold medals. Switzerland's Vreni Schneider is the only woman to have won three golds—achieved in 1988 and 1994. Another Swiss skier, Michela Figini, was the youngest Alpine gold medallist, aged 17 years 314 days, in winning the 1984 downhill. Austrian women, meanwhile, enjoyed a "grand slam" in the 1976 downhill winning gold, silver and bronze through Christl Haas, Edith Zimmermann and Traudi Hecher in that order.

By contrast, Costa Rica's Arturo Kinch was the only athlete or official from his country in 1980. He competed in the downhill and took a nasty spill. That did not prevent him trying the giant slalom where he missed a gate and fell. By now on crutches he had to be dissuaded from attempting the slalom.

In similar vein one report of the 1952 Oslo Games describes a "small Greek" who fell down eighteen times during the slalom event, rested against a flag-pole before deciding to sit down and finish the race backwards. Also in Oslo, attractive American skier, Andrea

"Andy" Mead Lawrence, won women's giant slalom gold despite falling—unthinkable in the modern age of split second victories.

In 1972, Spain won its first Alpine skiing medal through Francisco Fernandez Ochoa. Slalom victory for the man from Madrid was greeted with amazement. However, Ochoa was the son of a national ski coach and had spent all his early years in the mountains of Chile, skiing from the age of two onwards.

A Frenchman, Oreiller, whose name means "pillow" won the inaugural Olympic men's downhill in 1948. He also won the combined title and a bronze in the slalom at those Games in St Moritz. Before world war interrupted the Olympic programme a Norwegian teenager, Laila Schou Nilsen, won the 1936 Alpine Combined bronze. She held world speed skating records and only entered the skiing events at the Games because there were no skating events for women. Pigtailed Gretchen Frazer was America's first Alpine skiing gold medallist in 1948 in the slalom.

America was the scene in 1980 for one of the sport's biggest selection rows. Leonhard Stock skied for Austria in the downhill as a controversial, last-minute preference over world cup winner, Sepp Walcher, despite having suffered torn knee ligaments just three months earlier. It all had a happy ending on Valentine's Day with Stock taking gold and his team-mate, Peter Wirnsberger, winning silver.

Achieving adequate snow and weather conditions for the Games has always been a major concern for organizers. In 1968 helicopters were used for several days to pour 10,000 litres (2200 gallons) of water over the steeper sections of the giant slalom course to make it viable.

The 1952 Games downhill course incorporated the awesome "Steilhang" at Norfjell. This was made possible courtesy of thousands of military personnel who spent their time moving tons of snow from the top of the hill on metal boards, transferring it onto wooden boards in situ, spraying it with water and trampling it down.

Other Games' organizers resorted to moving snow in trucks. Small wonder that Lake Placid finally invested in millions of dollars worth of snow-making machinery in 1980. Temperatures fell so low in Lake Placid that the Austrian coach was forced to heat the inside of Annemarie Moser-Proell's ski boots with a hair dryer to keep her from getting frostbite.

Nearly every Games since 1980 has had similar weather problems although Lillehammer in 1994 was, perhaps, blessed with the best Olympic weather conditions of all time.

Equipment

Alpine skis are broader than their cross country counterparts. They are narrowest at the waist and broadest at the tip or shovel section. The metal edges are sharpened and skiers use the edges to help carve turns in the snow. Skis have a squared off rear end and an upturned tip. The bottom of the ski is flat. This surface is waxed before each race. The choice of wax can be crucial in events where gliding is important as different waxes are appropriate for icy or soft conditions. Skiers and their technicians must decide which wax is the best on the day. A wrong choice can lead to a disastrously slow performance.

The development of skis goes back over 5000 years. Skis started life as simple wooden supports to stop their wearer sinking in the snow. They were not designed to "slide" or travel on.

Modern-type skis originated from the Norwegian province of Telemark whose inhabitants developed a ski which could be steered at the end of the nineteenth century. Just like their current counterparts, these skis were also widest at the front and tapered towards the back but were thinnest at the middle or "waist". This effect meant that the ski had freedom to move as well as elasticity—an important feature when travelling over uneven ground.

A man called Sondre Norheim developed bindings, made out of willow birch, which fastened the toe and the heel. Sticks were used to brake and the Telemarkers soon learnt that beeswax, tar or pitch made the skis run faster.

Different woods, including hickory and ash, were used to create greater elasticity, durability and stability. Workers from the Alpine regions joined the Norwegians at the turn of the century and the secrets were passed on. Austria's Rudolf Lettner introduced metal strip in the middle of skis in 1928. Then came the brass or steel edges that helped in hard conditions. At first these were fastened using thousands of tiny screws until Christian Rubl, the first Lauberhorn downhill winner, experimented with a screwless version.

A German sports journalist, Hannes Marker, who had been injured in a ski accident, invented the safety bindings which, from the 1950s onwards, reduced the number of incidents of broken legs on the ski slopes. These new bindings snapped open when a skier fell.

Up to the 1958 world championships, all skis were made out of wood. Then some experts changed to skis with steel edges and plastic coatings. In 1960, the Frenchman Jean Vuarnet won the first downhill gold using metal skis.

Speeds of over 100kmph are commonplace in today's downhill skiing. So the skis have to have special qualities. Modern composites, including mainly carbon fibre, and moulding methods are used to create the optimum ski by the top manufacturers. And, as modern downhill courses have few changes in direction, the skis can be wider and don't need heavy edges. Downhill skis can vary in length depending on the skill of the wearer. For top downhillers, skis can be up to 2.25m (7ft 4.5in.)long.

On the eve of the 1976 Olympic Winter Games downhill in Innsbruck a ski manufacturer pulled off one of the biggest public relations stunts in Olympic history by announcing that Franz Klammer was going to use their new "wonder skis". The skis had a hole or "spatule" in the tip, supposedly to reduce wind balling under the normal, solid, upturned tip. "There are no wonder skis. Only facts", said Klammer's big rival, Bernhard Russi of France. Klammer went on to dethrone Russi.

Whether the "new" skis played any part, over twenty years ago, is a moot point. However, the difference between winning and losing in Olympic skiing in the 1990s can be measured in terms of mere hundredths of a second . Manufacturers and top racers are constantly searching for a technological edge whether in racing suits, helmets, poles, boots, bindings, ski wax or the skis themselves.

In the downhill, skiers wear an aerodynamic, tight-fitting racing suit with padding to protect the spine and lower back, ski-goggles and a helmet — the latter being compulsory. They also have rigid boots made of specially-moulded, synthetic material with internal padding. These enclose the ankle and the lower shin and are more inclined at the ankle than the normal recreational skier's boot. The boot fits into a binding which fixes both the toe and the heel but automatically snaps open if the skier has a crash.

Ski poles for downhillers and the super-G are aerodynamically curved whilst those for the giant slalom and slalom are straight. Each pole has a "basket" near the tip which prevents the pole from sinking too far into the snow.

Gate poles, originally made of bamboo, are now made of plastic and are equipped with a spring so that they tilt but do not snap back to hit the skier. Skiers in the technical events of the slalom and giant slalom wear "pads" or "guards" on their shins, knees and arms so that they can punch their body through the gates without being hurt. This dramatic technique and new equipment developments are designed to allow the skiers to find the best possible line between gates.

Throughout history there have also been many types of ski boot. Originally, these were often hand-made of leather with a flexible sole, the emphasis being on freedom of movement. This changed in the

1930s when new bindings fixed the toe and heel. Inner and outer double lacing was introduced as well as boots with inner shoes. This was followed by the introduction of buckles.

At the 1964 Olympic Winter Games, boots made of very stiff leather and stronger sides were introduced. These were uncomfortable but paid dividends for the top skiers. Later that decade, plastic boots first came onto the market. Lange, of the USA, manufactured the first plastic-shell boot. There were also boots of fibre-glass and polyurethane. Since that time engineers have worked to overcome a final problem—that of flexibility.

The 'rear-entry' boot, more simple fastenings and new materials for the shell have been amongst the constant improvements.

Rules and Regulations

Great skill, speed and courage are needed to tackle the courses in Alpine skiing in which there are five disciplines with separate races in each for men and women: downhill, super-G, giant slalom, slalom and Alpine combined (a combination of a downhill and a slalom).

The "blue riband" downhill is the fastest event with skiers reaching speeds of over 130kmph (80.5mph). Downhill courses also present the skiers with a number of jumps, flats, turns (marked out by gates) and concave slopes to test various skills. Competitors get the chance to try out the course on a number of training runs and a course inspection. However, on the day of the competition, only one run decides the winner in this event with the fastest time winning. Skiers are given a start number according to their FIS ranking, except the top 15 skiers where start numbers are drawn from a hat. This is because snow conditions can deteriorate quite quickly on the course and the best skiers are given the best conditions in which to race.

The course in Hakuba has a vertical drop of 800–1000m (2625–3281ft) for the men and 500-800m for the women. The men's downhill course is 3km—shorter than usual.

Similarly, the super-G only has one run. The course is not quite so steep as that for the downhill and there are a larger number of gates to negotiate through which both feet must pass. The super-G is a mid-way event between the downhill and the giant slalom.

In the giant slalom and slalom—called the "technical events" because the emphasis is on agility and technique to guide the skier down the course and through a tight series of gates as swiftly as possible—the winner is decided on the aggregate time for two runs. There can be as many as 45-65 gates on a slalom course for women and 55-75 for men. In the Super-G the number of gates is fixed at 10%

of the vertical drop with a minimun of 30 gates for women and 35 for men. The giant slalom site is 12-15% of the vertical drop. Start numbers for the second run are determined according the standings achieved on the first run. Both skis must pass through each gate but competitors can swing their bodies outside the poles.

Nagano Format

Each nation can enter four athletes per event up to a maximum of 22 athletes in total (maximum of 14 males or 14 females) for the Alpine skiing events. To qualify for the Games a skier must have been ranked within the top 500 of the International Ski Federation (FIS) points list in the November preceding the season in which the Games takes place. Many individual countries have stricter regulations than these for inclusion in their nation's team, including selection trials.

If no skier in a particular country has achieved this standard then that nation can enter one male and one female skier in one Alpine event each as long as they have no less than 140 FIS points at the same juncture.

Venue

The downhill and super-G races will take place in the Happo'one ski area on existing courses in Hakuba. These slopes extend eastwards from Mount Karamatsudake and have the Japanese Alps as the backdrop.

The men's downhill will start on the upper part of the Usagiaira course, ending on the Hakuba Kokusai course. The drop will be 840m (2756ft) whilst that for the women will be 780m (2560ft) starting on the upper part of the Kurobishi course and ending on the Sakka course. The super-G races will be on the same courses with lower starting points.

Giant slalom and slalom will be held at Shiga Kogen in Yamanouchi town—both on existing courses. Giant slalom will take place on the slopes of Mount Higashidate whilst the slalom races will be on the slopes of Mount Yakebitai. The latter will also play host to snowboarding during the 1998 Olympic Winter Games.

A Sporting Legend

Karl Schranz (AUT)

Karl Schranz is a trade-mark in skiing. World champion. World cup winner, the last Austrian to do so, back in 1969. He skied into history as the youngest Kandahar-winner (1957) and rose to fame clocking the fastest time at the world championships slalom in Badgastein (1958) — unofficially as a forerunner — thus stealing attention from the winner, Rieder — and the triple Olympic champion, Anton Sailer.

Schranz made headlines for nearly two decades. First as the "Wonderkind", then as the lonely wolf from Arlberg. He is one of the few all time "greats". He won almost everything everywhere but was haunted by bad luck in four Olympic Winter Games.

The heavy favourite always turned out to be a tragic hero. In 1960 (Squaw Valley) he was troubled by injury as well as equipment problems. Four years later Schranz, normally a bundle of energy, was weakened by influenza, taking only giant slalom silver on Tyrolean home-ground.

This, however, was just a prelude to an ironic Olympic fate which climaxed in 1968 and 1972. He smelt Olympic victory in a foggy Grenoble slalom for a few moments as a provisional 1968 winner, climbing to the top of the rostrum and looking down on second-placed Jean Claude Killy. Schranz kissed the gold and showed it to everybody until his celebrations turned sour.

Schranz, who had been allowed by the jury to repeat a first run which was cut short by an almost invisible marshall crossing the course, found himself disqualified for missing a gate on the re-run. He was stripped of the gold he had dreamed of for more than ten years. Delusion and frustration raged alongside a media-battle between France and Austria. But it was "Much Ado about Nothing". No winners, one loser — Schranz.

In Olympic terms it was the beginning of the end, which came in the countdown to the Sapporo Games. After winning the Streif-Double in Kitzbuehel, a rejuvenated 33 year old Schranz felt as strong as in his prime — not only as a skier but as a personality. So he dared to challenge his "best" enemy, the legendary IOC President Avery Brundage. Right ambition, wrong moment. The Eligibility Committee expelled "Karl the Great" from the Winter Games for having breached the amateur status rules, provoking hysterical reactions in his native country. He was not Schranz any more, he played the role of an Olympic martyr, who had fallen victim to a conspiracy. More than 200,000 people took to the streets to demonstrate but could not bring back his lost chance. Schranz and the IOC finally made peace, when Juan Antonio Samaranch later decorated the tragic hero with a special order of merit. It was a symbolic moment but no real compensation.

A Sporting Legend
Franz Klammer (AUT)

If you talk downhill, you must mention Franz Klammer. He is a man of records with 24 world cup downhill victories to his credit. World champion in the combined and world downhill runner-up 1974 (St Moritz), holder of the world record average speed in Schladming (111 kmph 1973), the longest winning-streak, a four times winner on the Streif-course (1975, 1976, 1977, 1984). And last, but not least, Olympic champion in 1976, coming from behind in one of the most thrilling Olympic pursuits to take the gold from the leader and defending champion, Bernhard Russi.

Victory, custom-made, in Innsbruck. Achieved in typical Klammer-manner. More rodeo than skiing. This undaunted "lad" from Mooswald, Carinthia, was Olympic champion and the people's choice. They nicknamed him "Kaiser Franz" as the undisputed no.1. He was always chuckling, always open-minded, rarely bad-tempered. A funny guy from sunny Carinthia — as if made to bring his region's characteristics to life.

But all of a sudden Klammer lost his golden touch. Prior to the 1978 world championships he was twice beaten at Kitzbuehel, his favourite course. This hit him mentally as much as his younger brother Klaus' bad fall which put a promising racer into a wheelchair. Just like his fans, the media wondered how deeply he had been affected by the tragic accident. He missed out on a medal in Garmisch, switched ski-brands and failed to qualify for the Lake Placid Games (1980). Already written off, he made a further change of equipment and then changed his attitude.

After 1173 frustrating days without a win Klammer turned things around, winning the Val d'Isere downhill. A star was reborn momentarily but could not strike gold, or any other medal, again. Every time he reached out, he was pushed back more or less painfully. Considered a hot favourite, Klammer suffered a fall in the very last practice session for the 1982 world championships downhill in Schladming. Nevertheless, he raced but finished well off the podium. He felt helpless in the downhill-lottery of Sarajevo 1984, having chosen the wrong skis. And in his last bid for a golden consolation, a big mistake destroyed his chances in Bormio 1985. At 34, the race against time and the clock was over. Nowadays Klammer only comes out of retirement to star in "legend races" all over America. Still admired for his youthful behaviour and dynamic skiing. Still rodeo-style, what else?

A Sporting Legend

Ingemar Stenmark (SWE)

Ingemar Stenmark, the son of a bulldozer driver in the Swedish Lapland village of Tarnaby, close to the arctic circle, was so dominant in slalom racing from 1976 to '80 that he became known as the "white god" and "Winter's Bjorn Borg".

He won the overall world cup in 1976, '77 and '78 and would have won in 1979 if the format had not been changed to include downhill—an event Stenmark did not race. Going into the 1980 Lake Placid Games the pressure on Stenmark was enormous. He had won bronze in 1976 but that was not deemed good enough by his countrymen. "The pressure I am under does not stop growing", he explained. "For my fans, victory is all that counts. A second place means nothing to them. The Olympic gold medal is the most important thing for me now".

Third after the first run of the giant slalom in Lake Placid, the tension mounted. Stenmark, however, did not disappoint. He re-found his rhythm on the second run to take victory and be congratulated by the King of Sweden who had travelled to America for the Games. Stenmark went on to win the special slalom two days later.

Stenmark's fluid style and single-minded determination were first spotted by coach Hermann Nogler when Stenmark was 13. By the age of 17 he was competing in his first world cup events. Stenmark, a loner who rarely socialized on the circuit, often trained by running alone or with his dog through the forests of Lapland. The superb technician also walked a tightrope and used a unicycle to help perfect his balance.

In Olympic season, Stenmark tapered down his training, methods more associated with the 1990s than the '70s. He always put emphasis on needing to enjoy his skiing, to feel that it was right. After his double gold he said: "I have nothing more to achieve. I ski just for fun now".

A Sporting Legend
Anne-Marie Moser-Proell (AUT)

She entered the world cup circuit as a 14 year-old girl more used to swinging down behind boys and brothers a couple of years her senior. Downhill's Charly Kahr, a famous talent scout, saw her potential on the spot. Here was a young girl who skied like a man. Another Alpine Manager, Hoppichler, followed Kahr's advice and put Annemarie Proell into the Silberkrug race in Badgastein in 1968. Caught by stage fright, the promising but inexperienced teenager lost control of her skiing. Yet, despite a series of falls, Proell did not abandon the race, finishing last, with tears running down her little face.

A year later Proell rose to the top as a runner-up to Isabelle Mir in St Gervais, France. A star was born. Her first world cup medal ever, a bronze in Val Gardena 1970, was a slight disappointment, but was followed by the kind of winning streak that turned the farmer's daughter from Kielnarl, Salzburg, into "La Proell", queen of skiing. She dominated the world cup like nobody had done before.

The Olympic Games, however, were different. In Sapporo in 1972, in the aftermath of the Schranz affair, "La Proell" suffered back to back shock defeats in the downhill and the giant slalom. Not until she took two world titles in St Moritz in 1974 could she restore her reputation as no.1. Then she took everyone by surprise twice. Firstly by secretly marrying Herbert Moser, a service-man, then by announcing her retirement in the countdown to the 1976 Olympic Games, leaving the door open to rumour and speculation. Was she fed up with skiing? Was she pregnant?

It turned out to be just a break, not more. As quickly as she had dropped out, Moser-Proell rejoined the circuit in 1976, struggling at first to regain her old strength but finally turning back the clock to add two more world titles (Garmisch 1978) and three more overall world cups to her impressive collection.

62 victories, six overall world cups and a dozen individual race titles, Moser-Proell was only spurred on by a last goal— going for Olympic gold at White Face Mountain in 1980.

Having won the pre-Olympics in 1979, the red carpet was already rolled out. And Moser-Proell rose to her last chance to crown herself the downhill queen of the mountains, finally fulfilling her Olympic ambitions. Dressed in a traditional outfit, called "dirndl" (Dirndl means young lady) she received the Olympic gold medal on Lake Mirror. What a symbolic sight! No wonder Moser-Proell was full of tears.

A Sporting Legend
Jean Claude Killy (FRA)

If the Austrians were "Kings of the Mountains" in the 1950s, the roaring '60s belonged to French success. Vuarnet, Périllat, Duvillard, Bozon, Bonlieu, Goltschel, Famose etc. were amongst the big names. Honore Bonnet, a true leader, had lifted the French to their highest level ever. But Bonnet also singled out the very best of them all—Jean Claude Killy, son of an Alsace man, turned Savoyarde, who ran a hotel in Val d'Isere.

Jean Claude Killy was a mixture of gambler and dare-devil. Supremely talented and mentally tough enough to overcome setbacks. Darkly handsome with a golden touch. Here was a winner beyond doubt. Bonnet used to predict: "Don't worry, in the end he will get there. He will be a winner." Killy was a skier for whom it was all or nothing. Bonnet just bided his time. He did not have long to wait. The break-through came in Portillo, 1966, where Killy took the world championship downhill in impressive style, a big boost for his self-confidence. Then he won the 1967 overall world cup to develop an aura of invincibility.

But it was on French "home slopes" in Grenoble that he fulfilled a nation's dreams and made history. It was here that he took an Olympic clean sweep. Killy came close to defeat twice, edging an aging Guy Périllat by a mere 0.08 seconds in the downhill, then went on to clinch the giant slalom. In the slalom he was declared the winner after the jury disqualified Austria's Franz Schranz for missing a gate. The decision was controversial but for Killy it was the gold and the triple-crown, driving everybody crazy in France.

Turning professional Killy converted gold into cash. But his fortune didn't bring luck. Killy lost his wife, the famous movie star Danielle Jaubert, who died from cancer. He turned back to sport....and the Olympic Games. He wanted to bring the Olympic Games to his home region of Albertville. Killy became the Bid's front-man. Totally committed, he travelled the world to lobby and orchestrate. And, with the prize won, he took centre stage once more. He handled the organization as smoothly and cleverly as he had once skied. His golden touch returned and his people acclaimed him as their hero again, a living legend.

A Sporting Legend
Anton ("Toni") Sailer (AUT)

Twenty. Tall and handsome. Dark hair, black eyes. A charming winner, idol and matinee hero. The 1956 Olympic Winter Games were struck by lightning in the shape of Toni Sailer— a tinsmith from Kitzbuehel on the gold-rush in Cortina d'Ampezzo. He swept the Alpine races of those Games— the first man ever to do so. Even more, he won by margins nobody would have expected and which nobody could believe. In the giant slalom, the very first race, he was ahead of Anderl Molterer, his compatriot, by more than six seconds. He was truly exceptional.

Sailer was the youngest of Kitzbuehel's "white wonder" team coached by Christian Pravda, himself a world downhill champion and Olympic racer in his own right. In the slalom Sailer edged out Chiharu Igaya. In the famous Tofana downhill, a steep, fast, demanding course running between dangerous-looking rocks, he opened up a big gap from runner-up Raymond Fellay of Switzerland. It was a remarkable victory because at the start Sailer had discovered a tear in his bindings, but kept cool. He repaired the damage within seconds and roared down to his third golden victory.

His sporting performance (triple Olympic gold and four world titles) combined with his good looks to make him an all-round favourite. The golden boy added three more world titles in 1958 before turning to a career as an actor and singer. He starred in at least 50 movies, some of which were box-office hits, especially in Japan, where Toni was worshipped like a god. Trying to be taken seriously as an actor, Sailer even entered the theatre once playing in "Death of a Salesman" in Luzern, Switzerland.

Sailer rejoined the alpine circuit at the end of the 1972 Olympic season as head coach to the Austrians, immediately putting them back on top— with Franz Klammer leading the pack, crowning Sailer's coaching career with gold in Innsbruck in 1976. Sailer, Olympic hero once and forever, will be in Nagano as chairman of the International Federation's Alpine Committee. Toni, from the Tyrol, will no doubt be admired as "Sailer-San".

A Sporting Legend

Rosi Mittermaier (GER)

She was always friendly. Always polite. A paragon of fair play. She embraced winners and consoled losers. Rosi Mittermaier could even laugh when she lost. This healthy Bavarian girl with pink cheeks, freckled face and short, brown hair was the daughter of an innkeeper running a mountain-hut in Winklmoosalm, close to the Austrian border of Salzburg and Tyrol.

Hers was a family of great ski-racers. A promising youngster, Mittermaier seemed to have the potential to follow in the footsteps of Christl Cranz, Mirl Buchner, Heidi Biebl or Barbi Henneberger. Yet as time passed nobody believed her to be a real winner. Her only strength appeared to be the slalom. In the dress rehearsal for the Olympic downhill in 1976, her younger sister, Evi, was runner-up and in the limelight. Mittermaier was last and hugely disappointed. It was a disaster.

So who would, rationally, have expected her to be centre stage in Innsbruck? Yet those Games created a totally different story. Rosi Mittermaier turned things upside down, surfacing as the fairytale heroine of the Alpine races. She had entered the Olympic Games as an underdog and left Innsbruck with two golds and one silver around her neck, coming close to an Olympic sweep in Sailer and Killy fashion. By a glimpse— a mere 12 hundredths of a second— she was beaten by Canadian Kathy Kreiner in the giant slalom, in between her wins in the downhill and the slalom.

Even the Austrians, hungry for more success after Klammer's downhill victory, adopted the Bavarian as their own golden girl. Risen from obscurity to popularity, Rosi Mittermaier retired at the end of that thrilling season. But the book was not yet closed. There was a love-story to come. Rosi married Christian Neureuther, a top ranked slalom racer from Garmisch-Partenkirchen. The "ideal couple" went on to have two children.

Contemporary Heroine

Deborah Compagnoni (ITA)

She cried with joy on the podium, danced at the Italian party and embraced happiness. In Sestriere, at the 1997 world championships, Deborahra Compagnoni was at her best in winning both the slalom and giant slalom titles. The Italian fans went wild and Compagnoni was extrovert as never before. She had peaked for the second time in a career which had been previously plagued by ups and downs.

Compagnoni, the daughter of an inn-keeper in Santa Caterina, Valtellina, near Bormio, first made headlines at home when she won titles and medals at the world junior championships. And, in the early years on the senior circuit, she converted that potential into gold in the 1992 Olympic super-G.

There was a price to pay, however. Her daring, masculine style of skiing lead to a torn cruciate ligament and put her out for almost a year. This was followed by the occasional kidney problem. Returning to form in 1994, she won the giant slalom at the Lillehammer Olympic Winter Games, followed by the world giant slalom title in 1996 in Sierra Nevada.

Only in Sestriere a year later, with her double gold, did Debbie risk taking the spotlight from her more illustrious Italian team-mate, Alberto Tomba. Not that he would have minded. Tomba had allowed the youngster to join his training camps early in her career. Obviously, she had watched, listened and learnt.

Contemporary Hero

Alberto Tomba (ITA)

They asked who on earth he was when Alberto Tomba won a bronze medal in the giant slalom at the 1987 world championships in Crans Montana. Tomba answered in his own way. The medal, it turned out, was only a curtain raiser for a subsequent series of world cup victories. And they were victories generated from, in skiing terms, an outrageously flamboyant lifestyle. Nobody had ever seen the like before. Tomba became "Tomba la Bomba".

This newcomer proved himself a great skier. He was also loud, charming, a media darling and sex symbol. Before long he was a heavyweight on the scene in more senses than one. The atmosphere on slalom courses changed overnight when the squarely-built Italian appeared. And the louder the din from the fans the more to his liking. Often trailing after the first run, he could turn things on their head in the second.

Tomba's rise coincided with the decline of former slalom king, Ingemar Stenmark of Sweden. The Italian burst onto the Olympic scene by winning two golds in Calgary in 1988. He followed with a gold and two silvers in the slaloms of Albertville and Lillehammer respectively.

Yet he always seemed to be off form in the world championships. It was not until 1996, in Sierra Nevada, that he won two titles as well as angering his hosts with some ill-judged pronouncements.

In the pre-Olympic season, Tomba missed more world cups than he raced. Nonetheless, he won in Schladming, took silver in Kitzbuehel and Madonna as well as bronze in the Sestriere world championships. He may not be as good as he was, but as long as Tomba races you cannot write him off.

Contemporary Hero
Michael von Gruenigen (SUI)

When Michael von Gruenigen joined the world cup circuit he was known as the brother of Christine von Gruenigen, already an established name. Although a consistent slalom racer, he was not considered good enough to win a major medal.

Dramatically, this orphan who was brought up by his uncle, has become the world no.1 in giant slalom. His stylishly outstanding and flawless performances have sometimes left his opponents speechless. In the last couple of years von Gruenigen has won back-to-back world cup overall trophies and the 1997 world giant slalom title—winning the latter by a large margin. Von Gruenigen has created a style which few can imitate.

More unusually, in Sestriere, this quiet family man used his new-found status to attack Tomba for cherry-picking during the preceding world cup season. "If everybody did the same, the world cup would not survive. Without its stars, it would collapse. It is unfair", he said. Since the outburst von Gruenigen has returned to the world he knows best— that of gentle wins rather than harsh words.

A Contemporary Heroine

Pernilla Wiberg (SWE)

There was a time when Alpine skiing was not a major consideration in Sweden. This was the cradle of top cross country skiers like Gunde Swan and Thomas Wassberg. Sweden had no history in Alpine events. There were no role models.

All that changed two decades ago with Ingemar Stenmark. The reserved but gifted skier took more titles than anyone else. Then came Pernilla Wiberg to emulate his skiing if not his personality. This quicksilver, outspoken, emotional, friendly and funny girl stormed to the top of the sport in aggressive style. She was Swedish dynamite attacking the gates with self-confidence and often coming from behind.

After a promising world cup tour, Wiberg blossomed at the 1992 Olympic Winter Games in Albertville, winning giant slalom gold. Two years later at the Lillehammer Games she won again, twice— in the slalom and the combined.

In the 1996/'97 pre-Olympic season, Wiberg finally took a long-desired overall world cup title as well as two individual victories. Equally, she put some of the specialists to shame by winning her first downhill title in Vail. But it is not enough to feed her hunger and when Wiberg sets specific goals she is almost unstoppable.

She now has her skiing sights set on Nagano. However, Wiberg also has talent in a different direction. She has risen up the Swedish pop charts as fast as she skis downhill. Her bright voice and personality have won over huge audiences at live events. Just as in her skiing, this stocky Swede, is the centre of attention.

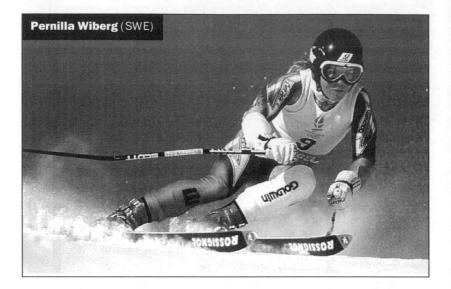

Pernilla Wiberg (SWE)

<table>
<tr><td>NAGANO SCHEDULE</td><td>Alpine Skiing</td></tr>
</table>

Venue: H1=Happo'one, course1; H2=Happo'one, course 2; Y=Mt Yakebitai; H=Mt Higashidate

Date	Description	Round	Start	Finish	Venue
8 Feb	Downhill (m)		10:15	12:15	H1
9 Feb	Combined downhill (m)		10:15	12:15	H1
10 Feb	Super-G (w)		10:15	11:45	H2
11 Feb	Combined slalom (m)		9:30	11:00	H1
			13:00	14:00	
13 Feb	Super-G (m)		10:15	12:15	H1
14 Feb	Downhill (w)		10:15	11:45	H2
15 Feb	Combined downhill (w)		10:15	11:45	H1
17 Feb	Combined slalom (w)		9:30	11:00	H1
			13:00	14:00	
18 Feb	Giant slalom (m)		9:30	11:30	H2
			13:30	15:30	
19 Feb	Slalom (w)		9:30	11:00	H
			13:00	14:00	
20 Feb	Giant slalom (w)		9:30	11:00	H2
			13:00	14:30	
21 Feb	Slalom (m)		9:30	11:30	Y
			13:00	14:30	

MEDALLISTS (by nation)

Country	Gold		Silver		Bronze		Total
	m	w	m	w	m	w	
AUT	12	9	12	11	14	9	67
SUI	6	11	10	6	8	6	47
FRA	8	3	4	7	7	6	35
ITA	7	3	5	1	2	4	22
USA	2	6	3	9	1	3	24
FRG	-	5	2	6	1	4	18
GER	3	2	1	2	-	1	9
NOR	4	-	3	-	5	1	13
CAN	-	4	-	1	2	3	10
SWE	2	2	-	-	3	-	7
LIE	-	2	1	1	3	2	9
ESP	1	-	-	-	-	1	2
YUG	-	-	1	1	-	-	2
LUX	-	-	2	-	-	-	2
JPN	-	-	1	-	-	-	1
NZL	-	-	-	1	-	-	1
SLO	-	-	-	-	1	2	3
CZE	-	-	-	-	-	1	1
URS	-	-	-	-	-	1	1

MEDALLISTS

Alpine Skiing [Men]

Year	Gold	Country	Points	Silver	Country	Points	Bronze	Country	Points

Downhill

Year	Gold	Country	Time	Silver	Country	Time	Bronze	Country	Time
1948	Henri Oreiller	FRA	2:55.0	Franz Gabl	AUT	2:59.1	Carl Molitor	SUI	3:00.3
							Rolf Olinger	SUI	3:00.3
1952	Zeno Colo	ITA	2:30.8	Othmar Schneider	AUT	2:32.0	Christian Pravda	AUT	2:32.4
1956	Anton Sailer	AUT	2:52.2	Raymond Fellay	SUI	2:55.7	Andreas Molterer	AUT	2:56.2
1960	Jean Vuarnet	FRA	2:06.0	Hanspeter Lanig	GER	2:06.5	Guy Périllat	FRA	2:06.9
1964	Egon Zimmermann	AUT	2:18.16	Leo Lacroix	FRA	2:18.90	Wolfgang Bartels	GER	2:19.48
1968	Jean-Claude Killy	FRA	1:59.85	Guy Périllat	FRA	1:59.93	Daniel Daetwyler	SUI	2:00.32
1972	Bernhard Russi	SUI	1:51.43	Roland Collombin	SUI	1:52.07	Heinrich Messner	AUT	1:52.40
1976	Franz Klammer	AUT	1:45.73	Bernhard Russi	SUI	1:46.06	Herbert Plank	ITA	1:46.59
1980	Leonhard Stock	AUT	1:45.50	Peter Wirnsberger	AUT	1:46.12	Steve Podborski	CAN	1:46.62
1984	William Johnson	USA	1:45.59	Peter Mueller	SUI	1:45.86	Anton Steiner	AUT	1:45.95
1988	Pirmin Zurbriggen	SUI	1:59.63	Peter Mueller	SUI	2:00.14	Franck Piccard	FRA	2:01.24
1992	Patrick Ortlieb	AUT	1:50.37	Franck Piccard	FRA	1:50.42	Guenther Mader	AUT	1:50.47
1994	Tommy Moe	USA	1:45.75	Kjetil Aamodt	NOR	1:45.79	Edward Podivinsky	CAN	1:45.87

Year	Gold	Country	Points	Silver	Country	Points	Bronze	Country	Points

Slalom

Year	Gold	Country	Points	Silver	Country	Points	Bronze	Country	Points
1948	Edi Reinalter	SUI	2:10.3	James Couttet	FRA	2:10.8	Henri Oreiller	FRA	2:12.8
1952	Othmar Schneider	AUT	2:00.0	Stein Eriksen	NOR	2:01.2	Guttorm Berge	NOR	2:01.7
1956	Anton Sailer	AUT	3:14.7	Chiharu Igaya	JPN	3:18.7	Stig Sollander	SWE	3:20.2
1960	Ernst Hinterseer	AUT	2:08.9	Mathias Leitner	AUT	2:10.3	Charles Bozon	FRA	2:10.4
1964	Josef Stiegler	AUT	2:21.13	William Kidd	USA	2:21.27	James Heuga	USA	2:21.52
1968	Jean-Claude Killy	FRA	1:39.73	Herbert Huber	AUT	1:39.82	Alfred Matt	AUT	1:40.09
1972	Francisco Ochoa	ESP	1:49.27	Gustav Thöeni	ITA	1:50.28	Roland Thoeni	ITA	1:50.30
1976	Piero Gros	ITA	2:03.29	Gustavo Thoni	ITA	2:03.73	Willy Frommelt	LIE	2:04.28
1980	Ingemar Stenmark	SWE	1:44.26	Phillip Mahre	USA	1:44.76	Jacques Lüthy	SUI	1:45.06
1984	Phillip Mahre	USA	1:39.41	Steven Mahre	USA	1:39.62	Didier Bouvet	FRA	1:40.20
1988	Alberto Tomba	ITA	1:39.47	Frank Woerndl	FRG	1:39.53	Paul Frommelt	LIE	1:39.84
1992	Finn Jagge	NOR	1:44.39	Alberto Tomba	ITA	1:44.67	Michael Tritscher	AUT	1:44.85
1994	Thomas Stangassinger	AUT	2:02.02	Alberto Tomba	ITA	2:02.17	Jure Kosir	SLO	2:02.53

Giant Slalom

Year	Gold	Country	Points	Silver	Country	Points	Bronze	Country	Points
1952	Stein Eriksen	NOR	2:25.0	Christian Pravda	AUT	2:26.9	Toni Spiess	AUT	2:28.8
1956	Anton Sailer	AUT	3:00.1	Andreas Molterer	AUT	3:06.3	Walter Schuster	AUT	3:07.2
1960	Roger Staub	SUI	1:48.3	Josef Stiegler	AUT	1:48.7	Ernst Hinterseer	AUT	1:49.1
1964	François Bonlieu	FRA	1:46.71	Karl Schranz	AUT	1:47.09	Josef Stiegler	AUT	1:48.05
1968	Jean-Claude Killy	FRA	3:29.28	Willy Favre	SUI	3:31.50	Heinrich Messner	AUT	3:31.83
1972	Gustav Thoeni	ITA	3:09.62	Edmund Bruggmann	SUI	3:10.75	Werner Mattle	SUI	3:10.99
1976	Heini Hemmi	SUI	3:26.97	Ernst Good	SUi	3:27.17	Ingemar Stenmark	SWE	3:27.41
1980	Ingemar Stenmark	SWE	2:40.74	Andreas Wenzel	LIE	2:41.49	Hans Enn	AUT	2:42.51
1984	Max Julen	SUI	2:41.18	Jurij Franko	YUG	2:41.41	Andreas Wenzel	LIE	2:41.75
1988	Alberto Tomba	ITA	2:06.37	Hubert Strolz	AUT	2:07.41	Pirmin Zurbriggen	SUI	2:08.39
1992	Alberto Tomba	ITA	2:06.98	Marc Girardelli	LUX	2:07.30	Kjetil Aamodt	NOR	2:07.82
1994	Markus Wasmeier	GER	2:52.46	Urs Kaelin	SUI	2:52.48	Christian Mayer	AUT	2:52.58

Super Giant Slalom (Super-G)

Year	Gold	Country	Points	Silver	Country	Points	Bronze	Country	Points
1988	Franck Piccard	FRA	1:39.66	Helmut Mayer	AUT	1:40.96	Lars-Borje Eriksson	SWE	1:41.08
1992	Kjetil Aamodt	NOR	1:13.04	Marc Girardelli	LUX	1:13.77	Jan Thorsen	NOR	1:13.83
1994	Markus Wasmeier	GER	1:32.53	Tommy Moe	USA	1:32.61	Kjetil Aamodt	NOT	1:32.93

Alpine Combined (Downhill and Slalom)

Year	Gold	Country	Points	Silver	Country	Points	Bronze	Country	Points
1936	Franz Pfnür	GER	99.25 pts	Gustav Lantschner	GER	96.26 pts	Emile Allais	FRA	94.69
1948	Henri Oreiller	FRA	3.27 pts	Karl Molitor	SUI	6.44 pts	James Couttet	FRA	6.95 pts
1988	Hubert Strolz	AUT	36.55 pts	Bernhard Gstrein	AUT	43.45 pts	Paul Accola	SUI	48.24 pts
1992	Josef Polig	ITA	14.58	Gianfranco Martin	ITA	14.9	Steve Locher	SUI	18.16
1994	Lasse Kjus	NOR	3:17.53	Kjetil Aamodt	NOT	3:18.55	Christian Nilsen	NOT	3:19.14

MEDALLISTS — Alpine Skiing [Women]

Downhill

Year	Gold	Country	Points	Silver	Country	Points	Bronze	Country	Points
1948	Hedy Schlunegger	SUI	2:28.3	Trud Beiser	AUT	2:29.1	Rese Hammerer	AUT	2:30.2
1952	Trude Beiser-Jochum	AUT	1:47.1	Annemarie Buchner	GER	1:48.0	Giuliana Minuzzo	ITA	1:49.0
1956	Madeleine Berthod	SUI	1:40.7	Frieda Dänzer	SUI	1:45.4	Lucile Wheeler	CAN	1:45.0
1960	Heidi Biebl	GER	1:37.6	Penpelope Pitou	USA	1:38.6	Traudi Hecher	AUT	1:38.9
1964	Christl Haas	AUT	1:55.39	Edith Zimmermann	AUT	1:56.42	Traudl Hecher	AUT	1:56.66

Year	Gold	Country	Points	Silver	Country	Points	Bronze	Country	Points
1968	Olga Pall	AUT	1:40.87	Isabelle Mir	FRA	1:41.33	Christl Haas	AUT	1:41.41
1972	Marie-Thérèse Nadig	SUI	1:36.68	Anne-Marie Proell	AUT	1:37.00	Susan Corrock	USA	1:37.68
1976	Rosi Mittermaier	FRG	1:46.16	Brigitte Totschnigg	AUT	1:46.68	Cynthia Nelson	USA	1:47.50
1980	Anne-Marie Moser-Proell	AUT	1:37.52	Hanni Wenzel	LIE	1:38.22	Marie-Therese Nadig	SUI	1:38.36
1984	Michela Figini	SUI	1:13.36	Maria Walliser	SUI	1:13.41	Olga Charvatova	CZE	1:13.53
1988	Marina Kiehl	FRG	1:25.86	Brigitte Oertli	SUI	1:26.61	Karen Percy	CAN	1:26.62
1992	Kerrin Lee-Gartner	CAN	1:52.55	Hilary Lindh	USA	1:52.61	Veronika Wallinger	AUT	1:52.64
1994	Katja Seizinger	GER	1:35.93	Picabo Street	USA	1:36.59	Isolde Kostner	ITA	1:36.85

Slalom

Year	Gold	Country	Points	Silver	Country	Points	Bronze	Country	Points
1948	Gretchen Frazer	USA	1:57.2	Antoinette Meyer	SUI	1:57.7	Erika Mahringer	AUT	1:58.0
1952	Andrea Mead Lawrence	USA	2:10.6	Ossi Reichert	GER	2:11.4	Annemarie Buchner	GER	2:13.3
1956	Renée Colliard	SUI	1:52.3	Regina Schoepf	AUT	1:55.4	Evgeni Sidorova	URS	1:56.7
1960	Anne Heggtveit	CAN	1:49.6	Betsy Snite	USA	1:52.9	B Hennerberger	GER	1:56.6
1964	Christine Goitschel	FRA	1:29.86	Marielle Goitschel	FRA	1:30.77	Jean Saubert	USA	1:31.36
1968	Marielle Goitschel	FRA	1:25.86	Nancy Greene	CAN	1:26.15	Annie Famose	FRA	1:27.89
1972	Barbara Cochran	USA	1:31.24	Daniele Debernard	FRA	1:31.26	Florence Steurer	FRA	1:32.69
1976	Rosi Mittermaier	GER	1:30.54	Claudia Giordani	ITA	1:30.87	Hanny Wenzel	LIE	1:32.20
1980	Hanni Wenzel	LIE	1:25.09	Christa Kinshofer	FRG	1:26.50	Erika Hess	SUI	1:27.89
1984	Paolette Magoni	ITA	1:36.47	Perrine Pelen	FRA	1:37.38	Ursula Konszett	LIE	1:37.50
1988	Vreni Schneider	SUI	1:36.69	Mateja Svet	YUG	1:38.37	Christa Kinshofer-Guetlein	FRG	1:38.40
1992	Petra Kronberger	AUT	1:32.68	Annelise Coberger	NZL	1:33.10	Blanca Fernandez Ochoa	ESP	1:33.35
1994	Vreni Schneider	SUI	1:56.01	Elfriede Eder	AUT	1:56.35	Katja Koren	SLO	1:56.61

Giant Slalom

Year	Gold	Country	Points	Silver	Country	Points	Bronze	Country	Points
1952	Andrea Mead Lawrence	USA	2:06.8	Dagmar Rom	AUT	2:09.0	Annemarie Buchner	GER	2:10.0
1956	Ossi Reichert	GER	1:56.5	Josefine Frandl	AUT	1:57.8	Dorothea Hochleitner	AUT	1:58.2
1960	Yvonne Ruegg	SUI	1:39.9	Penelope Pitou	USA	1:40.0	Giuliano Chenal Minuzzo		ITA
1:40.2									
1964	Marielle Goitschel	FRA	1:52.24	Christine Goitschel	FRA	1:53.11	Jean Saubert	USA	1:53.11
1968	Nancy Greene	CAN	1:51.97	Annie Famose	FRA	1:54.61	Fernande Bochatay	SUI	1:54.74
1972	Marie-Thérèse Nadig	SUI	1.29.90	Anne-Marie Proell	AUT	1:30.75	Wiltrud Drexel	AUT	1:32.35
1976	Kathy Kreiner	CAN	1:29.13	Rosi Mittermaier	FRG	1:29.25	Daniele Debernard	FRA	1:29.95
1980	Hanni Wenzel	LIE	2:41.66	Irene Epple	FRG	2:42.12	Perrine Pelen	FRA	2:42.41
1984	Debbie Armstrong	USA	2:20.98	Christin Cooper	USA	2:21.38	Perrine Pelen	FRA	2:21.40
1988	Vreni Schneider	SUI	2:06.49	Christa Kinshofer-Guetlein	FRG	2:07.42	Maria Walliser	SUI	2:07.72
1992	Pernilla Wiberg	SWE	2:12.74	Diann Roffe	USA	2:13.71	Anita Wachter	AUT	
1994	Deborah Compagnoni	ITA	2:30.97	Martina Ertl	GER	2:32.19	Vreni Schneider	SUI	2:32.97

Super Giant Slalom

Year	Gold	Country	Points	Silver	Country	Points	Bronze	Country	Points
1988	Sigrid Wolf	AUT	1:19.03	Michela Figini	SUI	1:20.03	Karen Percy	CAN	1:20.29
1992	Deborah Compagnoni	ITA	1:21.22	Carole Merle	FRA	1:22.63	Katja Seizinger	GER	1:23.19
1994	Diann Roffe	USA	1:22.15	Svetlana Gladischeva	URS	1:22.44	Isolde Kostner	ITA	1:22.45

Alpine Combined (Downhill & Slalom)

Year	Gold	Country	Points	Silver	Country	Points	Bronze	Country	Points
1936	Christel Cranz	GER	97.06 pts	Käthe Grasegger	GER	95.26 pts	Laila Schou-Nilsen	NOR	93.48 pts
1948	Trude Beiser	AUT	6.58 pts	Gretchen Frazer	USA	6.95 pts	Erika Mahringer	AUT	7.04 pts
1988	Anita Wachter	AUT	29.25 pts	Brigitte Oertli	SUI	29.48 pts	Maria Walliser	SUI	51.28 pts
1992	Petra Kronberbger	AUT	2.55	Anita Wachter	AUT	19.39	Florence Masnada	FRA	21.38
1994	Pernilla Wiberg	SWE	3:05.16	Vreni Schneider	SUI	3:05.29	Alenka Dovzan	SLO	3:06.64

CROSS-COUNTRY SKIING

Can Dæhlie make history?

by Tor Karlsen

Who can challenge Norway's Bjørn Dæhlie? Who can challenge Elena Valbe of Russia? Perhaps, more importantly, who can beat them? These Olympics can make Bjørn Dæhlie one of the greatest winter Olympians of all time. And he knows it. He shared the cross-country crown with Vegard Ulvang in Albertville in 1992. He kept it alone in Lillehammer two years later. In the world championships in Trondheim last winter, he was also the King. And as if to prove that he is the best cross-country skier of all time, he won the world cup, too. He dethroned Gunde Svan, the legendary Swede, once and for all.

To realize his ambitions Dæhlie will first have to fight against his old rivals. Men such as Vladimir Smirnov, Silvio Fauner, Mika Myllylae and, maybe, his fellow countryman Thomas Alsgaard.

Vladimir Smirnov of Kazakhstan has announced that this is his last season. He only has one Olympic gold and, of course, he wants to end his long and distinguished career with one or two more. On the other hand, he had a disappointing 1996/'97 season. Success eluded him at the world championships. In the world cup, he was ranked no. 9. Now the question is whether he can find the same form that made him so outstanding at the 1995 world championships in Thunder Bay.

Silvio Fauner, like Vladimir Smirnov, was not good last winter. In the world cup he finished at no.5. His Italian team-mate Fulvio Valbusa was the best Italian skier in 1996/'97 and was ranked third in the world cup. He could possibly be the strongest Italian in Nagano.

Contrary to Smirnov and Fauner, Mika Myllyla of Finland had a successful season last year. He was overall world cup silver medallist and he won the 50km gold medal in the world championship. He has been making great progress each year rising from 34th on the world cup lists in 1993 to the top three in 1997. He and his team-mate, Jari Isometsa, are both well-prepared for the Games in Nagano.

The Norwegian Thomas Alsgaard experienced some problems after he won the 30km free technique in Lillehammer. But in Trondheim, at the worlds, he was back after injuries and illness. Alsgaard is an outstanding free technician, and if he is in the right physical shape he may be a dangerous rival.

Looking at the results last winter, Italy's Stefania Belmondo will be the toughest rival for Elena Valbe. She finished second in the world cup. Katerina Neumannova of Russia had some very good races last season, but the strongest opponents for Valbe may be the other Russian girls. Nina Gavriluk, Olga Danilova and Larissa Lazutina are the top contenders.

The tracks in Nagano are some of the toughest ever in a major international championship. As Dæhlie says: "They are the toughest tracks I have ever raced. The uphills are long and continuous and very steep. The downhills are very tough too. In Lillehammer you could rest when going downhill. In Nagano you have to work as if you were going down an Alpine slope".

Who will benefit from this? A Smirnov in good shape or the Italians in super shape. But of course Dæhlie is a very strong climber himself.

Originally there was one major problem for the cross-country skiers in Nagano—the temperature. In a very short time, as the sun starts to warm, the temperature increases rapidly. The athletes drawn later in the starting order would have had to race under completely different conditions than their earlier counterparts. After some pressure the organizers agreed to start the competition earlier, and now the conditions will be much the same for all athletes. May the best racers win.

Background

Cross-country events carried skiing's banner at the early editions of the Olympic Winter Games despite opposition from some of the leading "Nordic" ski nations who felt it would detract from their own international events.

Two races—an 18km and a 50km—appeared on the programme of the inaugural Olympic Games in Chamonix in 1924. There was also a cross-country race as part of the Nordic Combined event in Chamonix. Ski-jumping completed the programme that year. Alpine skiing did not make its Olympic debut until 1936.

Gradually the men's programme of cross-country skiing at the Games has been extended to reach a total of four individual races and one relay. Women first participated in Olympic cross-country skiing as late as the Oslo Games of 1952 with a lone 10km race. A relay consisting of three 5km legs was added at the next Games. Very slowly, over the ensuing years, individual races at 5km, 15km and 30km have been added to the women's programme. And the modern-day relay has four participants rather than three.

Nordic or cross-country skiing is a direct competitive descendant of mankind's basic need to travel across snowy winter landscapes — either to hunt or to trade. The Olympic-style discipline involves racing over undulating terrain along a series of prepared tracks. Skiers set off at intervals and race against the clock rather than against each other, with the exception of the pursuit-style races.

This is one of the toughest disciplines of the Olympic Winter Games. It requires supreme fitness of a type akin to distance runners. Scandinavian and later Soviet bloc, athletes have dominated the sport for much of its history. Although there have been some exceptions.

On February 7, 1968, an Italian called Franco Nones, coached by a Swede, won the 30km cross-country ski race at the Olympic Winter Games in Grenoble. The victory was remarkable in that it marked the first time that a Nordic skiing race had been won by a non-Scandinavian at the Games. Sweden's Toini Gustafsson won the 5km and 10km individual golds for women at those Games as well as a relay silver. In 1976 American William Koch won a silver medal in the 30km race — the first American to win a cross-country medal of any type.

However, there have been occasions when even the mighty nations like Norway have faltered. In 1992 Vegard Ulvang ended an Olympic gold medal drought for Norway which had lasted 16 years by winning the 30km race.

In 1932 at Lake Placid the caterers took the classic 50km race seriously. Feeding stations along the course were stocked with oatmeal, gruel, oranges, water, lemons, rye bread, warm milk, raw eggs, warm tea, bananas, cold beefsteak and warm beef stock. What would today's sports scientists make of that?

In 1952 the Olympic torch relay brought the Olympic flame to the opening ceremony from Morgedal, Norway, rather than from Greece. The Morgedal valley is considered the cradle of competitive skiing. It was also the home of Thorleif Haug who won three golds and a bronze at the 1924 Olympic Winter Games.

Cortina D'Ampezzo in 1956 marked the entry of Soviet athletes into cross-country skiing for the first time at the Olympic Winter Games with their women taking first and second place in the 10km race. Since that date they — as well as those representing the

Bjorn Daehlie (NOR) on his way to a second gold in 1944

Vladimir Smirnov (URS) cheered on to 1994 50km gold

individual constituent nations after the break-up of the Soviet Union —have been successful in this sport at the Games. Nikolai Zimyatov won four golds. But Raissa Smetanina is one of the greatest with four individual golds over a remarkable, extended career between 1976 and 1992. Her compatriot Liubov Egorova won more golds—six—but now has a doping question-mark over her Olympic achievements after last year's world championships.

Perhaps the greatest cross-county Olympic accolades, however, belong to two Swedes. The first, Sixten Jernberg, won four golds, three silver and two bronze between 1956 and 1964—the last of these individually came when 12,000 spectators cheered him home at the end of the 50km marathon at Seefeld during the 1964 Olympic Winter Games of Innsbruck. At those Games he went on to win the relay gold.

The second, Gunde Svan, won two individual golds, a silver and a bronze. He will be remembered for his pre-race preparation and the way in which he was able to create such a psychological edge over his opponents. Now Norway's Bjørn Dæhlie has taken over the mantle of the most successful skier and will be competing in Nagano to extend his tally of five golds and three silver.

The 1984 Olympic Winter Games was marked by the performance of Finland's Marja-Liisa Haemalainen. She won a record three individual medals in one Games.

Cross-country skiing is generally well-known for its sportsmanship. In 1994 few will forget the sea of Norwegian flags and the roar of the crowd in Lillehammer as they willed Kazakhstan's Vladimir Smirnov across the line in the classic 50km race on the last day. Smirnov, one of the sport's consistently great and popular skiers, had never won an Olympic gold medal. With his advancing years, the knowledgeable crowd sensed that it might be his last hope. And they were prepared to give him all the support he needed even if it meant him beating one of their own.

Olav Oekern from Baerum was a good international skier, aged 28, in 1940. However, world war interrupted his career. He was sent to a German concentration camp and was skeletal on his return in 1945. At the 1948 Olympic Winter Games in St Moritz he finished 13th in the 18km and in 1952 he was 4th in the 50km race. The race was won by Finland's Veikko Hakulinen, a forestry worker, who almost missed the Games having injured a finger then badly cut his leg with an axe during the preceding summer.

Equipment

Cross-country skis are the lightest and slimmest of skis. Like all skis, the Nordic ski curves up at the tip. It is thicker and arched at the mid-section, or waist. A groove on the underside helps to keep the ski straight on the downhill sections of the trails. Skiers using the free technique (see below) use shorter skis and longer poles than those skiing in the classical fashion.

Competitors and their technicians must decide on the optimum wax for the base of their skis just as in all other skiing disciplines. In Nagano, temperatures will rise rapidly during the morning and, unlike European venues, there will be relatively high humidity.

There are specialized cross-country skiing boots which clip into bindings on the ski by the toe only. This leaves the heel free to move. The boots come up over the ankle but are not as rigid as alpine ski boots. Most skiers wear some form of head-gear because of the extreme cold in which they often compete. They also often wear sunglasses to avoid snow-blindness.

Rules and Regulations

Cross-country races take place in demanding terrain with the fastest skier winning the race. In Nagano there will be two types of race. Competitors in the more traditional events will set off at intervals of 30 seconds and race against the clock with the fastest time winning the race. In these events, coaches are permitted to run alongside their athletes at various stages to tell them the time they are making and where they stand in the rankings.

However, in two events, the men's 15km free technique and the women's 10km free technique, there will be a "pursuit format". This means that the race will take part in two sections. The men will begin by racing 10km in a classical style on the first day whilst the women will race 5km in classical style. At the end of the first section competitors are allotted starting times for the next day according to the rank they achieved on the first day, going off at relevant intervals. With the fastest skier starting first, the first person to cross the line wins. The second day's racing is in free technique.

The two different types of skiing style are "classical" and "free technique". The classical style is where skiers maintain their skis in parallel lines (except on the uphill stretches where a herringbone technique is applied) within the track whilst there is also a newer and faster, "skating" style of skiing which was developed in the late 1970s and is called the "free technique". The first real success for this skating style was in 1976 when American Bill Koch won a silver medal.

Interestingly, when a winter sports specialist was trying to explain skiing to de Courbertin in 1893 he said it was like "skating on snow". In Nagano, the classical style will be obligatory in the men's 10km and 30km and in the women's 5km and 15km. Two legs of each relay will also be in the classical style as will the first portion of the "pursuit" events. Skiers must use the free technique in all other events and sections of the relays.

One of the most exciting spectacles at the Games is the start of the cross-country relays. Instead of the staggered starts of the individual races, competitors on the first leg of each relay take part in a mass start, sprinting to try and establish a lead before they hand over to the next racer.

Nagano Format

There are ten events on the 1998 Olympic Winter Games cross-country skiing programme: men's 10km classic, 15km free/pursuit, 30km classic, 50km free and 4x10km relay; women's 5km classic, 10km free/pursuit, 15km classic, 30km free and 4x5km relay.

Each nation will be permitted a total of 28 athletes in the three Nordic events (cross-country, ski jumping and Nordic combined) including a maximum of 20 male and 10 female athletes. A country may enter up to four skiers per individual event provided that they are suitably qualified.

To achieve Nagano selection a cross-country skier must have gained at least one result better than 100 FIS (International Skiing Federation) points. If a nation has no skiers qualified under this rule, then one male and one female athlete may participate in the Games provided they have competed in at least five FIS-sanctioned events in the year preceding the Games and have scored some FIS points.

Venue

Cross-country skiing competition at the 1998 Olympic Winter Games will take place in Kamishiro to the east of Hakuba. There are three 5km circuits which will be used in combination for the varying events. A grandstand area has been constructed from which spectators will be able to see the start and finish of races as well as some interim sections.

A Contemporary Hero

Vladimir Smirnov (URS & KAZ)

Vladimir Smirnov, born on 7 March, 1964, in Sjutsjinsk, Kazakhstan, is one of the most popular cross-country skiers in the world. For many years his destiny was to be the second best. Apart from the 30km in the world championships in Lahti 1989, he never seemed to succeed in the big events. In the world championships, in Falun in 1993, he was momentarily announced as the winner of the 15km but a minute later was usurped by Bjørn Dæhlie of Norway. Then came the Olympic Games in Lillehammer and his favourite distance, the 30km. Smirnov had been preparing for this distance a whole year. Not for silver or for bronze but for gold. Yet he failed. He finished 10th and he was very disappointed. He thought it was the end. He did not want to ski any more. Only his wife, Valentina, gave him strength. She told him to pull himself together as it was only the first race. He listened to her. A couple of days later he got a silver medal at 10km. That gave him renewed strength and a new hope for gold. Three days later, he got another silver medal in the 15km pursuit start. That was steadily improving. And at last he succeeded. The Norwegian crowd, ten thousands of people round the track, were cheering him as if he was really a Norwegian. At last he proved that he was a winner. A year later, in Thunder Bay, he won three individual gold medals in the world championships.

A Contemporary Hero

Bjørn Dæhlie (NOR)

In Nagano Bjørn Dæhlie, born on 19 June 1967, has the chance to be the greatest Winter Olympian of all time. So far he has won four individual gold and two individual silver medals. The greatest of all time is speedskater Lidya Skoblikova who won six gold medals. Last winter Bjørn Dæhlie passed Gunde Svan as the greatest cross-country skier of all time.

His mother and father did not think that he would be the greatest skier when he was a little child. He did not like skiing at all. When the family wanted to ski in winter time, Dæhlie preferred to sit on a sledge. When he became interested in skiing, he started with ski jumping. His father was his trainer, but after a while Dæhlie sacked him from the job for not being ambitious enough for his son. "You are satisfied as long as a I am landing OK", chided Dæhlie.

At 14 Dæhlie quit ski jumping. He was afraid of the big hills. Suddenly, he found cross-country skiing more interesting and he soon revealed his great talent for the sport.

His first world cup race was in Holmenkollen, at 50km, in 1986 when he was still a junior. He finished 26th in that race. The first time he represented Norway was in December 1987. He finished 66th and thought that he would never be as good as the Swede Gunde Svan.

On 23 December, 1997, Dæhlie proved that he was even greater than Svan. On this day in Kiruna, Sweden, Dæhlie won his 31st world cup—2,541 days after his first victory in the world cup in Salt Lake City, 1989. Gunde's career ended with 30 world cup victories.

Dæhlie has won the world cup four times—in 1992, '93, '96 and '97. Of course, he is the biggest favourite in Nagano. He was number one in the Olympic Games in Albertville and in Lillehammer two years later. And he was the greatest at the world championships in Trondheim last year. Who can beat him in Nagano?

A Sporting Legend

Gunde Svan (SWE)

Gunde Svan, born on 12 January, 1962, was the King of cross-country skiing until Bjørn Dæhlie of Norway surpassed him last season. Svan introduced a new era in the sport. He understood how important details were and that small details could make the distinction between first and second best. Mentally he was also top dog, often shocking his rivals with his behaviour. Once, in Norway, he landed by helicopter just an hour before the start. With a skis "serviceman", unusual at that time, and a radar he started testing his skis. Everything was so professional and impressive that his rivals thought they only had second place and downwards to fight for. Svan was the winner even before the competition had started.

In the world championships in Seefeld, in 1985, he staged his biggest stunt ever. The day before the opening distance, 30km, he arrived at the stadium with only one pole—2.1m (6ft

10in.) long. He said that this pole gave him much more speed and his rivals were shocked and frightened. Svan won both the 30km and 50km without any problems.

Svan has two individual golds, a silver and a bronze from the Olympic Games. He ended his career at the 1991 world championships in Val di Fiemme by winning the 30km and by taking silver in the 15km and the 50km.

A Sporting Legend

Vegard Ulvang (NOR)

Vegard Ulvang, born on 10 October, 1963, is one of the most famous cross-country skiers of all time. He started a Norwegian cross-country revolution. When he won the gold medal at 30km in the Olympic Games in Albertville, he was the first Norwegian to win this distance in an international championship. In 1992 he also won the 10km, silver in the 15km and gold in the relay.

Vegard comes from the far North of Norway where the sun stays away in the winter time. He is well known as an adventurer. He has crossed Greenland on skis and, after the Olympic Games, and his three gold medals in 1992, he started climbing five of seven summits (the five highest mountains on five continents in five weeks) — Elbrus (5,645m/18.521ft) in Russia, Kilimanjaro (5,895m/19,341ft) in Africa, Puncak Jaya (5,030m/1650ft) in New Guinea, Anconcagua (6,959m/22,832ft) in South America and McKinley (6,194m/20,322ft) in North America. He succeeded in climbing the first three mountains, but because of a snow storm he had to stop when he was only a few meters from the peak of Anconcagua. After failing to reach the peak of Anconcagua he had to return to Norway. He had climbed McKinley earlier.

Vegard Ulvang is also known as one of the most outspoken athletes. A few years ago he had back problems and, after last season, he retired from cross-country skiing.

A Sporting Legend

Raissa Smetanina (URS)

Raissa Smetanina, born in 1952, is one of the greatest Winter Olympians of all time. She won four Olympic gold medals—two individual and two relay—five silver medals and one bronze. On the list of all-time greats, she is no. 5. The first gold medal she won was in 1976 at 10km, and the last was in the 4 x 5km relay in 1992, at the age of 39. She also won three individual gold medals from the world championships. Being at the top for more than 15 years, she wrote her name into ski history. Liubov Egorova (six golds) is, perhaps, a greater name than Smetanina, but being involved in a doping incident during the world championships in Trondheim last winter, Egorova's name will never be the same again.

A Sporting Legend
Sixten Jernberg (SWE)

Sixten Jernberg, born on 6 February, 1929, is called the greatest Olympic skier ever. From 1956 till 1964 Jernberg won four gold medals, three silver and two bronze. He also won four world championships between 1958 and '62. Jernberg had the important ability all top athletes dream about. He was the best when it came to the biggest events.

During his career he raced many splendid events. But one race above all others showed his greatness. That race did not take place in an Olympic competition. It was in the world championships in Lahti, Finland, in 1958. His toughest rival was Veikko Hakulinen from Finland. The distance was 50km and Hakulinen had already won the 30km. The weather was very cold and 50,000 people had found their place at the stadium to see their fellow countryman win another gold medal and to gain revenge after the Olympic Games in Cortina two years earlier. Then Hakulinen won the silver, 78 seconds behind Jernberg.

In Lahti, Jernberg started at no. 42 with Hakulinen at 43. Jernberg took the lead but when they were passing the stadium at 20km, Hakulinen was just 50m behind the Swede. The crowd was cheering for their man but suddenly something happened. Jernberg changed his speed. He started to run up the hill out of the stadium. Suddenly he was 60m and then 70m in front of Hakulinen before he disappeared into the forest.

Everyone was waiting for the report from 28km. Jernberg passed in 1:39.43. What about Hakulinen? The Finnish crowd was excited and quiet. Then they heard his time—1:40.10. Jernberg was in the lead by 27 seconds. Over those 8km he had been running 40 seconds faster than their hero. In the last 10km he was almost dancing along the tacks. In the end Jernberg won by 78 seconds—exactly the same number of seconds lead as in Cortina.

A Contemporary Heroine

Elena Valbe (RUS)

Elena Valbe, born on 20 April, 1968, is a born winner. She can win in free technique and in classic races. And she can win at all distances—5km, 10km and 30km. She is, of course, one of the biggest favourites in Nagano. Like a Siberian winter storm she swept into international cross-country skiing at the end of the 1980s. In 1989, she won the world cup. During the world championships in Val di Fiemme in 1991, Valbe became the queen. She won both the 5km and the 10km.

But, so far the Olympic Games have been a disaster for her. She does not have a single individual gold medal. In 1992 she won four bronze medals, but in Lillehammer she did not succeed at all. Last winter in the world championships in Trondheim she once more became the queen. Five gold medals are the final proof of her greatness. But apart from all the gold medals there is one thing she will be remembered for in Trondheim. The day after Liubov Egorova was sent home accused of doping and before the women's relay, Elena took the microphone at the stadium and, on behalf of the Russian team, she apologized for what happened. Of course, the Russian girls, without Egorova, won the relay. Elena says that this will be her last season. That means her last chance to win an Olympic gold medal.

Sixten Jernberg: cross-country legend from Sweden

MEDALLISTS *(by nation)*

Country	Gold		Silver		Bronze		Total
	m	w	m	w	m	w	
URS	11	17	8	16	12	13	77
NOR	19	2	21	6	11	5	64
SWE	18	3	12	2	11	2	48
FIN	10	8	13	8	17	10	66
ITA	2	3	3	4	5	3	20
RUS	-	3	-	1	-	1	5
GDR	-	2	1	-	-	1	4
KAZ	1	-	2	-	-	-	3
TCH	-	-	-	1	1	3	5
USA	-	-	1	-	-	-	1
SUI	-	-	-	-	3	-	3
BUL	-	-	-	-	1	-	1

NAGANO SCHEDULE

Cross-country skiing

Venue: **Snow Harp, Hakuba**

Date	Description	Start	Finish
8 Feb	15km classical (w)	9:00	10:30
9 Feb	30km classical (m)	9:00	11:00
10 Feb	5km classical (w)	10:00	10:00
12 Feb	10km classical (m)	9:00	10:30
12 Feb	10km free (w)	12:00	13:00
14 Feb	15km free (m)	9:00	10:30
16 Feb	4 x 5km relay (w)	10:15	11:45
18 Feb	4 x 10km relay (m)	10:15	12:15
20 Feb	30km free (w)	9:00	11:00
22 Feb	50km free (m)	9:00	12:00

| MEDALLISTS | | | Cross-country skiing [Men] | | | | | |

Year	Gold	Country	Time	Silver	Country	Time	Bronze	Country	Time
10,000m									
1992	Vegard Ulvang	NOR	27:36.0	Marco Albarello	ITA	27:55.2	Chriter Majback	SWE	27:56.4
1994	Bjørn Dæhlie	NOR	24:20.1	Vladimir Smirnov	KAZ	24:38.3	Marco Albarello	ITA	24:42.3
15,000m									
1924 (18km)	Thorleif Haug	NOR	1:14:31	Johan Gröttumsbraaten	NOR	1:15:51	Tipani Niku	FIN	1:26:28
1928 (18km)	Johan Gröttumsbraaten	NOR	1:37:01	Ole Hegge	NOR	1:39.01	Oedegaard	NOR	1:40:11
1932 (18km)	Sven Utterström	SWE	1:23:07	Axel Vikström	SWE	1:25:07	Veli Saarinen	FIN	1:25:24
1936 (18km)	Erik-August Larsson	SWE	1:14:38	Oddbjörn Hagen	NOR	1:15:33	Pekka Niemi	FIN	1:18:59
1948	Martin Lundstroem	SWE	1:13:50	Nils Ostensson	SWE	1:14:22	Gunnar Eriksson	SWE	1:18:06
1952	Hallgeir Brenden	NOR	1:01:34	Tapio Mäkelä	FIN	1:02:09	Paavo Lonkila	FIN	1:02:20
1956	Hallgeir Brenden	NOR	49:39	Sixten Jernberg	SWE	50:14	Pavel Kolchin	URS	50:17
1960	Hakon Brusveen	NOR	51:55.5	Sixten Jernberg	SWE	51:58.6	Veikko Hakulinen	FIN	52:03
1964	Eero Mäntyranta	FIN	50:54.1	Harald Grönningen	NOR	51:34.8	Sixten Jernberg	SWE	51:42.2
1968	Peter Thiel	GDR	47:54.2	Helmut Gerlach	GER	47:56.1	Klaus Ganter	GER	48:33.7
1972	Sven-Åke Lundback	SWE	45:28.24	Fjodar Simachev	URS	46:00.84	Ivar Formo	NOR	46:02.68
1976	Nikolai Bajukov	URS	43:58.47	Evgeni Beliaev	URS	44:01.10	Arto Koivisto	FIN	44:19.25
1980	Thomas Wassberg	SWE	41:57.63	Juha Mieto	FIN	41:57.64	Ove Aunli	NOR	42:28.62
1984	Gunde Swan	SWE	41:25.6	Aki Karvonen	FIN	41:34.9	Harri Kirvesniemi	FIN	41:45.6
1988	Mikhail Deviatiarov	URS	41:18.90	Pal Mikkelsplass	NOR	41:33.4	Vladimir Smirnov	URS	41:48.5
1992	Bjørn Dæhlie	NOR		Vegard Ulvang	NOR		Giorgio Vanzett	ITA	
1994	Bjørn Dæhlie	NOR	1:00:08.8	Vladimir Smirnov	KAZ	1:00:38	Silvio Fauner	ITA	1:01:48.6
30,000m									
1956	Veikko Hakulinen	FIN	1:44:06	Sixten Jernberg	SWE	1:44.30	Pavel Kolchin	URS	1:45:45
1960	Sixten Jernberg	SWE	1:51:03.9	Rolf Ramgard	SWE	1:51:16.9	Nikolai Anikin	URS	1:52:28.2
1964	Eero Mantyranta	FIN	1:30:50.7	Harald Gronningen	NOR	1:32:02.3	Igor Voronchikhin	URS	1:32:15.8
1968	Franco Nones	ITA	1:35:39.2	Odd Martinsen	NOR	1:36:28.9	Eero Maentyranta	FIN	1:36:55.3
1972	Vjateslav Vedenine	URS	1:36:31.5	Pal Tyldum	NOR	1:37:25.3	Johannes Harviken	NOR	1:36:32.44
1976	Sergei Saveliev	URS	1:30:29.38	William Koch	USA	1:30:57.84	Ivan Garanin	URS	1:31:09.29
1980	Nikolai Zimjatov	URS	1:27:02.8	Vasili Rochev	URS	1:27:34.22	Ivan Lebanov	BUL	1:28:03.87
1984	Nikolai Zimiatov	URS	1:28:56.3	Alexander Zavialov	URS	1:29:23.3	Gunde Swan	SWE	1:29:35.7
1988	Alexei Prokourorov	URS	1:24:26.3	Vladimir Smirnov	URS	1:24:35.1	Vegard Ulvang	NOR	1:25:11.6
1992	Vegard Ulvang	NOR	1:22:27.8	Bjørn Dæhlie	NOR	1:23:14	Terje Langli	NOR	1:23:42.5
1994	Thomas Alsgaard	NOR	1:12:26.4	Bjørn Dæhlie	NOR	1:13:13.6	Mika Myllylae	FIN	1:14:14.5
50,000m									
1924	Thorleif Haug	NOR	3:44:32	Thoralf Stromstad	NOR	3:46:23	Johan Gröttumsbraaten	NOR	3:47:46
1928	Per-Erik Hedlund	SWE	4:52:37	Johnsson	SWE	5:05:30	Sigurd Anderson	SWE	5:05:46
1932	Veli Saarinen	FIN	4:28:00	Väinö Liikkanen	FIN	4:28:20	Arne Rustadstuen	NOR	4:31:53
1936	Elis Viklung	SWE	3:30:11	Axel Wikström	SWE	3:33:20	Nils-Joel Englund	SWE	3:34:10
1948	Nils Karlsson	SWE	3:47:48	Harald Eriksson	SWE	3:52:20	Benjamin Vanninen	FIN	3:57:28
1952	Veikko Hakulinen	FIN	3:33:33	Eero Kolehmainen	FIN	3:38:11	Magnar Estenstad	NOR	3:38:28
1956	Sixten Jernberg	SWE	2:50:27	Veikko Hakulinen	FIN	2:51:45	Fedor Terentjev	URS	2:53:32
1960	Kalevi Hamalainen	FIN	2:59:06.3	Veikko Hakulinen	FIN	2:59:26.7	Rolf Ramgard	SWE	3:02:46.7
1964	Sixten Jernberg	SWE	2:43:52.6	Assar Rönnlund	SWE	2:44:58.2	Arto Tiainen	FIN	2:45:30.4
1968	Ole Ellefsaeter	NOR	2:28:45.8	Viatches Vedenine	URS	2:29:02.5	Josef Haas	SUI	2:29:14.8
1972	Pal Tyldum	NOR	2:43:14.75	Magne Myrmo	NOR	2:43:29.45	Vjatjeslav Vedenine	URS	2:44:00.19
1976	Ivar Formo	NOR	2:37:30.05	Gert-Dietmar Klause	GER	2:38:13.21	Benny Soedergren	SWE	2:39:39.21

Year	Gold	Country	Time	Silver	Country	Time	Bronze	Country	Time
1980	Nikolai Zimjatov	URS	2:27:24.60	Juha Mieto	FIN	2:30:20.52	Alexander Zavjalov	URS	2:30:51.52
1984	Thomas Wassberg	SWE	2:15:55.8	Gunde Swan	SWE	2:16:00.7	Aki Karvonen	FIN	2:17:04.7
1988	Gunde Svan	SWE	2:04:30.9	Maurilio De Zolt	ITA	2:05:36.4	Andy Gruenenfelder	SUI	2:06:01.9
1992	Bjørn Dæhlie	NOR	2:03.41.5	Maurilio De Zolt	ITA	2:04.39.1	Giorgio Vanzetta	ITA	2:06.42.1
1994	Vladimir Smirnov	KAZ	2:07:20.3	Mika Myllylae	FIN	2:08:41.9	Sture Sivertsen	NOR	2:08:49

4x10km relay

Year	Gold	Country	Time	Silver	Country	Time	Bronze	Country	Time
1936	Sulo Nurmela	FIN	2:41:33	Oddbjörn Hagen	NOR	2:41:39	John Berger	SWE	2:43:03
	Klaes Karppinen			Olaf Hoffsbakken			Erik Larsson		
	Matti Lähde			Sverre Brodahl			Artur Häggblad		
	Kalle Jalkanen			Bjarne Iversen			Martin Matsbo		
1948	Nils Oestensson	SWE	2:32:08	Lauri Silvennoinen	FIN	2:41:06	Erling Evensen	NOR	2:44:33
	Nils Taepp			Teuvo Laukkanen			Olaf Oekern		
	Gunnar Eriksson			Sauli Rytky			Reidar Nyborg		
	Martin Lundstroem			August Kiuru			Olav Hagen		
1952	Hasu Keikki	FIN	2:20:16	Magnar Estenstad	NOR	2:23:13	Nils Täpp	SWE	2:24:13
	Paavo Lonkila			Mikal Kirkholt			Sigurd Andersson		
	Urpo Korhonen			Martin Stokken			Enar Josefsson		
	Tapio Mäkelä			Hallgeir Brenden			Martin Lündstrom		
1956	Fedor Terentjev	URS	2:15:30	August Kiuru	FIN	2:16:31	Lennart Larsson	SWE	2:17:42
	Pavel Kolchin			Jormo Kortalainen			Gunnar Samuelsson		
	Nikolai Anikin			Arvo Viitanen			Per-Erik Larsson		
	Vladimir Kuzin			Veikko Hakulinen			Sixten Jernberg		
1960	Toimi Alatalo	FIN	2:18:45.6	Harald Gronningen	NOR	2:18:46.4	A Sheljukhin	URS	2:21:21.6
	Eero Mantyranta			Hallgeir Brenden			Gennadi Vaganov		
	Vaino Huhtala			Einar Ostby			Alexei Kuznetsov		
	Veikko Hakulinen			Hakon Brusveen			Nikolai Anikin		
1964	Karl-Ake Asph	SWE	2:18:34.6	Väinö Huhtala	FIN	2:18:42.4	Ivan Utrobin	URS	2:18:46.9
	Sixten Jernberg			Arto Tiainen			Gennadi Vaganov		
	Janne Stefansson			Kalevi Laurila			Igor Voronchikhin		
	Assar Rönnlund			Eero Mäntyrnta			Pavel Kolchin		
1968	Odd Martinsen	NOR	2:08:33.5	Jan Halvarsson	SWE	2:10:13.2	Kalevi Oikarainen	FIN	2:10:56.7
	Paal Tyldum			Bjarne Andersson			Hannu Taipale		
	Haral Groenningen			Gunnar Larsson			Kalevi Laurila		
	Ole Ellefsaeter			Assar Roennlund			Eero Maentyranta		
1972	Vladimir Voronkov	URS		Oddvar Braa	NOR	2:04:57.06	Alfred Kalin	SUI	2:07:00.06
	Yuri Skobov			Pal Tyldum			Albert Giger		
	Fjodor Simachev			Ivar Formo			Alois Kalin		
	Vjatjeslav Vedenine			Johannes Harviken			Eduard Hauser		
1976	Matti Pitkaenen	FIN	2:07:59.72	Pal Tyldum	NOR	2:09:58.36	Evgeni Beliaev	URS	2:10:51.46
	Juha Mieto			Einar Sagstuen			Nikolai Bajukov		
	Pertti Teurajaervi			Ivar Formo			Sergei Saveliev		
	Arto Koivisto			Odd Martinsen			Ivan Garanin		
1980	Vasili Rochev	URS	1:57:03.46	Lars Eriksen	NOR	1:58:45.77	Harri Kirvesniemi	FIN	2:00:00.18
	Nikolai Bazhukov			Per Aaland			Pertti Teurajarvi		
	Evgeni Beliaev			Ove Aunli			Matti Pitkanen		
	Nikolai Zimjatov			Oddvar Braa			Juha Mieto		
1984	Thomas Wassberg	SWE	1:55:06.3	Alexander Batuk	URS	1:55:16.5	Kari Ristanen	FIN	1:56:31.4
	Benny Kohlberg			Alexander Zivialov			Aki Karvonen		
	Jan Ottosson			Vladimir Nikitin			Harri Kirvesniemi		

Year	Gold	Country	Time	Silver	Country	Time	Bronze	Country	Time
	Gunde Swan			Nikolai Zimiatov			Lars Eriksen		
1988	Jan Ottosson	SWE	1:43:58.6	Vladimir Smirnov	URS	1:44:11.3	Radim Nyc	CZE	1:45:22.7
	Thomas Wassberg			Vladiir Sakhnov			Vaclav Korunka		
	Gunde Svan			Mikhail Deviatiarov			Pavel Benc		
	Torgny Mogren			Alexei Prokurorov			Ladislav Svanda		
1992	Terje Langli	NOR	1:39.26	Giuseppe Pulie	ITA	1:40.52	Mika Kuusisto	FIN	1:41.22
	Vegard Ulvang			Marco Albarello			Harri Kirvesniemi		
	Kristen Skjeldal			Giorgio Vanzetta			Jari Rasanen		
	Bjørn Dæhlie			Silvio Faunr			Jari Isometsa		
1994	Maurilio De Zolt	ITA	1:41:15.0	Sture Sivertsen	NOR	1:41:15.4	Mika Myllylae	FIN	1:42:15.6
	Marco Albarello			Vegard Ulvang			Harri Kirvesniemi		
	Giorgio Vanzetta			Thomas Alsgaard			Jari Raesaenen		
	Silvio Fauner			Bjørn Dæhlie			Jari Isometsa		
	Marco Albarello			Vegard Ulvang			Harri Kirvesniemi		
	Giorgio Vanzetta			Thomas Alsgaard			Jari Raesaenen		
	Silvio Fauner			Bjørn Dæhlie			Jari Isometsa		

MEDALLISTS — Cross-country skiing [Women]

5000m

Year	Gold	Country	Time	Silver	Country	Time	Bronze	Country	Time
1964	Claudia Boyarskikh	URS	17:50.5	Mirja Lehtonen	FIN	17:52.9	Alevtina Kolchina	URS	18:08.4
1968	Toini Gustafsson	SWE	16:45.2	Galina Koulakova	URS	16:48.4	Alevtina Koltchina	URS	16:51.6
1972	G Koulacova	URS	17:00.50	M Kajosmaa	FIN	17:05.50	H Sikolova	CZE	17:07.32
1976	Helena Takalo	FIN	15:48.69	Raissa Smetanina	URS	15:49.73	Nina Baldicheva	URS	16:12.82
1980	Raissa Smetanina	URS	15:06.92	Hilkka Riihivuori	FIN	15:11.96	Kveta Jeriova	CZE	15:23.44
1984	Marja-Liisa Haemalainen	FIN	17:04	Berit Aunli	NOR	17:14.1	Kvetoslava Jeriova	CZE	17:18.3
1988	Marjo Matikainen	FIN	15:04	Tamara Tikhonova	URS	15:05.3	Vida Ventsene	URS	15:11.1
1992	Marjut Lukkarinen	FIN	14:13.8	Liubov Egorova	EUN	14:14.7	Elena Valbe	EUN	14:22.7
1994	Liubov Egorova	URS	14:08.8	Manuela Di Centa	ITA	14:28.3	Marja-Liisa Kirvesniemi	FIN	14:36

10,000m

Year	Gold	Country	Time	Silver	Country	Time	Bronze	Country	Time
1952	Lydia Wideman	FIN	41:40	Mirja Hietamies	FIN	42:39	Siiri Rantanen	FIN	42:50
1956	Liubov Kozyreva	URS	38:11	Radya Eroshina	URS	38:16	Sonya Edstroem	SWE	38:23
1960	Maria Gusakova	URS	39:46.6	Liubov Baranova	URS	40:04.2	Radya Eroshina	URS	40:06
1964	Claudia Boyarskikh	URS	40:24.3	Eudokia Mekshilo	URS	40:26.6	Maria Gusakova	URS	40:46.6
1968	Toini Gustafsson	SWE	36:46.5	Berit Moerdre	NOR	37:54.6	Inger Aufles	NOR	37:59.9
1972	G Koulacova	URS	34:17.82	A Olunina	URS	34:54.11	M Kajosmaa	FIN	34:56.45
1976	Raissa Smetanina	URS	30:13.41	Helena Takalo	FIN	30:14.28	Galina Kulakova	URS	30:38.61
1980	Barbara Petzold	GDR	30:31.54	Hilkka Riihivuori	FIN	30:35.05	Helena Takalo	FIN	30:45.25
1984	Marja-Liisa Haemalainen	FIN	31:44.2	Raissa Smetanina	URS	32:02.9	Brit Pettersen	NOR	32:12.7
1988	Vida Ventsene	URS	30:08.3	Raissa Smetanina	URS	30:17.0	Marjo Matikainen	FIN	30:20.5
1992	Liubov Egorova	EUN		Stefania Belmondo	ITA		Elena Valbe	EUN	
1994	Liubov Egorova	URS	41:38.1	Manuela Di Centa	ITA	41:46.4	Stefania Belmondo	ITA	42:21.1

15,000m

Year	Gold	Country	Time	Silver	Country	Time	Bronze	Country	Time
1992	Liubov Egorova	EUN	42:20.8	Marjut Lukkarinen	FIN	43:29.9	Elena Valbe	EUN	43:42.3
1994	Manuela Di Centa	ITA	39:44.5	Liubov Egorova	URS	41:03.0	Nina Gavriluk	URS	41:10.4

Year	Gold	Country	Time	Silver	Country	Time	Bronze	Country	Time

20,000m

Year	Gold	Country	Time	Silver	Country	Time	Bronze	Country	Time
1984	Marja-Liisa Haemalainen	FIN	1:01:45	Raissa Smetanina	URS	1:02:26.7	Anne Jahren	NOR	1:03:13.06
1988	Tamara Tikhonova	URS	55:53.6	Anfissa Reztsova	URS	56:12.8	Raissa Smetanina	URS	57:22.1

30,000m

Year	Gold	Country	Time	Silver	Country	Time	Bronze	Country	Time
1994	Manuela Di Centa	ITA	1:25:41.6	Marit Wold	NOR	1:25.57.8	Marja-Liisa Kirvesniemi	FIN	1:26:13.6

4x5000m relay

Year	Gold	Country	Time	Silver	Country	Time	Bronze	Country	Time
1956 (3x5)	Sirkka Polkunen	FIN	1:09:01	Liubov Kozyreva	URS	1:09:28	Irma Johansson	SWE	1:09:48
	Mirja Hietamies			Alevtina Kolchina			Lisa Eriksson		
	Siiri Rantanen			Radya Eroshina			Sonya Edstroem		
1960 (3x5)	Irma Johansson	SWE	1:04:21.4	Radya Eroshina	URS	1:05:02.6	Siiri Rantanen	FIN	1:06:27.5
	Britt Strandberg			Maria Gusakova			Eeva Ruoppa		
	Sonya Ruthstrom			Liubov Baranova			Toini Poysti		
1964 (3x5)	Alevtina Kolchina	URS	59:20.2	Barbro Martinsson	SWE	1:01:27	Senja Pusula	FIN	1:02:45.1
	Eudokia Mekshilo			Britt Strandberg			Toini Poysti		
	Claudia Boyarskikh			Toini Gustafsson			Mirja Lehtonen		
1968 (3x5)	Inger Aufles	NOR	57:30	Britt Strandberg	SWE	57:51	Alevtina Koltchina	URS	58:13.6
	Babben Enger Damon			Toini Gustafsson			Rita Achkina		
	Berit Moerdre			Barbro Martinsson			Galina Koulakova		
1972 (3x5)	Lubova Moukhatcheva	URS	48:46.15	H Takalo	FIN	49:19.37	Inger Aufles	NOR	49:51.49
	Aleutina Olunina			Hilkka Kuntola			Aslaug Dahl		
	Galina Koulacova			Marjatta Kajosmaa			Berit Lammedal		
1976	Nina Baldicheva	URS	1:07:49.75	Liisa Suihkonen	FIN	1:08:36.57	Monika Debertshauser	GDR	1:09:57.95
	Zinaida Amosova			Marjatta Kajosmaa			Sigrun Krause		
	Raissa Smetanina			Hilkka Kuntola			Barbara Petzold		
	Galina Kulakova			Helena Takalo			Veronika Schmidt		
1980	Marlies Rostock	GDR	1:02:11.10	Nina Baldycheva	URS	1:03:18.30	Brit Pettrsen	NOR	1:04:13.50
	Carola Anding			Nina Rocheva			Anette Boe		
	Veronika Hesse			Galina Kulakova			Marit Myrmael		
	Barbara Petzold			Raissa Smetanina			Berit Aunli		
1984	Inger Nybraaten	NOR	1:06:49.7	Dagmar Schvubova	CZE	1:07:34.7	Pirkko Maatta	FIN	1:07:36.7
	Anne Jahren			Blanka Paulu			Eija Hyytiainen		
	Brit Pettersen			Gabriela Svobodova			Marjo Matikainen		
	Berit Anuli			Kvetoslava Jeriova			Marja-Liisa Haemaelainen		
1988	Svetlana Nagueikina	URS	59:51.1	Trude Dybendahl	NOR	1:01.33	Pirkko Maatta	FIN	1:01.53.8
	Nina Gavriliuk			Marit Wold			Marja-Liisa Kirvesniemi		
	Tamara Tikhonova			Anne Jahren			Marjo Matikainen		
	Anfissa Reztsova			Marianne Dahlmo			Jaana Savolainen		
1992	Elena Valbe	EUN	59.34.8	Solveig Pedersen	NOR	59:56.4	Bice Vanzetta	ITA	1:00.25.9
	Raissa Smetanina			Inger Nybraten			Manuela Di Centa		
	Larisa Lasutina			Trude Dybendahl			Gabriell Paruzzi		
	Liubov Egorova			Elin Nilsen			Stefania Belmondo		
1994	Elena Vaelbe	URS	57:12.5	Trude Dybendahl	NOR	57:42.6	Bice Vanzetta	ITA	58:42.6
	Larissa Lazutina			Inger Nybraten			Manuela Di Centa		
	Nina Gavriluk			Elin Nilsen			Gabriella Paruzzi		
	Liubov Egorova			Anita Moen			Stefania Belmondo		
1988	Svetlana Nagueikina	URS	59:51.1	Trude Dybendahl	NOR	1:01.33	Pirkko Maatta	FIN	1:01.53.8
	Nina Gavriliuk			Marit Wold			Marja-Liisa Kirvesniemi		
	Tamara Tikhonova			Anne Jahren			Marjo Matikainen		
	Anfissa Reztsova			Marianne Dahlmo			Jaana Savolainen		

Year	Gold	Country	Time	Silver	Country	Time	Bronze	Country	Time
1992	Elena Valbe	EUN	59.34.8	Solveig Pedersen	NOR	59:56.4	Bice Vanzetta	ITA	1:00.25.9
	Raissa Smetanina			Inger Nybraten			Manuela Di Centa		
	Larisa Lasutina			Trude Dybendahl			Gabriell Paruzzi		
	Liubov Egorova			Elin Nilsen			Stefania Belmondo		
1994	Elena Vaelbe	URS	57:12.5	Trude Dybendahl	NOR	57:42.6	Bice Vanzetta	ITA	58:42.6
	Larissa Lazutina			Inger Nybraten			Manuela Di Centa		
	Nina Gavriluk			Elin Nilsen			Gabriella Paruzzi		
	Liubov Egorova			Anita Moen			Stefania Belmondo		

FREESTYLE SKIING

Expression of a style & freedom

by Mik Barton

Nagano celebrates ten years of "Olympic" freestyle skiing since the first demonstration events in Calgary. To say the sport has "grown up" might seem an insult to some as freestyle is very much about the expression of a style and freedom to perform on challenging slopes.

Whether it is expressed through a jump, spin or somersault the freestyle skier is almost saying "my acrobatic ability is such that I can enjoy myself on any terrain the mountain dares to put in my way". Moguls and aerials are the two disciplines to receive Olympic recognition so far. Acro-ski and the head-to-head rodeo of the dual moguls are in the queue potentially for Salt Lake City.

Any skier above the intermediate level will encounter moguls on their holiday where snow mounds are formed by skiers consistently turning on the same spot on steep slopes. Once the skiers start to use these natural bumps to help execute the turn, the moguls take on exponential growth. Nowadays top competition runs are often started with a snow-cat and smoothed into shape by the skiers during training.

Canada, America, Sweden and France are the top moguls nations to watch out for in Nagano—with Jean-Luc Brassard of Canada almost certain to start as favourite. Sadly Sergei Shupletsov, who finished 2nd at the Lillehammer Games by just 0.34 points and was destined to become one of the best all-round skiers in the sport's history, was killed in a traffic accident a year later.

If anyone is to break the mould in Nagano, they will come from the home nation. Takehiro Sukamoto surprised everyone when he jumped straight from Continental Cup to a storming world cup victory at Meiringen last year. That was a warning shot across the bows of Europe and America; Daigo Hara also used home advantage

Nicolas Fontaine (CAN): continuing the Quebec tradition in the aerials

Moguls attire

at the pre-Olympic event. The host nation's top mogul skier is Yugo Tsukita who made the top 20 in last year's world cup standings.

In the women's competition the long-standing rivalry between Candice Gilg of France and American Donna Weinbrecht could be interrupted by Finland's Minna Karhu. The incredibly gymnastic Ludmila Dymchenko is sure to impress in the air but will need to work on her speed to challenge for a place. And for a good outside bet home-town support could just elevate Sapporo-born Tae Satoya to medal status.

In the aerials, the early world cup season will be a critical test period as the acrobatic ski jumpers perfect their most complicated tricks and decide whether to risk all in the quest for Olympic glory.

With a combination of single and double twists during three back somersaults the key is to watch for a noticeable change in the speed of rotation and the finishing point for each twist. Canada's Nicolas Fontaine, in the continuing Quebec tradition, is the nearest thing to a medal certainty. Of the up-and-coming nations, the Chinese have put a lot of effort into their development programme. Initial language difficulties created some humorous moments, but no-one doubts that they have to be taken seriously. Chinese determination paid off when Guo Dandon won her nation's first world cup gold medal at the start of the 1998 season in Mount Buller.

Background

Freestyle skiing first gained Olympic recognition at an IOC Session in May 1979 held in Nice, France. However, it was not until the 95th IOC Session in Puerto Rico ten years later that the decision was taken to add freestyle skiing to the Games programme by including races in the men's and women's moguls. In Barcelona in 1992 the 99th Session of the IOC added aerials to the list of full-programme events.

In practical terms this meant that moguls skiing made its Olympic competition debut in 1992 in Albertville whilst aerials had to wait until the Games of Lillehammer in 1994. As early as the Calgary Games of 1988 there were demonstration events in freestyle aerials whilst the ballet (or acro) element of freestyle skiing was a demonstration event in 1992.

The fact that freestyle belongs to the category of "judged" sports —like ice dancing and gymnastics—contributed to a degree of controversy over its debut in Albertville which continued in Lillehammer. First-time observers were also shocked by the sport's theatrical rock music accompaniments and organ overtures. But they were still caught by the novelty and the excitement.

Britain's Richard Cobbing, world silver medallist in aerials in 1993, took part in the Lillehammer Games aerials competition in 1994, finishing 10th. Earlier in his career he had won the World Games trampolining gold and had earnt a living, at one time, as a show diver.

In the final of the 1994 event Switzerland's Andreas Schoenbaechler was the surprise winner after qualifying in last place for the final. He held off a challenge from the Canadians Laroche and Langlois—part of the world-beating squad which had been nicknamed the "Quebec Air Force". Victory was even sweeter for Schoenbaechler as his nation had excluded him from any pre-Games funding, preferring to concentrate their resources behind their Alpine skiers who had a dismal Games.

Norway, previously almost unheralded in this sport, sprung two Lillehammer surprises. Stine Lise Hattestad won the women's moguls event whilst Hilde Synnove Lid picked up a bronze in the women's aerials which was won by Lina Tcherjazova of Uzbekistan.

Edgar Grospiron, who won the inaugural Olympic moguls gold in front of an ecstatic and adoring French home crowd in 1992, and Hattestad are the leading freestyle Olympic medallists to date. Both have a gold and a bronze apiece.

Equipment

Of all the freestyle disciplines, only acro-ski has really different equipment. For the event that relates to gymnastics on skis the athletes have extra-short, flexible skis and long, strong ski poles to somersault from. For the two disciplines you will see at Nagano there is not a huge amount of difference from standard equipment.

Skis are a bit shorter than normal to aid rotation in the aerial competition—and you will often see mogul skiers in ski suits with knee flashes to show off absorption and leg position to best effect.

One critical piece of freestyle equipment not worn by the skier is the sound system. It is not uncommon for up to 20 speakers alongside the piste to blast out more than 7000 watts of rock music for both aerials and moguls events. It is all part of the freestyle atmosphere, shouting loud to be noticed whether for a crash or a spectacle.

Rules and Regulations

Olympic medals will be awarded for two freestyle disciplines in Nagano: moguls and aerials.

In the first, scheduled for Iizuna Kogen on 8th and 11th February, skiers tear down a frightening 252m (827ft) bumps slope of up to 27 degrees—with points awarded for style, control and acrobatic manoeuvres.

The first thing to realize about a mogul skiing competition is that it is not a race. Speed only counts for 25% of the score. The quickest way from start to finish gate may be straight down the fall-line, but only the foolhardy and lucky would survive such an approach. Skiers must turn rapidly utilizing the terrain to score maximun points. Five judges award marks against strict criteria for the quality of skiing in difficult terrain (50%). Ignoring the moguls is the equivalent of a downhill skier cutting corners or a slalom skier missing out the more difficult gates. The last few turns are the ones to watch when a skier can be penalized heavily for forgetting to turn as they fly towards the finish.

Another two judges give the final 25% for the two compulsory aerials. Originally an exuberant expression of ability anywhere on the slope, the jumps now take place at pre-determined bumps that have been shaped for the purpose. The top 16 skiers after the elimination section qualify for a final which is judged in exactly the same way.

In the second Olympic freestyle event — the aerials (16th & 18th February) style in the air is the most important. Skiers launch themselves off a snow "kicker" — a concave ramp around 3.5m (10 ft 6in.) high set at an angle of 65 degrees — and perform complicated manoeuvres before touching down on the steep landing slope more than ten metres (33ft) below. The event and elements of the scoring system are related to high diving or trampolining, but freestyling aerialists have more time in the air than any other acrobatic sport. Triple somersaults with four twists are not uncommon.

A panel of seven judges, each looking at different aspects, award marks for take-off, height and distance (20%), form (50%) and landing (30%). Each score is then multiplied by the degree of difficulty of the jump and two different jumps are added together to give the final total. The top 12 competitors emerge from the elimination contest to take part in the final. Each skier has two jumps in the final.

The Nagano Format

A maximum of 135 athletes will take part in the freestyle skiing events at the 1998 Olympic Winter Games in Nagano. Each nation will be permitted up to 14 skiers—to include a maximum of eight men or eight women.

Every skier will have qualified by scoring points at any of the world championships, world cup or Continental Cup competitions in the period between August 1996 and January 1998.

Venue

Mt Iizuna, one of the five peaks of the Hokushin region, will play host to the 1998 Olympic Winter Games freestyle skiing competitions. This is a well-developed existing ski resort area on the outskirts of Nagano city. Bobsleigh and luge's Spiral track is located just 2km (1.24 miles) from the freestyle site.

A Contemporary Hero
Jean-Luc Brassard (CAN—moguls)

Jean-Luc Brassard set the sport alight with his stunning final jump at the Lillehammer Games and has maintained his position at the top of the sport ever since.

Innovation is the name of the game and that certainly helped the Canadian on his way to Olympic gold. Although only a quarter of the total score, a mogul skier's two aerial manoeuvres can easily create the greatest impact and that was certainly the case with Brassard's iron-cross backscratcher/cossack that has since been frequently imitated but rarely bettered.

The development of more complicated jumps and introduction of dual moguls (though not yet an Olympic discipline) has set the scene for some fascinating tactics in Nagano. Brassard's dominance in the single moguls has been more than equalled by Frenchman Thony Hémery in the head-to-head.

Helicopter (360°) jumps "with position" are all the rage and the 1997 season could even see double-helis (720°). Brassard's well-executed double-straight aerial that won in '94 works less well as a rushed triple and he has so far been much less comfortable on the rotation jumps.

A Contemporary Hero
Christian Rijavec (AUT—aerials)

Austria's Christian Rijavec faces a tough battle to break the American-Canadian domination of freestyle aerials, but as Switzerland's Andreus (Sonny) Schönbachler showed in Lillehammer a surprise is always possible on the big day of an

Olympic final.

Rijavec won the day at the close of last season's world cup campaign in Hundfjället, Sweden and was the top European at Nagano's pre-Olympic event. He also has five world cup gold medals to his credit.

Freestyle skiing is about performing to the limits of your ability—and not beyond. The trend is towards ever more complicated tricks leading in turn to greater margin of error and severity of judging. Last year's quad-twisting triple somersaults (double twist/single/single and single/double/single) could even be superceded by five twists in the new season. World cup leader Nicolas Fontaine spent the summer training such a manoeuvre on the water ramp in Blackcomb.

The extra risk involved means there will always be an opportunity for the skier with a perfectly executed simpler trick and a cool head to win through.

A Sporting Legend

Edgar Grospiron (FRA— moguls)

Edgar Grospiron was just what freestyle needed when he won the first Olympic gold. Born just up the road from Albertville, he was adored by the French crowd who supported him through the blizzard and partied long into the night in Tignes—seen by many as the spiritual home of freestyle and venue of the first world championships in 1986.

"Ga-ga" (the nickname comes from his French prénom rather than any English translation) was the hot favourite as long as he could keep a cool head. He was a real character and occasionally his over-confidence (some might say arrogance) got the better of him. His style exhibited the fine balance between control and exuberance that lay at the very foundations of freestyle skiing. At the 1992 Games, Grospiron became the local hero much valued in Olympic history.

He had finished third in Calgary, when mogul skiing was a demonstration event, but went on to win both subsequent world championships in 1989 and 1991. Although the Frenchman won the bronze in Lillehammer, he was clearly soon to be overtaken by the more disciplined mogul skiers we see today.

A Sporting Legend

Lloyd Langlois (CAN—aerials)

The Canadian winner of freestyle's first world championships, together with the remarkable Laroche family, dominated the opening years of the sport's history—and still continues to exert influence today. Having French as your native language was as good as having wings if you were an aerial freestyle skier. European French got the occasional look in, but it was really the Quebec Air Force that dominated in the early years—and may still do so in Nagano.

Langlois was 3rd at the Calgary Games, then concentrated more on the ski show circuit, before returning for another medal in Lillehammer. Considered a veteran in such a young sport, he may even hang in for the Nagano Games at the age of 35.

Often shunning the official team colours for his lucky yellow ski suit on the world cup circuit, the quiet presence of Lloyd Langlois has certainly supported more recent Quebecois talent like Nicolas Fontaine—both hail from the tiny town of Magog at the northern tip of the Appalachian Mountains.

Jean-Luc Brassard (CAN) starts as moguls' favourite

MEDALLISTS *(by nation)*

Country	Gold		Silver		Bronze		Overall
	m	w	m	w	m	w	total
FRA	1	-	1	-	1	-	3
CAN	1	-	1	-	1	-	3
USA	-	1	-	1	1	-	3
NOR	-	1	-	-	-	2	3
SUI	1	-	-	-	-	-	1
UZB	-	1	-	-	-	-	1
RUS	-	-	1	-	-	1	2
EUN	-	-	-	1	-	-	1
SWE	-	-	-	1	-	-	1

Freestyle skiing

NAGANO SCHEDULE

Venue: **Iizuna Kogen ski area**

Date	Description	Round	Start	Finish
8 Feb	Moguls (m & w)	elim	9:30	12:00
11 Feb	Moguls (m & w)	FINAL	12:00	13:30
16 Feb	Aerials (m & w)	elim	9:30	11:15
18 Feb	Aerials (m & w)	FINAL	10:15	11:45

MEDALLISTS

Freestyle skiing [Men]

Year	Gold	Country	Pts	Silver	Country	Pts	Bronze	Country	Pts
Moguls									
1992	Edgar Grospiron	FRA	25.81	Olivier Allamand	FRA	24.87	Nelson Carmichael	USA	24.82
1994	Jean-Luc Brassard	CAN	27.24	Sergei Shupletsov	URS	26.9	Edgar Grospiron	FRA	26.64
Aerials									
1994	Andreas Schoenbaechler	SUI	234.67	Philippe Laroche	CAN	228.63	Lloyd Langlois	CAN	222.44

MEDALLISTS

Freestyle skiing [Women]

Year	Gold	Country	Pts	Silver	Country	Pts	Bronze	Country	Pts
Moguls									
1992	Donna Weinbrecht	USA	23.69	Elizaveta Kojevnikova	EUN	23.5	Stine Hattestad	NOR	23.04
1994	Stine Hattestad	NOR	25.97	Elizabeth McIntyre	USA	25.89	Elizaveta Kojevnikova	URS	25.81
Aerials									
1994	Lina Tcherjazova	UZB?	166.84	Marie Lindgren	SWE	165.88	Hilde Lid	NOR	164.13

NORDIC COMBINED

By Kazushi Funaki

In the Nordic Combined, 1997 world cup champion Samppa Lajunen and fellow Finn Hannu Manninen will battle for the top spot with Japan's Kenji Ogiwara, the defending world title-holder, and world runner-up Bjarte Engen Vik of Norway.

Now, more than ever, it is crucial for Nordic Combined athletes to do well in the jumping portion because the competitive level in this first half of the event has considerably improved. The tough, hilly cross-country course in Hakuba makes it all the more difficult to overtake the jumping leaders in the latter event.

With new rules in the team contest, each Nordic Combined squad will be comprised of four members instead of three and each athlete will race 5 km—just half the distance required in the past—in the cross-country relay. Norway and Finland are the favourites alongside Japan.

Background

The Nordic Combined title was considered the ultimate, or "blue riband" event of the early versions of the Olympic Winter Games. It appeared on the programme of the inaugural Games in Chamonix in 1924 and has remained ever since. A Nordic Combined team event was added to the programme in 1988 in Calgary, Canada.

As in all the Nordic disciplines, the Scandinavian nations have often dominated this event. Indeed Norway took every single available medal in the event from 1924 to 1936 inclusive. However, Germany and Japan have emerged to challenge them in more recent decades. Germany won the inaugural team competition in 1988 whilst Japan took the team title four years later and again in Lillehammer in 1994

The Nordic Combined event consists of a ski-jumping competition followed by a cross-country race. Until 1952 the race always preceded the jumping competition. Since the Oslo Games the order has been reversed with start positions in the skiing race being determined by results achieved in the jumping competition. In this sense, the spectator appeal of the Nordic Combined has been increased because the first skier to cross the line wins the event.

These athletes are some of the most skilled at the Olympic Winter Games. The need to achieve excellence in both disciplines was never better portrayed than by Japan's Hidoki Nakano in 1972 in Sapporo. The host nation athlete won the jumping event but finished last in the cross-country race, leaving him 13th overall.

Ulrich Wehling of the former East Germany won the title at three successive Games—1972, '76 and '80. Georg Thoma, a 22 year-old German postman who was only 1.59m (5ft 2.5in) tall sprung the surprise of the 1964 Games in Squaw Valley. He won the Nordic Combined title and became the first non-Scandinavian to succeed in this way.

At the 1994 Lillehammer Games, Fred Lundberg of Norway delighted the home crowd by winning the individual title—the first Norwegian to do so since 1984. However, Japan took individual silver through Takanori Kono and went on to nudge the hosts into silver medal position in the team event, pointing perhaps to potential for 1998.

Equipment

For the ski jumping element of this event, participants use long, wide skis to help flight—although the length of ski and placement of the bindings are subject to new rules to prevent "overjumping" (see ski jumping section). For the cross-country section, skiers can employ free technique so they use shorter skis than the classical style cross-country skis. These have a smaller curvature at the tip but they are still arched and thicker at the waist than at either end. Choice of wax is crucial depending on the weather conditions and gliding wax will be applied to the whole base of the ski rather than "gripping" wax to the middle section as in classical races.

Racing takes place on specially-prepared cross-country terrain including many testing uphill sections. The 90m ski-jumping hill is used for the jumping section (see ski-jumping section).

Rules and Regulations

The Nordic Combined event consists of two jumps from the 90m (or "normal") hill on the first day followed by a 15km cross-country ski race on the second. As in a normal ski-jumping event, points are awarded to each competitor for distance and style. These points are totalled and are then used to determine the start order and interval between starts in the ensuing 15km race.

The athlete with the highest number of points starts the race first. Each subsequent racer starts out at an interval relating to their points difference behind the winner of the ski jump. For each 0.15 difference in points a second of delay is added to the start time of the next racer and so on. This means that the first past the post wins the event. There have been some dramatic finishes over past Games.

In the team event, four competitors take part for each nation. A team's results are not valid unless all four complete both events. As in the indivdual event, there are two jumps per competitor in the jumping section and the total points awarded to the team determines the start order once more for the cross-country relay which consists of four 5km legs. The winning team is the first which crosses the line.

Nagano Format

There are two events on the 1998 Olympic Winter Games Nordic Combined programme—an individual event (K90 ski jump and 15km cross-country) and a team event (K90 ski jump and 4 x 5km relay). Each nation is permitted a total of 28 athletes across the three Nordic disciplines of cross-country, jumping and Nordic Combined. Four athletes may be entered per nation in each event.

Athletes competing in Nagano will have qualified for the Games by finishing in the top 50 of at least one world cup competition in Nordic Combined in the 1996/'97 or 1997/'98 season. The deadline for entries being 11 January 1998. There are no exceptional circumstances in which one athlete per nation will be permitted if they have not reached the qualifying standard. The strictness of the criteria is based on safety in the ski jumping.

Venue

Nordic Combined will have a split venue at the 1998 Olympic Winter Games. The ski jumping will take place at the Hakuba Ski Jump Stadium in Happo whilst the cross-country element will be hosted by nearby Kamishiro.

A Contemporary Hero

Kenji Ogiwara (JPN)

One of the most unusual scenes of the 1992 Albertville Olympic Games took place on top of the medals podium for the Nordic Combined event. There, in the middle of the French winter resort, stood Kenji Ogiwara, celebrating Japan's team gold medal by shaking a bottle of champagne and spraying it Formula One-style.

Such an act was, perhaps, totally in character for one of the most popular competitors in the sport. In Japan, Ogiwara is like a rock star, attracting crowds of fans wherever he competes. Cheerful, funny, witty, tough—these are all facets of Ogiwara.

Born on December 20, 1969, in the hot spring resort of Kusatsu, Ogiwara mastered the "V" jumping style as a Waseda University student. Since then, he has won title after title, typically by taking a big lead in the jumping and running away from the pack in the cross-country leg.

He has a distinguished sporting résumé: three straight world cup titles from the 1992/'93 season; four world titles; and a second Olympic team gold medal in Lillehammer. There is, however, one medal missing from his trophy case, the Olympic individual gold. In Lillehammer, he stumbled on the jumping ramp to take sixth place in the first half of the individual event. Then he fought gallantly in the cross-country race but could climb no higher than fourth.

At 28, Ogiwara, now a resident of Nagano, has one more chance to grab Olympic glory and do it in front of a hometown crowd. Time advantages gained from the jumping results have tightened considerably but he has shown he can win whatever the conditions. Against a host of rising young stars, Ogiwara clinched the individual title at the 1997 world championships in Norway.

History provides Ogiwara with a reason for optimism. Fred Borre Lundberg's gold at Lillehammer was aided by the Norwegian's intense training at the Olympic jumping venue. If there is anyone who will know the Olympic in-run in Nagano, it will surely be Kenji Ogiwara.

Kenji Ogiwara (JAP) on skis

and in flight

A Sporting Legend

Ulrich Wehling (GDR)

Three-times Olympic gold medallist Ulrich Wehling of the former East Germany first mounted the Nordic Combined rostrum as a teary-eyed 19 year-old champion at the 11th Olympic Winter Games in Sapporo in 1972. Four years later in Innsbruck, Wehling was there again as the unrivalled "King of Skiing".

Wehling, who had never known what it was like to finish second, however, tumbled into third place for the first time at the 1978 world championships. With an injured shoulder, Wehling had fallen into a slump.

But, the king would be crowned again at Lake Placid in 1980, taking the lead after the jumping competition and then holding on through the cross-country race to become the first athlete outside of figure skating to win gold medals in three straight Olympic Winter Games.

In a competition that requires two completely different kinds of disposition for the jump and the cross-country, Wehling was the master.

He retired after his triumph in Lake Placid and is now engaged in sports-related research. He also serves as a coordinator for the Nordic Combined world cup events with the International Ski Federation.

MEDALLISTS *(by nation)*

Country	Gold	Silver	Bronze	Total
NOR	9	7	6	22
FRG	3	1	1	5
GDR	3	-	4	7
JPN	2	1	-	3
FIN	1	5	1	7
SUI	1	2	1	4
FRA	1	1	-	2
AUT	-	1	3	4
URS	-	1	2	3
SWE	-	1	1	2
POL	-	-	1	1

Nordic combined

NAGANO SCHEDULE

Venue: **Hakuba**

Date	Description	Start	Finish
13 Feb	K90m jump individual(m)	9:30	11:30
14 Feb	15km individual (m)	13:00	14:00
19 Feb	K90m jump—team (m)	9:30	11:00
20 Feb	4x5km (m)	13:00	14:30

Nordic combined

Year	Gold	Country	Points	Silver	Country	Points	Bronze	Country	Points
1924	Thorleif Haug	NOR	18.906	Thoralf Stromstad	NOR	18.219	Johan Gröttumsbraaten	NOR	17.854
1928	Johan Gröttumsbraaten	NOR	17.833	Hans Vinjarengen	NOR	15.303	John Snersrud	NOR	15.021
1932	Johan Gröttumsbraaten	NOR	446	Ole Stenen	NOR	436.05	Hans Vinjarengen	NOR	434.6
1936	Oddbjörn Hagen	NOR	430.3	Olaf Hoffsbakken	NOR	419.8	Sverre Brodahl	NOR	408.1
1948	Heikki Hasu	FIN	448.8	Martti Huhtala	FIN	433.65	Sven Israelsson	SWE	433.4
1952	Simon Slattvik	NOR	451.621	Heikki Hasu	FIN	447.5	Sverre Stenersen	NOR	436.335
1956	Sverre Stenersen	NOR	455	Bengt Eriksson	SWE	437.4	Franciszek Gron-Gasienica	POL	436.8
1960	Georg Thoma	GER	457.952	Tormod Knutsen	NOR	453	Nikolai Gusakov	URS	452
1964	Tormod Knutson	NOR	469.28	Nikolai Kiselyev	URS	453.04	Georg Thoma	GER	452.88
1968	Franz Keller	FRG	449.04	Alois Kaelin	SUI	447.99	Andreas Kunz	(ADE?)	444.1
1972	Ulrich Wehling	GDR	413.34	Rauno Miettinen	FIN	405.505	Karl-Heinz Luck	GDR	398.8
1976	Ulrich Wehling	GDR	423.39	Urban Hettich	FRG	418.9	Konrad Winkler	GDR	417.47
1980	Ulrich Wehling	GDR	432.2	Jouko Karjalainen	FIN	429.5	Konrad Winkler	GDR	425.32
1984	Tom Sandberg	NOR	422.595	Jouko Karjalainen	FIN	416.9	Jukka Ylipulli	FIN	410.825
1988	Hippolyt Kempf	SUI		Klaus Sulzenbacher	AUT		Allar Levandi	URS	
1992	Fabrice Guy	FRA	0.0	Sylvain Guillaume	FRA	48.4*	Klaus Sulzenbacher	AUT	1:06.3
1994	Fred Lundberg	NOR	0.0	Takanori Kono	JPN	29.5	Bjarte Vik	NOR	35.3

* time behind winner

Team

Year	Gold	Country		Silver	Country		Bronze	Country	
1988	Hans Pohl	FRG		Andreas Schaad	SUI		Guenther Csar	AUT	
	Hubert Schwarz			Hippolyt Kepmf			Hansjoerg Aschenwald		
	Thomas Mueller			Fredy Glanzmann			Klaus Sulzenbacher		
1992	Reiichi Mikata	JPN		Knut Apeland	NOR		Klaus Ofner	AUT	
	Takanori Kono			Fred Lundberg			Stefan Kreiner		
	Kenji Ogiwara			Trond Elden			Klaus Sulzenbacher		
1994	Taknori Kono	JPN		Knut Apeland	NOR		Hippolyt Kempf	SUI	
	Masashi Abe			Bjarte Vik			Jean-Yves Cuendet		
	Kenji Ogiwara			Fred Lundberg			Andreas Schaad		

SKI JUMPING

by Kazushi Funaki

The ski jumping competition at the Nagano Winter Games is likely to be a global showdown pitting the Japanese against the Europeans. Japan boasts a talented corps of top-level jumpers. They won the ski jumping Nations Cup crown last winter, followed by traditional powers Norway and Finland. Ski jumping is an unpredictable sport, in which the order of placings can be overturned in only moments, but Japan would seem to have an edge being able to train on, and become familiar with, the Nagano in-run.

Masahiko Harada is the main Japanese name. He won the large hill event at the 1997 world championships and already has two world gold medals and two silvers. Harada contributed to the team's silver medal at the 1994 Lillehammer Games. Experienced in top class competition, the 29 year-old veteran and master of the take-off should do well at Nagano where he will probably be making his final Olympic appearance.

Other key athletes from Japan include Kazuyoshi Funaki, Takanobu Okabe and Hiroya Saito who finished in 3rd, 4th and 5th places, respectively, in the 1996/'97 world cup overall rankings. With so many young and talented athletes, the competition within the Japanese team is perhaps the most fierce.

Last season, Primoz Peterka was the world cup overall champion with seven victories. The slender 18 year-old star from Slovenia—by no means a ski jumping power—who stands 1.80m (5ft 11in.) tall and weighs only 60kg (9st 6lb), still managed to take the jumping world by storm. If he can overcome his tendency of not leaning forward enough on some of his jumps, Peterka may surprise the world again in Nagano.

Austria's Andreas Goldberger also has the ability but his off-season admission to having used cocaine in the past has almost surely wrecked his chances.

German veteran Dieter Thoma, 29, has also set his sights on a gold medal. The three-times Olympian helped Germany win the team competition at the 1994 Lillehammer Games and comes with the ability to stretch a seemingly ordinary jump further down the hill.

Background

Ski jumping has been part of the Olympic Winter Games since 1924 in Chamonix. The longest jump registered there, from the 70m hill, was 49m. Since 1964 two events have been included on the Olympic programme—the normal hill and the big hill. From 1964 until '92 these were the K70 and K90 hills respectively—the distances denoting the critical landing point limit (K). These were changed to K90 and K120 in time for the 1992 Games. A team jumping title was added to the events in 1988.

That was also the year in which the flying Finn, Matti Nykanen, won both individual titles with some remarkable jumping during which he often seemed to threaten to jump far enough to land in the crowd at the far end of the out-run such was his talent. However, the victories of the man who ended his career with four golds and one silver, were overshadowed by an unexpected phenomenon in this sport of often aloof heroes.

Michael "Eddie" Edwards of Great Britain was last in both competitions in Calgary. He was a plasterer from Cheltenham with bottle-top glasses who had tried unsuccessfully for a career in Alpine skiing and had taken up ski-jumping by chance. Dubbed "The Eagle", Eddie captured the public imagination in North America and at home for his bravado as a jumping novice. Each time he jumped there was a gasp from the crowd as they feared for his safety. He became an overnight celebrity, appearing on US prime time chat shows as someone who epitomized the true, Olympic spirit. Since 1988 the FIS, skiing's international governing body, has increased the qualification level for ski jumping events.

In 1928 a Norwegian named Jacob Tullin Thoms was the defending champion and he jumped "too far". His 70m jump put him beyond the official landing area and ruined his landing form points. Thoms, landing on the flat ground, injured himself badly and could never ski jump again. Eight years later he won a silver in yachting during the 1936 summer Games.

On February 24th, 1952, 130,000 people packed into the famous Holmenkollen venue in Oslo to watch the ski-jumping competitions —a record Olympic crowd. Ski-jumping arenas have always been spectacular. Spare a thought, however, for those poor jumpers at the

Flying Finn Matti Nykanen

Japan has a host of talented jumpers, including Takanobu Okabe

Toni Nieminen (FIN): youngest ever gold medallist

1976 Innsbruck Olympic Winter Games where the 90m hill overlooked the local cemetery.

The weather threatened to play havoc with the 1968 ski jumping competition. Officials had to put salt on the hills as they had frozen overnight. They did not expect a sudden thaw and had to quickly set to removing the salt again before competition could begin hours late.

At the 1932 Lake Placid Games Norwegian brothers Sigmund and Birger Ruud both took part in the ski-jumping competitions. Birger won the gold (and did so again in 1936) and was first in the downhill section of the Alpine combined. Sigmund was already a silver medallist from 1928. Toni Nieminen of Finland won team gold at the 1992 Olympic Winter Games when he was aged just 16.

In 1994 Espen Bredesen of Norway jumped an Olympic record of 135.5m (445ft) from the 120m (394ft) hill. Japanese spectators at the 1998 Olympic Winter Games will be hoping for a repeat of the 1972 Sapporo Games 70m (230ft) hill event when the host nation took a clean sweep of the medals with Yukio Kasaya winning gold.

A new "V" style of jumping was introduced to the sport by Swede Jan Boklow in the late eighties. At first it was decried but now all the top jumpers employ it.

Equipment

The underside of the skis used by ski-jumpers have a groove in them to keep them straight down the in-run. The skis are also hollow inside and much wider (up to 11.5cm [4.5in.]) than their Alpine counterparts to allow more lift in flight. Ski-jumpers' boots are soft to allow the jumper to lean forward in flight and the boots are attached to the bindings only at the toe. Jumpers also wear specially-designed aerodynamic suits, gloves and obligatory helmets.

Ski jumping hills are basically specifically-constructed giant snow slides. They have an in-run of 109m (358ft) and 88m (289ft) in length respectively for the normal and large hills. The in-run starts at a height of 138m (453ft) for the large hill and 107m (351ft) for the small hill. The landing slope has a gradient of up to 37.5 degrees at its steepest point.

Rules and Regulations

Results in ski-jumping are achieved by adding points given by judges to each competitor for style and length. Each jumper has two jumps per competition. Length is judged in relation to the critical landing point for each hill. Two points are added for every metre beyond the critical (K) point. Style is calculated by the five judges awarding points on a scale of one to 20. Points are given for timing of the take-off, degree of perfection, stability, mid-air form and outline and overall balance as well as for the landing. The highest and lowest of the marks are discarded and the remaining three are totalled. These are added to the distance marks to give the result.

Skiers must land in a telemark position. If they fail to do so a maximum of four points can be deducted. Up to ten marks can be deducted for a fall.

In team competitions each team has four participants each of which has two jumps in the competition. The winner is decided by the total of points achieved by all four jumpers.

New rules have been added to the sport since 1994 to stop "overjumping". Ski jumpers are only allowed to use skis which are up to 80cm (2.6ft) longer than their own height. Bindings must now be placed no more than 57% of the ski length from the tip. Previously, jumpers could place these wherever they wished to gain advantage. And the ski suit worn by jumpers must be no more than 8mm (0.26in.) thick to stop air becoming trapped which was helping with lift and therefore distance.

Nagano Format

Each nation may enter up to 28 athletes in the three Nordic disciplines: cross-country skiing, jumping and Nordic Combined up to a maximum of 20 males and ten females. Four jumpers per event are allowed within these guidelines. There are three jumping competitions at the 1998 Games, all of them for men: the K90 and K120 individual events and the K120 men's team.

Every ski jumper will have qualified for Nagano by competing in world cup or skiflying competitions. In exceptional circumstances some may have qualified by being placed in the top half of the ranking list for the world junior championships or of the Continental Cup competitions. Both the 1996/'97 and 1997/'98 seasons formed the qualification period with the deadline for final qualification on January 11th, 1998

Venue

The 1998 Olympic Winter Games ski-jumping competitions will take place at the Hakuba Ski Jumping Stadium in Happo at the southern end of the Happo'one ski area. Two hills have been constructed specifically for the Games—the first of their type in Japan. Construction was completed in 1992.

A Sporting Legend
Matti Nykanen (FIN)

From the moment that the ski jumping competition was divided into two events—the normal hill and large hill—in 1964, a number of jumpers had attempted to win both gold medals in a single Winter Games. The first to succeed was Finland's Matti Nykanen in Calgary in 1988.

In the previous Winter Games in 1984 in Sarajevo, Nykanen won the silver on the 70m hill event and grabbed the gold on the 90m hill. Nykanen, at 24, famous for his superb technique and indomitable will, came to Calgary in 1988 with world cup overall victories in 1983, '85 and '86.

"The Flying Finn" was also a member of the Finland squad that won the team jumping event, being held for the first time in Calgary, to complete the ski jumping's first and only Olympic hat trick.

Notorious for his alleged love of alcohol and his fiery temper, Nykanen was excluded a number of times from the Finnish national team. His place in Olympic history, however, is assured by his ski jumping genius.

A Sporting Legend
Jens Weissflog (GDR)

Jens Weissflog has been blessed with a long and decorated ski jumper's career. Weissflog, born in 1964, began jumping at the age of eight in the former East Germany and, a decade later, was the world cup champion for the 1983/'84 season.

Aged 19, at the 14th Olympic Winter Games in Sarajevo in 1984, Weissflog soared to the top of the ski jumping world with the gold medal in the 70m hill event, adding the silver medal in the 90m jump.

Weissflog, however, then went through a prolonged slump and after the reunification of the two Germanys, reportedly experienced difficulty adapting to new training methods of Western coaches.

Approaching his late 20s, Weissflog concentrated on learning the innovative "V" style of jumping and, reunited with his old coach on the national team, made his triumphant comeback at the 1994 Lillehammer Games. Ten years after winning his first Olympic gold medal in Sarajevo, Weissflog claimed his second by taking the large hill competition in Lillehammer and then added a third as a member of Germany's winning team of jumpers.

A Sporting Legend

Toni Nieminen (FIN)

At the 16th Olympic Winter Games in Albertville, Finland, always a ski jumping power, brought its latest phenomenon to the Games: 16 year-old Toni Nieminen from Lahti. He promptly became the youngest ski jumper to win an Olympic gold medal.

As spectators moaned about the inclement weather conditions that enveloped the large hill jump, Nieminen nailed jumps of 122m (400ft) and 123m (403.5ft) for the gold medal. He also claimed a gold medal in the team event and a bronze medal in the normal hill jump.

Prior to Albertville, some ski jumpers were still using the traditional style of jumping with their skis held parallel during flight. But a growing number of competitors were beginning to use the "V" style of jumping. Nieminen had begun practising the "V" jump about a year before Albertville and had mastered the style by the time the Games came around.

Nieminen's Albertville success, however, hung like an albatross around his neck. The once national sports hero has, so far, failed to recapture those golden moments in Albertville.

MEDALLISTS *(by nation)*

Country	Gold	Silver	Bronze	Overall
NOR	9	10	7	26
FIN	9	4	3	16
AUT	3	6	7	16
GDR	3	3	3	9
GER	2	-	-	2
JPN	1	3	1	5
TCH	1	2	4	7
POL	1	-	-	1
URS	1	-	-	1
SWE	-	1	1	2
YUG	-	1	1	2
SUI	-	1	-	1
GER	-	-	2	2
USA	-	-	1	1

NAGANO SCHEDULE

Ski jumping

Venue: **Hakuba ski jumping stadium**

Date	Description	Start	Finish
11 Feb	K90m individual (m)	9:30	11:30
15 Feb	K120m individual (m)	9:30	12:30
17 Feb	K120m team (m)	9:30	12:00

MEDALLISTS

Ski jumping

Year	Gold	Country	Pts	Silver	Country	Pts	Bronze	Country	Pts
Special jump - 70m hill									
1924	Jacob Thams	NOR	18.960	Narve Bonna	NOR	18.689	Anders Haugen	USA	17.961
1928	Alf Anderson	NOR	19.208	Sigmund Ruud	NOR	18.542	Rudolph Burkert	CZE	17.937
1932	Birger Ruud	NOR	228.1	Hans Beck	NOR	227	Kaare Wahlberg	NOR	219.5
1936	Birger Ruud	NOR	232	Sven Eriksson	SWE	230.5	Reidar Andersen	NOR	228.9
1948	Petter Hugsted	NOR	228.1	Birger Ruud	NOR	226.6	Thorleif Schielderup	NOR	225.1
1952	Arnfinn Bergamm	NOR	226	Torbjorn Falkangar	NOR	221.5	Karl Holmström	SWE	219.5
1956	Antti Hyvarinen	FIN	227	Aulis Kallakorpi	FIN	225	Harry Glass	GER	224.5
1960	Helmut Recknagel	GER	227.2	Niilo Halonen	FIN	222.6	Otto Leodolter	AUT	219.4
1964*	Veikko Kankkonen	FIN	229.9	Toralf Engan	NOR	226.3	Torgeir Brandtzäg	NOR	222.9
1968	Jiri Raska	CZE	216.5	Reinhold Bachler	AUT	214.2	Baldur Preiml	AUT	212.6
1972	Yukio Kasaya	JPN	244.2	Akitsugo Konno	JPN	234.8	Seiji Aochi	JPN	229.5
1976	Hans-Georg Aschenbach	GDR	252	Jochen Danneberg	GDR	246.2	Karl Schnabl	AUT	242
1980	Anton Innauer	AUT	266.3	Manfred Deckert	GDR	249.2	Hirokazu Yagi	JPN	249.2
1984	Jens Weissflog	GDR	215.2	Matti Nykanen	FIN	214	Jari Puikkonen	FIN	212.8
1988	Matti Nykanen	FIN	229.1	Pavel Ploc	CZE	212.1	Jiri Malec	CZE	211.8
1992	not held								
Special jump - 90m hill									
1964	Toralf Engan	NOR	230.7	Veikko Kankkonen	FIN	228.9	Torgeir Brandtzäg	NOR	227.2
1968	Vladimir Beloussov	URS	231.3	Jiri Raska	CZE	229.4	Lars Grini	NOR	214.3
1972	Wojciech Fortuna	POL	219.9	Walter Steiner	SUI	219.8	Rainer Schmidt	GDR	219.3
1976	Karl Schnabl	AUT	234.8	Anton Innauer	AUT	232.9	Henry Glass	FRG	221.7
1980	Jouko Tormanen	FIN	271	Hubert Neuper	AUT	262.4	Jari Puikkonen	FIN	248.5
1984	Matti Nykanen	FIN	231.2	Jens Weissflog	GDR	213.7	Pavel Ploc	CZE	202.9
1988	Matti Nykanen	FIN	224	Erik Johnsen	NOR	207.9	Matjaz Debelak	YUG	207.7
1992	Ernst Vettori	AUT	222.8	Martin Hollwarth	AUT	218.1	Toni Nieminen	FIN	217
1994	Espen Bredesen	NOR	282	Lasse Ottesen	NOR	268	Dieter Thoma	GER	260.5
120m									
1992	Toni Nieminen	FIN	239.5	Martin Hollwarth	AUT	227.3	Heinz Kuttin	AUT	214.8
1994	Jens Weissflog	GER	274.5	Espen Bredesen	NOR	266.5	Andreas Goldberger	AUT	255
Combined jump									
1956	Juri Moshkin	URS	217.5	Sverre Stenersen	NOR	215	Bengt Eriksson	SWE	214
1964	Georg Thoma	GER	241.1	Tormod Knutsen	NOR	238.9	Nikolai Kiselev	SUI	233
90m team									
1988	Ari Nikkola	FIN	634.4	Primoz Ulaga	YUG	625.5	Ole Eidhammer	NOR	596.1
	Matti Nykanen			Matjaz Zupan			Jon Kjorum		
	Tuomo Ylipulli			Matjaz Debelak			Ole Fidjestol		
	Jari Puikkonen			Miran Tepes			Erik Johnsen		

*(80m)

Year	Gold	Country		Silver	Country		Bronze	Country	

120m team

Year	Gold	Country		Silver	Country		Bronze	Country	
1992	Ari-Pekka Nikkola	FIN	644.4	Heinz Kuttin	AUT	642.9	Tomas Goder	CZE	620.1
	Mika Laitinen			Ernst Vettori			Frantisek Jez		
	Risto Laakkonen			Martin Hollwarth			Jaroslav Sakala		
	Toni Nieminen			Andreas Felder			Jiri Parma		
1994	Hansjoerg Jaekle	GER	970.1	Jinya Nishikata	JPN	956.9	Heinz Kuttin	AUT	918.9
	Christof Duffner			Takanobu Okabe			Christian Moser		
	Dieter Thoma			Noriaki Kasai			Stefan Horngacher		
	Jens Weissflog			Masahiko Harada			Andreas Goldberger		

Hakuba ski jump venue

SNOWBOARDING

Snowboarding Grows Up and Joins The Olympics

by Shanti Sosienski

Is the Olympic Winter Games ready for snowboarding? The time has come where people no longer need to answer this question. The "fastest growing winter sport", as it has been dubbed by the media, will be a part of the Games for the first time in Nagano. The question that now remains is whether the young sport is ready to be thrust into such a spotlight.

The youthful winter activity with "attitude", seen over the last few years by the public in its "punk" form, has been quick to shed its image over the last year and step into the Olympic arena for the first time as a grown-up sport. Once a backcountry activity, banned at one time by many resorts, the Olympic version of the sport is only a small segment of what snowboarding has become today.

Giant slalom, a more traditional race, will be used to introduce snowboarding to the Olympic audience. As potential American Olympian and medal contender Betsy Shaw explains: "Giant slalom is really what snowboards were built for. They are perfect for that radius of a turn".

Some of the bigger names to look out for, along with Shaw, are Lisa Kosglow and Chris Klug, Austria's male and female power racers Dieter Happ and Christine Rauter, and Canadians "Jasey" Jay Anderson and Mark Fawcett.

The other form of snowboarding competition being highlighted at the Nagano Games is "half-pipe". To the unfamiliar eye this discipline might seem a little strange at first. Competitors ride up and down the sides of a U-shaped tube of snow, launching as high as possible into the air, spinning much like a freestyle skier and performing a variety of tricks which are judged and given marks.

Potential Olympians like Todd Richards, Daniel Franck, Terje

Haakonsen, Fabian Rohrer, Guillaume Chastagnol, Michele Taggart, Natasza Zurek, Tricia Byrnes, Jennie Waara, and many more have spent the last year trying to perfect these moves to earn a spot on their countries' national teams. But, unlike giant slalom where true competitors are easily picked out by the clock, half-pipe is a difficult sport to score. Like ice skating, it is a subjective event.

Background

Snowboarding is a very recent phenomenon. It emerged over the last ten years as a youth cult a little like inner-city skateboarding a decade before. The only difference was that this was an activity which took place on the same mountain slopes as more traditional Alpine pursuits. The friction between the two disciplines has often been raw but snowboarding has begun to win friends and influence ski authorities internationally. There is a recently-instituted world cup series organized by FIS (The International Ski Federation).

Snowboarding's inclusion for the first time in the Olympic Winter Games in Nagano in 1998 may prove to be one of the more visionary moves made by the IOC. Its Olympic inclusion constitutes a meteoric rise. The sport has not even been included as a demonstration event —as was its nearest winter counterpart, freestyle skiing. Much will depend on its reception by live and TV audiences alike as well as by the worldwide media.

There are a range of different disciplines in the sport. Those that are on show in Nagano will be the giant slalom and the half-pipe. Americans, Canadians and Austrians should be amongst the top contenders in this sport in Nagano.

Equipment

The vital piece of equipment in this sport is the board itself which is wide and flexible for the half-pipers but stiff and narrow for the giant slalom competitors. For both events the board, which is made of modern composites and/or wood, is ridden skateboard style but with fixed bindings.

Snowboarders use a slightly different style of boots for both disciplines. Those used in the giant slalom are akin to Alpine ski boots but with slightly more flexibility and greater rubber content. They must allow for edge control. The soft boots used in half-pipe whilst still coming up over the ankle have a greater degree again of flexibility to allow the ankle to move when executing skateboard-type manoeuvres. Ski suits and helmets are worn by the giant slalomists.

The giant slalom course is almost 1000m (3281ft) long with a drop in elevation of 290m (951ft) and an average gradient of over18 degrees. The course is laid out symmetrically, unlike its Alpine skiing counterpart, so as to give an equal chance whether a competitor skis with their right or left foot forward.

The half-pipe course looks as it sounds—like a pipe of snow cut in half. It is 120m (394ft) long and also has an average gradient of 18 degrees. The width between the rims is 15m (49ft) and the height of the rims is 3.5m (11ft 6in.).

Rules and Regulations

In the giant slalom event competitors negotiate the course through a series of gates. They race against the clock with the fastest time winning.

For the half-pipe competition, snowboarders ride up and down the U-shaped tube's sides to gain momentum and launch themselves in the air. They perform a series of manoeuvres or "tricks" in the air for which they are judged. There are five judges who award marks up to ten for items such as technique, rotation, height, landing and technical merit. The winner is the snowboarder with the highest points total.

Nagano Format

A total of 120 snowboarders will take part in the inaugural Olympic snowboarding competition in Nagano in 1998. Each nation is permitted a maximum of 14 athletes in this sport, including a maximum of eight males and eight females. Each nation may enter four competitors in each of the four events. There is a giant slalom and half-pipe event for men and women.

Athletes in this sport will have qualified for the Games between December 1996 and January 1998. As the sport is so young in competitive terms, the Federation Internationale de Ski (FIS) has made special arrangements for athletes to enter all of its competitions even if they are not affiliated to their own national ski association. Only athletes who have gained at least one FIS point in these competitions will be able to compete.

Venue

Snowboard's giant slalom event will take place on the slopes of Mount Yakebitai in Shiga Kogen. This venue is also hosting the Alpine skiing slalom and combined slalom.

The half-pipe competition will be held at Kanbayashi Snowboard Park—a top, existing snowboard venue in Yamanouchi Town.

A Contemporary Hero

Todd Richards (USA)

Last summer while most potential Olympians spent months sweating to achieve their goals through gruelling workouts, Todd Richards skateboarded. It is hard to believe that this summer sport, which entails a little board on wheels, could help make the 28 year-old a candidate for the Winter Olympic Games. Yet Richards explains that his less-than-traditional form of half-pipe training uses the same muscle groups as snowboarding. Richards claims that he is not the only one to use the method.

Others, however, may not have gone so far as doing without a coach. "Snowboarding and skating are individualistic sports", says Richards. "I have come this far without a coach, so I don't know why I would need one". To some this may appear to be a bold move. But after eight years of successful competition, Richards, a half-pipe specialist from Breckenridge, Colorado, who was born in December 1969, seems to have come out on top over nearly every other competitor in the world.

A Contemporary Heroine

Betsy Shaw (USA)

Few racers can say that they have been competing as long as Betsy Shaw. Nor have they held as many titles as the 29 year-old. Shaw has been competitively racing since 1989 and has placed in the top five in many of the competitions she has entered since 1993. Her dedication and consistent ability to stay focused on winning have helped her gain recognition in the snowboarding world as one of the most solid female giant slalom competitors making her a definite Olympic hopeful.

"The fact that snowboarding has made it to the Olympics is overwhelming", says the native of Manchester, Vermont. "I never thought I would see snowboarding come this far in my career". After a strong placing in the Grand Prix races (the American Olympic qualifiers) in the 1996/'97 season, Shaw is ready to take on the Games. Then she will retire. After nearly ten years of racing, no matter what results Nagano brings, she is ready for a quieter life at home.

A Contemporary Heroine

Nicola Thost (Ger)

Born in March 1977, this half-pipe specialist from Pforzheim in Germany has only been racing for four years. In that short time she has risen to impress the judges more than most other professional competitors. An international winner, Thost's speciality acrobatics are her strength—particularly her "backside 540".

"There's a special feeling you get when you do that one trick and push it to the other wall, and then do another trick", she explains. "I like the whole atmosphere at contests. It doesn't feel like a real fight. To me it's more to show yourself what is possible in snowboarding".

A Contemporary Hero

Martin Freinademetz (Aut)

Martin Freinademetz likes to win, especially when it comes to snowboarding. Born in December 1969, he grew up next to the ski-lift in the Austrian Tyrol and he has snowboarded for the past twelve years. Seven of those have been in competition where he has won titles at all levels. "I have won every possible snowboard title up to the international level", he says. "If I win a gold medal in the Olympics that will be the ultimate".

But, despite his desire to rule the racing world, Martin still loves freeriding. "The more I compete and the more professional everything gets, the less time I have for freeriding, but I think there's nothing better than a powder day in the backcountry".

NAGANO SCHEDULE

Snowboarding

Venue: **Y=Mt Yakebitai; K=Kanbayashi Snowboard Park**

Date	Description	Round	Start	Finish	
8 Feb	Giant slalom (m)		9:30	10:30	Y
			13:00	14:00	
9 Feb	Giant slalom (w)		9:30	10:30	Y
			13:00	14:00	
12 Feb	Half pipe (m & w)	elim	9:30	13:00	K
	Half pipe (m & w)	FINAL	13:00	14:30	K

Street-cred on the slopes

Top contender Martin Freinademetz (AUT)

PART FOUR
The Olympic Family and Movement

THE IOC: A VAST AND COMPLEX GLOBAL ORGANIZATION

by Michele Verdier

Introduction

What is the Olympic Movement? Who organizes the Organizing Committees? And who ensures that the Games are run in the best possible conditions for the athletes of the world? Who is responsible for promoting the ideals of Olympism worldwide on a permanent basis?

Inevitably the answers to such enormous questions lie within an interlocking series of vast and complex global organizations which make up the Olympic Movement.

The administrative structures of the International Olympic Committee (IOC) and the Olympic Movement have evolved parallel to the development of Olympic sport, now more than a century old. Over time, they have grown and adapted to the environment of the society in which sport exists, and have incorporated prevailing new technology and methods along every step of the way.

Today the IOC alone has a permanent headquarters split between Olympic House and the Chateau de Vidy in Lausanne, Switzerland, and employs around 80 full-time staff. It is equipped with the latest information technology, which enables it to follow events all over the world as they happen, around the clock. All a far cry from the days at the turn of the century when Baron Pierre de Coubertin, the man responsible for reviving the modern Olympic Games, worked single-handed from his home using just handwritten correspondence and the telegraph as means of communication.

The Olympic Movement is often graphically depicted as a pyramid. The IOC is at the tip. Two of the sides are occupied, one by the International Federations (IFs) governing a sport included on the programme of the Games of the Olympiad (summer) or Olympic Winter Games, the other by the National Olympic Committees (NOCs), which number 197. Inside this pyramid are the organizing committees elected by the IOC Session (or annual conference), whose task is to set up the practical side of the Games that they have been chosen to host. The pyramid also contains the organizations and the athletes who agree to be guided in their activities by the Olympic Charter.

The International Olympic Committee

The IOC is not a state but, in its operation, it possesses the structures of a typical modern democratic state. In the words of the "Olympic Charter", the set of rules which fixes and governs the activities of the Olympic Movement and which is to some extent its constitution, the IOC is the "supreme authority of the Olympic Movement".

It is a non-governmental, non-profit organization in the form of an association, with the status of a legal person. It is financed entirely by private income, essentially from the negotiation of exclusive television rights and marketing programmes, to the exclusion of any state subsidy. Moreover, the IOC retains only 10% of these revenues, and distributes the majority to its partners, namely the IFs and NOCs — through the so-called Olympic Solidarity fund — and the organizing committees (60%).

As the charter says, the IOC's role is, among other things, "to lead the promotion of Olympism; to encourage the organization and development of sport and sports competitions; to collaborate with the competent public or private organizations and authorities in the endeavour to place sport at the service of humanity; to ensure the regular celebration of the Olympic Games; to fight against any form of discrimination affecting the Olympic Movement; to lead the fight against doping in sport; to take measures, the goal of which is to prevent endangering the health of athletes; and to see to it that the Olympic Games are held in conditions which demonstrate a responsible concern for environmental issues".

The IOC fulfils these tasks through three elected elements: the Session (or annual conference), the Executive Board and the President himself— all supported by an administrative nerve-centre in Lausanne.

The Session is the "annual general assembly" or conference of all 96 IOC members. It constitutes the legislative power of the Movement, and as such is the supreme organ of the IOC, a kind of "Olympic parliament". Its agenda is established by the Executive

Board and President. But its work generally revolves around adopting, modifying and interpreting the Olympic Charter. The Session may delegate all or some of its powers to the Executive Board. Any rule change or adoption of a new text requires the consent of at least two-thirds of the members present at the Session.

An IOC member is elected by all the existing members during the Session. They receive no salary for their work. In practical terms, to be chosen as an IOC member, a person must have had a career in sport (actively or as a voluntary or salaried administrator or senior office holder) or be a person of considerable influence within their own country. In reality, many IOC members fulfil both sets of criteria. They are generally recommended to the Session for membership by the President and Executive Board who will have researched them thoroughly in advance.

Members take an oath on joining the IOC and they must be able to speak at least one of the languages used at IOC meetings including French, English, German, Russian, Spanish and Arabic. The two official Olympic languages are French and English. Not every participating Olympic nation has a member. Some have two because they have organized an Olympic Games in the past; such is the historical fashion in which membership has grown over the years. Baron Pierre de Coubertin's original inspiration for the IOC's membership was based on that used to select Stewards at Henley Royal Regatta— a rowing event in Britain.

Those members elected before 1966 are members for life. Members elected since 1966 must finish at the end of the year in which they celebrate their 80th birthday. Members may tender their resignation at any time. They are the IOC's ambassadors to their own country, and not the reverse. They must attend the Sessions, participate in the work of the commissions to which they have been appointed, inform colleagues about the situation of Olympism in their country of origin and represent the President whenever asked to do so.

The Session also elects, through a secret ballot, eleven of the IOC members to form the Executive Board: the President, four vice presidents and six other members. A simple majority, that is to say half the members present plus one, is required. Together with the President, the Executive Board holds the executive power. It is the IOC's "government" or "cabinet", and its members begin their mandates at the end of the Session which elected them. They are elected for a four-year term.

An ordinary member of the Executive Board may stand for

election as vice president. All outgoing members, including vice-presidents, must wait for one year before being eligible to seek a new term, whether as an ordinary member or directly as vice president. This rule was established to ensure two elements indispensable to the IOC: continuity of action (hence stability), and renewal (to bring in new blood and new ideas).

It is the Executive Board which has ultimate responsibility for the daily workings of the IOC, approves the internal organization, organization chart and administrative regulations; is responsible for financial management and prepares the annual report. It establishes the agenda for the Sessions and recommends people for election as IOC members. Convened by the IOC President, the Executive Board meets four or five times a year.

"Primus inter pares", the President is elected by secret ballot for an eight-year term by the IOC members. He or she may be re-elected for successive four-year terms. If he or she is prevented from fulfilling his or her duties, he or she is replaced by the most senior vice president until a new President is elected at the next Session. The President presides over all the activities of the IOC and represents it permanently. Since 1980 Juan Antonio Samaranch has been an executive President for the IOC because of the complexity of the post although he does not receive a salary.

To perform the tasks assigned to him by the Olympic Charter, the President sets up permanent or ad hoc Commissions and working groups whenever this appears necessary. These Commissions, often split into sub-commissions and working groups, meet at most once a year. The latest Commission to be set up by the IOC addresses issues related to sport and the environment. The President appoints the members, who do not have to be (and often are not) members of the IOC. Delegates of the IFs and NOCs also sit on the Commissions, together with representatives of the professions concerned, particularly for the media (press and radio/television) and medical commissions. There is an athlete representative on every IOC Commission.

The Commissions are consultative bodies which give opinions and make recommendations. They have no decision-making powers. They submit reports to the Executive Board which examines these and in turn makes recommendations to the Session for a final decision.

The IOC also has a consultative body called the Congress. Convened by the President at fairly regular intervals, it is a discussion forum which brings together the IOC, IFs, NOCs, athletes, referees, media and all recognized associations dealing with sport or sports activities, in a format decided in advance by all the partners. This "university of ideas" allows the main orientation and development of the Olympic Movement to be identified. Its recommendations and final motions are studied by an ad hoc commission, which reports to the Executive Board and Session. The resulting concrete measures are incorporated into the Olympic Charter, and thus allow the Olympic Movement to perpetuate itself and secure its permanence, while ensuring necessary renewal and progress.

The "IOC system" is vast and flexible in order to perform its mission, which is composite and on a global level. But it needs thorough coordination. This is provided by the central administration based in Lausanne, since 1915, and, more precisely, at the Chateau de Vidy since the end of 1967.

A director general (responsible more specifically for political, legal and financial issues), and a secretary general look after, among other things, general administration, protocol and the organization of all the meetings, and provides a link with the Olympic Museum. They are the right hand of the President. The director general and secretary general are assisted in their tasks by a team of directors responsible for specific areas.

The IOC has a permanent staff of around 80 people, representing some 15 nationalities and the administrative structure more or less parallels the commissions, all the directors being responsible for one or more commissions which correspond to their field of activity.

Equipped with a powerful data processing system and communications and information networks (in particular a wire to seven world and national agencies enabling it to follow global developments in real time 24 hours a day) linked to the four corners of the globe, the administration can perform the mission entrusted to it on behalf of the Movement, with maximum efficiency and a minimum number of permanent staff.

One of the key words of the Olympic Movement is independence. Each of its component parts, while included in a coherent whole, still retains its autonomy and sovereignty.

The International Federations

The International Federations governing a sport on the programme of the Games of the Olympiad and the Olympic Winter Games have an administrative structure comparable to that of the IOC, at least in terms of technical codification and rules of the sport in question. The IFs also have a permanent headquarters, an administration, executive board or committee and a general assembly or congress. They all have established constitutions, charters or rules which define their activities and missions as their sports have become codified and organized, some in a structured form even before the IOC was created.

They are also responsible for overseeing the technical correctness of the sports competitions at the Olympic Games. They help and advise the Organizing Committee as well as providing key technical personnel. They also set the competition rules and format.

Over the years, the winter and summer IFs have joined together within umbrella bodies promoting and safeguarding their common interests, particularly vis-a-vis the IOC and organizing committees. Thus the Association of Summer Olympic International Federations (ASOIF) and the Association of International Winter Sports Federations (AIWF) have come into being. It is through them that the funds from television rights are distributed among the IFs which form these associations, according to their own independently-formulated systems.

The National Olympic Committees

There are a total of 197 National Olympic Committees representing 197 countries. The NOCs represent the IOC in a given territory and their essential role is to form and enter the national teams which will represent them at the Olympic Games and to ensure the development of the Olympic Movement in the country for which they are recognized.

They are each vastly different in their size, scope and cultural background. Some NOCs are merged with the sports ministry, others are simply administered from the home of the president or secretary general whilst others again have their own administration and sophisticated technical, coaching, medical, marketing and sponsorship departments. They are similarly grouped together within an umbrella body, the Association of National Olympic Committees (ANOC), which provides an interface with the IOC and the organizing committees. In order to take into account regional and specific disparities, continental associations have also been set up for each of the continents: Africa, America, Asia, Europe and Oceania.

A permanent dialogue is maintained between the three pillars of the Olympic Movement, for organizing the Olympic Games but also for developing the Olympic Movement. Annual or two-yearly meetings are held between the IOC and ASOIF, IOC and AIWF and IOC and ANOC. All the problems of the Olympic Movement are discussed there, respecting the independence and autonomy of each partner, with the ultimate goal of working with the chosen organizing committees to stage the best summer and Winter Games possible for the athletes of the world.

Over the past 100 years the Olympic Movement has successfully ensured its survival by maintaining cohesion and unity. Only unity between the IOC, IFs and NOCs has enabled this atypical movement to run world sport in the service of the fundamental ideals on which the Olympic phenomenon is built. The Movement is now looking forward to the next Millennium.

CITIES BIDDING TO HOST THE OLYMPIC WINTER GAMES

Year	Bidding cities	Host cities
1924		Chamonix
1928	Davos	
	Engelberg	
	St-Moritz	St-Moritz
1932	Bear Mountain	First priority
	Denver	
	Duluth	
	Lake Placid	Lake Placid
	Minneapolis	
	Montréal	
	Yosemite Valley 1	
	Yosemite Valley 2	
1936		Garmisch-Partenkirchen
1940		First priority given to Sapporo (withdrawn) Transerred to St-Moritz—after a disagreement transferred again to Garmisch-Partenkirchen but due to war the Games were not held.
1944	Cortina d'Ampezzo	
	Montréal	Not held due to war
1948	Lake Placid	Should have been awarded to
	St-Moritz	London but as London was not suitable for Winter Games it reverted to St-Moritz.
1952	Cortina d'Amezzo	
	Lake Placid	
	Oslo	Oslo
1956	Colorado	
	Cortina d'Ampezzo	Cortina d'Ampezzo
	Lake Placid	
	Montréal	
1960	Garmisch-Partenkirchen	
	Innsbruck	
	Squaw Valley	Squaw Valley
	St-Moritz	
1964	Calgary	
	Innsbruck	Innsbruck
	Lahti	
1968	Calgary	
	Grenoble	Grenoble
	Lahti	
	Lake Placid	
	Oslo	
	Sapporo	

Year	Bidding cities	Host cities
1972	Banff	
	Lahti	
	Salt Lake City	
	Sapporo	Sapporo
1976	Denver	Denver withdrew in 1974 after
	Sion	referendum
	Tampere	Games attributed to Innsbruck.
	Vancouver	
1980	Chamonix	Both Chamonix and Vancouver
	Lake Placid	withdrew leaving Lake Placid
	Vancouver	as the only candidate
1984	Göthenberg	
	Sapporo	
	Sarajevo	Sarajevo
1988	Calgary	Calgary
	Cortina d'Ampezzo	
	Falun	
1992	Albertville	Albertville
	Anchorage	
	Berchtesgaden	
	Cortina d'Ampezzo	
	Falun	
	Lillehammer	
	Sofia	
1994	Anchorage	
	Lausanne	
	Lillehammer	Lillehammer
	Östersund	
	Sofia	
1998	Aoste	
	Jaca	
	Nagano	Nagano
	Östersund	
	Salt Lake City	
2002	Graz	
	Jaca	
	Östersund	
	Poprad Tatry	
	Quebec	
	Salt Lake City	Salt Lake City
	Sion	
	Sotchi	
	Tarvisio	

OLYMPIC SOLIDARITY

By Dick Palmer

The beginnings of Olympic Solidarity go back to 1961. Count Jean de Beaumont, one of the IOC Members in France, had the idea of an Olympic Aid Commission whose aim would be to assist those National Olympic Committees (NOCs) most in need. The notion was that a fund would be established to be supported by the IOC, donations from companies, organizations and individuals and by the richest NOCs. In 1963 the IOC created a Commission to assist underprivileged NOCs but later, sadly, due to lack of funds, it was decided not to continue.

In 1968 during a meeting of NOCs a programme described as Olympic Solidarity was formed. Thus began the movement and, of course, the name. The IOC after some initial misgivings adopted the concept in 1971 and set up an Olympic Solidarity Commission. Prominent in those early stages were Count Jean de Beaumont, Giulio Onesti of Italy and Raoul Mollet of Belgium (who developed a system of help and assistance, particularly by sports experts such as coaches, for developing NOCs).

Olympic Solidarity had its first home in Rome under the guidance of Onesti, the then President of CONI (The Italian Olympic Committee) and the first President of ANOC (the worldwide Association of National Olympic Committees). Its first Director was Edward Wieztoric from Poland. However, in 1979, Wieztoric left and the offices of Solidarity moved to Lausanne, Switzerland.

In 1980 Juan Antonio Samaranch became President of the IOC. He quickly realized both the potential and importance of Olympic Solidarity. President Samaranch's philosophy was (and is) based on the strength of the three pillars of the Olympic Movement (the IOC, the International Federations and the NOCs) and Olympic Solidarity clearly had a pivotal role in strengthening the status, role and work of the NOCs.

283

Significantly President Samaranch, in 1981, appointed fellow Spaniard Anselmo Lopez to be the Director of Olympic Solidarity. He has been an inspired choice. A man of impeccable integrity, Lopez is himself a highly successful businessman who has brought his business acumen to bear on the development of Olympic Solidarity.

Continental Associations have been given a key role in the formation of Olympic Solidarity policies and on how the funds (made available through the television revenues for Olympic Games) are made available to NOCs. Each NOC in the Olympic Movement has benefited from Solidarity grants. Six athletes and two officials from each NOC have their expenses paid to the Games. Each NOC has an annual subvention for its administrative costs. NOCs are able to call on experts to run sports coaching courses in their countries for high level athletes and for national coaches. The Itinerant School for Sports Administration (a particular initiative of Anselmo Lopez) has run hundreds of courses to improve the efficiency and administrative skills of the NOCs. In many ways it is the Olympic Movement's most effective form of Olympic education.

But Olympic Solidarity has to cope with a changing world just like all other aspects of sport. Recently there has been a marketing initiative to try to improve the marketing skills of NOCs in the developing world to help them attract further and vital funds from sponsors. Olympic Solidarity scholarships are now given to promising athletes, who lack opportunities in their own countries, to enable them to train and thus compete with the best in the world. Already results at recent Olympic Games and world championships give testimony to the benefits of this scheme.

And so from its early, perhaps tentative, beginnings Olympic Solidarity has become an indispensable part of the National Olympic Committees. By strengthening the work of the NOCs it is fortifying the basic framework of the Olympic Movement. Long may it play this vital role.

THE OLYMPIC FIGHT AGAINST DRUGS IN SPORT

by John Goodbody

The International Olympic Committee has struggled with persistent and lengthy determination to rid sport of drug-taking. As the guardian of the ethics of the Olympic Movement, it has been in the forefront of this battle, not only at the Games every four years but also for the panoply of sport, in all its variety of competitions across the world.

Quite rightly, the IOC has taken on itself the responsibility to co-ordinate the work against doping: to sponsor conferences; to accredit laboratories; to establish a definitive list of banned substances and, above all, to give sport the moral leadership, which it has so desperately needed.

Because the Olympic Games are the most widely-publicized event on the sporting calendar, positive tests at the Games receive extraordinary publicity. The most notorious case of doping at the Games, the banning of Ben Johnson, of Canada, three days after his men's 100m victory in the sport of athletics over Carl Lewis in 1988, became such a "cause celebre" only because it had taken place at the Olympic Games. Such global interest would not have occurred if this positive test had been recorded at even the world athletics championships, let alone a grand prix meeting.

Drug-taking in sport is not a new phenomenon. There had been reports of competitors using dope in the 19th century, pre-dating even the founding of the Modern Olympic Games in 1896. These included canal swimmers in Amsterdam in 1865 and six-day cyclists 14 years later. It is believed that Dorando Pietri, the Italian who collapsed at the finish of the 1908 Olympic marathon, may have taken strychnine, then commonly used as a stimulant when taken in small doses. There were also reports that empty ampules and syringes were found in the dressing-room at the 1952 Olympic Games in Oslo during the skating events.

However, the decisive moment for the IOC occurred in 1960, when Knud Jensen, a Danish cyclist, died during the road race, a collapse almost certainly caused by taking stimulants. The following year, an IOC Medical Commission was set up in Athens under the presidency of Sir Arthur (later Lord) Porritt. Some drugs tests were carried out on cyclists at the 1964 Games, the first occasion these had occurred at the Games. Three years later, with the resignation of Sir Arthur and his replacement by Prince Alexandre de Merode of Belgium, the Commission was reconstituted. It was this commission, which had charge of the first drugs tests to be carried out across the sports for the 1968 Games in Grenoble and Mexico.

The original impetus for instituting testing was to combat the growing use of stimulants. In 1967, Tommy Simpson, the 1965 world champion and Britain's greatest-ever cyclist, had died during the Tour de France on Mont Ventoux. Amphetamines were found in his clothing. However, properly regularized dope tests can easily identify whether competitors have taken stimulants and since the early '70s their use has declined. As Sir Arthur Gold, the former chairman of the British Olympic Association, said of testing at events: "Those who get caught are either the careless or the ill-advised."

The greatest problem that the IOC, and particularly the doping sub-commission of its medical commission, has faced has been the use of hormone drugs. They began to be widely employed in the early '60s. In 1973, Hal Connolly, the former Olympic hammer champion, wrote that from 1964 to '72: "like all my competitors I was using anabolic steroids as an integral part of my training in the hammer throw."

What was not perceived in the '70s was the wide-spread use to which anabolic steroids could be put. Initially, it was thought that only sports like the throwing events in athletics, weightlifters and the heavier divisions of the combat sports would benefit by adding increased muscle bulk. However, competitors in other disciplines found that the drugs enabled them to recover more quickly from intensive exercise, and that a whole range of activities could benefit, from long-distance running to swimming, from sprinting to cycling.

The first problem was one of detection. The IOC owed much to Professor Raymond Brooks of St. Thomas's Hospital, London, who discovered a foolproof method of analysis. This was employed at the 1974 Commonwealth Games in New Zealand. The scientific results satisfied the IOC, who in April 1975, banned the use of anabolic steroids. In 1976, eight weightlifters were found positive for drug offences in Montreal, seven of them for anabolic steroids.

However, there remained a further problem. That same year, Professor Arnold Beckett, then a member of the IOC Medical Commission, wrote: "A competitor may take anabolic steroids during training, discontinue their use a week or so before a particular event and still have an advantage at least in weight, from the drug misuse. Yet a urine sample collected at the event does not show a positive result. If international sports federations decide to introduce random testing at various events throughout the year, thereby making it difficult to establish a continuous anabolic steroid schedule, this should constitute a deterrent."

Sadly there was a lack of initiative for many years by the international federations to set up a programme of out-of-competition testing. In athletics, the centrepiece of the summer Games, there were more than 140 drug offences world-wide, many involving Olympic champions or world record-holders, even before the case of Ben Johnson focussed the minds of the officials of both the sport and the Olympic movement.

What was of such concern in the Johnson case was not that the sprinter was found positive, it was rather that at the subsequent judicial inquiry, Johnson and other leading Canadian athletes admitted that they had been taking hormone drugs for several years without being caught. They also disclosed what had been rumoured for several years: that competitors were now using substances like human growth hormone (HGH), which was not prohibited because no satisfactory test had been agreed.

There have been very few cases of proven drug taking during the Olympic Winter Games although suspicions have always surrounded the use of "blood-doping" in some of the distance skiing events.

In 1976 in Innsbruck, the Soviet Union female cross-country star Galina Koulakova, winner of five medals at previous Games, was tested after winning 5km bronze. She was found to have traces of a banned substance from the use of a nasal spray for a streaming cold. Her medal was taken away but the offence was considered trifling enough to permit her to continue in the 10km race and the relay where she earned another bronze and gold respectively.

Also at the 1976 Winter Games Hans-Georg Aschenbach of the former East Germany won the 70m ski jump event. He later admitted to having taken anabolic steroids for several years. He described waiting for his doping result at those Games as "the worst hours of his life" because he was so afraid he was going to be found out.

Two days before the opening ceremony of the 1988 Olympic Winter Games the Soviet Union's Nikolai Gulyaev was cleared to compete in the speed skating events where he won a gold. This was despite having been caught passing steriods to a Norwegian skater two months earlier. He protested his innocence by saying that a trainer had given him the package and he was unaware of its contents.

Czechoslovkia's Frantisek Pospisil admitted during the 1976 ice hockey tournament that he had been taking codeine to combat a virus when he was called for a random test after a game against Poland. The IOC expelled Pospisil and declared the match result void.

More recently, outside of the Games, Liubov Egorova of Russia, Olympic multi-medallist was sent home from a recent cross-country world championships for allegedly failing a doping test. And Great Britain's Mark Tout—who led the Olympic two-man bobsleigh event in Albertville in 1992 after two runs—was banned from the sport for life last year for taking anabolic steroids.

The dismantling of the 'Iron Curtain' in 1989-'90 had earlier provided further evidence of the extent of general drug-taking in sport. Everyone had suspected that the former East Germans had been taking drugs but what was not fully understood was the extent of the state's involvement across the range of Olympic disciplines.

Since 1990 the IOC has made strenuous efforts to standardize penalties for drug abuse throughout the sports. It has also looked at a Court of Arbitration for sport to limit the need for expensive legal cases. And, as the international federations have begun increasing the number of out-of-competition tests, so some of the loopholes have begun to be closed.

Another would have been shut if the findings of Professor Manfred Donike of Germany had been accepted. The head of the Cologne laboratory believed he could identify whether someone had taken hormone drugs even if he had stopped taking them several months before a test. He called his method the 'steroid profile'. However, this stalwart of the IOC Medical Commission died in August 1995 before he was able to convince his colleagues on the unquestioned validity of his research.

Perhaps the IOC should now consider building a laboratory at its HQ in Lausanne, where a team of technicians could continue both this work and other research initiatives to counter the increasingly sophisticated methods of the drug users. It would be a continuation of a duty which it has discharged so keenly over the last 35 years.

THE NEXT OLYMPIC CENTURY*

by Richard Palfreyman

Sydney, with its landmark Opera House, is set to take the Olympic Movement into the next century when it hosts the Games of the year 2000 from September 15 to October 1 during the normally mild and sunny antipodean Spring. The Australian city was chosen as host in September 1993 by the IOC during its Session in Monte Carlo.

70% of the Sydney venues are already in place. An Aquatics centre was opened in October 1994 at Sydney Olympic Park. The area, at Homebush Bay, will also stage athletics, baseball, cycling, tennis and archery. It is being built on former industrial land whose rehabilitation is seen as a major environmental triumph. The Athletes' Village will be the first to house all the athletes from every sport in one place. It will feature recycling, improved energy efficiency and solar power.

Sydney Harbour is the focus of other venues including sailing, football, basketball, weightlifting, judo, table tennis, triathlon (making its Olympic debut) and taekwondo. Ferry services will link the venues. Visitors will be able to enjoy a range of accommodation as well as superb public transport networks. The cost of staging the Games is likely to be A$2 billion but the Australian economy should benefit by A$7.3 billion.

Meanwhile, in 1998, the Olympic Family looks forward to the last Olympic Winter Games of this Millennium in Nagano, Japan. Nagano was selected as host city by the IOC during its Session of June 1991 in Birmingham. Salt Lake City, USA, beaten in that Birmingham vote, was later selected to host the Olympic Winter Games of 2002.

Salt Lake City, USA, is at the centre of the Wasatch Mountains "front" on the Western slopes of the Rocky Mountains and will host the 2002 Olympic Winter Games. There will be approximately 70 medal events across seven sports. NBC TV have already bought the US television rights for $545 million

* More information on both venues will be available in the Official Companion to Sydney to be published in mid 2000.

289

There is only one international event that exerts sufficient power to unite the people of the world. Where the only conflict is one of sporting endeavour.

The Olympic Games.

It is the continual support and co-operation of the Worldwide Olympic Partners that make this possible. Their experience, products and technology provide direct support for staging the Games. And National Olympic Committees are able to help their teams with advanced training facilities and technical assistance.

This universal partner support enables the world's athletes to compete in the spirit of friendship, solidarity and fair play synonymous with the Olympic Movement.

For many the pursuit of excellence remains a distant dream. With the help of the Worldwide Olympic Partners, athletes at the Olympic Games will realise that dream.

e Pursuit
Excellence

The Worldwide Olympic Sponsors

INTERNATIONAL OLYMPIC COMMITTEE

International Olympic Committee
Chateau de Vidy, 1007 Lausanne,
Switzerland
Tel: (41.21) 621 61 11
Fax: (41.21) 621 62 16

Museum and Olympic Study Centre
Villa Olympique, 1 Quai d'Ouchy,
1006 Lausanne, Switzerland
Tel: (41.21) 621 65 11
Fax: (41.21) 621 65 12

INTERNATIONAL OLYMPIC SPORTS FEDERATIONS

(Winter Games)

(Sequence: by sport. C=Founding
date; A=Number of affiliated national
organisations)

Biathlon

UIPMB: Union Intrnationale de
Pentathlon Moderne et Biathlon
(C: 1948 A: 72)
Airport Center, Postfach 1,
5071 Wals Himmelreich, Austria
Tel: (43.662) 85 58 50/1
Fax: (43.662) 855 05 05/ 855 05 18

Bobsleigh

FIBT: Fédération Internationale de
Bobsleigh et de Tobogganing
(C: 1923 A: 48)
Via Piranesi 44B, 20137 Milan, Italy
Tel: (39.2) 757 33 19
Fax: (39.2) 738 06 24 / 70 12 47 43

Curling

WCF: World Curling Federation
(C: 1966 A: 31)
c/o Messrs Waltham Electronic
GmbH, Anzinger Strasse 11, 81671
Munich, Germany
Tel: (49.89) 416 72 17
Fax: (49.89) 416 72 27 / 49 50 11

Ice Hockey

IIHF: International Ice Hockey
Federation
(C: 1908 A: 50)
Tödistrasse 23, 8002 Zurich,
Switzerland
Tel: (41.1) 281 14 30
Fax: (41.1) 281 14 33

Luge

FIL: Fédération Internationale de
Lude de Course
(C: 1957 A: 41)
Rathausplatz 9, 83471
Berchtesgaden, Germany
Tel: (49.8652) 669 60
Fax: (49.8652) 669 69

Skating

ISU: International Skating Union
(C: 1892 19 A: 64)
Promenade 73, 7270 Davos-Platz,
Switzerland
Tel: (41.81) 410 06 00
Fax: (41.81) 410 06 06

Skiing

FIS: Fédération Internationale
de Ski
(C: 1924 A: 86)
Blochstrasse 2, 3653
Oberhofen/Thunersee, Switzerland
Tel: (41.33) 244 61 61
Fax: (41.33) 243 53 53

NATIONAL OLYMPIC COMMITTEES
(For forthcoming Games)
A complete list of National Olympic
Committees is available from the
IOC.

AUS:Australian Olympic Committee
Inc., Level 13,
The Maritime Centre
207 Kent Street
Sydney NSW 2000
Tel: (61.2) 931 20 75
Fax: (61.2) 931 20 98

USA: United States Olympic
Committee, Olympic House, 1750
East Boulder Street
Colorado Springs, Colorado 80909
Tel: (1.719) 578 45 42
Fax: (1.719) 632 41 80

OLYMPIC ORGANIZING COMMITTEES
(For forthcoming Games)
Sydney 2000, Sydney Organizing
Committee for the XXVII Olympic
Games (SOCOG)
Level 14, 207 Kent Street, Sydney,
NSW 2000. Australia.
Tel: (61.2) 9297 2000
Fax: (61.2) 9297 2020

Salt Lake City 2002, Salt Lake
Olympic Organizing Committee for
the Winter Games of 2002 (SLOC)
257 East 200 South, Suite 600, Salt
Lake City / Utah 84111, USA
Tel: (1.801) 322 20 20
Fax: (1.801) 364 76 44

293

Olympic Museum Lausanne
Where the Olympics come alive every day

The Olympic Museum in Lausanne, Switzerland.
Here's where you'll discover the fullest, fascinating source of
Olympic information and inspiration.

Here's where the most memorable, moving moments in Olympic competition
come alive before your eyes, in vivid sound and pictures.

Permanent and temporary exhibitions, an auditorium, video library,
cafeteria and shop plus a terrace with a breathtaking view of
the Alps and Lake of Geneva : all there for you.
So plan your visit today !

OLYMPIC MUSEUM
LAUSANNE

Opening times : May 1 to Sept. 30 Monday to Sunday from 10 a.m. to 7 p.m.
Oct. 1 to Apr. 30 Tuesday to Sunday from 10 a.m. to 6 p.m.
Every Thursday to 8 p.m.

Car park: Hôtel Beau-Rivage and Pl. de la Navigation
1, Quai d'Ouchy, CH - 1001 Lausanne
Information: (021) 621 65 11

Authors and Editors

EDITORS:

Bryn Vaile won Olympic gold in yachting's Star class in Korea in 1988. He is a sportswriter, sports marketing and PR consultant.

Caroline Searle is a former sports journalist who worked for the British Olympic Association for seven years as its Public Affairs Director. Both are partners in Matchtight Media—a sports publications, sponsorship and public relations agency.

AUTHORS:

The History Section:

Joseph Metzger: Chief sports editor, since 1979, of "Die Presse", Austria's leading, quality daily newspaper. Also a freelance contributor with the Austrian state television company. A renowned expert on winter sports

Morley Myers: A member of the IOC Press Commission since 1980, is one of Britain's most experienced sports journalists and this year received the Olympic Order for his services to Olympism. Has worked for over 30 years reporting international sport, first with Reuters and then United Press International before turning freelance. Has attended six Olympic Winter Games in addition to eight summer Games.

The Nagano Section:

Wilf O'Reilly: 1991 World short track speed skating champion and winner of two gold medals when the sport was demonstrated at the 1988 Olympic Winter Games in Calgary. Competed at the 1992 and 1994 Olympic Winter Games. Now coach to the Dutch national short track speed skating team and a successful businessman.

The Sportsfile:

Thore-Erik Thoresen: A sports journalist since 1965 who joined Norway's leading daily paper, Aftenposten, in 1974. Has covered biathlon on a national and international level since 1977.

Ingeborg Kollbach: Began work straight from school in 1967 with SID (Sports Information Dienst, the German sports news agency). Has covered three Olympic Games and four Olympic Winter Games. Now runs her own press agency and is the press officer for the International Bobsleigh and Tobogganing Association (FIBT).

Hakan Sundstrom: Joined Sweden's central news agency, TT, in 1970. Has reported on every curling world championship for men since 1971. A former general secretary of the Swedish Curling Association who has been media relations officer for the World Curling Federation since 1995.

John MacKinnon: Former sports journalist who now works for Hockey Canada.

Harro Esmarch: Has written several publications on the sport of luge and a history of the bobsleigh. Has attended every world and European bobsleigh and luge championships since 1967. Press officer of the International Luge Federation (FIL) since 1989.

Debbie Becker: Is a founding member of USA Today - a leading American newspaper. She joined the staff in 1982 for its first publication and has covered Olympic sports since 1984 with specialities in gymnastics and figure skating. A former Division I athlete.

Dick Kiers: Leading Dutch journalist with ANP, the country's press agency. Has covered the sport of short track for a number of years and is an acknowledged international expert.

Mette Bugge: A sports journalist for the last 20 years with Aftenposten, Norway's leading daily paper. Covers a variety of sports but, more particularly, long track speed skating. Attended the last three Olympic Winter Games. Married and mother of two children.

Joseph Meztger: Author of the Alpine skiing chapter. (See above)

Tor Karlsen: Cross-country skiing specialist who writes for Asten Posten, Norway's leading daily paper.

Mik Barton: was a journalist during freestyle's Olympic debut in 1992. Enjoyed a brief competitive career himself before switching to judging for which he now holds a FIS licence.

Kazushi Funaki: Deputy editor of the sports department at Kyodo news - Japan's leading press agency based in Tokyo. In charge of Nordic and Alpine skiing coverage for Kyodo. Has covered the Olympic Winter Games, world championships and world cups for over a decade. Has contributed both ski jumping and nordic combined material for this publication.

Shanti Sosienski: Associate editor for "Snowboarding Online", a regularly updated internet magazine on the sport. Covers extreme sports in general. Lives in Seattle.

The Olympic Family and Movement:

John Goodbody: Chief sports news correspondent of the The Times of London and a leading authority on drugs in sport.

Michele Verdier: The IOC's Information Director. A talented multi-linguist who has often been the IOC's public image in making media statements during the Games.